The Singing of the New World

In *The Singing of the New World* Gary Tomlinson offers histories of ancient music long since silent: the songs of the Indians that Europeans met in the sixteenth century. Merging recent cultural history, early European accounts, archaeological findings, and rare indigenous documents for the Mexica (or Aztecs), the Incas, and the Tupinamba of lowland Brazil, Tomlinson explores the place of singing in these societies. He details the expressive and ritual ends it was expected to fulfill before and after the coming of the *conquistadors*. Musical practices and the cultural ends they served come alive across a spectrum that reaches from the cosmogonic geometry of Inca ritual song through the immanent sacred materiality of Mexican *cantares* to the interconnections of singing, speaking, and eating in Tupinamba cannibalism. A final chapter considers the fears mutually and repeatedly inspired by the expressive powers of American and European song.

GARY TOMLINSON is Annenberg Professor in the Humanities at the University of Pennsylvania. He is the author of many books and articles on topics ranging from Renaissance music to jazz, including *Monteverdi and the End of the Renaissance*, *Metaphysical Song: An Essay on Opera*, *Music in Renaissance Magic*, and *Music and Historical Critique: Selected Essays*.

New perspectives in music history and criticism

GENERAL EDITORS
JEFFREY KALLBERG, ANTHONY NEWCOMB, AND RUTH SOLIE

This series explores the conceptual frameworks that shape or have shaped the ways in which we understand music and its history, and aims to elaborate structures of explanation, interpretation, commentary, and criticism which make music intelligible and which provide a basis for argument about judgments of value. The intellectual scope of the series is broad. Some investigations will treat, for example, historiographical topics, others will apply cross-disciplinary methods to the criticism of music, and there will also be studies which consider music in its relation to society, culture, and politics. Overall, the series hopes to create a greater presence for music in the ongoing discourse among the human sciences.

Published titles

LESLIE C. DUNN AND NANCY A. JONES (eds.), *Embodied Voices: Representing Female Vocality in Western Culture*

DOWNING A. THOMAS, *Music and the Origins of Language: Theories from the French Enlightenment*

THOMAS S. GREY, *Wagner's Musical Prose*

DANIEL K. L. CHUA, *Absolute Music and the Construction of Meaning*

ADAM KRIMS, *Rap Music and the Poetics of Identity*

ANNETTE RICHARDS, *The Free Fantasia and the Musical Picturesque*

RICHARD WILL, *The Characteristic Symphony in the Age of Haydn and Beethoven*

CHRISTOPHER MORRIS, *Reading Opera Between the Lines: Orchestral Interludes and Cultural Meaning from Wagner to Berg*

EMMA DILLON, *Medieval Music-Making and the 'Roman de Fauvel'*

DAVID YEARSLEY, *Bach and the Meanings of Counterpoint*

DAVID METZER, *Quotation and Cultural Meaning in Twentieth-Century Music*

ALEXANDER REHDING, *Hugo Riemann and the Birth of Modern Musical Thought*

DANA GOOLEY, *The Virtuoso Liszt*

BONNIE GORDON, *Monteverdi's Unruly Women: The Power of Song in Early Modern Italy*

GARY TOMLINSON, *The Singing of the New World: Indigenous Voice in the Era of European Contact*

The Singing of the New World

Indigenous Voice in the Era of European Contact

GARY TOMLINSON

CAMBRIDGE UNIVERSITY PRESS
Cambridge, New York, Melbourne, Madrid, Cape Town, Singapore, São Paulo, Delhi

Cambridge University Press
The Edinburgh Building, Cambridge CB2 8RU, UK

Published in the United States of America by Cambridge University Press, New York

www.cambridge.org
Information on this title: www.cambridge.org/9780521110174

© Gary Tomlinson 2007

This publication is in copyright. Subject to statutory exception
and to the provisions of relevant collective licensing agreements,
no reproduction of any part may take place without the written
permission of Cambridge University Press.

First published 2007
Reprinted 2008
This digitally printed version 2009

A catalogue record for this publication is available from the British Library

ISBN 978-0-521-87391-8 hardback
ISBN 978-0-521-11017-4 paperback

Cambridge University Press has no responsibility for the persistence or accuracy of URLs for external or third-party Internet websites referred to in this publication, and does not guarantee that any content on such websites is, or will remain, accurate or appropriate.

CONTENTS

	List of illustrations	*page* viii
	Introduction: Raised voices	1
1	Unlearning the Aztec *cantares*	9
2	Metonymy, writing, and the matter of Mexica song	28
3	*Cantares mexicanos*	50
4	Musicoanthropophagy: The songs of cannibals	93
5	Inca singing at Cuzco	124
6	Fear of singing	168
	Appendix	202
	Works cited	204
	Index	213

ILLUSTRATIONS

2.1 Mixtec *teponaztli*, probably fifteenth century. © The Trustees of
The British Museum. 35
2.2 Song volutes with drumming, rattling, and dancing from the
Codex Borbonicus (probably mid-sixteenth century). Bibliothèque
de l'Assemblée Nationale Française, Paris, Y120, p4; printed by
kind permission of Akademische Druck- und Verlagsanstalt,
Graz, Austria. 36
2.3 Song volute in bas-relief, Xochicalco (probably ninth or tenth
century). 37
2.4 Song volute from a wall fresco at Teotihuacan (seventh or eighth
century). Mural fragment with tassel headdress priest, 400–600,
$38\frac{3}{16} \times 27\frac{9}{16}$ in. Fine Arts Museums of San Francisco, Gift of Jack
Tanger, 1986.74. 38
2.5 Olmec song volute from a cylindrical seal (seventh century BCE).
Courtesy Christopher Von Nagy. 38
2.6 Music writing from the *Cantares mexicanos*. Biblioteca nacional,
Mexico City, Ms. 1628 bis, f. 26v. 43
2.7 Tupinamba song from Léry, *Histoire d'un voyage faict en la terre du
Brésil* (Geneva, 1585), Daniel Garrison Brinton Library, University
Museum, University of Pennsylvania. 47
4.1 Tupinamba captive singing before his execution, from Léry,
Histoire d'un voyage faict en la terre du Bresil (Geneva, 1594), Robert
Dechert Collection, Rare Book and Manuscript Library,
University of Pennsylvania. 100
4.2 Tupinamba dance with maracas, from Staden, *Warhafftige Historia
und Beschreibung* (Marburg, 1557), Van Pelt Library, University of
Pennsylvania. 112
4.3 Tupinamba dance with maraca, from Léry, *Histoire d'un voyage
faict en la terre du Brésil* (Geneva, 1594), Robert Dechert Collection,
Rare Book and Manuscript Library, University of Pennsylvania. 113
4.4 Tupinamba dance with maracas, from Léry, *Histoire d'un voyage*,
as translated into German in Theodor de Bry, *Dritte Buch Americae*
(Frankfurt, 1593). 114

List of illustrations

4.5 *Ahouai* tree and rattles, from Thevet, *Les Singularitez de la France antarctique* (Paris, 1558), Robert Dechert Collection, Rare Book and Manuscript Library, University of Pennsylvania. 115

5.1 Inca Cuzco, from *Ancient Cuzco: Heartland of the Inca* by Brian S. Bauer © 2004. By permission of the author and the University of Texas Press. 140

5.2 Iunio / Haucai Cusqui: June sun festival, from Guaman Poma de Ayala, *Nueva corónica y buen gobierno*, p248 GKS 2322 4to. Courtesy of the Royal Library, Copenhagen, Denmark (www.kb.dk/elib/mss/poma). 146

5.3 Deziembre / Capac Inti Raimi: December sun festival, from Guaman Poma, *Nueva corónica y buen gobierno*, p260 GKS 2322 4to. Courtesy of the Royal Library, Copenhagen, Denmark (www.kb.dk/elib/mss/poma). 147

5.4 Abril / Camai Inca Raimi: April Inca festival, from Guaman Poma, *Nueva corónica y buen gobierno*, p244 GKS 2322 4to. Courtesy of the Royal Library, Copenhagen, Denmark (www.kb.dk/elib/mss/poma). 149

5.5 Fiesta de los Ingas / Varicza Aravi del / Inga canta co[n] su puca llama: Inca singing with sacred llama, from Guaman Poma, *Nueva corónica y buen gobierno*, p320 GKS 2322 4to. Courtesy of the Royal Library, Copenhagen, Denmark (www.kb.dk/elib/mss/poma). 163

INTRODUCTION: RAISED VOICES

The eons-old human silence on the archipelago that would become Bermuda was broken, as far as we know for the first time, about 1505. It was probably in that year that the Spanish adventurer and slaver Juan de Bermúdez, returning from one of many trips he made to the new Spanish settlements in the Caribbean, happened upon the islands. Bermuda presented to the Europeans a unique prospect. Nowhere else in the New World, from the Amazon basin to Hudson Bay, did they walk a landscape unsettled by humans before them. Far off the shores of North America, farther from the Antilles, farther still from Europe, the archipelago marked its isolation even in the restricted range of terrestrial fauna that had managed to reach it; a species of skink seems to have been the largest non-flying vertebrate native to it, competing with small amphibians, ubiquitous crabs, and flocks of migratory birds.

Once voyages to the New World became a regular occurrence – as they did with astonishing rapidity after 1492 – the discovery of Bermuda was inevitable. It lay in the midst of the return course sailors charted from the Caribbean, bathed in the green waters and temperate trade winds of the Gulf Stream. In the decades after its discovery, Spanish, Portuguese, and other seamen continued to sail near the archipelago. Some foundered on its ring of protective reefs, others navigated safely into its calm bays to rest and replenish supplies. Their visits are attested in travel accounts, in hints from European archives of settlement projects, on early Atlantic maps, and in some few traces later discovered on Bermuda itself, most famously an enigmatic carving left in a rock above the ocean on the south shore, dated 1543. The more fortunate visitors left behind pigs – a population that grew, offering easy provisions for later visitors – and went on their way.

For a hundred years, however, the Europeans did not linger on the islands. Only in 1609, with the providential delivery on the Bermudian reefs of the storm-tossed *Sea Venture* out of Plymouth, did settlement of the islands finally begin.

It is a surprising sidelight to early exploration of the New World that it took a century for settlement of Bermuda to take hold. These were years in which Europeans pursued, with aggressive and zealous force, colonizing projects from the Bolivian Andes to Canada, from rain-forested Caribbean islands to the rugged, arid hinterlands of Mexico. The delay is explained in part, no doubt, by the conditions of Bermuda itself. Its reefs were treacherous, and it afforded scant supplies of fresh water. Still, the islands lay along the richest trade route known to sixteenth-century Europe. Their disadvantages could not have outweighed their potential advantage as either a respite for the Spanish fleet, loaded down with New World plunder, or a well-placed hideaway for the French, Dutch, or English corsairs that increasingly preyed on it. The advantage was apparent to European rulers, and as early as 1527 a first project was afoot to settle the islands. But this and whatever projects followed came to nothing; there is no solid evidence that settlers managed to reach the islands in the sixteenth century. It is as if the Europeans, not finding the islands already populated, could not quite imagine peopling them themselves.

Instead their imaginings of Bermuda took a different turn. Through the late sixteenth century the word spread that the archipelago was enchanted, an Isle of Devils or *demoniorum insulam*. This certainly had much to do with the lack of an indigenous population. The Europeans twisted the absence of Indians on Bermuda into a haunting presence of – something else.

Early seventeenth-century reports, from the time when settlement finally began, memorialize these tales even as they debunk them. In 1603, when the galleon of Diego Ramirez ran aground on its reefs, he and his crew at first quailed at the "shrieking and din" of "the devils reported to be about Bermuda"; but they soon recognized the noise as voices of less uncanny origin: "The headlands are undermined at water level with the haunts of nocturnal birds, which remain in their caves by day . . . These birds sally forth at nightfall with such an outcry, and varying clamor, that one cannot help being afraid."[1] In 1610 *A True Declaration of the Estate of the Colony in Virginia* could treat the hauntings as widely rumored, only summarily to disenchant them: "These Islands of the Bermudos have ever been accounted an enchanted pile of rocks, and a desert habitation of Devils; but all the Fairies of the rocks were but flocks of birds and all the devils that haunted the woods were but herds of swine."[2] The next year saw the first production of *The Tempest*, set on a magic island fashioned after Bermudian reports.

It is a fact not enough remarked that the demonic presence on Bermuda was known, above all else, by its *voice*. A shadowy glimpse in the Bermudian cedar forests of what turned out to be a pig could lend credence to the hauntings, but it was first of all the shrill cries, heard even far offshore, that announced devilish presence. The identification of the source of these cries – the bird in question is the cahow, or grey-and-white petrel, now nearly extinct – finally laid to rest their otherworldly repute, but at the same time it underscored the sonic, aural, and finally vocal stimulus that gave rise to demonic imaginings in the first place. Shakespeare remembered this stimulus, in more benign form, in famous lines of his play: "Be not afeard," Caliban says, ". . . the isle is full of noises, / Sounds and sweet airs

---

[1] Quoted from Henry C. Wilkinson, *The Adventurers of Bermuda: A History of the Island from Its Discovery until the Dissolution of the Somers Island Company in 1684* (London: Oxford University Press, 1958), pp. 22–3.

[2] Quoted from Jean Kennedy, *Isle of Devils: Bermuda under the Somers Island Company, 1609–1685* (Hamilton, Bermuda: Collins, 1971), p. 26.

that give delight and hurt not. / Sometimes a thousand twangling instruments / Will hum about mine ears; and sometimes voices . . ."

The transformation in the European imagination of cahows into devils no doubt involved many things – ancient myths of sirens, associations of euphony with heaven and cacophony with hell, and so forth. But from beneath this already heavy cultural baggage it bespoke an atavistic need: to hear voice where there was none. The Europeans' breaking of the Bermudian silence summoned an answering cry. In the absence of Indians, they heard it as extra-human.

This cry was no mere speech but instead something more, a raised voice recognized as distinct from speech in its intonation, patterned rhythmicization, and tautological excess – all features familiar from other, less raucous birdsong. Early visitors recognized the cry as non-speech, even anti-speech, in its escape from a semantic order within which its powers might have been defined and tamed. It was exactly this indistinct semanticism of the demons' calls that one of Ramirez's sailors could not abide. On hearing the cahows he cried out: "What is this devil trying to tell me? Out with it! Let's hear what it is!"

These basic features of heightened voice open out a latitudinarian space broader than the space of speech and in some ways independent of speech's particular powers. One consequence of this, to glance forward to theoretical areas I will touch upon later, is to revise the metaphysics of speech and writing Derrida analyzes, expanding it to a tripartite division of writing, speaking, and vocalization all told – in which speech plays an important but by no means encompassing role. Another consequence is to pose questions of the relevance to early experiences in the New World of Lacanian ruminations on desire that separate voice from signification and leave it to one side, so to speak, as a remainder of the signifying encounter with others.

The imagining by European visitors of demons' cries on Bermuda projected their own fantasies of encounter, and it is an important first step in the direction I wish to take in this book to realize that such fantasies coalesced especially under the impetus of raised voices. Everywhere else the Europeans went they encountered indigenous populations and did not need to fabricate voices. Instead they found themselves face to face with people not merely speaking but lifting up a vocal din in ritual, communal affirmation, massed threat, or colloquy with the divine (or demonic). The newcomers recognized in the din an activity familiar from their own societies: singing. The special powers of voices heightened in song, experienced in all the encounters (and invented on Bermuda, let us say, where they were not), resounded through the early contact period and still resonate in its record.

Yet it would not seem so, to read recent scholarly literature from many disciplines on the early New World. The inattention in this literature to the powers of heightened voice – of song, more specifically – is not absolute, to be sure, but it is widespread. It has resulted in a body of work that overlooks not only a fundamental aspect of early encounters but also an important perspective on indigenous American societies. To understand certain of these societies by listening for the voices they raised at the moment of contact is, in a phrase, the project of the book that follows.

The inattention to heightened voice within current study of the contact period, which might be called a resistance to listening, does not reflect a scarcity of information in early European accounts of the New World. These, to the contrary, make room almost obsessively for comment, short or long, about singing, dancing, music-making, and all manner of ceremonial chants, calls, and cries. These testimonies from the sixteenth and seventeenth centuries regularly attain a level of detail and vividness that beckons with the prospect of hearing, if dimly, the 500-year-old song of indigenous Americans.

The resistance to listening, I have come to think, originated elsewhere, from two other causes, the one bespeaking disciplinary agendas and prerogatives of musicology, the other reaching deeper. The musicological limitation comes down to a squeeze-play, so to speak, determined by old dichotomies of oral and written cultures. Despite the considerable expansion in purview of each discipline in recent decades, ethnomusicology still concerns itself mainly with living (and often putatively unwritten) traditions, musicology overwhelmingly with the written music of the European classical tradition. There is, in addition, a third, neodisciplinary space, the study of popular music and global pop, which has as its primary object the recorded song of the last century or so. This three-way division leaves little obvious space for a music that does not survive in a living, sounding tradition, or on record or CD, or written in a performable notation.

Scholars of ancient musical traditions – of Greece or India or China, to name a few – have always fallen between the cracks of these disciplinary agendas. Scholars of premodern and early modern Europe, meanwhile, are attending more than ever before to soundscapes beyond the preserved archive of music writing. If the traces of sixteenth-century American music-making are more fragmentary and perhaps more jealous of their secrets than even the remains of these other musics, it nonetheless wants only a sustained and judicious effort of listening to hear them tell at least some of their tale.

In this effort, what do we listen for? Not, to be sure, for the moment-to-moment performative realities of long-silent musics. Though efforts have been made to reconstruct such performances, the traces on which they are based are too imprecise to enable them to be much more than the playing out of modern-day ethnic allure and ethnographic fancy. This limitation will come as a disappointment to some; they need to be alerted now to the fact that no CD of reconstituted Aztec or Inca song awaits them tucked in the back cover to this book, no transcribed music is to be read in its pages.

This impossibility of reliably reconstructing musical performance has been a basic force shaping musico-historical study of the societies I scrutinize. It has created certain recognizable categories of work. On the one side are descriptions of the general nature of music-making in these societies – the kind of culling and analysis of early Spanish or Portuguese accounts witnessed in Robert Stevenson's *Music in Aztec and Inca Territory* or Samuel Martí's *Canto, danza y música precortesianos*. It has encouraged, for another part, organological analyses of surviving musical instruments from these cultures, a materialist, archaeological orientation with a long heritage (cf. R. and M. d'Harcourt, *La Musique des Incas et ses survivances*, 1925; Martí, *Instrumentos musicales precortesianos*, 1955) recently augmented by Dale A. Olsen's *Music of El Dorado: The Ethnomusicology of Ancient South American Cultures*. And, of course, the impossibility of performative reconstruction has never stood in the way of ethnographic studies of music in present-day societies related to, and in some cases descended from, the societies I discuss here. Ellen B. Basso, David M. Guss, Anthony Seeger, Lawrence E. Sullivan, Greg Urban, and many other anthropologists and ethnomusicologists have had fascinating things to say about the place of music in these societies; some of these writers will be cited below.

As much as I have profited from these approaches, my own moves along different lines. In the first place, my study is resolutely historical rather than ethnographic. This may seem a strange qualification for me to start with, since I have argued in several other writings that there is little to distinguish history and ethnography at the deepest levels of method and aspiration. At more superficial levels, however, their differences in sources and approach – in the traces of others encountered as the stimulus to thought and the immediate manner of this encounter – are evident enough. (In part because of these differences, most ethnomusicologists and anthropologists have been rightly circumspect about reading much historical depth into their conclusions. Such "upstreaming," whereby traditional societies today are seen to reflect ancient societies, was a favored method of earlier generations of scholars; I have avoided it here except in carefully delimited instances.)

In the second place, I have wished to till a fertile middle ground between the most general accounts of music-making in the societies I study and the always frustrated desire to know exactly how the music went. In this middle ground we might nurture textured and unexpectedly specific accounts of uses to which song was put, of expectations for its efficacies, of the sense of world embodied in it. (This place and efficacy of song in given societal circumstances I like to call *songwork*.) We might understand these things in the light of interactions of one indigenous group with others or with the European newcomers. We might, then, savor the achievements of song in specific situations both indigenous and colonial. This is not the place for an all-out methodological analysis of this middle ground and our ways of approaching it; I hope that the essays that follow will exemplify both with sufficient clarity to make unnecessary such analysis. It needs to be said, however, that my orientation here is one that has rarely been pursued in a historical musicology of societies from which no performable music writing survives.

In sum: What we can still hear in certain songs from these societies, if we listen intently in this space between the beckoning phantasm of a reconstructed performance and the encyclopedic rehearsing of contemporary testimony, is the nuanced cultural work they were designed to accomplish. This musical force, synonymous neither with performance itself nor with the broadest views of music-making, is a *supraperformative* force, linked to societal and expressive particulars and yet audible even in the absence of specific recuperable sounds.

I mentioned above a second explanation for the resistance to listening to the raised voices of New World Indians, an explanation less caught up in parochial disciplinary distinctions than this musicological one. Singing and its musical offshoots arguably form one of three fundamental modes of human cultural expression, alongside speaking and writing (that is, plastic inscription broadly conceived). As such, and like its counterparts, singing is everywhere. But by this very ubiquity it is spread thin in our perceptions. A category always with us, it tends to turn transparent, hence become invisible to our gaze. (For an easy test of this transparency, pull off your shelf books taking up, passingly or more, singing and song. Rarely will you find a heading for either in their indexes. "Music," a more technical, less widespread, finally more palpable coinage, is indexed somewhat more often, but even this category tends at least to translucency.)

The frequency itself of the appearance of song in the cultural remains of the indigenous Americans has paradoxically reduced commentators almost to silence. The transparency of singing is noteworthy in scholarly analyses of even the best-known sources I will linger over in the chapters that follow: a unique eyewitness account of the Inca in celebration, the moving and fascinating song texts from sixteenth-century Mexico, Montaigne's essay "Of Cannibals." Yet these again and again bespeak the songwork at stake. The cosmogonic powers of singing ripple through the Inca ritual; the Mexican *cantares* open unanticipated vistas on the immanence of the sacred in the materials of Aztec rite and in the Nahuatl language itself; and the Tupi songs Montaigne reports undo his own analysis of cannibal culture and those of his European contemporaries, suggesting very different possibilities.

Attended to in another way than has been our custom – *listened* to – such sources reveal much about special powers of singing. These powers in turn tell stories about the self- and world-making practices of the societies that deployed them. Rendering opaque the singing in such sources, then, does not merely compensate for an overdetermined scholarly inattention. It brings adjusted views of the societies all told that sang in these ways and for these purposes. In the chapters that follow it will suggest three distinct patterns, differing from one another and from European patterns, of relations among song, the material world, and metaphysics.

It must be remembered, meanwhile, that the sources I have used in this book are never pure indigenous expressions. Often they were mediated, at the moment of their production, by the novel presence of Europeans; more often still they were created by the Europeans themselves; always they are read today through the dimming, altering scrim of colonial histories and modern historiographies. Even as we attempt to hear indigenous song and all it might reveal, we need also to gauge, against the backdrop of modern historiographical agendas, the changes wrought in both song and context by the European conquerers and colonizers.

Altogether these are complex matters leading to unexpected places: to the fealty structures sustaining Inca rulership, the economics of cannibalism, the intricacies of Nahuatl grammar, the differential politics and psychology of colonized and colonizers. The strand connecting all these discussions, however, is the fundamental role of singing as a constitutive element in the making of both indigenous and colonial worlds. It is in this latter sense that I intend the gerund of my title. I have of course wished to pay detailed, varied attention to an activity of peoples of the Americas, a nominative practice pertaining to their societies: the singing *of*, belonging to, the New World. At the same time the gerund exercises its verbal function, for the kinds of singing I describe are also acts of world- and self-making. Through them Americans and the Americas were sung – shaped, molded, even created – both before and after European contact. Through them indigenous powers were unfolded that continued to make the world in non- (or anti-) European ways even in the bleakest moments of conquest and early colonization. Students of many varieties of premodern song, especially in Native North American and indigenous Australian societies, will recognize this world-constituting power. I have long urged that we uncover its disguised persistence in modern worlds as well. It is a primary – perhaps *the* primary – way in which song and by extension music continue to be one of our fundamental expressive capacities.

One more word, finally, about the "New World." I do not use this handy phrase without an awareness of its Eurocentric dangers (i.e., new to whom?). The care with which I have lingered over indigenous traces should make this clear. I use it instead to mark out a time and place where to some a world could seem new even as, for others, it reached back to moments of divine creation – a time and place marked, more dramatically than most, by a border separating a before from an after. Our difficulty in seeing back past this border does not lessen our obligation to try. By the same token, our nuanced appreciation of the politics of representing others should not dislodge, from the heart of the humanities, the imaginative empathy involved in such representation.

The chapters of the book were conceived as separate essays toward the effort of listening described above, but this does not render them independent of one another. The first two, in particular, form a prolegomenon for the third, a lengthy interpretation of sixteenth-century Nahuatl songs. At the same time I have hoped with chapters 1–2 to clear the ideological ground, so to speak, for chapters 4 and 5, occupied respectively with Brazilian and Peruvian matters. Chapter 6, finally, takes as its subject the ever fraught colonial mediation of song, attempting to bring to general account and even theorize some sonic effects of the early meetings of Europeans and Americans; these meetings, at the same time, run as a more or less explicit subtext through all the earlier chapters.

Chapters 1 and 2 rework material published in two earlier essays, "Unlearning the Aztec Cantares," in *Subject and Object in Renaissance Culture*, edited by Margreta de Grazia, Maureen Quilligan, and Peter Stallybrass (Cambridge: Cambridge University Press, 1996), pp. 260–86, and "Ideologies of Aztec Song," in the *Journal of the American Musicological Society* 48 (1995), pp. 343–79; the first part of chapter 4, on Montaigne, was published in an earlier version as "Montaigne's Cannibals' Songs" in the journal *repercussions* 7–8 (1999–2000), pp. 209–35. I am grateful to the publishers of these volumes for permission to rework these materials here. The generous support of a MacArthur Fellowship extended into the early formulation of this project and certainly facilitated it. The aid of the series editors of New Perspectives in Music History and Criticism, Jeffrey Kallberg, Ruth Solie, and Anthony Newcomb, and of the Music Editor for Cambridge University Press, Victoria Cooper, was welcome and opportune. In hunting down illustrations Elaine Bernstein offered an expertise I appreciate and know well from other projects.

I am grateful also to many colleagues and students who have helped me more directly in conceiving and writing these essays. The Colonial Dialogues seminar at the University of Pennsylvania deserves preeminent mention here, having for the last decade provided a welcoming haven for this work. Among its members special thanks go to Nancy Farriss, Ann Farnsworth-Alvear, Tom Cummins, and Greg Urban. Cummins, Farriss, and also Gordon Brotherston read the manuscript through and offered invaluable comments on it. Many

The Singing of the New World

students heard much about these ideas over the years and helped me to sharpen them; four who wrote venturesome PhD dissertations with me that intersected with agendas here are Jose Buenconsejo (writing on the Philippines), Olivia Bloechl (Native North America), Paja Faudree (Mexico), and Ruth Rosenberg (Corsica). Finally, Juliet Fleming offered unflagging encouragement and focusing conversation across the last years of this project. Without the second, it would have amounted to much less; without the first, it might never have coalesced into a book at all. To her, and to my children Julia, Laura, and Dave, this book is lovingly dedicated.

A word concerning some technical matters: Of the various names used for indigenous inhabitants of central Mexico, *Aztec* is the most common but the one with the least indigenous authority. It is customarily applied these days to the tributary empire that spread its influence out from the capital of Tenochtitlan through the fifteenth century. The local nation that ruled this empire, which had migrated into central Mexico from the north two centuries earlier, knew itself as the *Mexica*. The language of the Mexica, and hence the lingua franca of their dominion, was Nahuatl; they and indigenous speakers (or singers) of Nahuatl in general are often called *Nahuas*.

The orthography of indigenous New World languages has a complex history half a millennium old. For both Nahuatl and Quechua, the two languages most met with here, I have employed a modernized version of Franciscan hispanized spelling. This is easily legible for readers of Romance languages, with only a couple of unexpected pronunciation twists in Nahuatl: *x* is pronounced *sh*, and *tl* is pronounced as in a*tl*as (it does not add a syllable to the end of a word). Nahuatl accent falls on the penultimate syllable. Thus *xochicuicatl* yields something like *shoo-chee-**kwee**-cahtl*.

This modernized Franciscan orthography is relatively well standardized for Nahuatl, but not for Quechua, where it is displaced in some recent writings by a more phonetic, less hispanized spelling. I have compromised, as most writers do, on a common-usage orthography that varies to embrace the most familiar forms of different words and is therefore somewhat inconsistent. Thus I use *huaca*, not *waka*, *quipu*, not *khipu*, and Guaman Poma, not Waman Puma, but *taki*, not *taqui*. I hope that the inconsistency of orthography is compensated for by the recognizability of individual words across many of the studies that employ them.

All citations from primary sources retain original spellings. Except where I note otherwise, all translations are my own.

1

Unlearning the Aztec *cantares*

By now, scholars have moved far to restore the writing of pre-Columbian America; not so its singing.

Recent developments in archaeological, codicological, and anthropological interpretation, abetted by an upsurge in attention to indigenous America in the years before and after the Columbian quincentenary of 1992, have brought us to a fuller comprehension than ever before of the varieties of expression and conception encoded in American scripts. Scholars have reread familiar but insufficiently grasped indigenous texts, and they have recognized and begun to interpret traces rarely before thought by Europeans to be writing at all. They have shown much-traveled dichotomies of nonliterate versus literate or oral versus written societies to be based on limited judgments of what constitutes meaningful script. They have broken down long-held Western biases that extol the flexibility and semantic richness of phonetic above all other writing. And, most provocatively, they have uncovered orders of meaning that do not coincide with European notions of time, space, and human movements through them.[1]

---

[1] Perhaps the most challenging and synoptic among recent readings of American scripts is Gordon Brotherston's *Book of the Fourth World: Reading the Native Americas through Their Literature* (Cambridge: Cambridge University Press, 1992); more technical, less venturesome, but of consummate interest is Joyce Marcus, *Mesoamerican Writing Systems: Propaganda, Myth, and History in Four Ancient Civilizations* (Princeton: Princeton University Press, 1992). Other important essays are collected in Elizabeth Hill Boone and Walter D. Mignolo, eds., *Writing without Words: Alternative Literacies in Mesoamerica and the Andes* (Durham, NC: Duke University Press, 1994). For a newly deepened view of Andean writing, see two provocative works on the Inca knotted *quipu*: Gary Urton, *Signs of the Inka Khipu: Binary Coding in the Andean Knotted-String Records* (Austin: University of Texas Press, 2003), and Frank Salomon, *The Cord Keepers: Khipus and Cultural Life in a Peruvian Village* (Durham, NC: Duke University Press, 2004). I will return to the *quipu* and in particular to Salomon's work in chap. 5. For indigenous writing in colonial Mexico, and for much else as well, Serge Gruzinski, *La Colonisation de l'imaginaire: Sociétés indigènes et occidentalisation dans le Mexique espagnol, XVIe–XVIIIe siècle* (Paris: Gallimard, 1988, trans. Eileen Corrigan as *The Conquest of Mexico: The Incorporation of Indian Societies into the Western World, 16th–18th Centuries* [Cambridge: Polity Press, 1993]); and James Lockhart, *The Nahuas after the Conquest: A Social and Cultural History of the Indians of Central Mexico, Sixteenth through Eighteenth Centuries* (Stanford: Stanford University Press, 1992). With a few exceptions, notably two articles in *Writing without Words* (Mark B. King's "Hearing the Echoes of Verbal Art in Mixtec Writing" [pp. 102–36] and John Monaghan's "The Text in the Body, the Body in the Text: The Embodied Sign in Mixtec Writing" [pp. 87–101]), all these studies pay at most fleeting attention to song.

In the meantime American voices have remained largely silent. Of the singing that was so often associated with the inscribed traces of American cultures we hear little. As I have noted in my Introduction, this is not because the legacy of native American song is meager. To the contrary, it assumes many forms: portrayals in pre-contact and early colonial picture codices of humans and gods singing and playing instruments; preserved instruments themselves, now mostly sitting mute in museum collections; countless reports of indigenous singing, dancing, and ceremony, some rivaling modern-day ethnographies in care and detail; even substantial bodies of song texts recorded in alphabetized native languages.

In the midst of such riches, what forces – beyond the considerable difficulties, encountered likewise in many other musicological endeavors, of reconstructing historical soundscapes whose clamor has long since faded – keep us from hearing native singing throughout the Americas? The essays in this book aim to listen for this song and at the same time to engage the historiographic quandaries such listening provokes.

If, to set out on this path, we begin with writing rather than singing, this is for two reasons. The remnants of American soundscapes from the sixteenth century survive, as I have indicated, in large part as written traces, pictographic or alphabetic. Some measure of these sources must be taken as part of the act of listening. More generally, the natures of these inscribed traces from the New World have stimulated, in the realm of recent humanistic theory, significant challenges to Eurocentric habits of thought ingrained over five centuries. Read in a certain manner, these traces delimit the boundaries of a soundscape and bring into question the habits that have deafened us to it.

This suggests, meanwhile, several reasons why we start by revisiting Jacques Derrida's critique of *logocentrism*, the hoary ideology in which the powers of writing all told were circumscribed while the prestige of alphabetic writing in particular was guaranteed. First, some few scholars of New World writing have seized upon this critique, which marks the emergence of a poststructuralism from its structuralist antecedents, in order to encounter anew, and with invigorating results, American scripts.[2] Second, Derrida's analysis of

---

[2] For three studies whose reliance on poststructuralist insights is explicit, see Brotherston, *Book of the Fourth World*; and Elizabeth Hill Boone, "Introduction: Writing and Recording Knowledge" and Walter D. Mignolo, "Afterword: Writing and Recorded Knowledge in Colonial and Postcolonial Situations," both in *Writing without Words*, ed. Boone and Mignolo, pp. 3–26 and 293–313 respectively. For an earlier overview see also Gordon Brotherston's "Towards a Grammatology of America: Lévi-Strauss, Derrida and the Native New World Text," in *Literature, Politics and Theory: Papers from the Essex Conference 1976–84*, ed. Francis Barker, Peter Hulme, Margaret Iversen, and Diana Loxley (London: Methuen, 1986), pp. 190–209. Mignolo's poststructuralism is, at least, ambivalent. He rejects Brotherston's call for a grammatology of New World writing, ascribing to Brotherston – mistakenly, I think – the advocacy of Derrida as a "model" for understanding American writing and the view that Derrida's "thesis . . . is . . . automatically relevant to account for Mesoamerican and Andean writing practices before the conquest" (p. 303). In my reading Brotherston instead guardedly advocates Derridean argument as a starting point for critique of our general, Europe-inflected notions of the relations between writing and speech; with this use of Derrida Mignolo has no quarrel (see p. 304). Mignolo's idea of "rereading Derrida's grammatology *from* the experience of the Americas" (p. 303) would be more feasible in a situation where the hegemony of Western language ideologies did not weigh heavily on us. Since, in my view (and clearly enough in Mignolo's as well), it remains burdensome, we need to bring analytic strategies for exposing its hidden structures together with careful study of native American traces. On these parallel paths I set out below, with a reconceptualization of song in mind.

Unlearning the Aztec cantares

Jean-Jacques Rousseau's *Essai sur l'origine des langues* highlights some general terms from which we might build a parallel analysis that might allow singing, as opposed to writing, to emerge.

Third – turning back on these first two points – a full elaboration of song in the midst of Derridean critique can realign poststructuralist terms themselves. Rousseau's *Essai* is as much about singing as it is about speech, and more about singing than about writing. Pursued in a certain direction, Derrida's analysis not only rearranges the relation of writing and speech in Western language ideologies; it also points up ideological pressures that have led us to subordinate song to speech. One of the preliminaries necessary to enable a hearing of now silent songs is this rescue of singing in general from the logocentric prison-house guarded over by speech. Among its consequences is the nudging of singing into alliance with writing, over against speech and its venerable privilege.

If, finally, I take the Mexica of Tenochtitlan and the surrounding territories, commonly known as the Aztecs, as the particular society that is my touchstone for this analysis, it is because the surviving traces of Aztec song are more abundant than those from any other New World culture of the early contact period. These traces culminate in collections of sung words written in alphabetized Nahuatl in the late sixteenth century. This and the following chapter point toward the new reading of these *cantares* I offer in chapter 3.

Reading Derrida reading Rousseau

A most durable lesson of Derrida's *De la grammatologie* is that the connections and distinctions we tend to perceive between speech and writing are not natural and given in human communication but rather constructed in complicity with an ancient and widely dispersed metaphysics of presence.[3] This metaphysics uniquely valued the spoken word as the place where a divine being and meaning were most directly revealed; it was, in this way, speech- or sound-centered – *logocentric* or *phonocentric*. With the emergence through the Renaissance (and especially in the Cartesian moment at its end) of something approximating a modern subjectivity, the metaphysical emphasis shifted from a divine presence in logos to an individual, reflective self-presence there (see *OG*, pp. 16, 97–8); but still the spoken word was exalted. As it has continued to be: From Rousseau through Hegel to Saussure, writing has been considered an indirect representation of a presence found embodied in speech. It has been seen as a sign of a sign of presence.

In a historical convergence that is not accidental, the period of the emergence and development of this modern, logocentric subjectivity is also the period of Europe's growing contacts with and subjugation of vast stretches of the non-European world. It is the period of Europe's first sustained encounter with many forms of nonalphabetic writing, including Chinese characters, Egyptian hieroglyphs, and Mexican pictographs. In dealing with such

---

[3] Jacques Derrida, *De la grammatologie* (Paris: Les Éditions de Minuit, 1967), trans. Gayatri Chakravorty Spivak as *Of Grammatology* (Baltimore: Johns Hopkins University Press, 1976). All citations in the text below will be from Spivak's translation, abbreviated *OG*.

writing, Derrida argued, logocentrism operated as language ethnocentrism and language teleology (*OG*, pp. 76–81). *Language ethnocentrism*, in that phonetic writing, while subordinate to speech, could nevertheless be raised over all other writing systems, since it aimed to inscribe the sound or *phonos* of speech and thus represented presence-in-speech more faithfully than nonphonetic writing systems. *Language teleology*, in that Europeans quickly incorporated the nonalphabetic scripts they studied in a vision of historical progress toward phoneticism, a progress then correlated with a presumed societal evolution. For Rousseau, the three kinds of writing apparent to him – pictographs or hieroglyphs, ideographs, and alphabet – "correspond fairly accurately to the three different states in terms of which it is possible to consider men assembled into nations. The depiction of objects suits savage peoples; signs of words and propositions, barbarian peoples; and the alphabet, civilized peoples."[4]

Derrida's analysis of Western language ideology gravitates toward the eighteenth century, a period, he asserts, when questions as to writing's place first irrupted from within logocentrism (see *OG*, p. 98).[5] Derrida devoted the lion's share of his book to a reading of Rousseau's *Essay* because he found there "the most energetic eighteenth-century *reaction* organizing the defense of phonologism and of logocentric metaphysics. What threatens is . . . writing" (*OG*, p. 99).

It is not only writing that threatens, however; singing threatens as well, letting that word stand here both for what is customarily heard as song and also, metonymically, for all heightened uses of voice. This threat is discernible in Rousseau's *Essay* but obscured, ultimately, by Derrida's emphasis on writing. (Indeed, a sustained attention to song of the sort pursued in the following essays can be offered as a global adjustment of Derrida's grammatological project.[6]) Singing and writing come into contact with speech from different

---

[4] Both the ethnocentrism and the teleology have continued to run strong in general analyses of writing; see, for example, the literature reviewed in Boone, "Introduction." I read Rousseau's *Essai sur l'origine des langues* in the translation by Victor Gourevitch in Jean-Jacques Rousseau, *The First and Second Discourses Together with the Replies to Critics and Essay on the Origin of Languages* (New York: Harper, 1986), hereafter cited in the text as *Essay*, and in Jean-Jacques Rousseau, *Essai sur l'origine des langues*, edited by Charles Porset (Bordeaux: Guy Ducros, 1970). For the quotation here see p. 250 of the Gourevitch translation (for Derrida's analysis of this passage see *OG*, pp. 291–302). For another view of Derrida's analysis of Rousseau, see John Neubauer, *The Emancipation of Music from Language: Departure from Mimesis in Eighteenth-Century Aesthetics* (New Haven: Yale University Press, 1986), chap. 6. Yet another, famous reaction to Derrida's account is Paul de Man, "The Rhetoric of Blindness: Jacques Derrida's Reading of Rousseau," in *Blindness and Insight: Essays in the Rhetoric of Contemporary Criticism*, 2nd edn. (Minneapolis: University of Minnesota Press, 1983), pp. 102–41. I agree with Neubauer (pp. 88, 102) that de Man's reading is marred by a willful ahistoricism of method that is imputed to Rousseau as well.

[5] The fact that this historical localization is questionable does not affect, I think, the cogency of Derrida's analysis. The difficulties in Western language ideology that Derrida sees emerging in the eighteenth century were broached earlier, in Renaissance humanist conceptions of language that themselves evolved and shifted under the impact of late Renaissance awareness of non-European languages and cultures.

[6] Such an adjustment has to date taken shape especially in the dialogue between Derridean theory and ideas of voice derived from Lacanian psychoanalysis; see Mladen Dolar, "The Object Voice," in *Gaze and Voice as Love Objects*, ed. Renata Salecl and Slavoj Žižek (Durham, NC: Duke University Press, 1996), pp. 7–31: "if for Derrida the essential [sic] of the voice lies in auto-affection and self-transparency, as opposed to the trace, the

sides, from the side of its potency as embodied, nonsemantic *phonos* on the one hand and from the side of its semiological mechanics on the other. Writing converges on speech from this semiological vantage while diverging in its orientation toward hand rather than voice; singing draws near in the voice it shares with speech while drawing apart in the resistance of its special powers to specific semiosis. By virtue of the characteristic difference from (or surplus over) speech that each carries, they challenge the preeminence of speech within the logocentric scheme. So song, just as powerfully as the writing Derrida stresses if in a different way, grants leverage against the prevailing logocentric ideology. Song and writing together function as speech's dual others, as traces that shape its meanings and powers while it shapes theirs.

Derrida locates a reflection of this problematic alterity of writing and singing in Rousseau's use of the word *supplément*. This word can signify both an addition (or surplus or completion) and a substitution (or replacement or displacement; *OG*, pp. 144–5). This ambivalence or dualism, replicating the general grammatological relation of *différance* by which the meaning of one sign depends on / is shifted on to another, opens a rift in Rousseau's defense of phonologism. For Derrida the rift is a window on the dispersed operation of the metaphysics (Rousseau's and ours) that, by suppressing the dualism inherent in the supplement, has constructed for the West ostensibly natural and universal relations among song, speech, and writing.

For us the rift will expose this, and also something more specific: an ideological apparatus or, to speak thus, myths within our language beliefs that have helped to determine Western conceptions of the Aztecs since the sixteenth century. The terms that sustain this apparatus will at the same time help us to unmake it by the token of their supplementarity. They are four: song, poetry, metaphor, and writing.

Song

The dual logic of the supplement undoes Rousseau's attempts to assign song an unequivocal role in his history of languages. Rousseau understood song to be an addition to speech imitating its accents by a certain permanence not found in it. This permanence seems a matter not only of sustained intonation but also of a codified, restricted system of intervals not heard in speech – in other words, a scale: "The different inflexions which we give to the voice in speaking, form intervals which are not at all harmonic, which form no parts of the system in our music, and which consequently not being expressed in notes, are not properly a tune for us," he wrote in the *Dictionary of Music*. Because it requires this codification, it would appear, "The tune does not seem natural to mankind." It is an artifice added to supplement the speech of civil societies, and in this spirit it may be provisionally denied to

---

rest, the alterity, and so on, for Lacan that auto-affection is where the problem starts. Derrida's deconstructive turn deprives the voice of its ineradicable ambiguity by reducing it to the ground of the illusory presence, while the Lacanian account tries to disentangle from its core the object [voice] as an interior obstacle to self-presence." Hence "the phonocentric bias is maybe not the whole story of the metaphysical treatment of the voice. There exists a different metaphysical history of voice, where the voice, far from being the safeguard of presence, is considered dangerous, threatening, and possibly ruinous" (p. 16). On this voice see below, chap. 6.

"savages": "Tho' the savages of America sing, because they speak, yet a true savage never sung."[7]

At the same time, however, Rousseau envisioned song as the point of origin of speech, as a primordial imitation of the passions from which speech first arose: "Together with the first utterings, the first articulations or the first sounds were formed, depending on the kind of passion that dictated either of them. . . . thus verse, song, speech have a common origin . . . the first speeches were the first songs" (*Essay*, p. 276). In this notion that the first language was sung, he extended a European strain of thought with ancient roots, in which the speaking voice reached back through history to merge into the passionate idyll of song: "In a language which would be completely harmonious, as was the Greek at the beginning, the difference of the speaking and singing voices is null: We should have the same voice for speaking and singing. Perhaps that may be at present the case of the Chinese," Rousseau wrote, again in the *Dictionary*.[8] For Rousseau, then, song was not only a supplementary accretion on speech in civil society; it was also a supplementary *displacement* of speech at its beginnings, before civil society. It was the voice's first, natural, most primitive and authentic expression and simultaneously artificial, unnatural to the human voice, and unknown to savages.

Inevitably, the place of Rousseau's savages in this reasoning is as equivocal as the place of song itself. Because song is not natural to humankind but a civilized artifice, "a true savage never sung." But because song displaces speech at its origin, aboriginal peoples or those closer to them than Europeans in Rousseau's estimation remain nearer the passionate origins of speech/song. Their present-day discourse may even still merge speech with song, as (Rousseau opined) in the Chinese case. The primal, authentic speech-force of melody survives in Rousseau's world only insofar as it is given voice by others less advanced than Europeans.

This equivocation in regard to non-Europeans divides song against itself. Civilized peoples systematize melody in the distinct intervals of scales, in effect creating a phenomenon inaccessible to savages, but at the same time they slide farther and farther away from an aboriginal song displacing speech. It is not much to the point here that Rousseau's dilemma arose in part from his advocacy of melody and his polemic against part writing, harmony, and theorists of harmony like Rameau. But in the course of this polemic the dilemma ramified into another distinction in Rousseau's thought: the distinction of *song*, the enactment of melody, from *music*, the degraded realm of harmony, far from authentic imitation of passions. In chapter 19 of the *Essay* Rousseau traced a European evolution by which "singing gradually became an art entirely separate from speech; . . . the harmonic aspects of sounds caused the inflections of the voice to be forgotten; and . . . music, restricted to the exclusively physical effect of combinations of vibrations, finally came to be deprived of the moral

---

[7] See Jean-Jacques Rousseau, *Dictionnaire de musique* (Paris, 1768; facsimile edn., Hildesheim: G. Olms, 1969), s.v. "chant"; William Waring's translation of the *Dictionnaire*, from which I quote, renders Rousseau's *chant* as "tune" (*A Complete Dictionary of Music* [London: J. French, 1779], p. 451). This material is quoted in *OG*, p. 197; for related material see Rousseau's *Essay*, p. 289.

[8] See Rousseau, *Dictionnaire*, s.v. "voix" (*Dictionary*, trans. Waring, s.v. "voice," p. 464); quoted in *OG*, p. 198.

effects it used to produce when it was doubly the voice of nature" (*Essay*, p. 293). Music is for Rousseau a privileged depravity limited to only the most advanced societies. Harmony, as Derrida puts it, is "the evil and the science proper to Europe" (*OG*, p. 212).

So, in counterpoint with Rousseau's views on melody, grounded in the logocentric valuation of speech and its origin in song, "music" emerges as an exclusionary principle. It takes shape as a conception that cannot embrace song fully but instead must overlap partially and uncomfortably with it, denying some versions of it its name. This music is an exemplary outgrowth of Western metaphysics, one anticipated in views earlier than Rousseau's and elaborated in later ones.[9] It is an ideological mechanism whose unceasing, noisy operation will eventually drown out whole realms of others' singing. The supplementary equivocation so marked in Rousseau's construction of song is, at least, a control for turning down the machine.

Poetry and metaphor

In separating song from speech, Rousseau's evolution of music divides song from poetry as well. It proposes for the kinds of song it embraces a system of intervals that distinguishes civilized song from savage utterance. In the same motion it pushes poetry away from song and closer to a body of rhetorical theory that historically had been allied especially with speech and oratory. Of this civilized poetry, figurative language – metaphor – was a crucial identifying feature: figurative language viewed as a supplementary surplus added on to literal, rational language. Within the ideology of music, poetry is no longer determined by its melody; it is defined by its tropes.

This poetic phylogeny is undone, however, by a supplementary ambivalence of poetry and metaphor similar to that of song. Rousseau identified poetry with song at the origins of language: "The first stories, the first declamations, the first laws were in verse; poetry was discovered before prose; it had to be so, since the passions spoke before reason did. The same was true of music: at first there was no music other than melody, nor any other melody than the varied sound of speech; accents made up the song..." (*Essay*, p. 276; quoted in *OG*, p. 214). Poetry shares with song a fullness of passion not found in more rational speech. It cannot be only a refinement on speech but must simultaneously mark the origin of speech. The early interceding of reason and philosophy between passions and speech is antithetical to poetry and song and threatens to destroy them: "once Greece abounded in Sophists and Philosophers it no longer had famous poets or musicians. In cultivating the art of convincing, that of moving [the emotions] was lost" (*Essay*, p. 291; quoted in *OG*, p. 201).

Just as language originated in song and poetry, so the earliest language was figurative, not literal. Rousseau depicted this first language in a much-quoted historical fable:

> A savage, upon meeting others, will at first have been frightened. His fright will have made him see these men as larger and stronger than himself; he will have called them

---

[9] For some later ramifications of this ideology, see Gary Tomlinson, "Musicology, Anthropology, History," *Il saggiatore musicale* 8 (2001), pp. 21–37.

> *Giants*. After much experience he will have recognized that, since these supposed Giants are neither bigger nor stronger than he, their stature did not fit the idea he had initially attached to the word Giant. He will therefore invent another name common both to them and to himself, for example the name *man*, and he will restrict the name *Giant* to the false object that had struck him during his illusion. This is how the figurative word arises before the proper word does. (*Essay*, pp. 246–7; quoted in *OG*, p. 276)

Metaphor is thus imbued with supplementary ambivalence: it is at once a de-rationalizing ornament added as surplus to rational speech and a primal link between language and passion *before* rational speech. Rousseau writes: "Just as the first motives that moved man to speak were passions, his first expressions were Tropes. Figurative language arose first, proper meaning was found last. . . . At first men spoke only poetry; only much later did it occur to anyone to reason" (*Essay*, p. 246; quoted in *OG*, p. 271).

Here again, as in the case of the linkage of melody and speech, Rousseau turned to the "barbarians" of his own world for an example: "The genius of the oriental languages, the oldest ones known to us, completely contradicts the didactic development they are imagined to have followed. These languages are in no way methodical or reasoned; they are lively and figurative" (*Essay*, p. 245; quoted in *OG*, p. 273). Imprecision and irrationality of style are linked with less than fully civilized languages. (And not only by Rousseau; Condillac made the same association in his *Essai sur l'origine des connaissances humaines*, Derrida noted, and offered an example we will recall in considering Mexican song: "Even now, in the southern parts of Asia, pleonasms are considered as an elegance of speech." See *OG*, p. 273.) At the same time imprecise, irrational metaphor forms a truer expressive language than any rational speech.

In this the poetry of primitive language would seem to be exalted above modern, rationalized poetry, just as primitive song could seem more authentic than civilized music. Except that by an imperious sleight of hand Rousseau allowed himself an escape: "Since the illusory image presented by passion showed itself first, the language answering to it was invented first; subsequently it became metaphorical, when the enlightened mind recognized its original error and came to use expressions of that first language only when moved by the same passions as had produced it" (*Essay*, p. 247; quoted in *OG*, p. 276). Enlightened Europeans created metaphor, even though savages had first naturally deployed it, by joining it only with the passions appropriate to it. "The *Essay* thus describes at the same time the advent of the metaphor and its 'cold' recapture within rhetoric," Derrida comments (*OG*, p. 276).

There is more at stake here than a chronological narrative. In a movement exemplary of the whole European construction of others over the last half millennium, Rousseau attributed metaphor to savages even as he withdrew it from them, recovering it for control by Europeans. He allowed savages to construct their linguistic world, but with tools delimited and defined by Europeans. A similar strategy motivates poetic/aesthetic readings of Mexican song, as I will relate. Meanwhile it is important to remember that Rousseau's movement *is* a sleight of hand, not a substantive resolution of the dilemma of the supplement. How can the savage's giant both mark the emergence of figurative before proper language and also reserve for a later, rational consciousness the discovery of metaphor?

Writing

Rousseau's views of writing, finally, are caught up in much the same dilemma of supplementarity. Here it is the pictograph that stands in place of cherished melody, the alphabet in place of despised harmony. This devaluing of alphabetism is unexpected. In Rousseau's logocentrism, writing as a whole is an addition to speech that more or less distantly reflects the presence embodied in voice. Alphabetic writing is the calculus that comes closest to inscribing the spoken accent. It is *phonography*, a representation of speech sounds themselves, and hence closer to the presence of speech than other writing systems. For this reason, as we have seen, it is for Rousseau the most advanced writing, appropriate to "civilized people."

But what of a writing that narrows the signifying distance between speech and things? Pictography, if it claims no ability to inscribe sounds, inscribes things themselves. It also writes gestures, which Rousseau believed to be a preverbal language, universal and independent of convention, in which primitive people expressed their needs and, less so, their passions. (The original speech/song of these peoples was, in the historical scheme of the *Essay*, a supplement to earlier communicative gesture. It arose in order to express passions more fully and effectively than gesture could; see the *Essay*, chaps. 1–2.) Pictography and phonography stand in different relations to the original language of gesture. The modern spoken word signified by the conventions of alphabetic writing is farther from the passionate origins of language than the gesture signified by a pictograph. As Rousseau put it in the *Essay*, "The original method of writing is not to depict sounds but the objects themselves, either directly as did the Mexicans, or by allegorical figures as the Egyptians did in ancient times. This state corresponds to passionate language" (*Essay*, p. 249; quoted in *OG*, p. 237).

So, while phonography is the writing closest to modern speech, it has taken a step with that speech away from the articulation of passion at the source of languages. It is farther from that passion than pictography and its associated gesture. In the terms of supplementarity, writing is both a surplus brought to speech, recording its sound, and the record of gesture, a pre-phonic substitute for speech at or before its origin. In a way the alphabet cannot, pictography can displace speech, substituting for it at the point of its emergence from gesture – at the very point, that is, where speech was still song.

An unexpected alliance of song and pictography thus emerges in the supplementary play of Rousseau's historical schema. The writing that touches a preverbal gesturalism, that approaches primordial passion more closely than phonography, is not the civilized alphabet but aboriginal pictographs. Song is connected to this pictography in its prosodic, impassioned gesture and dissociated from the precise semantics revealed by the alphabet.

In the play of the supplement the demand of Western metaphysics for an unequivocal and universal positioning of song, writing, metaphor, and poetry is undone. The working of logocentrism, which would make those things familiar by setting them in fixed relation to speech – a relation, usually, of accretion – is replaced by a different operation of fluid interrelations between speech and its others. Song's unsettling otherness from speech thus partakes of the alterity hardwired in the grammatological structure of meaning. Poetry, too, is understood here neither as a canonized "literature" nor as "primitive" song itself, object of nostalgic European attempts at capture and literary domestication, but rather as any number of heightened utterances that will always slip, in some measure, out of reach of either of these Western projects. This slippage suggests why the alterity of song and poetry cannot be assuaged from within metaphysics, by appeal to constructs such as "aesthetics," "the sublime," or even "music."

Neither will it be assuaged by the development, parallel to and as it were from within alphabetic writing, of separate writing systems for song – that is, music notations. As westerners have understood and deployed these, they work within the ideology of music to separate song from poetry and fix the relations between them. In the same motion they push poetry toward speech, toward speech's own, phonetic writing (alphabetism), and toward its "literatures." In Europe's encounter with non-European others, music notations reflect an absence within alphabetism, an outgrowth of the egregious insufficiency of phonetic writing to encompass the otherness of song/poetry; we will see two examples later. Music notation in its familiar form works in tandem with the logocentrism that has determined our orderings of speech, song, and writing. It records and represents from within these European orders, in the process excluding other music notations that do not. Which is finally only to say that music writing, like the other phenomena we have treated here, must find its own supplementary flux.

Ideologies of Aztec song

Since the sixteenth century, logocentric patterns have shaped European views of indigenous Americans. They have worked steadily to graft on to Americans regimens of communication that have no necessary indigenous purchase. Described within these regimens, native cultures were evaluated according to teleological evolutionary schemes that have become more and more firmly entrenched across the last four centuries. The European domestication of Mexican speech, song, and writing exemplifies a broadly dispersed discursive adjunct to the European conquest, colonization, enslavement, and even extermination of native Americans.[10]

Writing

Almost from the first moment of contact the Europeans worried over Mexican picture writing. The most common way of familiarizing this unknown script was by assimilating it to a cryptic writing nearer to home: Egyptian hieroglyphs. Peter Martyr pointed up the similarities of the two systems as early as 1530 (*Decade* IV; see Keen, p. 64), only nine years after the fall of Tenochtitlan, and they were noted again by numerous writers over the next

---

[10] For the following overview I rely on numerous reports on the Aztecs dating from the sixteenth to the twentieth century and on Benjamin Keen's valuable survey of them, *The Aztec Image in Western Thought* (New Brunswick: Rutgers University Press, 1971); see also Jorge Cañizares-Esguerra's *How to Write the History of the New World* (Stanford: Stanford University Press, 2001). Further references to Keen and Cañizares-Esguerra will be given in the text.

two centuries (by André Thevet, for example, in his *Cosmographie universelle* of 1575; see Keen, p. 152).

At least by the middle of the seventeenth century, however, the attempt to identify the two systems was challenged. The Jesuit Athanasius Kircher, always ready to express (at length) a view on any arcane topic, denied that Mexican pictographs carried the kind of secret meanings Egyptian hieroglyphs did (*Oedipus Aegyptiacus*, 1652–4; see Keen, p. 208; Cañizares-Esguerra, p. 97). The gulf opened here between Mexican and Egyptian writing did not undermine the familiarizing intent behind their earlier identification. Instead it marked the emergence of an evaluative scale of writing systems, from pictography through hieroglyphs and ideographs to alphabetism, on which Mexican pictography could be at once comprehended and devalued.

The scale was affirmed by those, like Cornelius de Pauw (*Recherches philosophiques sur les Américains*, 1768; see Keen, p. 261; Cañizares-Esguerra, pp. 29–32) and William Robertson (*History of America*, 1777; Keen, pp. 281–2; Cañizares-Esguerra, pp. 39–43), who adopted something akin to Kircher's dismissive attitude toward Mexican writing. Robertson noted the Mexicans' inability to progress from pictographs to hieroglyphs and the alphabet, ascribing it to the brief duration of their empire. The scale was accepted also by those others, like Juan José de Eguiara y Eguren (*Biblioteca mexicana*, 1755; Keen, p. 224; Cañizares-Esguerra, pp. 210–13), Gian Ricardo Carli (*Lettere americane*, 1780; Keen, p. 271; Cañizares-Esguerra, p. 43), and Francisco Javier Clavigero (*Storia antica del Messico*, 1780–1; Keen, p. 298; Cañizares-Esguerra, pp. 235–49), who insisted that the Mexican pictographs were not merely literal renditions of things but also carried symbolic meanings as subtle as those of Egyptian writing. Carli adduced the scale near the end of his point-by-point refutation of de Pauw's views: "We must conclude that, beyond representative figures, there were [in Mexican writing] also conventional signs apt for explaining ideas; which is the second step toward the perfection of letters that express the sounds of words."[11]

It remained only for a nineteenth-century rearguard action to pursue farther the case for Mexican pictographic complexity, emphasizing in the glyphs not only ideographic symbolism but also an incipient phoneticism that had long been recognized in some of the codices. This took the form of a rebus writing and was deciphered especially by J.-M.-A. Aubin (*Mémoire*, 1849; see Keen, p. 340). It brought the conceptualization of Mexican writing close to the point where it remains today in accounts like those of Miguel León-Portilla, with their confident distinctions of pictographs, ideographs, and phonetic glyphs.[12]

Views such as these have the power only to shift the Aztecs from one position to another on the eighteenth-century scale of linguistic evolution. They do not undermine the authority itself of the scale. Derridean critique with its supplementary flux, instead, loosens the bond

---

[11] Carli links these hieroglyphs, if in uncertain relation, to Aztec song, to "the use of the Areito or historical songs, which were taught from generation to generation, passing down with them the annals and facts of the nation." [Gian Ricardo Carli], *Lettere americane*, 2 vols. (Cosmopoli, 1780), I, pp. 225–6.

[12] León-Portilla discusses Aztec writing in several works; for a recent overview see his study *The Aztec Image of Self and Society: An Introduction to Nahua Culture*, ed. J. Jorge Klor de Alva (Salt Lake City: University of Utah Press, 1992), pp. 52–5.

of writing to speech created through Western alphabetic phonography. It facilitates the understanding of writing systems that engage orders of reality other than speech differently than alphabetism. Pictography, in this broadened conception, does not take its place in an evolutionary queue, awaiting the forces of enlightenment that will nudge it toward phoneticism. Instead it defines its own set of valences between utterance and the world. We will return below, with the examples of speech and song glyphs, to these valences as they may have formed in the Mexican world.[13]

Song and poetry

Mexican song too was brought under the sovereignty of logocentric thought. More precisely: Mexican *song* was incorporated into this thought by means of the European invention of Aztec *poetry* and *music*. The repression of song's ambivalent supplementarity was the driving force of this invention. It came more and more to impose, across the seventeenth, eighteenth, and nineteenth centuries, a Europeanized view of indigenous American song as a compound of speech and a separate, more or less straightforward addition to it. It divided the unified performance of Mexican singing between two familiar European discursive practices, in the process obscuring less familiar ties to other forms of utterance and to the world that made this song meaningful in its indigenous contexts. It ushered Mexican song into the realm of poetry, aligned in the early modern period especially with oratory and in later centuries more and more with a new category, Literature. (It is a poignant irony that the voices of a civilization so often dismissed for its lack of letters should ultimately come to sing only under the aegis of Literature.) Meanwhile it set apart the elements of Mexican song "added" to speech – its *songish* elements – as a substandard, primitive, and in any case essentially unknowable form of another European category, Music.

This dissection of Mexican song set in slowly after the first Euro–American contacts. Some of the earliest Europeans in Mexico, men like the friar Vasco de Quiroga, could hear in native song echoes of the pastoral Golden Age that would later unsettle Rousseau's evolutionary schemes. The most substantial accounts from the sixteenth century, some of them almost ethnographic in their on-the-scene observation and detailed reportage on society and culture, adopt a related stance. Toribio de Benavente (called Motolinía, "he is poor," by the Indians for his humble Franciscan habit), Bernardino de Sahagún, Diego Durán, and others of this period depict Mexican song as an activity integrated into a broader setting of (idolatrous) festival, ceremony, and religious observance. They tend not to use words like "poetry" and "music" at all, preferring to call the songs *cantares* or to refer to the usual ensemble of dance, song, and drumming with the Taino word *areito*.[14]

---

[13] The history of the development of Mesoamerican writing systems may be seen to reverse the logocentric teleology. That is, it moves in the broadest view from the phoneticism of Maya glyphs to the generally iconic usages of Mixtec and Aztec writing. For the outlines of large cultural shifts that may have militated for this history, see John M. D. Pohl, "Mexican Codices, Maps, and Lienzos as Social Contracts," in *Writing without Words*, ed. Boone and Mignolo, pp. 137–60, esp. pp. 155–6. From such outlines scholarly views of the cultural efficacy (rather than inadequacy) of post-Classic Mesoamerican writing are beginning to emerge.

[14] For Quiroga's references to Mexican song, from his legal brief of 1535 entitled "Información en derecho," see Vasco de Quiroga, *La Utopía en América*, ed. Paz Serrano Gassent (Madrid: Historia 16, 1992), p. 218; also Keen, *The*

Already in the waning sixteenth century, however, as the shock of unfamiliarity of Mexican society wore off – and as a new, bleak stage of the colonization that we will examine in chapter 6 set in – European observers began to graft their own categorical distinctions of poetry and music on to autochthonous practices. Diego Muñoz Camargo, writing his *Historia de Tlaxcala* in the last quarter of the century, assimilated the Nahuatl language to European poetic traditions, extolling it in part because "one can easily compose verses in [it] according to the rules of meter and scansion" (quoted in Keen, p. 129). Michele Zappullo, writing in 1603 in the vein of condemnatory writers like Francisco López de Gómara, asserted that the Mexicans possessed neither music nor letters, in one motion dismissing the Mexicans and imposing on them the European division of the two (see his *Historie di quattro principali città del mondo*, cited in Keen, pp. 140–1).

By the middle of the next century the Europeanized view was prevalent. Eguiara y Eguren celebrated "the love of the Mexicans for poetry and oratory" (quoted in Keen, p. 224). And Joseph Joaquín Granados y Gálvez, in his dialogues of 1778 entitled *Tardes americanas*, discussed separately and at some length ancient Mexican music and poetry. On the one side he praised the consonance and melodiousness of the music, its ensemble of voices and instruments ably concerted so as not to overwhelm the words, and its varied and delightful melodic figures capable of inducing ecstasy in its listeners. He compared the Mexican musicians to celebrated musicians of ancient Greece, and he distinguished three styles of Mexican "compositions," warlike, pathetic, and grave, that harken back to Plato's well-traveled descriptions of modal ethos. On the poetic side, although he could not find in Mexican poetry all the genres practiced in the ancient European world, he succeeded in locating at least the "mathematical" (i.e., astronomical) style of Manilius, the tragic and comic modes of Seneca and Euripides, and the heroic style of Silius Italicus.[15]

By around 1900, finally, in the wake of intensive new source studies led by Eduard Seler and Francisco del Paso y Troncoso and with the recovery, of paramount significance, of

---

Aztec Image, p. 108. For Motolinía's account see *Memoriales de Fray Toribio de Motolinía*, ed. Luis García Pimentel (Mexico: published by the editor, 1903), bk. 2, chap. 26; although it remained unpublished until Pimentel's edition, this account was widely known in manuscript, echoed in Francisco López de Gómara's *Istoria de las Indias y conquista de Mexico* of 1552 (see Robert Stevenson, *Music in Aztec and Inca Territory* [Berkeley and Los Angeles: University of California Press, 1968], p. 105), and taken over almost verbatim in Juan de Torquemada's massive *Monarchia indiana* of 1615 (see the facsimile reprint of the 1723 edition [Mexico, 1943], bk. 14, chap. 11). Sahagún's remarks on song are scattered through his huge Nahuatl compilation known as the *Florentine Codex* (see Fray Bernardino de Sahagún, *Florentine Codex: General History of the Things of New Spain*, ed. and trans. Arthur J. O. Anderson and Charles E. Dibble, 13 vols. [Santa Fe and Salt Lake City: School of American Research and University of Utah Press, 1950–82]) and his Spanish *Historia general de las cosas de Nueva España*, ed. Angel María Garibay K. (Mexico: Editorial Porrúa, 1956), abstracted from the *Florentine Codex*; for particularly rich descriptions of song and dance *in situ* see the accounts of merchants' banquets in either work, bk. 9, chaps. 8–10. For Durán's account, from his *Historia de las Indias de Nueva-España e islas de la tierra firme*, see Stevenson, *Music in Aztec and Inca Territory*, pp. 109–10. Stevenson's book gives a useful overview of many early accounts on pp. 85–120.

[15] See Joseph Joaquín Granados y Gálvez, *Tardes americanas: Gobierno gentil y catolico: breve y particular noticia de toda la historia indiana* (Mexico, 1778), pp. 88–90. On Granados y Gálvez's work in general see Cañizares-Esguerra, *How to Write the History*, pp. 230–4.

the manuscript of alphabetized Nahuatl song texts entitled *Cantares mexicanos*, Mexican utterance was well on the road to consolidation under the category Literature. The capstone of this whole history would wait another half century. Father Angel María Garibay K.'s monumental *Historia de la literatura náhuatl*, published in 1953–4, divided and classified prehispanic Mexican speech/song according to the Western genres that had defined Literature in the first place: religious poetry, dramatic poetry, epic poetry, lyric poetry, didactic prose, historical prose, and fiction ("imaginative prose"). Meanwhile prehispanic "music" was left in its own Western camp, the province of conservatory-oriented modernist composers with a nationalist and archaeological bent such as Carlos Chávez.

In these ways the European invention of Aztec music and poetry depended on the denial of song's supplementary dualism – on the preeminence of its supplementing-by-addition to speech and the submergence of its supplementing-by-substitution for speech. But this second *différance* of song was not entirely repressed; its propensity to surface is evident, after all, in the possibility of views like Vasco de Quiroga's.

Another such surfacing occurs in the *Idea de una nueva historia general de la America septentrional* of Lorenzo Boturini Benaducci (1746), a précis for a larger work on ancient Mexico never completed. Boturini viewed prehispanic Mexico through the lens of an earlier work that aimed at nothing less than describing in general terms the life-cycles of all societies: the *Scienza nuova* of Giambattista Vico (1725; rev. edn. 1744). In Vico's view, all societies passed through three ages, divine, heroic, and human or rational. The divine and heroic ages were distinct stages in a pre-rational "poetic wisdom" – by which Vico meant to suggest the imaginative, creative impulse of the primitive mind, in the spirit of the Greek *poiesis*, not some modern literary category. Poetic wisdom shaped every aspect of society and thought – logic, morals, economy, politics, and so forth. It expressed these things in the forms of fables, hieroglyphic writing, and especially song. It was superseded by natural reason only in the third, human age.

Following the lead of Vico's poetic wisdom, Boturini in his *Idea* emphasized songs to a degree unusual in earlier Mexican studies.[16] He did not, however, accept Vico's estimation of the historical age that American societies had attained at the time of the European invasions; from this difficulties sprang. Whereas Vico regarded the Americans as still in their heroic age when the Spaniards arrived, Boturini wished to portray the Mexicans, at least, as more advanced. He discerned all three of Vico's ages in the history of Mexico, dating the last of them from the establishment of Toltec society in 660 CE. In the process he extolled the sophistication of the Mexicans' writing, the truths garbed as fables in their pantheon of gods and their *teoamoxtli* or divine book, and the refinement and subtlety of their poetry.

On this last point Boturini was unequivocal; once he completed his history, he claimed, European "poets would drink, in the *cantares*, the nectar of the Indian Parnassus." Boturini

---

[16] Keen, *The Aztec Image*, pp. 225–37, discusses Boturini's work and his dependence on Vico; see also Cañizares-Esguerra, *How to Write the History*, pp. 135–55. For Boturini I use the facsimile edition of the *Idea de una nueva historia general de la America septentrional* (Paris: Genet, 1933). For my own consideration of Boturini, Vico, and Rousseau and further secondary literature on Boturini, see "Vico's Songs: Detours at the Origins of (Ethno)Musicology," *The Musical Quarterly* 83 (1999), pp. 344–77.

devoted most of a lengthy chapter to the Mexican *cantares*. He ascribed them to poets of the heroic age, distinguished their different genres according to European models, and described the poetic means, including their "elevated metaphors and allegories," that made them "una óptima Poesía." He singled out for special praise the poems of King Nezahualcoyotl, who ruled Texcoco shortly before the Spanish invasion.[17]

Boturini's dilemma is all too clear: How can the Mexicans have traversed some eight centuries of their human and rational age and still embody the truths of their culture in the pre-rational form of poetic wisdom? How can primordial, sung poetic wisdom display all the aestheticized refinement and evolutionary unfolding of "una óptima Poesía"? How can a voice like Nezahualcoyotl's represent the poetic, heroic age almost a millennium after its end? Boturini, wishing simultaneously to hear song as pre-rational, heroic utterance and to assert the rational attainments of the Mexicans, instead stumbled upon the supplementary dualism of song that would soon plague Rousseau. The *cantares*, for him, bore the dual burden of aboriginal utterance and post-rational refinement.

Metaphor

Metaphor is the final Western construct that has captured and held Aztec utterance. The earliest European notices of Mexican songs already called attention to their frequent and difficult metaphors. Diego Durán wrote that "all their *cantares* are made up of such obscure metaphors that there is hardly anyone who understands them." Sahagún also reported on the obscure meanings of songs he knew; for him this amounted to Satan's attempt to conceal their idolatry. He reserved the word *metaphoras* – and the Nahuatl coinage *machiotlahtolli* (approximately "sign-speech") that he used interchangeably with it – for his admiring observations on the *huehuetlahtolli*, the "elders' talk" or ritualistic speeches delivered on various civic and domestic occasions. The mestizo chronicler Juan Bautista Pomar, writing his *Relación de Tezcoco* in 1585 and possibly himself the compiler of a collection of *cantares* entitled *Romances de los señores de la Nueva España*, closely related to the *Cantares mexicanos*, admired the many truths to be gleaned from such songs but admitted that it required a "great linguist" to understand their images. Another mestizo writer, Fernando de Alva Ixtlilxochitl, a descendant of the kings of Texcoco and the first great propagandist for their wisdom and learning, absorbed European conceptions of poetry and figurative language from the Franciscans at their College of Tlatelolco. He described the songs as "very obscure, being allegorical in form and adorned with metaphors and other figures of speech."[18]

---

[17] For Boturini's "Indian Parnassus" remark see p. 160 of the *Idea*; the *cantares* are discussed in chap. 15. For an earlier account of Nezahualcoyotl's songwriting abilities that Boturini knew, see Torquemada, *Monarchia indiana*, bk. 2, chap. 45.

[18] Durán's quotation comes from his *Historia de las Indias de Nueva-España*; I take it from Angel María Garibay K., *Historia de la literatura náhuatl*, 2 vols. (Mexico: Editorial Porrua, 1953–4), I, p. 74; see also the translation of this passage in its larger context in Fray Diego Durán, *Book of the Gods and Rites and The Ancient Calendar*, trans. Fernando Horcasitas and Doris Heyden (Norman: University of Oklahoma Press, 1971), pp. 299–300. For Sahagún see his *Florentine Codex*, ed. Anderson and Dibble, I, p. 81. Pomar's remark is quoted by John Bierhorst in

Later writers continued to call attention to the metaphors of Nahuatl songs, whether admiringly[19] or with the view that they reflected the roundabout tautologies of an impoverished language.[20] Particularly in the latter, negative assessment we are reminded of Rousseau and Condillac on the imprecisions and pleonasms of less than fully civilized languages. In the coexistence of both views we are brought again to face the ambivalence of metaphor-as-supplement. Figurative language is a pre-rational confusion of savage and barbarous tongues and, at the same time, a civilized transcendence of reason in poetry. (Or again, in Rousseau's imperious attempt to resolve the dilemma, it is a natural impulse not meriting the name "metaphor" until brought under the control of European rationality.)

It was left for Garibay to exalt the positive interpretation of Mexican metaphor and dispel the last suspicions of Nahuatl expressive inadequacy. He did so, not unexpectedly, by bringing Nahuatl metaphors under the umbrella of a European aesthetic made universal (in language that looks all the way back to the seventeenth-century theorist of metaphor Emanuele Tesauro): "The metaphor is the mother of all beauty. In essence it comes to be the nucleus of all poetry. . . . Nahuatl poems teem with [metaphors]."[21] But in effect this only reiterates Rousseau's evasion of metaphor's supplementarity through the arrogation of all metaphor to Europe. Metaphor, for Garibay, is not so much a speech-act that might be rethought at or beyond the boundaries of Europe's "poetry" as it is the engine of the poetic ideology.

It is a powerful engine. Garibay's conception of Nahuatl metaphors has been dispersed by now through many accounts, scholarly and popular, of Aztec culture. To judge from these, its attraction is the result especially of a specific technique Garibay identified as central to Nahuatl figurative language. He called this technique *difrasismo* or diphrasis.[22] It is the joining of two concepts in grammatical apposition to signify a third: for example, *in atl in tepetl*, literally meaning "water and hill" but metaphorically "town" or "settlement." The most famous of the *difrasismos* Garibay identified is an expression that, for his followers, came to signify poetry itself in indigenous culture: *in xochitl in cuicatl*, approximately "flower and song."

In this technique of diphrasis Garibay countered the negative valuation of Nahuatl pleonasms. He upheld the literary status and the figurative subtlety of Mexican "poetry" and even found for it an indigenous name. Some of his followers have gone farther. Miguel León-Portilla, Garibay's most important disciple, has seen in the metaphorical naming of poetry the reflection of a whole indigenous humanism and aestheticism; writers like Birgitta Leander and Luis Alveláis Pozos have followed his lead. They propose the existence of a noble, melancholic, stoic, and philosophic facet of Aztec society opposed to its

---

Cantares mexicanos: Songs of the Aztecs (Stanford: Stanford University Press, 1985), p. 17; Ixtlilxochitl's *Relaciones históricas* are quoted by Keen, *The Aztec Image*, p. 199.

[19] See for instance Boturini, *Idea*, pp. 2, 6, 88, 96, 162, and Granados y Gálvez, *Tardes americanas*, p. 94; also Thomas F. Gordon, *History of Ancient Mexico* (1832), cited in Keen, *The Aztec Image*, p. 350.

[20] For example, Francisco G. Cosmes, *La dominación española y la patria mexicana* (Mexico, 1896); Eugène-Emmanuel Viollet-le-Duc, in Désiré Charnay, *Cités et ruines américaines* (Paris, 1863); and Edward J. Payne, *History of the New World Called America* (London, 1904); all cited in Keen, *The Aztec Image*, pp. 435, 438, and 445 respectively.

[21] Garibay, *Historia*, I, p. 76.   [22] Ibid., I, pp. 18–19, 67.

warfare, human sacrifice, and cannibalism. They link this view of life built around *xochicuicatl* to the great university supposedly sponsored at Texcoco by Nezahualcoyotl and his son Nezahualpilli, the story of which is traceable back through Boturini's *Idea* and other sources to Ixtlilxochitl. They imagine fifteenth-century poet-philosopher-rulers in Mexico musing on the ephemerality of mortal existence, rulers like Prince Tecayehuatzin of Huexotzinco, for example, or, signally, Nezahualcoyotl himself, likened in recent accounts to Alexander the Great, Lorenzo the Magnificent, and the psalm-singing King David. They even advance some of the *cantares* as the work of Nezahualcoyotl and others like him. In Davíd Carrasco's summary of this interpretation, the poet-philosophers "used language, instead of blood, to communicate and make offerings to the gods.... They preserved honored traditions, produced and read the painted manuscripts, and developed refined metaphors and poems to probe the true foundations of human existence." They devised "techniques to open the depths of the human personality to the illusive world of truth. The main technique was the creation of *in xochitl, in cuicatl,* or flowers and songs."[23]

The linchpin of this construction of Aztec poetic humanism has been the *Cantares mexicanos* or *Mexica Songs* that I have already mentioned more than once, the most important of the repositories of song texts in alphabetized Nahuatl surviving from the sixteenth century. The collection has abetted the humanist interpretation not least because the headings of some of its songs have encouraged readers to consider them the work of the Texcocan kings and other like-minded rulers. It has done so also because it has been construed to be a chief source, along with the other, closely related collection of song texts mentioned above, the *Romances de los señores de la Nueva España,* of the diphrasis and *xochicuicatl* imagery singled out by Garibay and basic to León-Portilla's poetic humanism. So even those scholars – writers like David Damrosch – who do not put much stock in the ascriptions of particular *cantares* to specific prehispanic rulers nevertheless tend to ground their readings of the texts in León-Portilla's and Leander's humanism, aestheticism, and belle-lettrism.[24]

Among post-Garibay writers on the *cantares*, some have begun to challenge the ideology of poetry imposed on the songs. James Lockhart, for example, in *The Nahuas after the Conquest,* judiciously urges that the *cantares* be considered songs rather than poems, since European notions of poetry have in recent times been associated with "regular meter, fixed line, rhyme, the primacy of the written form, and a relative divorce from music and dance,

---

[23] For an influential statement of Léon-Portilla's views, see his *Aztec Thought and Culture*, trans. Jack Emory Davis (Norman: University of Oklahoma Press, 1963), esp. pp. 74–9; also Birgitta Leander, *In xochitl in cuicatl: flor y canto, la poesía de los Aztecas* (Mexico: Instituto Nacional Indigenista, 1972), and Luis Alveláis Pozos, *Los cantos de Nezahualcóyotl* (Toluca: Instituto Mexiquense de Cultura, 1989). For Carrasco's words see his *Religions of Mesoamerica: Cosmovision and Ceremonial Centers* (San Francisco: Harper, 1990), pp. 79–80. For Boturini's description of the university at Texcoco, see his *Idea*, p. 142; for Ixtlilxochitl's, his *Historia de la nación chichimeca*, ed. Germán Vásquez (Madrid: Historia 16, 1985), p. 136 (chap. 36); and for Torquemada's, his *Monarchia indiana*, bk. 2, chap. 41.

[24] See David Damrosch, "The Aesthetics of Conquest: Aztec Poetry Before and After Cortés," *Representations* 33 (1991), pp. 101–20.

none of which apply to Nahuatl song."[25] Lockhart notes also that Nahuatl has no word for "poetry," thus casting aside the interpretation, from Garibay on, of *in xochitl in cuicatl* as a diphrasis with this meaning.

Anything but judicious, instead, is John Bierhorst's rereading of the *cantares*; but it too challenges the poetic ideology guiding interpretation of the songs. Bierhorst's two-volume transcription, translation, and analysis of the *Cantares mexicanos* manuscript, complete with a dictionary/concordance of its idiosyncratic vocabulary, is by any measure the most significant study of the corpus since the work of Garibay, and arguably the most significant since the recovery of the manuscript more than a century ago. (I will have much recourse to Bierhorst's work in chapter 3 below.) Bierhorst dismisses the prehispanic authorship of the *cantares*, dating most of them from well into the colonial period. He questions the tradition of ascribing poems to Nezahualcoyotl and other pre-Cortesian luminaries. Like Lockhart, he doubts whether the use of *in xochitl in cuicatl* to mean "poetry" reaches any farther back than Garibay himself.[26]

Bierhorst's achievement is marred, however, by his single-minded interpretation of the *cantares* as "ghost-songs" intended (in the manner of certain more recent native North American practices to which we will return in chapter 6) to revive spirits of dead heroes to combat the Spaniards. This interpretation comes to be the tail that wags the whole of his edition, driving the translation at countless points, twisting the definitions in his dictionary in directions not elsewhere attested, even affecting his grammatical and orthographic analyses of these difficult texts. The only aspect of his work untouched by it is his transcription of the manuscript itself, which has been recognized as authoritative. The ghost-song interpretation as a whole, in Bierhorst's unqualified form, has been rejected by both Lockhart and León-Portilla and has found limited support elsewhere.[27]

Largely forgotten in the hubbub of interpretive debate, however, has been the value of Bierhorst's project as a corrective (even if not entirely plausible) to earlier views. Here at last is an attempt to understand the *cantares* as an indigenous colonial discourse, a sung discourse in which the Mexica tried to construct an efficacious vision of their altered world and the strangers among them. Bierhorst seeks to understand the *cantares* as embodiments of other-than-European ideologies. He reads them as the reflections of colonial experience they no doubt are, and we must not gainsay the importance of the gesture.

Neither is it gainsaid in one more recent study, Amos Segala's *Literatura náhuatl*.[28] Segala labors mightily toward what reconciliation is feasible between the Garibay and Bierhorst views of the songs. He distrusts their attribution to pre-conquest rulers and heroes, reading them instead as ambivalent products of the colonial period. For Segala, the songs are rooted

---

[25] Lockhart, *The Nahuas*, p. 393.
[26] Bierhorst, "General Introduction," *Cantares mexicanos*, esp. pp. 17, 97–9, and 103–9. Bierhorst's companion volume to this work is *A Nahuatl–English Dictionary and Concordance to the Cantares mexicanos, with an Analytical Transcription and Grammatical Notes* (Stanford: Stanford University Press, 1985).
[27] See James Lockhart, "Care, Ingenuity, and Irresponsibility: The Bierhorst Edition of the Cantares Mexicanos," *Reviews in Anthropology* 16 (1991), pp. 119–32; and Miguel León-Portilla, *Fifteen Poets of the Aztec World* (Norman: University of Oklahoma Press, 1992), pp. 41–4.
[28] Amos Segala, *Literatura náhuatl* (Mexico City: Grijalbo, 1990).

Unlearning the Aztec cantares

in traditions reaching back to the indigenous priests' schools, the *calmecac*, but at the same time issue the "last cry" of a society undergoing cataclysmic transformation in the second half of the sixteenth century. His interpretation attempts, probably, to harmonize views too divergent not to clash. But by domesticating Bierhorst's views – by drawing them, in qualified form, into the mainstream of discussion of the *cantares* – it productively questions the presumptions of earlier accounts.

All three of these writers, Lockhart, Bierhorst, and Segala, have challenged the literary, poetic ideology that has long guided interpretation of the *cantares*. None of them, however, has questioned the putative preeminence of metaphor in the songs. To appreciate the supplementary analysis of metaphor discussed above – to meet head-on Rousseau's aporia – is to begin to sense the familiarizing power this trope has exercised on conceptions of Aztec figurative language. It is to scrutinize the relations of language to the world imposed by the discovery of metaphors in the speech of others. It is to wonder whether the dichotomy of literal and figurative all told is as transparent and universal as the supposed preeminence of metaphor makes it seem. All of which issues a question of some importance to postcolonial historiography: Has the history of European-American colonialism, with its dispersion of Western metaphysics, been a history also of the overlaying of metaphorical views of language, psyche, and the world on different indigenous views?[29]

The poststructuralist view of language as unending sign-chain, with meaning produced in deferral from one sign to another, might also weaken the power of metaphor in Western conceivings of others. Metaphor, in its tropological operation, would seem to match better the leap from signifier to signified of Saussurean semiology than the slippage from signifier to signifier of grammatology. The very proximity of the signs between which meaning arises in grammatology suggests that another trope will be more broadly helpful in comprehending different language uses, a trope of displacement from one entity to other contiguous ones: metonymy. From this vantage, the pervasive metaphoricity of modern Western culture might well appear a measure of our inability to perceive propinquities in the world more readily apparent – or simply more prized – in many other cultural settings. Perceiving these contacts between things might be a matter of traversing the world linguistically in a different way than we customarily do, of linking signs with signs rather than separating them, indeed finally of bringing nearer to one another than is our wont the realm of signs and the realm of things. A shift of emphasis from metaphor to metonymy enables some of these other shifts. I will pursue this shift of emphasis, with the *Cantares mexicanos* ever more firmly in mind, in chapters 2 and 3.

---

[29] One recent writer who would answer this question with a resounding "yes" is Eric Cheyfitz. In *The Poetics of Imperialism: Translation and Colonization from "The Tempest" to "Tarzan"* (New York: Oxford University Press, 1991) he opposes views broached in recent years that metaphor works as a figure of intercultural communication, and he traces some of the ways European perceptions of and actions toward indigenous Americans were driven by metaphorical conceptions of language. See chap. 6, esp. pp. 104–9.

2

Metonymy, writing, and the matter of Mexica song

The most basic European technology at work in the *Cantares mexicanos* is the alphabet. To pursue a metonymic understanding of these songs we need to begin with it.

The *Mexica Songs* are preserved in one section of a modest, late sixteenth-century miscellany now in the Biblioteca Nacional of Mexico City (MS 1628bis). It records the texts of ninety-one songs in a Nahuatl alphabetized according to the rules of Spanish orthography. The genesis of the manuscript is obscure, the dating of its contents, as I suggested in chapter 1, warmly debated. The *cantares* section seems to have been copied from earlier alphabetized sources between 1582 and 1597. The preponderance of evidence suggests that its songs, whatever their connections back to earlier traditions might be, mainly reflect singing practices of the 1550s through the 1570s or –80s.

The transformation of sung Nahuatl into alphabetized words – of performed utterance into fixed inscription – brings to bear on these songs various regimens of Western writing. At the same time it seems to weaken other, indigenous regimens. What is entailed in reading these words as traces of indigenous culture is, clearly, something different from what is involved in reading Milton's or the *National Enquirer's* or even a trouvère's words as traces of their respective authors and cultures. The *cantares* do not merely reflect in writing an oral practice; they do not (more specifically) record an oral tradition that lived in the midst of a larger context that included notions of alphabetic writing. Instead they inscribe oral practices of a people for whom alphabetic writing had recently and dramatically become conceivable.

Writing always effects an alteration of spoken or sung language, of course, a change we tend to imagine as a fixing or solidification. But in the instance of the *cantares* and other early Nahuatl documents this solidification granted to the language an independent material volume of a sort that must have been foreign to indigenous linguistic usage. The inconceivability of this particular volume in the Nahua mind – or, put positively, the existence there of other valences among utterance, inscription, and the world, other kinds of solidity – challenges at a deep level expectations of linguistic commonality that are basic to our usual modes of reading and historical understanding.

Metonymy, writing, and Mexica song

This is not to endorse the general analyses of the differences between oral and written cultures advanced by scholars such as Walter J. Ong and Jack Goody.[1] These, notwithstanding the many insights they yield into relations of speech and writing and perceptions of the world involved in each, are too sweeping, too near to older teleological views, too prone to structuralist reification, and too distant from specific language practices in particular situations to be of much help here. Instead we must locate in the meeting of Nahuas and Spaniards the borderlines of different manners of linguistic registering of the world. When Nahuatl was written in Latin characters its ties to a whole view of reality were subtly undone. It was, so to speak, pushed from one inscriptive terrain toward another.

The ties that were thus loosened seem once to have brought prehispanic, spoken or sung Nahuatl into intimate contact with the material world. What we might imagine as its ephemeral, immaterial orality was probably experienced by the indigenous singer or speaker as something more like a voluminous intersection of numerous worldly realms in the structures of Mexica life. Prehispanic Nahuatl, Serge Gruzinski has maintained, "in addition to expressing itself through oral speech and the ritual word, . . . adopted an architectural, iconographical, choreographical, liturgical, musical, ornamental vocabulary that makes doubtful and inevitably partial any attempt at exegesis in our writing."[2] From this multiple intersection with the social and material world indigenous Nahuatl seems to have gained a semantics somewhat distinct from that of European written languages. What might seem to us its ephemerality as an unalphabetized language needs to be understood within the larger context of its worldly connections, its entailments in structures other than song or speech.

Such worldly contact is evident even at the level of basic grammatical formations. (I will have more to say in chapter 3 about some less basic aspects of Nahuatl grammar.) Nahuatl is an agglutinating language, laden with prefixes, infixes, and suffixes, building up lengthy compound words and stringing them together to put across messages of syntactic or conceptual complexity. Even the most basic kernels of this complex grammar, however, the units that Western linguists present for pedagogical convenience as their stems or roots, are not absolutive or abstract in the sense customary in Indo-European languages. They do not have the semantic generality and neutrality we expect in Indo-European roots. Instead of infinitives, the simplest form of a Nahuatl predicative word already assumes a substantive: *cuica* means not "to sing" but instead "he/she/it sings." Instead of absolute nouns, the simplest form of a substantive includes a predicate: *cuicatl* means not simply "song" but something closer to "it/there is a song" (it can also signify the plural: "they/there are songs"). The most basic words are, in J. Richard Andrews's term, "sentence-words," and

---

[1] See among their many writings on the subject Ong, *The Presence of the Word: Some Prolegomena for a Cultural and Religious History* (Minneapolis: University of Minnesota Press, 1981), chaps. 2 and 3; and Goody, *The Interface between the Written and the Oral* (Cambridge: Cambridge University Press, 1987), chap. 1.

[2] Serge Gruzinski, *Man-Gods in the Mexican Highlands: Indian Power and Colonial Society, 1520–1800*, trans. Eileen Corrigan (Stanford: Stanford University Press, 1989), p. 18.

he warns us against eliding this difference in our necessarily Westernizing translations.³ The irreducibility to absolute grammatical abstraction of these sentence-words might well reflect a smaller distinction between the linguistic denotation of things and the actions involving them than we habitually presume. It is, perhaps, the marker of a material volume fixed in the language and the perceptual modes underlying it.

The solidification brought about by alphabetic writing fostered in Nahuatl a different sort of materiality than this, one at odds with its autochthonous connectedness to things. The material inscription of spoken or sung *phonos* limned an independent, representative linguistic system running parallel to the things it denoted. Bringing this technology to bear in Mexico could not but have situated Nahuatl utterance in the world in new and unanticipated ways. In its written form the language must have come to seem more like Latin or Spanish, more a means of representing a reality separate from it than a constituent part of reality. The pre-contact valences pertaining between words and things were altered, twisted toward modern Western valences.⁴

Mesoamerican cultures had their own systems of writing, of course. These rich pictographic systems, preserved on innumerable archaeological monuments, in the few prehispanic painted codices that remain, and, in altered forms, in many colonial documents, seem only to underscore the (for us paradoxical) material immateriality of indigenous Nahuatl. They inscribe the world in a palpable, substantial medium not itself distanced from the things it encodes. Gruzinski has written eloquently, in *La Colonisation de l'imaginaire*, of the ritual substance the painted codices assumed in prehispanic times and of the rupture of their bond to the broader world that occurred when, after the conquest, their contents were alphabetized. The transference from painting to writing was in his view precisely a loss of the materiality that connected the codices both to the world and to the ritual speech and song they recorded.⁵

Inga Clendinnen, in her interpretive study *Aztecs*, pursues a slightly different line of thought. She analyzes the indigenous view as one in which the experienced world was made up of ephemeral images of a somewhat more stable and enduring sacred reality behind and beyond them. Thus natural, material things in the world – butterflies, quetzal plumes, obsidian knives, tamales – were from the start images of a more real reality; they had the same ontological status as pictures in the codices. "Our art–nature distinction," Clendinnen writes, "lapses where nothing is 'natural'"; in such a view "our

---

³ *Introduction to Classical Nahuatl* (Austin: University of Texas Press, 1975); see for instance p. 204.
⁴ On the degree to which our presumption of the separateness of words and things continues to underpin our narratives of discovery see Mary C. Fuller, "Ralegh's Fugitive Gold: Reference and Deferral in *The Discoverie of Guiana*," *Representations* 33 (1991), pp. 42–64; esp. pp. 45–7. On the solidification of representational linguistic modes in early modern Europe see Michel Foucault, *The Order of Things: An Archaeology of the Human Sciences* (New York: Vintage Books, 1970), chaps. 2 and 3; and Gary Tomlinson, *Music in Renaissance Magic: Toward a Historiography of Others* (Chicago: University of Chicago Press, 1993), chap. 6. For related issues in the development of logic and dialectic see Walter J. Ong, *Ramus: Method and the Decay of Dialogue* (Cambridge, MA: Harvard University Press, 1958).
⁵ Serge Gruzinski, *La Colonisation de l'imaginaire: Sociétés indigènes et occidentalisation dans le Mexique espagnol, XVIe–XVIIIe siècle* (Paris: Gallimard, 1988), pp. 77–8.

world is not the measure for the 'real', but a fiction, . . . its creatures and things called into transitory existence through the painting and the singing of an elaborate pictorial text."[6]

This formulation smacks of a familiar Platonism – Clendinnen even calls the perceived Mexica world "a representation composed out of representations" (p. 214) – and may seem suspect as an interpretation of a Mesoamerican mentality. Nevertheless there are important notions lurking in it: the idea of the parallel constitutive powers of painting and singing and the suggestion that the art–nature dichotomy that has served as a basis for Western aestheticism might not be relevant to indigenous perceptions. (Clendinnen does not pursue very far the implications of this latter notion; it comes at the beginning of a chapter on Aztec "aesthetics.") We may rescue these ideas and alienate Clendinnen's formulation from its Platonic associations with two related qualifications. First, we might insist on the palpable and substantial, not ephemeral constructive powers of indigenous singing and painting. Clendinnen herself seems to acknowledge the substantiality of Mexica song when she alludes to native "worlds sung into existence" (p. 349).

Second, more broadly, we might note that Clendinnen's idea of a fictive, made world need not entail its immateriality but could just as easily, in the absence of Platonic ontologies, suggest the opposite. That is, we might see the whole indigenous world – godly and human realms, pictures, words – as pervasively materialized. This would shift Clendinnen's dichotomy of mundane ephemerality vs. supramundane solidity toward a fully material, fully voluminous, and (by the way) fully sacred dichotomy: a dichotomy between material presence and (material) absence, between palpable fullness and privation, between "precious tactile splendour and emptiness."[7] Such a shift would have the advantage of distancing us from the suspiciously familiar, nostalgic, and melancholic version of ephemerality that has, as we saw in chapter 1, played a large role in interpretations of the *cantares*. And it would seem to be warranted even in some explicitly sacred indigenous ceremonies, with their emphasis on *ixiptlayotl*, the incarnation (not "impersonation" or "representation," as it is often described) of deities by chosen humans.[8]

At any rate, whatever the material status of pictures and things and sacred truths, Clendinnen suggests that the relation of pictures and things to one another was intimate in Aztec perceptions. The materiality of quetzal plumes and the materiality of pictographic glyphs were equivalent. This equivalence once more conflates the distance between language – now written – and things. Glyphic writing did not set itself apart from the world

---

[6] Inga Clendinnen, *Aztecs* (Cambridge: Cambridge University Press, 1991), p. 214.
[7] See Gordon Brotherston, "Nezahualcóyotl's 'Lamentaciones' and Their Nahuatl Origins: The Westernization of Ephemerality," *Estudios de cultura náhuatl* 10 (1972), pp. 393–408; see p. 402.
[8] We should strive to understand literally Jacques Soustelle's assertion that in *ixiptlayotl* ceremonies "it was the god himself who died before his own image and in his own temple" (see Jacques Soustelle, *Daily Life of the Aztecs on the Eve of the Spanish Conquest*, trans. Patrick O'Brian [Stanford: Stanford University Press, 1961], p. 98). In translating the notion of *ixiptlayotl* Clendinnen wavers between "god-representation" or "god-image" (*Aztecs*, pp. 77, 99) and the more effectively defamiliarizing "god-presenter" (pp. 104, 110). She summarizes our perceptual problems in dealing with this phenomenon on pp. 251–3. For a good discussion of similar issues in the colonial period see Gruzinski, *La Colonisation*, pp. 325–6.

it presented but rather was of it, its paint absorbed back into it. Its syntax was the syntax of things, not a separate system by which things might be represented. In this integrated place in the world, this location in the midst of material entities, glyphic writing resembled sung or spoken Nahuatl.[9]

Against this backdrop, the alphabetization of the *cantares* worked to fix these songs on a Western grid of relations between language and the world. It embedded the songs in a system of graphemes that give themselves over as representing reality at one remove rather than participating materially in it. It connected the songs to a network of our assumptions about reading including the dual nature of language, spoken (or sung) and written, and the primacy, within the written, of alphabetic technology.

Here we circle back to the poetic and literary ideology that has guided most interpretation of the *cantares*, for this too was enabled by the alphabetization of the songs. Their manner of inscription has encouraged us to read them as literature – as, more specifically, written poetry the loss of whose sung medium affects its meaning in no essential way. This turning away from the performed, songish traits of the *cantares*, which seems an inevitable result of the inscriptive technology that brings them to us, breaks down any number of other metonymic connections of these songs to the indigenous world.

Other than their many references to singing, accompanimental instruments, and so forth and some enigmatic sequences of syllables that record percussion cadences – we will return to all these features – the songish traits of the *cantares* do not ostensibly survive in their written form. In this circumstance discussion of them is, to say the least, difficult. In the face of such inscrutability many interpretations of the songs have chosen simply to leave "musical" matters to one side, with only the most peripheral mention. Other accounts have dwelled on their musical aspects separately from their "poetic" features and in general fashion, reproducing colonial descriptions of indigenous singing, information on Aztec organology, and so forth in hope of shedding light on performances of such poems. Some few accounts, finally, have attempted specific interpretations of the percussion cadences – interpretations that, in the absence of much evidence apart from the cadences themselves, can bring little insight as to the exact relations of sung words and percussive accompaniment.[10]

---

[9] With regard to Mesoamerican writing and painting Arthur G. Miller has developed this dichotomy of representation and presentation along different lines (see *The Mural Painting of Teotihuacán* [Washington, DC: Dumbarton Oaks, 1973], pp. 26–8). He sees the two-dimensionality of Mesoamerican images as "presentational" in opposition to "representational" Western perspectival technique. Presentational painting eschews Western naturalism and with it the "intermediary step between the painted image and what it represents, i.e., what it symbolizes." It forges a direct, symbolic connection between the image and the idea of what it depicts and is distanced from the world by this unmediated connection ("Teotihuacán painting . . . is a presentation whose meaning is *in the image* and not anywhere else"). This is a more expressly Platonic view even than Clendinnen's. We might adjust it to the view espoused here by suggesting that the unmediated connection of image and what it depicts must function, in a world observed as fully materialized, to draw image and world together rather than to separate them; the image conveys a part of the world in its iconic, semantic, and material substantiality.

[10] For examples of general avoidance of musical matters see Garibay, *Historia*, I, pp. 79–83, and Karttunen and Lockhart, "La estructura de la poesía náhuatl vista por sus variantes," *Estudios de cultura náhuatl* 14 (1980), pp. 15–64; Garibay attempted, unsatisfactorily, to redress the absence of music from his *Historia* in his later *Poesía náhuatl* (3 vols., 1964–8; rpt. Mexico City: Universidad Nacional Autónoma, 1993), the project of

Such accounts obscure a very basic aspect of the *cantares*. They approach these song texts as if music and poetry were from the start in some way distinct and separable in them. But is it plausible to think that the creators of such songs, while they evidently could imagine the songs written in pictography, ever imagined their words as spoken rather than sung? The distinction of poetry and music emerged only as an artifact of the alphabetic inscription that prised the words of the *cantares* apart from their sung delivery. This technology set up a hierarchy in which recitable, writable words were the primary means of signification and singing only a feebly signifying conveyance for them.[11] In this view of the *cantares* we can read, translate, and analyze their words with scant attention to their songish features, reassuring ourselves all the while that we possess most of what is essential.

The temptation of such reassurance is great. Even Gruzinski, so perceptive on the nature of indigenous language and the differences between painted and alphabetic transmission, sometimes succumbs to it. In *La Colonisation de l'imaginaire*, for example, he contrasts the *cantares* with pictographic expressions because the *cantares* were "easily fixed" in alphabetic writing with only "a crystallization and a Christianization of the oral tradition" as the result.[12] It is as if the crystallization were not a fundamental metamorphosis, as if it didn't alter the significance of the *cantares* at every point. Here again the nonsongish, European materiality of the *Cantares mexicanos*, its palpable presence as a book of poems in alphabetic writing, limits our hearing, leading us to push the specifically indigenous sung materiality of its contents to the edges of our thought.

Elsewhere Gruzinski voices a different position, one closer to the subtlety of his analysis of pictography. He suggests the profound mutation involved in the alphabetization of Nahuatl: "The reduction to alphabetic writing leads one to believe that the medium . . . is simply the vehicle of the idea of which it is in fact an integral part, from which it is so indissociable as indeed to be the idea."[13] To view the *cantares* in a modern literary-poetic guise, apart from their songish nature, does not merely render them less vividly communicative than they once were. It brings about more basic changes. It places them in a paradigm of linguistic significance, a vision of the relations of words, music, and the world, distant from their origins. It relishes their ability to speak with unfamiliar accents even while aggressively familiarizing them, even in the absence of singing and instrumental accompaniment (not to mention dance, ritual circumstances, etc.). To enable the *cantares* to

---

translating both the *Cantares* and the *Romances* repertories that he left incomplete at his death; see esp. II, pp. xxxviii–xl. Samuel Martí's discussion of the *cantares* in *Canto, danza y música precortesianos* (Mexico: Fondo de cultura económica, 1961), pp. 118–51, is a compilation of primary and secondary sources heavily indebted to Garibay's *Historia*; Robert Stevenson's *Music in Aztec and Inca Territory* (Berkeley: University of California Press, 1968) is a more thorough survey of colonial testimony and organological evidence with, however, less to say concerning the *cantares*. Most commentators, including Martí, pp. 140–8, and Stevenson, pp. 46–54, offer speculation on the percussion cadences; for a recent attempt to interpret them and review of other attempts see Bierhorst, *Cantares mexicanos*, pp. 72–9.

[11] I have argued elsewhere that alternatives to this hierarchy existed even within early modern Europe; see *Music in Renaissance Magic*, chap. 4.

[12] *La Colonization de l'imaginaire*, p. 77.   [13] *Man-Gods*, pp. 18–19.

speak in a manner less familiar to us we should seek the conflation suggested by Gruzinski of their medium and their significance – elements that it is a habitual gesture of modernity, after all, to separate.

In restoring to these songs a foreign voice we should seek also, more broadly, the conflation of language and the world implied in Clendinnen's view of the pictographic codices. Where there is no space between words or pictures and things in the world, neither can there be any separable ontological niche for sung words. These then take a position alongside pictures, words, and material objects. Sung words and the things that came along with them in the Mexica world – the introductory finger-whistling; the deep intonations of the upright, hand-beaten drum *huehuetl*; the resonant, wooden thong of the mallet-beaten log-drum *teponaztli*; perhaps the rhythmic clatter of rattles, the scratchy whisper of rasps, the low wail of conch trumpets; the synchronized kinetics of dance; the torchlit incandescence of jeweled, plumed, flowered, and painted costume – all these elements of Mexica song that we insist on setting apart as "music" or in some other category were engaged in immanent material reality as fully and in the same manner as words and pictures. They were as fully pregnant with sacred truths as any other material things. In overarching terms, as John Monaghan has recently emphasized in regard to Mixtec codices, both utterance and painting might need to be rethought as connected to bodily gesture through a whole system of linguistic, pictographic, and danced choreographies.[14]

In this situation writing itself does not stand aloof from reality, a set of conventional symbols for its representation. Instead its symbolic powers are predicated on material reality and always on the verge of being absorbed back into it. A musical case in point from Monaghan's Mixtec culture area is a fifteenth-century wooden *teponaztli* preserved in the British Museum (see Figure 2.1). Unlike most surviving *teponaztlis*, which tend to be carved in anthropomorphic or biomorphic guises, this instrument is written – extensively carved with pictographs in the manner of the Mixtec painted codices. It depicts a battle between the warrior-kings Four Wind (upper left) and Five Rain (upper right). It tells another, more general story too: of the assimilation of pictographic writing to the drumming this

---

[14] See John Monaghan, "The Text in the Body, the Body in the Text: The Embodied Sign in Mixtec Writing," in *Writing without Words: Alternative Literacies in Mesoamerica and the Andes*, ed. Elizabeth Hill Boone and Walter D. Mignolo (Durham, NC: Duke University Press, 1994), pp. 87–101, esp. 87–91. Monaghan argues from linguistic evidence that dance, in Mixtec understanding, was a kind of embodied singing related to prayer; in thus merging dance with song Monaghan suggests that our customary notion of dance is a Western category in need of a critique similar to mine above of poetry, song, and so on. He does not, however, allow for any separation of song and speech within Derrida's analysis of logocentrism: "But if we are now coming to the realization that these [Mixtec] texts cannot be understood apart from their performance, the focus on song and chant betrays our logocentricity. Were these texts only put into words? Is that the way they were 'read'?" (p. 89). In this he misses the supplementary role of song in regard to speech I have endorsed in chap. 1. A rethinking along Monaghan's lines for the Nahua culture-areas would start from Alfredo López Austin's magisterial *The Human Body and Ideology: Concepts of the Ancient Nahuas*, trans. Thelma Ortiz de Montellano and Bernard Ortiz de Montellano, 2 vols. (Salt Lake City: University of Utah Press, 1988). For similar issues in Inca culture with suggestive remarks on sound and song see Constance Classen, *Inca Cosmology and the Human Body* (Salt Lake City: University of Utah Press, 1993), esp. pp. 68–73; also chap. 5 below.

Metonymy, writing, and Mexica song

Figure 2.1   Mixtec *teponaztli*, probably fifteenth century

instrument was made for and the singing it was intended to support. We do not know the particulars of this story – why *these* pictographs on *this* drum? – but we can assume that the union of the two was not happenstance. Here musical instrument and pictographic codex coincide for a moment in a fashion that was probably perceived to enhance the expressive potency of both. Writing and singing join together in the bodily, and very material, discipline of playing.

Several Mesoamerican cultures have left suggestive traces, in pictographic writing, of the worldly materiality of their songs. These are the elaborate volutes extending from the mouths of singing figures pictured in the codices, on painted murals, and elsewhere. Figure 2.2 reproduces a famous example, from the *Codex Borbonicus*, a calendar-book most likely of Mexica origin from shortly after the time of the conquest. The glyph in question is the decorated volute or scroll extending upward from the mouth of the smaller deity pictured.

Elaborate volutes such as this reach far back in Mesoamerican pictography. Many examples are carved on the central pyramid at Xochicalco, dating probably from the ninth or tenth century CE and showing the incursion northward of late Classic Maya styles (see Figure 2.3). Earlier still, many more are painted in the murals of Teotihuacan, dating from the seventh or eighth century CE (Figure 2.4). The glyphs are present even at one of the earliest

35

The Singing of the New World

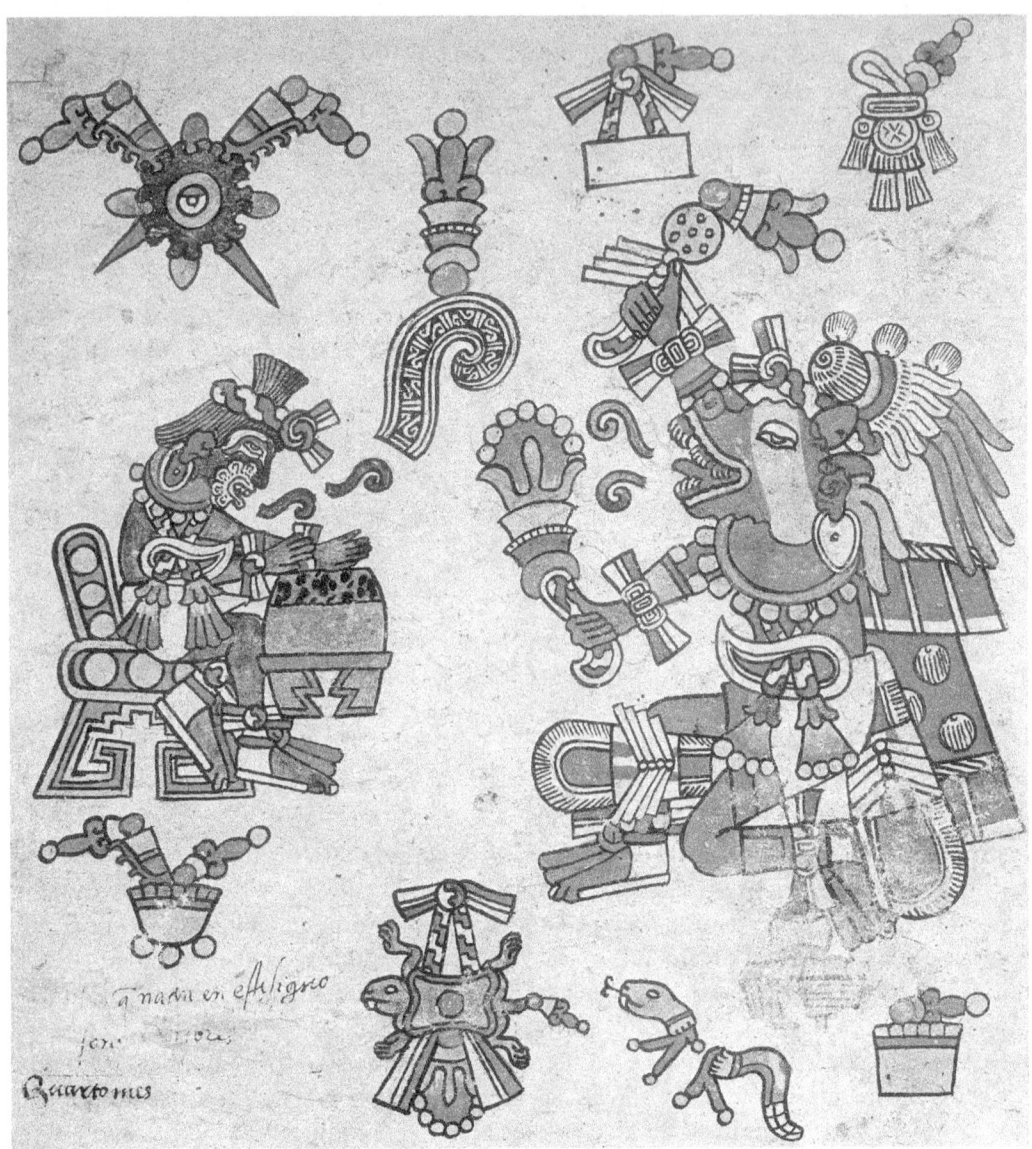

Figure 2.2 Song volutes with drumming, rattling, and dancing from the *Codex Borbonicus* (mid-sixteenth century)

moments of American writing archaeologists have yet discovered. The recent uncovery of an Olmec name-seal from about 650 BCE shows a bird singing what seems to be the name of an Olmec king (Figure 2.5).

The interconnected, integrated world-conception of indigenous Mexican culture – its conflating force, seen from a European perspective – operates at many levels in song glyphs.

Metonymy, writing, and Mexica song

Figure 2.3   Song volute in bas-relief, Xochicalco (probably ninth or tenth century)

First is the contiguity of speech and song. We can tell that the glyph in Figure 2.2 represents song, not speech, since the singer accompanies himself on the *huehuetl*. (Another, less direct hint was provided by an early Spanish commentator on this calendar-book, who wrote beneath the figures, "those born under this sign are singers.") By the same token, the larger deity also must be singing; he accompanies himself with a rattle. But his glyph, unlike his companion's, is utterly simple and unornamented. It is clear even from this page, then, that the contrast of plain and ornate volutes does not in any straightforward manner convey the difference between speech and song.

Indeed, while we know that the Mexica distinguished clearly between these vocal functions, speech (*tlahtolli*) and song (*cuicatl*), we also know that rhetorically heightened, ritualized speech occupied an important enough place in elite Mexica culture to help bridge the gap between the two. This heightened speechifying took the form of the *huehuetlahtolli* or "elders' talk" so admired by Sahagún for its sensible wisdom. The distance seems to have been bridged also in linguistic practices that set elite Nahuatl apart from its more plebeian usages, which included a complex syntactic formality and perhaps even modest tonal elements. In its patterned formality heightened speech probably pushed at the boundary of song in Mexica culture, even while maintaining some distance from it in its lack of instrumental accompaniment, associated dance, and, probably, elaborate melody. In this light,

The Singing of the New World

Figure 2.4 Song volute from a wall fresco at Teotihuacan (seventh or eighth century)

Figure 2.5 Olmec song volute from a cylindrical seal (seventh century BCE)

perhaps the most that can be said of plain and ornate volutes alike is that they pictured the unbroken spectrum inhabited by both ritual speech and song at the same time as they shifted along it in ways difficult for us to interpret.

A second integration evident in the volutes is the union of song and paint. The paint in the codices was, as I have suggested along with Gruzinski, a solid, voluminous presence binding the glyphs to the material things they depicted. It was the medium through which the glyphs took on a materiality equivalent to things outside the codices, through which they came even to be presentations rather than representations of the world. The volutes, especially ornate ones like those in Figures 2.2, 2.3, and 2.4, drew song (and speech) into this loop of contiguous substances. From our perspective they seem to materialize song, conflating it with painted substance in the encoding of the world. From the indigenous perspective they probably affirmed something so self-evident to the Mesoamerican mentality as to be unnoticed: the cognate materialities of paint and song.

Along the way they must also have affirmed the material linkage of song to other things that can appear in paint. The third connection evident in the ornate volutes is a case in point: they joined song with seashells, feathers, precious stones, and especially flowers. In fact the ornate volutes most often include indigenous images of flowers; iconographers among students of Mesoamerica have worked to identify particular species thus depicted. In this the ornate volutes presented song blossoming, connecting song to another of the material substances basic to Mexica ritual. We will follow in chapter 3 some of the implications of this particular material bond in the *cantares*.

The flowers in the volutes may even have had a quite specific ritual significance, one that indicates a fourth material union expressed in the song glyphs. Abraham Cáceres has argued that the flower atop the volute in figure 2.2 is the *heimia salicifolia*, *xonecuilli* in one of its Nahuatl names, one of a number of hallucinogenic plants employed in Mexica ritual to aid the priests in their shamanic contacts with sacred realms.[15] This interpretation is in some of its particulars more than a little speculative, to be sure; but the identification of *xonecuilli* in the song glyph seems well founded. It hints at a sacred reality immanent in the worldly materiality of the glyph. It suggests a final, sweeping embrace that might have operated in this volute, a hallucinogenic embrace of song, flower, and paint together as avatars of sacred truths.

The joining of flower and song in painted volutes can be interpreted, then, as a powerful manifestation of the integrated and material sacrality of the indigenous world. But it also anticipates precisely the "flower-and-song," *xochicuicatl* imagery of the *cantares*, and it might seem to lead us back toward the humanistic interpretations of Aztec culture we examined in chapter 1. So it does, for example, in Cáceres's work.

Viewed from a metonymic perspective, instead, the connected materialities of song, flower, and paint turn this interpretation on its head. They have the effect of denying altogether a place for Garibay's or León-Portilla's metaphorical play in indigenous

---

[15] "*In xochitl, in cuicatl*: Hallucinogens and Music in Mesoamerican Amerindinan Thought" (PhD dissertation, Indiana University, 1984), chap. 2.

sensibilities. The idea that flower and song could be a metaphor for poetry and for a wider poetic philosophy depends on the perception of flowers and song as disjunct parts of reality. In a manner basic to all metaphor, that is, it requires a perceptual separation of things that may then be linked in the trope.

There is little evidence of such separation in the Mexica mentality. It seems to be another ghost of European habits of thought. Instead of disjunction, what we sense here is connection: not a seamless merger of all things into all other things, to be sure, but rather a dovetailing of certain phenomena in the world between which Western modes of thought perceive gaps. Our effort should not be to divide Aztec flowers from Aztec song so we can put them together again in a metaphorical emblem. It should be to see, however hazily, a perception of the world in which flower and song were always already connected; in which flower was in contact with song and therefore able to present it in some aspect, while song was adjacent to flower and likewise able to present it; in which the question of the connections of parts to a whole stood in place of the question of relating unrelated things. Our effort, once again, should be to see a culture not of metaphors but of metonymies. These are the concomitants of a material world seen as a varied, rich, but nonetheless narrowly integrated whole.

This view pushes us toward a reconsideration of Garibay's notion of *difrasismo*. It is a metaphorical notion that needs to be remade in antimetaphorical terms of proximity and the partial habitation of one thing in another: not *difrasismo* so much as a redoubled *monofrasismo* of a sort we do not easily comprehend. Likewise, and more generally, the whole European discovery of complex metaphors at the heart of Nahua discourse, a discovery dating back to earliest colonial times, as we saw in chapter 1, needs to be questioned. Along with it the metaphorical foundation of the *xochicuicatl* interpretation of the *cantares* needs to be reimagined. How do the juxtapositions of different (to us, sometimes, distant) objects in these songs function? What is their relation to the world when they appear as confirmations of perceived affinities rather than as poetic images spanning distance in ingenious ways? How then do we rethink the world they reflect?

Among writers on Aztec culture Clendinnen comes as close as anyone to dissolving Western categories that yield metaphors. "The puzzle," she writes,

> is to know when [the Mexica] were speaking, as we would say, "merely" metaphorically, and when they were speaking literally, simply describing the world as they knew it to be. In certain tropes, as when maize is invoked as human flesh, we casually take the linked concepts to be so widely separated that we assume we are dealing with metaphor and the cognitive *frisson* of overleaping difference. Then comes the jolting recognition that the Mexica might well have been stating a perceptually unobvious but unremarkable truth: maize was flesh.

Here our parsing of the world is, for a moment, effectively challenged. But not for long: Clendinnen still holds out the possibility that the Mexica perceived a duality of literal and figurative relations between language and the world. Still she assumes that the Mexica "lived by" metaphors: "On other occasions," she continues, "... they might well have been 'speaking metaphorically.' In a differently conceptualized world concepts are differently distributed. If we want to know the metaphors our subjects lived by, we need first to know how language scanned actuality."[16]

We should push farther Clendinnen's insights. It seems likely that the duality of literal and figurative language is all told a Western importation to the Mexica mentality; that the indigenous construction of the world connected things to other things in a network of extraordinary, more than Western complexity and intimacy; that the expression of one thing in another was, therefore, a real connection – a metonymic one, again, involving the interplay of adjoining parts of a whole; and that the surmounting of distance and difference basic to metaphorical understandings of the world was not the issue it seemed to the Spaniards. It seems likely, to recall the old vocabulary of Lucien Lévy-Bruhl's pluralistic sociology, that the Mexica mentality before European contact was a mentality of *participation* more than one of *causality*.[17]

If this carries Clendinnen's view of indigenous metaphor farther than she might take it, it nonetheless affirms her most general thesis about the place of the individual in pre-contact Mexica culture. Clendinnen argues that the individual subject was a "highly vulnerable social construct" in Mexica life, "made or unmade through a series of public acts." In a manner foreign to emergent early modern subjectivities in Europe, the Mexica self was permeable, opening out to fortifying, terrifying, sustaining, and destructive sacred powers and defined by its changing relations to them embodied in ritual.

This view of the self originated in conjunction with an eschatology widely dispersed through Mesoamerica that involved a cyclic world order and periodic destructions of the cosmos. The Mexica harped with particular insistence on this eschatology; though they lived in relative abundance, as Clendinnen says, elaborating earlier views of Jacques Soustelle, "they represented themselves as . . . toiling along a windswept ridge, an abyss on either hand."[18] The fluid Mexica view of individual subjectivity is apparent also in the

---

[16] *Aztecs*, p. 287. Clendinnen's indecisiveness is apparent also in comparing pp. 143 and 182, where she accepts "metaphors" as pervasive ways all societies conceive the world and themselves, with p. 251, where she faces "the implication that [a] metaphor might not be metaphor at all." In her discussion of the *cantares* Clendinnen pronounces metaphors a basic technique of Mexica poetry (p. 215) but also glimpses a less familiar view, where she senses "a marvellous concreteness in what we would call 'metaphors'" (p. 220).

[17] On Lévy-Bruhl see S. J. Tambiah, *Magic, Science, Religion, and the Scope of Rationality* (Cambridge: Cambridge University Press, 1990), pp. 84–92. In *Man-Gods*, p. 21, Gruzinski touches on an insight similar to Clendinnen's: "The Nahua perceived totalities," he writes, "even if it meant confusing, as sometimes happened, the signifier with the signified, the object with its representation." Gruzinski returns to the subject in *La Colonisation*, pp. 325–6, broaching it now as a fundamental indigenous mode of perceiving reality and correcting (p. 330) his earlier imputation of confusion to the Mexica.

[18] *Aztecs*, pp. 143, 29. For the sources of Clendinnen's image see *Florentine Codex*, ed. Anderson and Dibble, VI, pp. 101, 125. For Soustelle, in *Daily Life of the Aztecs*, Mexica existence was perilous at the most fundamental level, for "their fragile world was perpetually at the mercy of some disaster" (p. 101). This threat configured every ritualized gesture of Mexica society as "a continually renewed white-magic operation, a perpetual collective effort without which nature itself would be destroyed" (p. 147). "The common task," Clendinnen writes in developing Soustelle's view, "was to sustain a social order sufficiently in harmony with the 'natural' order to exist within it, with women and men pursuing their separate and dangerous paths, to maintain humankind's precarious purchase on existence" (p. 209).

(to us) vague borders of selfhood in the complex Aztec pantheon, where a deity seemingly distinct and individual at one moment can reemerge as a single aspect of a different deity at another. And it is evident in the permeable borders between sacred and human selves in Aztec ritual, where chosen humans, as I remarked before, became this god or that.[19]

This notion of subjectivity sits well with the integrated, metonymic Mexica world vision. The permeable boundaries of Mexica selfhood echo and redouble the operative adjacencies at the edges of things. The self takes its place in the numberless proximities that allow the connections I outlined before among song, flower, paint, words, and world. The "eclipse of subjectivity" Clendinnen finds at crucial moments of Mexica life, the "deep cultural predilection" she perceives among the Mexica "for seeking the sacred through the extinction of self,"[20] is the most basic ritual confirmation of the participation of human flesh and life-force in a cosmos of contact and affinity. It might therefore better be called an expansion or unfolding or dilation of the self than its extinction or eclipse. Mexica woman and Mexica man opened out at every point – like maize, *teponaztli*, and glyph – to the material world around them. They touched this world and merged in some degree with it in their speeches, their dances, their painted books, and their songs.

Music writing

Consider again the ornate song glyph we have analyzed from the *Codex Borbonicus* (Figure 2.2), and think of it for a moment as music notation. It does not answer, of course, to post-Medieval Western requirements of such notation. It does not enable the more or less precise re-creation of a specific song-act. Rather, as I have argued, it presents the palpable, worldly volume of indigenous Mesoamerican utterance. It conveys through the tangible medium of paint, itself laden with cultural values and meanings, a meeting of sung language and the world in their coextensive material substance. It is, then, more properly *music substantiation* than *music notation*.

In the manuscript of the *Cantares mexicanos* (and in the related manuscript the *Romances de los señores de la Nueva España*) there appears a music writing closer than this to European expectations. It takes the form of percussion cadences, indicated by the four syllables *ti*, *to*, *qui*, and *co*, written between the headings of some of the songs and the song texts themselves (for an instance from the *Cantares mexicanos*, see Figure 2.6). We do not know much about the origins of this syllabic notation. The syllables probably reflect mnemonic practices for teaching, disseminating, and preserving percussion cadences within oral traditions of Mexica song, and it is certainly plausible to think that their use reaches back to the time before European contact. The syllable system was clearly dispersed more widely than in

---

[19] Clendinnen is particularly eloquent on the permeability of borders between sacred and mundane realms and the role of ritual in controlling border-crossings; see esp. *Aztecs*, pp. 50–4. She discusses the fluid identities of Mexica deities on pp. 248–9.

[20] *Aztecs*, pp. 258–9; on the warrior's escape from subjectivity see p. 150.

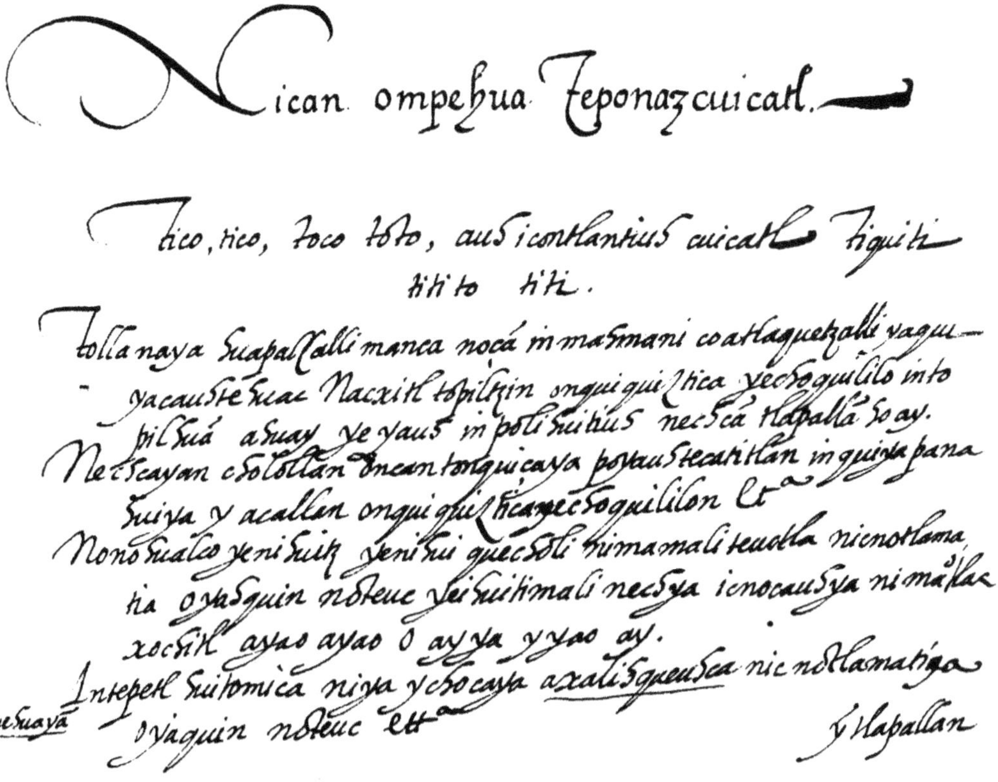

Metonymy, writing, and Mexica song

[handwritten manuscript:]

Nican ompehua teponazcuicatl.

tico, tico, toco toto, auh icontlantius cuicatl tiquiti
titi to titi.

Tollanaya huapalcalli manca noca in mamani coatlaquetzalli yaqui-
yacauhtehuac Nacxitl topiltzin onquiquiztica yechoquililo into
pilhua ahuay ye yauh in polihuitiuh necca tlapalla ho ay.
Nechcayan cholollan oncan tonquicaya poyauhtecatitlan inquiyapana
huiya y acallan onquiquizticayecchoquililon et°
Nonhualco yenihuih yenihui quetzalli humamali teuctla nicnotlamatia oyahquin noteuc yehuitima li necya icnocauhya nimatlac
xochitl ayao ayao o ay ya y yao ay.
xehuaya Intepetl huitomica niya ychocaya axalihqueuhca nicnotlamatiya
oyaquin noteuc et° y tlapallan

Figure 2.6 Music writing from the *Cantares mexicanos*

these manuscripts – widely enough so that by the middle of the seventeenth century a genre of colonial Mexican song, the *tocotín* or *tocontín*, could be named after it.[21]

---

[21] For seventeenth- and eighteenth-century accounts of *tocotines*, see Bierhorst, *Cantares mexicanos: Songs of the Aztecs* (Stanford: Stanford University Press, 1985), pp. 88–90, and Stevenson, *Music in Aztec and Inca Territory*, pp. 165–6. The most specific comment we have as to the significance of the syllables comes from a mid-seventeenth-century description of a *tocotín* by the Jesuit Andrés Pérez de Ribas; he wrote that "Those three syllables in the word Tocontín are like pitches which imitate the sound of the little drum, and therefore some call the dance by this name" (trans. Bierhorst, ibid., p. 89). See Andrés Pérez de Ribas, *Historia de los triumphos de nuestra santa fee . . . en las missiones de la provincia de Nueva-España* (Madrid: Alonso de Paredes, 1645), p. 640 (*recte* 740): "Essas tres sylabas de la palabra, Tocontin, son como puntos, que guarda el son del tamborcito, y por esso llaman algunos con esse nombre a este baile." The account is tantalizing but unsatisfying for at least two reasons: It associates the syllables only with the *teponaztli*, Pérez de Ribas's "little drum," while they are clearly applied to both *teponaztli* and *huehuetl* in the *cantares*; and it specifies three pitches, whereas the *teponaztli* was constructed and (according to sixteenth-century accounts) the *huehuetl* was played so as to produce two. Nonetheless, Pérez de Ribas's account has suggested to scholars the attractive hypothesis that the vowels of the syllables might signify two different pitch levels, leaving the consonants to determine somehow rhythmic patterns. One playing-out of this hypothesis is explored by Bierhorst (*Cantares mexicanos*, pp. 72–9); others, alongside less probable possibilities (such as Vicente Mendoza's hypothesis, later taken up by Garibay, that

We can be confident, in any case, that the songs of Mexica ritual were prepared through careful oral teaching. An instance is described in some detail in Sahagún's *Florentine Codex*:

> First the ruler announced what song should be sung. He commanded the singers to rehearse and practice the song and [to prepare] the *teponaztli*, the rubber drum hammers, and the *huehuetl*, and all the properties [costumes? regalia?] used in the dance. And [he determined the kind of] dance, who would give the pitch, who would lead, who would beat the *teponaztli*, who would play the *huehuetl*. All was first arranged, so that nothing would be left out.

Motolinía, in his *Memoriales*, also attests to this concern for carefully planned performance. He notes that both old, hallowed sacred songs and newly devised songs were sung in Mexica festival, then adds, "The singers decided some days before the festivals what they would sing ... and if there were to be new songs and dances they gathered in advance so there would be no imperfections on the festival day." As to the sacred songs, these seem (again according to the *Florentine Codex*) to have been "read" from the codices kept in the *calmecac*, or priests' school: "Especially there was [in the *calmecac*] teaching of songs which they called the gods' songs [*teocuicatl*] inscribed in books."[22] Here pictographic writing seems to have come into direct and fascinating relation with performed song. No example of such a songbook has survived, but from the few codices that remain we must imagine the relation to be one in which general themes and ritual functions for the songs were conveyed on painted pages, with the particulars of the songs' performance left to be passed along through careful oral pedagogy.

This tradition of oral transmission needed to convey not only the sung words of the songs; it needed also to teach the drumming, especially of *huehuetl* and *teponaztli*, that was habitually associated with them. It would have been an easy and natural step in this teaching to devise an oral system for reciting and practicing drum cadences. Such systems are known today in the most complex surviving oral traditions of musical instruction; a foremost example is the classical tradition of India. The recited drum cadences would have drawn the drumming to the heart of the oral transmission as a whole.

Whether or not the syllabic system itself looks back on prehispanic origins, it must have arisen in a tradition of oral transmission such as this. Against this background, it was subtly transformed by its alphabetization. In the *cantares* manuscript it is no longer one component in an oral and pictographic pedagogy but instead comes to seem the product of an absence created by the alphabetization of the song texts themselves. Only their inscription,

---

the syllables represent four pitches of a pentatonic scale), are reviewed by Stevenson, *Music in Aztec and Inca Territories*, pp. 46–54. In the Epilogue to chapter 3 below, we shall see that in some areas this syllabic notation lived on as a guide to percussive performance into the eighteenth century.

[22] For these quotations see Fray Bernardino de Sahagún, *Florentine Codex: General History of the Things of New Spain*, ed. and trans. Arthur J. O. Anderson and Charles E. Dibble, 13 vols. (Santa Fe and Salt Lake City: School of American Research and University of Utah Press, 1950–82), VIII, pp. 55–6, and III, p. 67; and Toribio de Motolinía, *Memoriales de Fray Toribio de Motolinía*, ed. Luis García Pimentel (Mexico: published by the editor, 1903), bk. 2, chap. 26.

after all, prizes these words apart from their sung medium, which comes then to require a writing of its own. Their writing presses the demand for a music notation answering to the European requirement of song-act reconstructibility; alphabetic writing prescribes a role for music writing. Music notation in the West is fundamentally defined by this bond to and alienation from alphabetic "word notation"; it is the product of a gap (and hence a felt lacuna) introduced by the alphabet.[23] On the other hand, in the music notation of the *Codex Borbonicus*, the song volute, there is no such absence. There song is rendered complete, in its full indigenous materiality, without response to any Western demand for precise reconstitution in performance.

Writing down the syllabic percussive cadences thus brought them within the gravitational control of European inscriptive technology. The Western expectation that word writing and music writing would aspire to the telos of more or less exact reconstructibility was mapped on to a system that had once functioned within indigenous contexts of ritual preservation and oral/pictographic dissemination. This mapping resulted in the transformation of a Mexican *music enunciation* (the orally transmitted syllabic cadences) into a European *music notation*, and carried with it the corollary judgment – almost inevitable, it would seem – that the first is only a preliminary or as yet inadequate version of the second. The sense of this failure suffuses the many scholarly attempts that have been made over the years to "decipher" the syllabic notation of the *Cantares mexicanos*, to find out what it really means so as to reconstruct how the Nahuas really played.[24]

The European control exercised by the writing of the percussive syllables in the *Cantares mexicanos* might be dramatized by comparison with an explicit irruption of European music notation, also linked to an attempt to alphabetize indigenous song, concerning another American locale. This is the account of Tupinamba singing from Jean de Léry's *Histoire d'un voyage fait en la terre du Brésil*, first published in 1578 and reprinted frequently thereafter.

In recent years Léry's book has been a *carte de visite* of sorts for repeated meditations on European encounters of Americans by Michel de Certeau, Frank Lestringant, Stephen Greenblatt, and others. De Certeau in particular focuses on passages recording Léry's ravishment by Tupinamba song. In his view these moments in Léry's experience of the Tupinamba betray in paradigmatic fashion a presence of others' voices that transgresses ethnographic and historiographic attempts to capture and discipline them through writing. As de Certeau puts it, we cannot fully "replace with a text what only a voice that is other

---

[23] Leo Treitler adumbrates this view in stressing that the earliest music notation of Gregorian chant aimed not to define a sequence of pitches but instead to write the melodic inflections of individual syllables of sung words; see "The Early History of Music Writing in the West," *Journal of the American Musicological Society* 35 (1982), pp. 237–79, esp. p. 244. These inflections were absent, of course, from the alphabetic writing of the chanted words and syllables – an absence recuperated, then, by music notation. For more technical detail on the subject, see Leo Treitler, "Reading and Singing: On the Genesis of Occidental Music-Writing," *Early Music History* 4 (1984), pp. 135–208.

[24] See for examples Garibay, *Historia*, I, pp. 80–1; Samuel Martí, *Canto, danza, y música precortesianos* (Mexico: Fondo de Cultura Económica, 1961), pp. 140–8; Stevenson, *Music in Aztec and Inca Territory*, pp. 46–53; and Bierhorst, *Cantares mexicanos*, pp. 72–8.

could reveal." The bodied voices of others will always escape full domestication in our writing.²⁵

De Certeau's ideas intersect at several points (if obliquely) with Derrida's critique in *Of Grammatology*. His point of departure is the relation between writing and speech, and he shares with Derrida the conviction that Western categories of self and other have been formed in the matrix of this relation. But where Derrida concentrates on the place of writing as a supplementary force undoing speech's claims to priority and full presence, de Certeau focuses instead on the escape of the New World voice from the confines of Europe's alphabetic regimen. Léry's writing creates both an object (the Tupinamba of Brazil) and a discipline within which it is defined (ethnology). Even as it does so, however, it cannot avoid registering the sonic excess by which Tupinamba voices escape its sovereignty. These voices sound at the margins of Léry's account as a "ravishing" of the text and a "calling" of its author. In the midst of ethnological objectification, de Certeau asserts in Lacanian fashion, they signal "the insurmountable alterity from which the subject's desire is modeled."²⁶

De Certeau comes closer than most writers to taking account of the fact that the rapturous Tupinamba voice is crucially not the speech Léry shared with the natives but their song he overheard. ("What comes from the mouth or goes into the ear can produce ravishment. Noises win over messages, and singing over speech."²⁷) Léry himself, instead, registered the supplementarity of song, the excess by which it transgresses speech, in the form of his writing. He did so first, in the earliest editions of his travelogue, by italicizing the brief Tupinamba song texts. He did so more strikingly in later editions, from 1585 on, by introducing music examples in European notation for the five Tupinamba songs (see Figure 2.7). Here we follow a step-by-step acknowledgment of the lacuna opened by phonetic writing. We progress from a distinction of song *within* alphabetization (by means of italics for the sung words) to an attempt to close, with music notation, the absence made palpable *by* alphabetization. But if in the *Cantares mexicanos* alphabetization construes an indigenous system as inadequate, here it is European notation that fails in the face of the other. Léry's readers gain little hint even from his desperate music-notational measures (first published thirty years after the event!) of how Tupinamba singing could have awakened in him the strong emotions he describes: fear, wonder, transporting delight. His writing technologies cannot keep Tupinamba song from escaping his and his readers' control.

So, also in the 1585 edition, another European regimen intruded, this time a conceptual one. Hard on the heels of his description of one of the songs, where he had in earlier editions suspected that the singers were possessed by Satan, Léry now broke off to

---

²⁵ See Michel de Certeau, "Ethno-Graphy: Speech, or the Space of the Other: Jean de Léry," in *The Writing of History*, trans. Tom Conley (New York: Columbia University Press, 1988), pp. 208–43 (for the quotation, p. 212); Stephen Greenblatt, "Introduction," in his *Marvelous Possessions: The Wonder of the New World* (Chicago: University of Chicago Press, 1991); and Frank Lestringant, "The Philosopher's Breviary: Jean de Léry in the Enlightenment," *Representations* 33 (1991), pp. 200–11. For Léry's *Histoire* I have used the facsimile of the 1580 edition, edited by Jean-Claude Morisot (Geneva: Droz, 1975), and the translation of it by Janet Whatley, *History of a Voyage to the Land of Brazil, Otherwise Called America* (Berkeley and Los Angeles: University of California Press, 1990). See also chap. 4 below.

²⁶ De Certeau, "Ethno-Graphy," p. 236.   ²⁷ Ibid., p. 235.

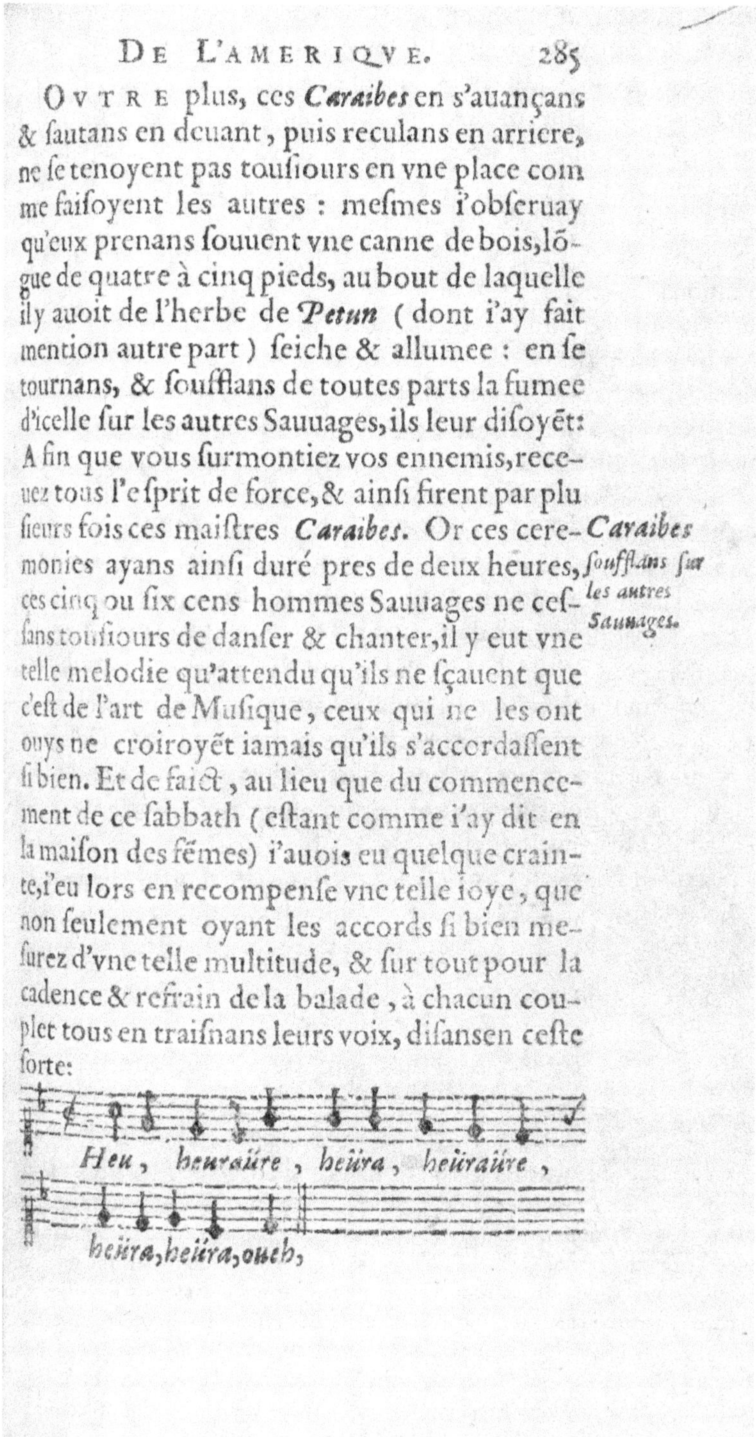

> DE L'AMERIQVE. 285
>
> OVTRE plus, ces *Caraibes* en s'auançans & fautans en deuant, puis reculans en arriere, ne se tenoyent pas tousiours en vne place comme faisoyent les autres : mesmes i'obseruay qu'eux prenans souuent vne canne de bois, longue de quatre à cinq pieds, au bout de laquelle ily auoit de l'herbe de *Petun* (dont i'ay fait mention autre part) seiche & allumee : en se tournans, & soufflans de toutes parts la fumee d'icelle sur les autres Sauuages, ils leur disoyēt: A fin que vous surmontiez vos ennemis, receuez tous l'esprit de force, & ainsi firent par plusieurs fois ces maistres *Caraibes*. Or ces ceremonies ayans ainsi duré pres de deux heures, ces cinq ou six cens hommes Sauuages ne cessans tousiours de danser & chanter, il y eut vne telle melodie qu'attendu qu'ils ne sçauent que c'est de l'art de Musique, ceux qui ne les ont ouys ne croiroyēt iamais qu'ils s'accordassent si bien. Et de faict, au lieu que du commencement de ce sabbath (estant comme i'ay dit en la maison des fēmes) i'auois eu quelque crainte, i'eu lors en recompense vne telle ioye, que non seulement oyant les accords si bien mesurez d'vne telle multitude, & sur tout pour la cadence & refrain de la balade, à chacun couplet tous en traisnans leurs voix, disansen ceste forte:
>
> *Caraibes soufflans sur les autres Sauuages.*
>
> Heu, heuraüre, heüra, heüraüre, heüra, heüra, oueh,

Figure 2.7 Tupinamba song from Léry's *Histoire d'un voyage* . . .

introduce learned material on witchcraft and the witches' Sabbath from Jean Bodin's *De la démonomanie des sorciers*.[28] Where the Tupinamba before had been merely *enragés* they now became *Démoniaques* – as if the deployment of a technical, even clinical, terminology (complete with upper-case D) could redress the limitations of a notational regimen. The sonic excess of song that escaped constraint by notation was disciplined instead by recourse to an abominated European diabolism. The analytic categories of this evil, more and more fully developed in Europe through the sixteenth century, were made to compensate for the inability of alphabetic writing and its attendant music writing to capture performed utterance and rationalize affective response.

Léry's gesture toward Bodin and the black Sabbath exemplifies the most common conceptual mechanism by which Europeans sought to bring an indigenous American imaginary under the aegis of a Christian supernatural. It has been analyzed by several writers, recently and notably Serge Gruzinski and Fernando Cervantes for central Mexico and Sabine MacCormack for Inca Peru.[29] Its connection to song has seldom been remarked, but it runs deep. This automatic and repeated European association of American song with things diabolical reacts to the unsettling transgression inherent in others' singing.[30]

I will return in chapter 6 to these issues. Here it is enough to note that the whole constellation is related also to European technologies of writing. The surplus of song over speech was brought home forcefully by an absence at the heart of alphabetism, the writing most closely bound to the sound of speech. At the moment of generating a musical notation – at moments like those in the Carolingian Middle Ages, of capital importance for European music history, or like the one marked in successive editions of Léry's *Histoire* – alphabetic writing declares this absence, proclaims an insufficiency evident especially in the presence of song. Through music writing it labors to capture in its own inscriptive terms an aspect of sung utterance that escapes it.

The escape unsettles in part because of what it tells us about our speech and our writing. Song powerfully lays bare the illusion by which phonetic writing could support a universal

---

[28] On Léry's use of Bodin and for an interpretation along other lines of its significance, see Greenblatt, *Marvelous Possessions*, pp. 15–19.

[29] See Gruzinski, *La Colonisation*; Fernando Cervantes, *The Devil in the New World: The Impact of Diabolism in New Spain* (New Haven: Yale University Press, 1994); and Sabine MacCormack, *Religion in the Andes: Vision and Imagination in Early Colonial Peru* (Princeton: Princeton University Press, 1991).

[30] One writer who has begun to analyze this association for Inca territories is Juan Carlos Estenssoro Fuchs, "Los bailes de los indios y el proyecto colonial," *Revista andina* 10 (1992), pp. 353–89. The transgression of others' songs is felt not only across wide cultural distances; it occurs constantly in the context of narrower differences as well. Its intrusion in familiar European repertories has repeatedly animated Carolyn Abbate's studies of nineteenth-century opera. There the transgression has the force to thwart the monologic aspirations of a unilateral compositional authority, to breach conventional narrative strategies, to "destroy language" and with it the presence of enacted character, and even to undo the structures of power associated with visually identified gender; see her *Unsung Voices: Opera and Musical Narrative in the Nineteenth Century* (Princeton: Princeton University Press, 1991) and "Opera; Or, the Envoicing of Women," in *Musicology and Difference: Gender and Sexuality in Music Scholarship*, ed. Ruth A. Solie (Berkeley: University of California Press, 1993), pp. 225–58. See also Gary Tomlinson, *Metaphysical Song: An Essay on Opera* (Princeton: Princeton University Press, 1999), esp. chap. 4.

metaphysics of presence in spoken speech. It is bound to speech/*logos* usually by a semantics and always by a dimension of *phonos*. But its *phonos* exceeds speech and remains always farther alienated than it from alphabetic writing. (What would Western writing have been like had it from its beginnings answered to singing rather than speaking?) Because of this distance, singing, chanting, and intonation in general mark experiences of Europeans in America that are not reduced and domesticated, but rather exposed and exacerbated, by the exegetical technology the Europeans brought. Song is the open question that undoes the metaphysical pretensions of phonetic writing. It clears a space for other disruptions of familiar connections of language and the world.

To return to prehispanic and early colonial Mexica song: We cannot hope to hear it again except in the echo of a surplus that overwhelms the forces in the West mobilized to control song all told. There we sense a realm allied to but beyond speech that eludes the effort of phonetic writing to represent utterance. We hear, then, new resonances of song in paint and pictography – writing in its extra-phonetic dispensations – in flower, feather, book, and finally world. In unlearning what we thought we knew about Aztec singing, we productively unlearn other things as well. To follow through this process, we need now to examine in some detail the *Cantares mexicanos*.

3

Cantares mexicanos

To read outward from the alphabetic traces of the Nahuatl *cantares* toward the world at large in which they arose is, in one view, an instance of what the historian forever attempts in approaching written documents. Viewed differently, however, the special nature of the *cantares* sources draws the exercise away from the historian's usual practice, and this for two reasons we have dwelled on in the previous chapters. First, these texts represent not poems or literature in our usual sense – they represent nothing at all, finally, to be *read* – but songs to be sung, drummed, and danced. This draws them into the special orbit of the countless thousands of other song texts that have come down to us in legible writing but with few hints of the ways they were once sung. Second, the alphabetization of these sung words pulled them away from their indigenous world, in which there was no alphabet and no phonetic writing, toward different cultural horizons. Of those countless thousands of songs, the majority came to be preserved in writing systems proximate or native to the cultures that sang them; not so the *cantares*. On account of both these conditions, we need to read these songs, paradoxically, so as to alienate them from the very medium of their writing.

Such a reading is not tantamount to a reconstruction of the original modes of performance of the *cantares*. Reconstructions of this sort have been attempted, of course; but they inevitably need to rely on any number of specifics we are not in a position to recover. Our knowledge of almost all the exact particulars of the sixteenth-century performance of these songs is severely limited by the sources that bring them to us. This is not to say that these speculations are not intriguing, or that we should abandon the desire to know more about performance particulars. I will have something to say about them below, and it is not unlikely that new sources will emerge that will shed more light on them. Nevertheless, this kind of reconstruction is not the primary aim here.

It is possible to approach the *Cantares mexicanos* with different goals in mind. Between knowledge of performative particulars of the Nahuatl *cantares* and the broadest generalizations about the place of ritual song and dance in Aztec culture there is a third level of investigation that has been paid relatively little attention. Here we discern how the *cantares* once opened out to touch the world, how their sung and drummed performance answered to a constellation of expectations concerning their expressive powers and their entailments with the non-songish things around them. Call it a *supraperformative* level, where we can glimpse not so much the specific manner in which a song was presented as what work its performance was expected to achieve. Behind and beneath this, in turn, we perceive the unspoken conditions of musical and ritual knowledge on which these expectations were founded. At this nexus of songwork, fixed between the most specific practices of song and dance and archaeological cultural values, a sung texture of indigenous and colonial aims emerges.

The Nahuatl *cantares* have much to reveal about this supraperformative level. To see how this is so we start – where else? – by reading: reading the words of a song that exemplifies a prominent strain in both of the main manuscripts preserving these songs, the *Cantares mexicanos* and the *Romances de los señores de la Nueva España* (see Example 1).[1]

---

[1] Throughout this chapter the translations from Nahuatl are my own. However, they are, like all but the earliest translations from this difficult corpus, much indebted to their predecessors. These include especially the translations of Garibay and Bierhorst: see Angel María Garibay K., *Historia de la literatura Náhuatl*, 2 vols. (Mexico City: Editorial Porrúa, 1953–4) and *Poesía Náhuatl*, 3 vols. (1964–8; 2nd edn., Mexico City: Universidad Nacional Autónoma, 1993); and John Bierhorst, *Cantares mexicanos: Songs of the Aztecs* (Stanford: Stanford University Press, 1985). Other translations I have consulted include those of Miguel León-Portilla, scattered through his many books on Aztec thought and culture, and, from the nineteenth century, the pioneering work of Daniel G. Brinton, *Ancient Nahuatl Poetry, Containing the Nahuatl Text of XXVII Ancient Mexican Songs* (Philadelphia, 1890; rpt. New York: AMS Press, 1969). Bierhorst provides a concordance of the translations available of each song in the "Commentary" section of *Cantares mexicanos*, pp. 429–514. In order to translate these songs, the texts must first be analyzed orthographically, a process which is necessarily tantamount to a grammatical analysis. My analysis is much indebted to Bierhorst's "Analytical Transcription" of the manuscript, in *A Nahuatl–English Dictionary and Concordance to the Cantares mexicanos with an Analytical Transcription and Grammatical Notes* (Stanford: Stanford University Press, 1985), pp. 425–678. For reasons I have outlined in chap. 1, this is a resource to be used with caution; but, in conjunction with Bierhorst's authoritative diplomatic transcription of the manuscript, in *Cantares mexicanos*, it is nevertheless valuable. For the manuscript itself I use the facsimile edition published in 1994 by the Instituto de Investigaciones Bibliográficas of Mexico City, ed. José G. Moreno de Alba and Miguel León-Portilla. Many dictionaries and grammars have been invaluable to me in approaching these songs; the most important deserve general mention here: Alonso de Molina, *Vocabulario en lengua castellana y mexicana* (Mexico, 1571; facsimile edn., Madrid: Ediciones Cultura Hispanica, 1944), hereafter referred to in the text; Frances Karttunen, *An Analytical Dictionary of Nahuatl* (Norman: University of Oklahoma Press, 1992); Horacio Carochi, *Grammar of the Mexican Language with an Explanation of Its Adverbs* (1645), ed. and trans. James Lockhart (Stanford: Stanford University Press, 2001); J. Richard Andrews, *Introduction to Classical Nahuatl* (Austin: University of Texas Press, 1975); Thelma D. Sullivan, *Compendium of Nahuatl Grammar*, trans. Thelma D. Sullivan and Neville Stiles (Salt Lake City: University of Utah Press, 1988); and James Lockhart, *Nahuatl as Written: Lessons in Older Written Nahuatl, with Copious Examples and Texts* (Stanford: Stanford University Press, 2001).

Example 1: *Cantares mexicanos*, no. 81, ff. 68r–v

Xopancuicatl
Strophe 1
Noopehua noncuica çā nicuicanitl *huiya*	1
mantemaco xochitl ma yca onahuielo a yca	2
ontlamachtilo in tlp̄ca *ohuaya ohuaya*.	3

2
Can monecuiltonol ticuicanitl *huiya* ca mach in	4
ticyamaceuh xochitl *aya* ca mach in ticyaitac in	5
cuicatl tictemaca ye nican xochimecatl in	6
mocamacpa quizticac tonteahuiltia *yaya* ica	7
onnetlamachtiloya in tlp̄ca *aye aha ohuaya*	8
ohuaya.	9

3
Quetzalpapalocalco ompa ye nihuitz *ayao* ye	10
nictoma ye nocuic *ahuaya onhuiya*.	11

4
Nepapan xochitl ỹ nepapan tlacuilolli ye noyol in	12
nicuicanitl *ayao* ye nictoma ye nocuic *ahuaya*	13
ohuaya.	14

5
Achi yhuic tonahuiya *o* achin ic tonpahpactinemi	15
toyollo in tlp̄cqui ye niyohyontzin	16
nixochiehelehuiya *o* nixochicuihcuicatinemi,	17
ohuaya, ohuaya.	18

6
Nicnehnequi nicehelehuiya in icniuhyotl in	19
tecpillotl achi cohuayotl nixochiehelehuiya *o*	20
nixochicuihcuicatinemi *aya ohuaya ohuaya*.	21

7
Nihualchoca nihualicnotlamati çan nicuicanitl	22
huiya tlaca ahnicuicaz in noxochio *ohuaya* maic	23
ninapantiaz cano ximohuaya *ohuaya*	24
nihuallaocoya *ohuaya ohuaya*.	25

8
Çan no iuhqui xochitl *aya* ypan momati in	26
tlp̄cqui çan cuel achic tocontotlanehuiya *a* in	27
xopanxochitlo xonahahuiyacan *ohuaya*	28
nihuallaocoya *ohuaya ohuaya*.	29

Summer Song
I begin; I sing. I am the singer. Huiya! Let flowers be given so that there is pleasure, so that there is joy on earth. Ohuaya, ohuaya!

Where are your riches, singer? Huiya! Wherever did you get your flowers? Aya! Wherever did you discover the songs you give? Here flower twines are flowing from your mouth. You give pleasure, aya! All on earth are content. Aye aha ohuaya ohuaya!

I come from the house of the quetzal-plume butterflies. Ayao! I loose my songs. Ahuaya onhuiya!

My heart is a multitude of flowers, a multitude of painted pictures. I am the singer. Ayao! I loose my songs. Ahuaya ohuaya!

With them briefly we are content, o, briefly we go giving joy to our hearts on earth. I am Yohyontzin. My cravings are flowers. O! Here, there, everywhere I am singing flowers, ohuaya, ohuaya!

I covet, I crave friendship, nobility, a little comradeship. I flower-crave, o! I am singing flowers. Aya ohuaya, ohuaya!

I come weeping; I come grieving – I, the singer. Huiya! Let me not carry off my flowers. Ohuaya! Let me be adorned [in them?] as I die, there in the place where all are shorn. Ohuaya! Here I am sad. Ohuaya, ohuaya!

So it is with flowers. Aya! So are they known on earth. Only for a moment do we borrow, ah!, the summer flowers. May you rejoice! Ohuaya! Here I am sad. Ohuaya, ohuaya!

Cantares mexicanos

Notes to Example 1

The *Xopancuicatl* here transcribed from f. 68r–v of the *Cantares mexicanos* is a particularly well-attested song, as Bierhorst has reported (*Cantares mexicanos*, p. 497). In addition to the text on f. 68, lengthy passages from it recur in three other songs. Song 75 of the *Cantares*, f. 64v, comprises strophes 1–4 and 7–8 of Song 81 in the order 1, 2, 7, 8, 3, 4. Song 25 of the *Cantares*, ff. 18v–19r, presents the remaining two strophes of song 81, 5–6, as its own strophes 3–4. Finally, strophes 5–6 occur once more on ff. 2v–3r of the *Romances de los señores de la Nueva España*. In these several occurrences the song presents a rich example of the processes of centonization that seem to have played an important role in the formation of the corpus of *cantares* as a whole.

It is not surprising that these versions of the text present a thicket of variants small and large. For my version I have taken the text on f. 68r–v as primary. The notes below explain all the instances where I have accepted readings from the other texts or diverged from the primary text in significant ways; they also detail a few important variants I have not accepted. I have not reported variants that fall within the bounds of normal orthographic deviations in the period – e.g., *in* for *yn* or the inconsistent appearance of *-h-* to indicate a glottal stop – or all variants in the indication of repeated words at the ends of strophes.

In the Nahuatl texts here and below I have italicized the major vocables. I have not, however, followed Bierhorst in italicizing the frequent vocable infixes and suffixes (e.g., line 5, tic*ya*maceuh . . . tic*ya*itac).

Title: Molina, *Vocabulario*, gives "verano" for *xopan*; hence my "Summer Song." Garibay gives the etymologically accurate but circumlocutory "Canto de tiempo de verdor"; less satisfactorily, Bierhorst reads the *-pan* suffix of *xopan* in a narrowly locative sense, yielding "a song of green places." The closely related song 75 is entitled *Xochicuicatl*, "Flower Song."

Line 1: Song 75 opens with the imperative instead of indicative (*Xompehua xoncuica çā ticuicanitl*: "Begin! Sing, singer!"), thus postponing until later the change of voice that occurs with strophe 2 of Song 81. The indicative I have retained seems more in keeping with the first-person emphases later in the song. The first word is a variant for the more usual *nompehua*.

Line 5: Before *in ticyaitac*, song 81 repeats *in ticyamaceuh* from lines 4–5. This is probably a scribal error stimulated by the repetition of *ca mach*; it is not found in song 75, and I delete it here.

Line 7: *tonteahuiltia* from song 75 replaces the corrupt reading *tontecuiltia* from song 81.

Lines 8–9: The vocables here begin *ayc aha* in the original; since *ayc* is not a normal vocable in the *Cantares*, I have followed Bierhorst in correcting it to *aye*. The vocables here are presented in simpler form in song 75: *ohuaya Et.^{a}*

Line 11: The vocables here are indicated only by *Et.^{a}*. I supply them from song 75.

Lines 11–12: Song 75 presents no strophe-break here; however, the extended vocables ending line 11 and the parallel phrases in lines 10–11 and 13–14 both confirm the break indicated in song 81.

Line 12: *Nepapan xochitl ỹ* is not present in song 81, but supplied from song 75. This is probably another scribal oversight caused by repetition (of *nepapan*); the addition creates a characteristic paired locution.

Line 14: *Ohuaya* from song 75; song 81 gives only *o*.

Lines 15–16: The reading from song 25, *nonahuiya . . . ompahpactinemi noyollo* ("I am content . . . he gives pleasure to my heart"), seems less straightforward than the reading here retained.

Line 20: *achi cohuayotl* ("a little comradeship") is not present in song 25, though it is found in the *Romances*. This third noun-phrase, ending the series *in icniuhyotl in tecpillotl*, seems uncharacteristic, especially with its qualifier *achi*; but I accept the weight of two attestations.

Line 23: Song 75 has the plausible *toxochio* ("our flowers").

Lines 25–6: Song 81 presents no strophe-break here. It is called for, however, by the strophe-ending vocables of line 25 and the repetition of lines 24–5 in lines 28–9; I supply it from song 75.

The Singing of the New World

Preliminary considerations and speculations on performance

This song brings together many features that are typical of the *cantares*.[2] Most obvious are formal traits, and first among these is the division of the words into sections. (These are marked off by hanging indents in the manuscript; see Figure 2.6 in chapter 2 above.) Frances Karttunen and James Lockhart have called these sections "verses," Bierhorst prefers "stanzas," while Miguel León-Portilla chooses the somewhat more descriptive "unities of expression" (*unidades de expresión*). I will follow Robert Stevenson in calling them "strophes."[3] This term avoids the ambiguities of "verse," which can refer both to a single line of poetry and to a section of a song. It avoids also the implications of León-Portilla's "unities," a necessary caution since the unity of theme across each strophe is not always marked (see for example strophe 5 in Example 1). Finally, for the musicologist "strophe" hints, better than the other possibilities, at a musical organization in which certain elements of melody and rhythm were recycled for each new section of words; for reasons I will say more about, this seems to me the most likely general performative organization for these songs.

The strophes are punctuated at their ends by sequences of non-lexical words or vocables.[4] This feature is common in the *cantares* – common enough, indeed, to make one wonder whether strophe-ending vocable formulas were not intended to be sung even in those places where the scribes have not indicated them. At any rate, here, as in the majority of the songs, they are expressly indicated. Here also we can see that the strophe-ending vocables tend to be similar across the whole song; they function, that is, as a refrain. The refrain that recurs most often in the songs – we might even think of it as a repertory-wide refrain, binding many songs of this tradition together – is the repeated *ohuaya* of the present song. We will return below to these refrain vocables and the many others that occur within the strophes.

The strophes are grouped here, and normally throughout the *cantares*, in pairs. In each pair they are connected by a repetition of the words at their ends that usually extends back into the strophe to include more than just the final vocables. Each of the pairs of this song, strophes 1–2, 3–4, 5–6, and 7–8, shows this internal relationship. As Karttunen and Lockhart have pointed out, the connection of paired strophes can be strong, with lengthy repeated

---

[2] The formal and stylistic features of the *cantares* here discussed have been described at length especially in two important articles from the early 1980s: Frances Karttunen and James Lockhart, "La estructura de la poesía náhuatl vista por sus variantes," *Estudios de cultura náhuatl* 14 (1980), pp. 15–64; and Miguel León-Portilla, "Cuícatl y tlahtolli: Las formas de expresión en náhuatl," *Estudios de cultura náhuatl* 16 (1983), pp. 13–108. For a more recent summary of Lockhart's views see James Lockhart, *The Nahuas after the Conquest: A Social and Cultural History of the Indians of Central Mexico, Sixteenth through Eighteenth Centuries* (Stanford: Stanford University Press, 1992), pp. 392–401. See also Bierhorst, *Cantares mexicanos*, General Introduction, esp. chaps. 3–4. In referring to songs from the *Cantares mexicanos* I will follow Bierhorst's numbering of them and also cite the folios they occupy in the original manuscript.

[3] Robert Stevenson, *Music in Aztec and Inca Territory* (Berkeley: University of California Press, 1968), pp. 48ff.

[4] Like Bierhorst, I italicize vocables for easy spotting. For the most part this is a straightforward procedure, though there are numerous places where either a questionable reading in the manuscript or the pervasive use in Nahuatl of weakly semantic particles makes the judgment difficult.

material sometimes even embracing most of the strophe, or it can be briefer and weaker. In Example 1 the connection is strongest between strophes 3 and 4 and 5 and 6. Paired strophes are often of approximately equal length, but they need not be: strophes 1 and 2, of dramatically different length, are nevertheless bound by a pair-refrain. Karttunen and Lockhart show also that by far the most usual number of strophes in these *cantares* is the number found in the present poem, eight, grouped in four pairs.[5]

The local refrain of the strophe pair can involve vocables that come before the general vocable refrain that ends all strophes of the song. Three instances occur in Example 1; see strophes 3–4, 5–6, and 7–8. All three are somewhat unusual in that the vocables unique to each pair do not lead directly into the general vocable refrain but come before additional lexical material. For example, the strong repeated element binding strophes 3–4 begins with the vocable *ayao* but then returns to lexical material "ye nictoma ye nocuic" before ending with the vocable refrain.

All these formal features suggest that the performances of these songs involved musical repetition synchronized to the sectional structure of the words sung. Let me put this the other way around, capturing more accurately the nature of these texts: The sectional structure of the alphabetized texts probably reflects a sectional organization of their original presentation; the presence of verbal refrains almost certainly reflects some sort of musical repetition. There is only indirect evidence to make such assertions, but it is strong. Worldwide, clear divisions in written song texts again and again have reflected sectional, repeating musical structures in their performance. Indeed, the fixed poetic forms often associated with these written textual divisions spring up historically, in most cases, as nothing other than signals of performed musical repetitions of various kinds, more or less complex. We see such a development in the crystallization of the fixed song forms of the European Middle Ages, and it was likely traced also by any number of ancient song traditions, European and otherwise. The circumstantial case for such musical repetition grows even stronger when we consider the refrain structures of the *cantares*. Examples can be found in song repertories of such systematic repetition of specific words *without* musical repetition, but they are few and far between, and they usually appear as selfconscious divergences within a context of refrains involving repetition of both words and the manner of their singing.

The most likely musical organization of the *cantares*, then, was some sort of strophic form, one we can see reflected in the format of their written words. Given the varied lengths of the strophes of these songs, however, this must have been a rather flexible affair. Over the metrical accompaniment of the drums, the melodies might have been built up out of cellular units repeated (and perhaps elaborated) as often as needed to accommodate the words (this would accord with practices in many other song traditions). Perhaps the melodies entailed formulas for beginning and ending the strophes. In this way the differing lengths of the strophes would not disallow melodic repetition.

Such speculation raises the question of a poetic meter in these texts. Several scholars, including Garibay, León-Portilla, and Karttunen and Lockhart, have sought to discern traces

[5] Karttunen and Lockhart, "La estructura," pp. 18–20; Lockhart, *The Nahuas*, pp. 396–7.

of regular meter – mostly, by their own admission, with only equivocal results.[6] It is worth emphasizing, however, that the texts themselves need not evince any metrical structure in order for their performances to have done so. Strongly metrical accompanimental patterns can remain unambiguous while supporting even quite free sung recitation. Conversely, it is also possible to sing words possessing no strong metrical regularity of their own so as to conform to the marked meter of such accompanimental patterns.[7]

Bierhorst suggests that the melodic style itself of the songs may have been a "recitative-like" chant over the metrical patterns of the drums, in the manner of some more recent Native North American traditions.[8] But we need not presume that the melodies were simple, unadorned, declamatory, or monotonal in nature. Neither the variable length of the strophes nor the lack of apparent poetic meter in the words militates against the possibility of an elaborate, even florid melody for the *cantares*. The longer vocable refrains of some of the songs might in particular signal places where complex, perhaps rapturous singing stepped to the fore.

The fundamental accompaniment to the singing of the *cantares* consisted of drumming on the *huehuetl* or the *teponaztli* or both together. The drum cadences indicated for many of the songs by the syllabic notation discussed in chapter 2 – the four syllables *ti, to, qui,* and *co* in various combinations – are short enough that they would have had to be repeated many times across a single strophe, not to mention a whole song. The longest songs are divided into sections consisting each of a number of strophes (Bierhorst calls them "cantos"). These sections sometimes are headed each by a new drum cadence – song 61 in the *Cantares mexicanos* (ff. 46r–48v) is a good example – suggesting that variety in these brief, repeated patterns was sought across the span of longer songs. The variety is indicated occasionally even across shorter spans: Song 44 (ff. 26v–27v), for example, consists of two sections, each of ten strophes. The second is accorded a drum cadence different from the first, but even the first incorporates two cadences; its heading reads: "Tico tico toco toto; auh ic ontlantiuh cuicatl [i.e., and when the song is ending:] tiquiti titito titi" (see again Figure 2.6 in chapter 2).

We have little to guide us in guessing at the precise synchronization of the singing and drumming. If the model of a cellular melodic structure built over metrical drumming is right – and given, again, the variety of strophe lengths present within single songs – some resynchronizing of melodic and rhythmic patterns might well have been necessary near the end of each strophe to bring it to a satisfactory close. Perhaps the vocable refrains joined with repeated melodic formulas to function as a sung signal for this realignment with the

---

[6] See Garibay, *Historia*, I, pp. 60–4, and *Poesía náhuatl*, I, pp. xxxviii, and II, pp. xxxiii–xxxviii; Karttunen and Lockhart, "La estructura," pp. 28–33; and León-Portilla, "Cuícatl y tlahtolli," pp. 37–40.

[7] Here, then, I would disagree with the assertion of Karttunen and Lockhart ("La estructura," p. 33) that it is necessary first to understand the "internal structure of the verse itself" in order then to illuminate the meter of the percussion accompaniment. As songs (and not read poems), the *cantares* may well have employed their percussion accompaniment, rather than any linguistic features, as the fundamental determinant of their meter. The difference of opinion is, however, probably moot, since we are close neither to deciphering the percussion syllables nor to perceiving some clear meter in the language of the song texts.

[8] Bierhorst, *Cantares mexicanos*, pp. 44–5.

drums. It is possible also that a heading like that of song 44 bows to this sort of consideration; it could indicate a shift to the second cadence not somewhere near the end of its ten-strophe "canto" but rather at the end of each strophe.

Direct evidence as to the circumstances in which these *cantares* were performed is sparse.[9] One contemporary testimony that seems to come close to them occurs in Sahagún's *Relación del autor digna de ser notada*, the brooding treatise he included in book 10 of his *Florentine Codex*.[10] It departs from the ethnographic reportage of most of the codex to detail in pessimistic tones the failure, as the septuagenarian Sahagún saw it in 1576, of the College of Tlatelolco he had helped to found many years before and indeed of the Christian mission in central Mexico all told. Gloomily Sahagún relates the breakdown of the systems by which the Spaniards had once policed the idolatrous practices of the Mexicans. In the midst of this narrative, and as evidence of the natives' backsliding, he comes to speak of their songs:

> In this way they sing when they wish and celebrate their feasts as they wish and sing the ancient songs they were wont to sing in the days of their idolatry – not all of them but many of them. And no one understands what they say as their songs are very obscure. And if, after their conversion here, they sing some songs they have composed, which deal with the things of God and His saints, they are surrounded by many errors and heresies. And even in the dances and *areitos* many of their ancient superstitions and idolatrous rituals are practiced, especially where no one resides who understands them. This happens most frequently among the merchants when they hold their feasts, entertainments, and banquets.
>
> This continues; every day it grows worse. And there is no one who strives to remedy it because it is not understood, except by a few, and they do not dare tell.

Here we have a miniature sketch of the *cantares'* performance as entertainments for more or less prosperous natives in the midst of drinking and other revelry. Sahagún suggests, in tones reflecting his dark suspicions, that the songs were sung in private circumstances out of earshot of the colonial authorities who wished to police them. He adds the usual

---

[9] For one general account of the performance situation of the songs, see Bierhorst, *Cantares mexicanos*, pp. 70–2. Note that Bierhorst's particulars are mainly drawn from passages, in sources such as Motolinía and Durán, which describe grand public ceremonies and may not be relevant to the *cantares* tradition. Bierhorst shows some awareness of this problem, but other attempts to illuminate the performance of the *cantares* do not. They draw willy-nilly on the whole spectrum of accounts of Mexica culture, as if one type (or era) of native music-making were interchangeable with any other. It is debatable, at least, whether early accounts attempting to describe the music-making of grand public ceremonies of the Aztecs can tell us much about the *cantares*, which seem to have thrived, as we will see, either in more intimate circumstances or in expressly Christian processions and festivals. Moreover, many of these early accounts themselves evince a similar confusion, swerving between the author's firsthand experience and testimony, variously collected, about ancient practices; see for example the chapter on song and dance in Fray Diego Durán, *Book of the Gods and Rites and The Ancient Calendar*, trans. Fernando Horcasitas and Doris Heyden (Norman: University of Oklahoma Press, 1971), chap. 21.

[10] Fray Bernardino de Sahagún, *Florentine Codex: General History of the Things of New Spain*, ed. and trans. Arthur J. O. Anderson and Charles E. Dibble, 13 vols. (Santa Fe and Salt Lake City: School of American Research and University of Utah Press, 1950–82), I, pp. 74–85; for the citation here see p. 81. This account occurs also in Sahagún's *Historia general de las cosas de Nueva España*, ed. Angel María Garibay K. (Mexico: Editorial Porrúa, 1956), pp. 578–85.

complaint about the songs' incomprehensibility: even had they heard them, the authorities would have been hard pressed to understand them. He acknowledges the living tradition of *cantares* composition in colonial times and recognizes that the singers incorporated Christian elements in their new songs, even while he despairs of the doctrinal correctness of these elements.

Sahagún specifies also that merchants' banquets provided a customary venue for singing of the *cantares*. This is an important clue, for the *Florentine Codex* devotes the lion's share of an entire book to merchants' celebrations. Here, amid rituals for setting out on and returning from journeys and for buying slaves and preparing them for sacrifice, is a three-chapter description of a merchant's banquet (bk. 9, chaps. 7–9). Sahagún's *Relación* suggests that it might bring us closer than any other source to the prehispanic origins of social practices in which the *cantares* we have were later performed.

The account tells of an affair lasting all night and through the next day and involving visions induced by hallucinogenic mushrooms, augury using decapitated fowl, offerings to Huitzilopochtli of flowers, tobacco and copal incense, and much else. A number of particulars look forward to the specifics of the *cantares*. There are offerings of "shield-flowers" (*chimalsuchitl* = *chimalxochitl*), mentioned often in the *cantares* (see for instance Example 9 below). Specific genres of songs are called for that reappear among the later *cantares*, including the *xopancuicatl* we have already encountered.[11] More generally, the rituals of the banquet gravitate toward the central place of the *huehuetl*, which, as we shall see, is repeatedly, even habitually, emphasized in the *cantares* texts (see below, Examples 5, 9, 11, etc.). The *teponaztli* too is called for, and both drums are used to accompany singing and dancing that last through the night into the next morning.

If this account of merchants' banquets indeed portrays the kind of circumstances that persisted in Sahagún's idolatrous song-feasts, we gain a sense of the performance of the *cantares* that is at odds with the public, even community-wide religious song-and-dance celebrations described in many early accounts of the Mexica. We sense something more intimate in dimension and private in intent. Unlike the public ceremonies, here singers could accompany themselves on the drums – in another merchant's ritual, the *Florentine Codex* refers to *teponazcuicanime*, or teponaztli-singers[12] – and a single singer playing a drum, with perhaps a second drummer playing along, might have constituted all the musicians needed for a typical performance. Singing by the whole group, if involved some of the time (could the refrains especially have been sung *en masse*?), was probably not the rule. Dancing to the musicians' songs, instead, more often involved the whole group. The elaborate costume and regalia of larger ceremonies probably gave way to the intimate paraphernalia of a different

---

[11] Three other genres mentioned in the *Florentine Codex* and represented among the *Cantares mexicanos* are the regional or ethnic Hexotzincan songs (*uexotzincaiotl*) and Chalcan songs (*chalchicacuicatl*) and the "plain-style" (*tlamelauhcaiotl*) song; see *Florentine Codex*, ed. Anderson and Dibble, X, p. 40; for xopancuicatl (= supancuicatl) and one further type not found in the *Cantares mexicanos*, the Anahuac song (*anaoacaiotl*; "world-song"), see p. 41. For more on generic distinctions in the *cantares* see below.

[12] See ibid, p. 45. For a singer accompanying himself on the *huehuetl* pictured in the *Codex Borbonicus*, a manuscript probably not far removed chronologically or geographically from the tradition of the *cantares*, see chap. 2 above, Figure 2.2.

kind of ritual: tobacco pipes, plates of mushrooms, birds for sacrifice, shared flowers, and chocolate.

This intimate scene of performance that so worried Sahagún was not, however, the only circumstance in which the *cantares* were sung. We have evidence also of more public performances of some of the songs at least, performances viewed with approval and even organized by the Spanish authorities. Some of this evidence comes from the manuscript of *Cantares mexicanos* itself. A section in the middle of the manuscript preserves a group of lengthy songs, several concerned, more explicitly than any other songs in the anthology, with Christian themes and Biblical stories. These songs come close to the kind of content found in the *Psalmodia Christiana*, a collection of Nahuatl songs on Christian themes devised by Sahagún in collaboration with Nahua scholars in the 1560s and published in 1583.[13] They stand apart from the rest of the *cantares* also in being supplied with headings that are more informative than usual, specifying such information as composers' names and dates of composition.

Three of these headings give particulars about the performances of the songs they begin:

Song 56: Female apparition [epiphany?] song [*Cihuaixnexcuicatl*], in which the holy word is set out. It was sung at the feast of the holy spirit. The singer Cristóbal de Rosario Xiuhtlamin composed it in August of the year 1550.

Song 58: Here begins a casting-out song [*Tequihquixtilizcuicatl*] in which the holy word is translated. Thus was celebrated the feast of San Felipe, when His Majesty's gift arrived from Spain – the coat of arms that he presented to the city of Azcapotzalco Tepanecapan in the year 1564. The one who composed it was Don Francisco Plácido, governor of Xiquipilco, and the year in which it was sung was 1565, when the governor of Azcapotzalco was Don Antonio Valeriano.

Song 61: Here begins a children song [*Pilcuicatl*], or little-children song [*Piltoncuicatl*] that used to be sung there at the church in Mexico at the feast of St. Francis. It was composed in our lifetime when we were living there at the church and were still little children.[14]

The first of these headings associates its song with a Christian festival but does not recall a specific public performance; the second instead seems to do so; while the third connects its song not only to a Christian festival but also to the church school in Mexico. The latter two headings bespeak particularly clearly Spanish participation in the phenomenon of the *cantares*.

These indications of public performance and Spanish participation are seconded by entries in an important source that chronicles events of the 1560s. This manuscript, entitled *Anales de Juan Bautista*, is a copy from the 1580s of a Nahuatl journal kept by a native scribe, notary, or painter in Mexico. It commemorates many Catholic festivals and in several entries names the genres of specific songs sung to celebrate them. A few of these are identical or

---

[13] For the Nahuatl text and English translation, see *Bernardino de Sahagún's Psalmodia Christiana*, trans. Arthur J. O. Anderson (Salt Lake City: University of Utah Press, 1993).

[14] For these headings I follow Bierhorst's translation with minor modifications. See *Cantares mexicanos*, pp. 258–9, 268–9, and 286–7.

similar to genres encountered also in the *Cantares mexicanos*. The songs referred to in the *Anales* were performed in ceremonies of an ostentatiously public nature involving processions, stagings in the patios of churches and palaces, and on a few occasions the spectacular *volador* ceremony, in which Indians costumed as birds and tied to ropes spun down from the top of a high pole.[15]

The author of the *Anales* comes especially close to the songs preserved in the *Cantares mexicanos* at two points. He recalls a performance on June 1, 1564 of a *tequiquixtilizcuicatl*, a type otherwise only attested as song 58 of the *Cantares* (see above). The designation, translated by Bierhorst as "bringing-out song," is probably better rendered as "casting-out song"; it seems to refer in the *Cantares* example to the main theme of the song, the sins of Adam and Eve and their expulsion from Eden. It is possible that a whole miniature tradition of such expulsion songs existed; conversely, could these two songs be one and the same?

In his entry for September 1567, meanwhile, the chronicler writes of a *pipilcuicatl* taught to the people of the church at the instigation of Fray Pedro de Gante and sung then for the public celebration of the feast of St. Francis. The designation is again unclear, but Garibay has taken it to mean a "children's song";[16] this would make it synonymous with the designations for song 61 in the *Cantares* (see above). Both song 61 and the song of the *Anales* were associated with the church school in Mexico; both were composed for performance at the feast of St. Francis. Arthur J. O. Anderson has suggested, with good reason, that they may be the same song.[17]

Whatever the direct connections between the preserved song texts and the songs mentioned in the *Anales*, certain generalizations can be securely drawn from these fragments of evidence. It is clear that there existed a kind of expressly Christian *cantar* meant for public performance, a sort of song not distant in use or evangelizing intent from the overtly Christian songs of Sahagún's *Psalmodia*. It is clear also that the *Anales* supply tantalizing details of such performances and that several songs of this kind are preserved in the *Cantares mexicanos*.

It cannot be coincidental, meanwhile, that these several preserved songs associated with public church festivals also mark the deepest incursion into the *cantares* repertory of Christian themes and Biblical topics. References to Christ, Mary, and a Christian God are found elsewhere in these song texts, but nowhere else are Biblical events and the stories surrounding Christmas and Easter elaborated in detail. This fact might finally help us to understand the dichotomy of performance settings, private/Mexican on the one hand and public/Mexican-Spanish on the other, that emerges from the evidence we have. The *cantares* repertory as it has come to us seems to include a mixed body of songs intended variously

---

[15] For a facsimile, transcription, and Spanish translation of the *Anales* see Luis Reyes García, *Cómo te confundes? Acaso no somos conquistados? Anales de Juan Bautista* (Mexico: Ciesas, 2001); for an earlier description of the manuscript, Garibay, *Historia*, II, pp. 328–33. For the most important references to songs in the *Anales* see in the Reyes edn. pp. 148–51, 154–5, 164–5, 196–7, 220–1, 296–9, and 326–7. On the *volador* ceremony see Bierhorst, *Cantares mexicanos*, pp. 66–9.

[16] Garibay, *Historia*, II, p. 331.   [17] *Sahagún's Psalmodia Christiana*, trans. Anderson, pp. xxii–xxiii.

for one or the other of these settings. It is a repertory seemingly divided in its original presentation between a kind of song authorized by the colonizers and another kind not so authorized. It is likely that this second category remained closer than the first to indigenous themes; perhaps – though this is hard to discern – it remained closer to native modes of performance as well.

Whether or not it did so, we should not mistake even these less Christianized *cantares* for a simple extension of pre-contact practices into the new colonial world. The songs of merchants' banquets guarded from the ears of the Spaniards and the most lavish displays of Christian themes in Nahua song were reverse sides of the same coin. The secret song festivals that Sahagún feared as well as the public processions celebrating Christian festivals were indelibly marked as expressive gestures of a colonial society.

Themes and genres

Both Karttunen and Lockhart and León-Portilla have remarked that the conceptual logic of the *cantares* does not typically unfold in a linear or narrative fashion across individual songs. León-Portilla finds instead "processes converging on an approach that shows from diverse angles the key theme of the composition," while for Lockhart and Karttunen "it is as if the verses were arranged around a center – a theme, a feeling, a character, or all those together – to which they stand in a similar, direct relation rather than relating to one another."[18] The individual strophes often seem, indeed, to orbit around the theme or set of themes of the song they make up rather than pursuing a progressive elaboration, narrative or lyrical, of the topics at hand. This tendency is evident in Example 1 in the loose semantic relations of strophe 3 to strophe 4 and strophe 5 to strophe 6. Karttunen and Lockhart have also suggested that, because of this nonlinear tendency, the order of strophes in the *cantares* is often less important than their relevance to the main theme of a song.[19] We may well see ramifications of this in the processes of centonization by which six of the strophes of Example 1 were reordered to form another song, while the remaining two reappeared in two more songs (see the notes to Example 1).

It is tempting to discover in this feature of the *cantares* something more consequential still: what we might call a *conceptual parataxis* bearing a deep kinship to the patterns of Nahuatl itself. In chapter 2 we saw that the basic predicative and nominative elements in the language are sentence-words, not absolutive words dependent on other words around them to complete a thought. The valences of Nahuatl utterance thus seem to connect out to the extra-linguistic world around as much as they bind sentence-words tightly to one another. In this circumstance the language functions without the same degree of hypotaxis or grammatical subordination found in Spanish or English. In the *cantares* and in many other texts – Sahagún's *Florentine Codex* comes quickly to mind – this creates the impression of an accumulation of relatively independent thoughts, loosely bound to one another in syntax and meaning – a paratactic organization, in other words. In addition, the *cantares* in

---

[18] See León-Portilla, "Cuícatl y tlahtolli," p. 42; Karttunen and Lockhart, "La estructura," p. 16.
[19] Karttunen and Lockhart, ibid.

particular are notorious for their inconsistent deployment even of the indicators of grammatical subordination and independence that Nahuatl provides. From this pervasive parataxis comes the aphoristic tone of much alphabetized Nahuatl. From it also, no doubt, sprang European reactions to the *cantares* that we examined in chapter 1: the early criticisms of their pleonasms and, from Garibay on, the championing of diphrasis as their most characteristic rhetorical turn. Setting aside such evaluative agendas, we might glimpse in the large-scale conceptual organization of the songs a play of patterns reaching very deep in Nahua language and thought alike.[20]

At the same time, however, we must be wary of overemphasizing the nonlinearity of thought in the *cantares*. Example 1 can also help us in this. It displays the kind of straightforwardly linear elements that occur in many songs, for example the questioning of the singer of strophe 1 by a second voice in strophe 2; or the maxim-like elaboration, in strophe 8, of the hint of the transience of flowers in strophe 7; or – this across the border of adjacent strophe pairs – the apparent reference at the beginning of strophe 5 back to the songs of strophe 4. Though it may play a smaller role than we are accustomed to, conceptual hypotaxis is by no means unknown to the Nahua mentality or inexpressible in Nahuatl grammatical forms.

Lockhart has summed up the themes central to the corpus of *cantares* and at the same time highlighted its special place in world traditions of song. "The great idiosyncrasy of Nahuatl song" for him resides in its "combination of themes of ethnic pride, battle, martial glory, and the divine not with epic narrative but with an intricate lyricism of flowers, birds, music, friendship, the refinements of nobility, and the pathos of ephemerality."[21] From his list we can see that Example 1 is typical but by no means exhaustive of the range of themes the *cantares* explore. It features singing, flowers, the desire for friendship, and the pathos of the transience of life. It hints at the birds elsewhere ubiquitous (see line 10), and it adds two other frequent topics not mentioned by Lockhart but which play an important if lesser role in the lyricism he describes: butterflies and painted pictures.[22]

Missing from Example 1 is any allusion to ethnic pride or the glories of warfare. This is a reflection of the genre the song represents. It is a *xopancuicatl*, a summer or green-season song (see the notes to Example 1). There are seven other songs so titled in the *Cantares mexicanos*. In their themes and vocabulary they bear a close relation to another genre, the *xochicuicatl* or flower song. These genres are close enough, indeed, that song 75 can be called a *xochicuicatl* rather than *xopancuicatl* notwithstanding the fact that it comprises nothing other than six of the strophes of song 81 reordered. Throughout the *Cantares mexicanos*, the themes of warfare and its glories play only a small role in songs headed *xopancuicatl* and *xochicuicatl*.

---

[20] To point up such parallels is not to revert to any strong version of Sapir-Whorf linguistic relativism; for a review of "neo-relativist" positions connecting language, thought, and culture that have recently emerged see Jane H. Hill and Bruce Mannheim, "Language and World View," *Annual Review of Anthropology* 21 (1992), pp. 381–406.

[21] James Lockhart, *The Nahuas*, p. 398.

[22] Lockhart's description of *cantares* themes is not itself exhaustive, as he is well aware. In particular, precious stones and gems, water in its many aspects – raining, drizzling, snowing, etc. – and shining or resplendent sunlight provide sources of evocative vocabulary in many of the songs. Other general themes not signaled here are represented by a group of comic and/or erotic songs in the *Cantares mexicanos*.

They emerge into full view in several other kinds of songs, most particularly the *yaocuicatl*, the enemy or war song. These war songs tend to share the vocabulary characteristic of summer and flower songs, but they merge it also with their own images: of weapons, shields, eagles and jaguars, dusty battlefields, and chalk and feather regalia. In a similar way the *icnocuicatl*, song of misery or grief, seems to steer the vocabulary of the *xopancuicatl* in a direction emphasizing the sentiments of loss and bereavement signaled in its title.

Such topical generic distinctions, however, by no means provide a systematic categorization of the corpus of *cantares*. In the first place, not all the songs are given titles of any sort. In the second place, the titles signify different kinds of things, so comparing them is often a matter of apples and oranges. While *xochicuicatl* or *yaocuicatl* or *icnocuicatl*, for example, might indicate the general thematic content of songs they head, *teponazcuicatl* (*teponaztli* song) seems to refer instead to the specifics of percussive accompaniment, or perhaps to ritual circumstances in which such accompaniment came to the fore. Ethnic titles such as *otoncuicatl* (Otomi song), meanwhile, might refer to the themes of a song, its place of origin – even its original language, before it was translated into Nahuatl by the singers or writers – or all of these. The exact significance of still other titles remains unclear; *melahuac cuicatl*, for instance, means a song in some manner straight or plain and is, for Molina, the equivalent of *canto llano* or plainchant. Given this disparity of aim in the different names for song types, we are left with a situation in which a single song might carry two or even three titles – for instance *Mexicaxopancuicatl tlamelauhcayotl* (a plain-style Mexica summer song) or *yaoxochicuicatl* (war-flower song) – or in which one song might appear twice under different titles: song 43, a *melahuac cuicatl*, turns up later in the manuscript as a section of song 62, an *icnocuicatl* (see ff. 26r–v and 49v–50r).

The sharing of themes among these song types is asymmetrical. A *yaocuicatl* or *icnocuicatl* might take over the topics and vocabulary of a *xopancuicatl* or *xochicuicatl*, while the reverse is less likely. This suggests a conclusion that is difficult to avoid in reading this corpus of songs, no matter its wide range of topics: that the vocabulary of flowers, precious stones and metals, birds, and singing – the thematic lexicon central to the *xopancuicatl* or *xochicuicatl* – defines the topical centerpoint of the *cantares* as a whole, and that other songs with more specialized content diverge from this center only while remaining in varying degrees under its influence. While we can reach this conclusion without embracing Garibay's notion that flowers and song together made up an indigenous Nahua category of poetry (see chapter 1), it is nevertheless easy to see, on working through these songs, how this ideology of *in xochitl in cuicatl* arose. Avoiding the ideology allows the themes of flower and song to speak for themselves; they will have much to tell us below.

If the topics just named form the heart of the allusive *cantares* vocabulary, there is one element among them that is paramount. This is song itself. The *cantares* focus on the conditions, enactment, and consequences of song, and they do so with a regularity that is, if not unique, at least distinctive among song traditions of the world. Look again at song 81 in Example 1: After its opening apostrophes to the singer, by the singer himself and another voice (strophes 1–2), each successive strophe but the last one returns to the singer's actions and identity. In this the song gives a concentrated exposition of these themes, but one that is by no means unique or unsurpassed among the *cantares*. In fact, across the whole repertory preserved in the *Cantares mexicanos* and *Romances* manuscripts, it is a rare song that does not allude to acts of singing or drumming or, more typically still, describe itself as such an act.

Despite such prevalence, the very notion of singing and the singer as a theme in the *cantares* can go unnoticed. Lockhart, for instance, in his efficacious summary of *cantares* themes quoted above, mentions music but does not specify singing. More tellingly, León-Portilla, in the important article to which I have referred several times, "Cuícatl y tlahtolli: Las formas de expresión en náhuatl," devotes more than a page to the enumeration of the themes of the *cantares*, even listing the musical instruments they frequently name; but of the theme of singing itself there is no mention. These are further instances, no doubt, of the transparency of song in our own cultural perceptions that I remarked in the Introduction above.

We have no reason to believe that singing was similarly invisible to the Nahuas, every reason to believe the opposite. Whatever else the supraperformative analysis of the *cantares* pursued here will entail, it will certainly require a rendering opaque of this category, so basic to their conceptual lexicon.

Singing things

Anything but transparent or invisible, song in the *cantares* attains weight and substance. The act of singing and its consequences are rarely described here in the spiritual or technical terms familiar to modern Western sensibilities; somewhat more often they are cast in emotional terms, also familiar. Most often, instead, they are given volume through a set of associations with (other) material things. Because of their foreignness to our perceptions, we have tended to understand these associations as images – metaphors, similes, and the like – elaborating fancifully on material reality rather than firmly grounded in it. The language and grammar in which they are expressed, however, suggest something different.

In the opening strophe of Example 1 the singer hints that his song is a spreading of flowers. His questioner in strophe 2 confirms the suggestion with a bodily specificity that leaves little justification for disconnecting metaphorically the flowers from the somatic act of song: "nican xochimecatl in mocamacpa quizticac – here flower-twine is flowing from your mouth." The words call to mind the flowery volutes of the pictographic tradition, discussed in chapter 2. They seem almost a verbal epitome of images like the one reproduced there from the *Codex Borbonicus* – a codex painted in all likelihood in the valley of Mexico in the very decades that saw the rise there of the post-conquest *cantares* tradition. Like those painted and carved volutes, the song-act described in song 81 makes utterance palpable; it describes a vocalization of congealed, voluminous riches. ("Can monecuiltonol ticuicanitl," the questioner begins strophe 2: "Where are your riches, singer?")

This singing of flowers is an almost ubiquitous theme in the *cantares*, and the lexicon conveying it comprises some of the most characteristic vocabulary of the songs. It wants a willful twist of modern interpretation to read the song and flowers joined in these passages as some recognizable image of a third category, poetry. Time after time, instead, the singer sings forth blossomings, showers, and festoons of incarnate flowers.

In strophe 6 of the lengthy song 52, a *xochicuicatl* "in the plain style of the Chalcans,"[23] the theme appears with a bodily detail similar to that of song 81:

Example 2

Ytzmolini xochitl, celia, mimilihui, cueponi *yeehuaya* mitecpa onquiça in cuicaxochitlin tepan tictzetzeloa ticyamoyahuaya ticuicanitl Et. [i.e., *ohuaya*] (f. 33v)	Flowers appear; they sprout, unfold, burst into bloom, yeehuaya! From your belly flow song-flowers; then you shake them out, you scatter them, you the singer! Ohuaya!

Song 34, instead, ends with a more typical development of the theme, with no reference to the singer's body. Here, in a manner that remains unspecified, the singer generates both song and flowers in the material world he passes through:

Example 3

Çan nohuian nõne'nemi *yehuaya* nohuian nontlatoa *yehuaya* xochitl ycuepoya cuicatl yyahualiuhcã *aya* in oncã nemia noyollo *ahuayya ohuaye* cuix tictlamitazque [*yehua ohuaya*]. (f. 22v)	Everywhere I go along, yehuaya, everywhere I give voice, yehuaya, there is a blooming-place of flowers, there is a welling up of song. Aya! There lives my heart. Ahuayya ohuaye! Will we see it end? Yehua ohuaya.

Note: *Nontlatoa* (< *tlahtoa*) is most often to be translated as "I speak." In encountering it in the *cantares*, however, we need always to bear in mind the secondary meaning Molina gives: "chirriar, gorgear o cantar las aves." In a corpus where birds are prominent musicians (as we will see), and in the midst of selfconscious reflections on the act of singing, the meaning of *tlahtoa* often seems to inch from speech toward song even for human voices; for this reason I translate it here as "give voice."

In hinting at the transitoriness of life this passage helps us to make a distinction important to the thematics of the *cantares* between ephemerality and immateriality. Flowers endure only briefly, like human lives, but are not for this any less corporeal. Evanescence here is not tantamount to transcendent immateriality. Perhaps, indeed, it was exactly the evanescent materiality of flowers that encouraged their intimate connection to singing in the Nahua mind. Where the fleeting sounds of song have recurrently suggested to the West its supermundane entailments – its elevation above the somatic in the chain of being – they seem to have been conceived in Mexico instead as a link to other animate materials and affirmation of their transitoriness.

The verbs associated with the flowers produced by the singer, when they are not verbs generally linked to flowers (e.g., *cueponi* in Example 2, burst into bloom), are borrowed from other expressly material acts: shaking down, as of fruit from a tree (*tzetzeloa*); the twisting together of fibers to make rope (*malina*); or raining, drizzling, or snowing (for instance *tzetzelihui*, related to *tzetzeloa*). The opening strophes of song 80, called a *xochicuicatl cuecuechtli* or Ribald's Flower-Song, present a rich amalgam of such words:

---

[23] This qualification of the song occurs not in its title but in a sectional head in the manuscript two folios before it; the heading refers to songs 51–3, a *yaocuicatl*, the *xochicuicatl* here cited, and an *icnocuicatl*; see f. 31v. Not surprisingly, we have little idea what elements of theme or style the heading might signal.

Example 4

Hue nache niehcoya nihuehuetzcatihuitz ye nixcuecuech *aya* xochitl y ye nocuic momamalina ça nicyatotoma *ho ohuaya ca* nicalle.	I arrive; I come laughing, I, the lech. Aya! Flowers are twisted together in my song; I let them loose, ho ohuaya, I who own the house [?]
...	...
Hohuaya haya tzetzelihui xochitlon yca ahuialo ya ohiya yean.	Hohuaya haya! Flowers drizzle down, and thereby all are happy. Ya ohuiya yean!
Nepapan xochitla nictzetzeloa *ho ho* noncuicamanaco xochitla yhuinti *huaya ho* nixcuecuech *ha*. (ff. 67r–v)	I shake down myriad flowers. Ho, ho! I song-spread; the flowers get drunk. Huaya ho! I am the lech, ha!

In the midst of this rich lexicon, song itself materializes in the word *noncuicamanaco*. It joins the combinatory stem for song (*cuica-*) into a compound whose verbal foundation is *mana*, a word specifically connoting the laying or spreading out of flat, material things. From the examples Molina uses to gloss this verb we gain a sense of song patted out like a corn tortilla or, perhaps more aptly, laid as an offering on an altar. The connotations are expressly material – and difficult to capture in the shorthand of translation.

Finally, the singer produces flowers not only by singing but by drumming as well. In passages such as Example 5 the drum, like the singer's body in other passages, is the material matrix from which flowers are born:

Example 5

Ma xicyahuelintzotzona moxochihuehueuh ticuicanitl i *yeehuaya* ma izquixochitli man cacahuaxochitli, ma ōmoyahuaya maontzetzelihui ye nica huehuetitlano man tahuiyacani *ohuaya ohuaya*. (f. 19r)	Strike well your flower-drum, singer! Yeehuaya! Let there be tree blossoms and cacao flowers; let them scatter and drizzle down here beside the drum. Let us rejoice, ohuaya, ohuaya!

These examples and others like them suggest that, for the creators of the *cantares* and their original audiences, the producing of flowers through acts of singing and drumming was something other than an elegancy of poetic image, something tending more toward a perceived, palpable reality. *Song flowered*, to put the matter almost as directly as it might be rendered in Nahuatl. In the expression of this truth in the *cantares* we uncover an unanticipated crease in the Nahua world, a fold bringing into contact different points than are brought close in our world. Contiguities emerge where we find gaps; unmediated metonymies appear, as I suggested in chapter 2, where we labor toward overleaping metaphor. Nahua song was florid in a manner distant from our sensibilities, in touch with the flowers one could see and smell all around. Its envelope of sound was a snow-shower of blossoms.

And not only blossoms, for song assumed other material forms as well. If flowers were the precious things that most frequently poured from the singer's lips and drum, they were joined by turquoises, jewelry, precious metals, metal bells, brightly colored bird feathers, butterflies, and even painted pictures. The song in Example 1 hints at these other riches in its allusions to the singer's origin in the "house of quetzal-plume butterflies" and its equating of the flowers in his heart with painted pictures there (strophes 3–4), but there is no unequivocal affirmation, of the sort found here for flowers, that song issues *as* these things. Other songs are more explicit.

After flowers, precious stones and jewels are the material guise songs most commonly assume. In Example 6 a singer celebrates the songs that come to him from god; but these are anything but ethereal. Instead they accumulate – through the act itself of singing? – as a heft of gemstones and jewelry:

Example 6

Çan nocōtlapehpenia mocuic *ohuaye*	I gather your songs, ohuaya;
nichalchiuhnepanoa *yeehuaya*	I turquoise-heap, yeehuaya,
nicmaquiznepanoan . . . (f. 34v)	I bracelet-heap them . . .

Elsewhere, other songs, these too coming to the singer from god, are likened not only to turquoises and jewels, but also to the long, brilliant-green quetzal tail-plumes favored in Aztec feather-work:

Example 7

O anca iuhquin chalchiuitl *ohuaya* çan ca	Oh, therefore as turquoises, ohuaya, as
yuhquin cozcatl in quetzallin patlahuac ypan ye	jewels and broad quetzal plumes
nicmatia yectli ye mocuic *aya* tota Dios	I know your good songs, aya, oh God,
ypalnemoani . . . (f. 18v)	our father, giver of life . . .

Here the crucial word connecting songs to these materials is *nicmati[a]*, "I know." Like words for knowing in most languages, the root of this word, *mati*, covers a broad range of secondary meanings, including find out, feel, and taste. It is tantalizingly suggestive but imprecise as to the relation perceived between the songs and the other precious things named. On this point one more song, instead, is clear:

Example 8

In chalchihuitl *ohuayee*	They are turquoises, ohuaye! Your words, ah!,
onquetzalpi'pixauhtimania yn *a* motlatol *huia* . . .	are quetzal-plume-drizzling down, huia!
(f. 9v)	

The words of the singer fall softly as gems transformed into a feather-drizzle. Here the verb, derived by elaborate compounding from *pihpixahui*, to drizzle or snow, enriches the lexicon of falling materials we already remarked in the case of flowers. (We will return below to compounds such as this.)

Less frequently than precious stones, songs can take the form also of shining metals. "Teocuitlatzitzilin i nocuic," chants the singer of song 4, "A gold jingle-bell is my song" (see Example 17 below, strophe 2). Such instances are particularly intriguing because of the nature of the metal objects involved. In her recent survey of the rise of metallurgy in ancient west Mexico, archaeologist Dorothy Hosler concludes that preceding cultures passed on to the Mexica a belief in the sacred powers of jingling metals, and that these powers arose from both the colors and the sounds of the objects involved. Metal bells in particular, in this compelling interpretation, materialized together sacred substance and sacred sound. Their appearance in the *cantares* among the objects song brought forth seems to represent the tail end of a centuries-old Mexican ideology surrounding the metallurgic arts.[24]

In these examples, the mixing of material substances is typical. The shifting vocabulary captures the polymorphous stuff of solidified song. Yet another song ends with a long strophe that dwells on both flowers and other materials, including turquoises and jewelry. Its distinctive verbal and nominative compounds, represented in this translation through hyphenated English constructions, build a rich web of reference connecting song to precious matter:

Example 9

Yca ye ninapanao tlaocolxochicozcatlon nomac ōmanian elcicihuilizchimalxochitlon nicehuaya in tlaocolcuicatl oo nicchalchiuhcozcahuicomana yectli yan cuicatl nicahuachxochilacatzoa y nochalchiuhuehueuh ilh.^{tl} ytech nictlaxilotia in nocuicatzin in nicuicani ye niquincuilia in ilh^c chaneque o çacuantototl quetzaltzinitzcantototl teoquechol in on tla'toa quechol in quicecemeltia in tloq̄, etc.^a (f. 5r)	I dress myself in a sad-flower-necklace; in my hands lie my sighing-shield-flowers. I raise a sad song; I turquoise-necklace-offer up a good song. I pull a sprinkle of flowers from my turquoise huehuetl. I, the singer, hold up my dear song to the sky; I take it from the sky-inhabitants: the zacuan-bird, the quetzaltzinitzcan-bird, the divine quechol – the quechol who sings, who entertains the Ever-Present, [the Ever-Near.]

The passage is remarkable, first, for the regalia the singer dons and carries. The long, nominative compounds in the first two lines join flowers to other materials (necklace, shield); but at the same time they connect both to emotional states. The second of these compounds in particular, *nelcicihuilizchimalxochitlon*, suggests that these mournful emotions are materialized much as the things they join. Its first component, *nelcicihuiliz-*, derives from *elcihcihuiliztli*, a sigh. But this word in turn starts from *elli*, the liver, thought by the Mexica to be a bodily source of animating substances and strong (especially negative) passions. To this it joins *ihcihui* to give the sense of "liver-panting" or, more generally, "gut-panting." Behind the whole formation stands the related *ihiyotl*, a fundamental, airy, vital substance in Mexica psychophysiology, emanating from the liver.[25]

Meanwhile, the strophe affirms song's material substance in two ways. The singer delivers his song of sadness *in the form of* a string of turquoises. The compound that expresses this

---

[24] Dorothy Hosler, *The Sounds and Colors of Power: The Sacred Metallurgical Technology of Ancient West Mexico* (Cambridge, MA: MIT Press, 1994), chap. 8.

[25] See Alfredo López Austin, *The Human Body and Ideology: Concepts of the Ancient Nahuas*, trans. Thelma Ortiz de Montellano and Bernard Ortiz de Montellano, 2 vols. (Salt Lake City: University of Utah Press, 1988), I, pp. 191–2, 232–6. On the *ihiyotl* see also Jill Leslie McKeever Furst, *The Natural History of the Soul in Ancient Mexico* (New Haven: Yale University Press, 1995), chaps. 19–23.

idea (*nicchalchiuhcozcahuicomana*) infixes nominative elements in its verbal base (*nichuicomana*) for an overall effect that is not captured in a translation – more normal than mine – such as "I offer it as emeralds and jewels." Finally, while the song is uttered in these material forms, it is drummed forth as a shower of flowers from a *huehuetl* itself fashioned of turquoise. (The strophe ends with clear suggestions as to the origins of the singer's song; we will return below to consider the role of the birds invoked here.)

Examples 7 and 8 above show quetzal plumes as the material form assumed by songs. Elsewhere this assimilation of song to plume can be as simple as an asserted identity, as on f. 31r, where the singer intones "Y niquetzal ... nicuicatl – I am a quetzal plume ... I am a song." More typically the plumes are drawn into the matrix of lush compounds that describe the song-act and its consequences:

Example 10

Nohuian nõne'nemi nohuian nontla'tohua	Everywhere I go along, everywhere I give
nicuicanitl *huia*, in quetzalizquixochitl	voice – I the singer, huia! – truly the quetzal-
ca ye ontzetzeliuhtoc	plume-tree-blossoms are sprinkling down. They
xochiithualco *yehua* papalocalitec	are in the flower-court, yehua, of the butterfly-
y yaoo ayahue ohuaya etc (f. 11r–v)	house, y yaoo ayahue ohuaya!

Here the plumes merge with flowers as the stuff of song. In an earlier passage from the same song, instead, the singer/drummer looses god's hymns as quetzal plumes alone – only to be echoed by a bird singing flowers:

Example 11

Yn tlaca'ce otemoc *aya* huehuetitlan ye nemi in	By god! He has come down, aya! The singer is at
cuicanitl *huia* çan quiquetzalintomaya	the drum, huia! He quetzal-plume-looses them,
quexexeloa *aya* ycuic ipalnemoa	he disperses, aya, the songs of the giver of life.
quiyananquilia in coyolyantototl oncuicatinemi	The jingle-bell-bird answers – goes along
xochimana man *aya* toxocha	singing, flower-spreading. May they, aya, be our
ohuaya ohuaya. (f. 9v)	flowers, ohuaya, ohuaya!

In this fertile mixing of song-flowers with other precious substances, finally, even butterflies, another instance of ephemeral materiality like flowers, can take shape:

Example 12

Aquin nehua nipapatlantinemi *yehuaya*	Who am I? I am soaring about, yehuaya! I
notlatlalia nixochincuicã cuicapapalotl *aya* ...	compose; I flower-sing. It is a song-butterfly,
(f. 11v)	aya ...

The paint of the Aztec codices, as we saw in chapter 2, seems to have functioned as a material bond between the semantic content of those books and the world around – an assertion, in color, not only of the ritual presence embodied in the codices but also of the metonymic Mexica construction of reality. It is doubly fascinating, then, to find song congealing in the *cantares* into writing, painted pictures, and even screenfold codices. Songs, in the first place, can be written or painted – the crucial verbs are the related *ihcuilihui* and *cuiloa* – as in this strophe, bristling with martial allusions:

Example 13

Oceloihcuiliuhquĩ a mocuic
quahuintzetzeliuhtoc moxochiuh *aya* in
tinopiltzin yehuan maceuhquiya chimalcocom
aye mohuehueuh ticyahuelintzotzona *ahuayyao*
(f. 23v)

Your song is jaguar-painted, your flowers are
eagle-drizzling down, aya.
Oh prince, here is the dancer. Your huehuetl
shield-roars, aye. You strike it well, ahuayyao.

In another strophe, the painter of songs is the Christ child himself:

Example 14

Ac ypiltzin? Ach anca ipiltzin yehuayan Dios
jesu chr̃o: can quicuiloã tlacuiloa quicuiloã
cuicatl *a ohuaya ohuaya*. (f. 7v)

Who is this child? Is it the child of God,
yehuayan, Jesus Christ? For he paints, he paints
pictures, he paints songs, a ohuaya ohuaya.

The writing that limns songs can be joined to other materializations, as in Example 13, where the painted song falls as flowers, or here, where the quetzal plumes are not to be thought of as feather pens but as one aspect of the polymorphic appearance of the flower-song:

Example 15

Ỹ maoc toncuicaca antepilhua *huiya* ỹ maoc
ticahuilti yn ipalnemoa onquetzalycuiliuhtimani
xochicuicatl *y ahuayyo* Et. (f. 34v)

Let us sing, you princes, huia! Let us entertain
the giver of life. The flower-song is being
quetzal-plume-written, y ahuayyo!

Several passages in the *cantares*, finally, allude to songbooks. When the singer intones "tocõyaitquitihuitz in mocuicaamoxtlacuilol – you come carrying your songbook-painting" (f. 63r), it is tempting to believe that the reference is to the pre-Cortesian, pictographic songbooks mentioned by Sahagún's informants (see chapter 2) rather than to the European music writing increasingly known among the Indians. In either interpretation, however, this phrase seems to signal not an instance of song materializing through performance into a book, but the (nonetheless intriguing) proposition of some sort of book from which songs might be sung.

Elsewhere, instead, the case is different, and paintings and songbooks alike enter into the kaleidoscopic play of solidifying song:

Example 16

Chalchiuhtlacuilolli o in cuicaamoxtli
onquetzalxilohuitoliuhtoc in yectlon cuicatl
xochinpapalocalli ya yc ompa hualtemo in
cuicatl ompa niccaquia nicuicanitl *yehua* . . .
(f. 52v)

Turquoise-paintings and songbooks are quetzal-
plume-milk-corn-twisting down; good songs
descend from the flower-butterfly-house. I, the
singer, hear songs from there, yehua . . .

The relation of writing and singing here cannot be a painting of song, as in Examples 13–15, or a description of a book from which songs might be performed. Instead the paintings and songbooks, like the flowers, gems, and plumes elsewhere, come swirling down as the material manifestation of the song-act itself. Writing, rather than serving its familiar

Cantares mexicanos

function as a stimulus or *aide-mémoire* for music, is summoned into existence by singing; paint appears as it is sung.

This association of song with pictographs seems to underscore the gesturing of both outward, toward the other, natural materials so prominent in the *cantares* and codices alike. The incessant allusions to the singing of flowers (and other materials) in the *cantares*, in other words, may be not merely a recollection in post-conquest songs of the ancient song glyphs but something lodged even deeper in the Nahua mentality: an affirmation that the things that mattered most in these realms of expression – flowers, gems, metals, feathers, painted pictographs, and uttered words alike – were interwoven in a weft of materiality so tight that each gained its signifying powers through its contact with the others.

Look once more at Example 1. In line 17 there occurs a suggestive compound word that tests our ability to hear the material connections of Nahuatl song: *nixochicuihcuicatinemi*. Karttunen and Lockhart draw attention to this compound, which occurs three times in the *Cantares mexicanos* and *Romances*;[26] but, in a rare misreading, they distort its component parts. They translate it as "ando cantando poesía," evidently construing it as a compound of *cuica* (sing) with the *xochicuicatl* read by interpreters in the Garibay tradition to mean poetry.[27] In fact, the compound joins *xochitl* (flower) with *cuihcuica*, the verb *cuica* with a reduplicated first syllable (to which is appended the auxiliary verb *nemi*, here an indicator of progressive action).

Reduplication of this sort is ubiquitous in Nahuatl. Most often it carries the general semantic message of intensification or distribution, marking an extreme or repeated version of the action connoted by the root. But words with reduplicative prefixes can also move off into distinct, if related, semantic territory. The closest Molina comes to *cuihcuica* is *cuicuicani* for cricket (*grillo*). Extrapolating from this, Bierhorst translates our compound "I'm ... flower-chirping." This is no more satisfactory than Karttunen and Lockhart's gloss, since it does not take full account of the glottal stop that the scribe took pains to record – extraordinarily – by the *-h-* that ends the reduplicated syllable. In all likelihood the glottal stop does not refer to crickets, but instead marks the verb as indicating repetition across many distinct instances. (*Cuihcuica*, then, might be etymologically prior to Molina's *cuicuicani*, defining the cricket as incessantly singing, an "always-singer.") Garibay, for his part, recognized this when he encountered the compound in translating the songs of the *Romances*. But, in a revealing act of dematerializing Nahua song, he omitted the flowers altogether from his translation: "yo ando constantemente cantando."[28]

Since they do not face its superabundant materiality, none of these translations can capture the rich connotations of *nixochicuihcuicatinemi*. Altogether the compound adds up to something like, "I am singing flowers here, there, and everywhere," or "I go about singing flowers over and over," or, following Garibay, "I am singing flowers constantly." The luxuriant, evanescent production brought about by the singer proclaims itself in the snowballing agglutination of his utterance.

---

[26] *Cantares mexicanos*, ff. 18v and 68r; for the *Romances* instance, see Garibay, *Poesía náhuatl* I, p. 6 . The compound occurs once more in the *Romances*, this time without the *ni-* first-person pronominal prefix; see ibid., p. 7.

[27] See Karttunen and Lockhart, "La estructura," p. 28.   [28] See Garibay, *Poesía náhuatl* I, p. 6.

The Singing of the New World

A grammar of metonymy

Nahuatl itself was stretched, strained, and rebuilt in order to express this semantic matrix of song and things. The rich, allusive compound words found in the *cantares* – compounds especially of nouns and verbs, of the sort exemplified by *nixochicuihcuicatinemi* – represent a high-water mark of such agglutination in the language all told. Or at least so said the great seventeenth-century Nahuatl and Otomi linguist Horacio Carochi. Of the *cantares* he took no notice in his *Arte de la lengua mexicana* of 1645 until he came to his chapter on compounding nouns with verbs and other nouns. There he singled out the special compounds of the songs even as he advised against such excess:

> I note that the words to be compounded are usually two in number; occasionally there may be three . . . ; and one is not to go beyond that. The Indians of old were restrained in compounding more than two words. Those of today are excessive, and all the more if they speak of sacred matters; although in poetic language the ancients were extravagant too, as will be seen by the following:
> 1. *Tlāuhquechōllaztalēhualtòtōnatoc.*
> 2. *Āyauhcōçamālōtōnamēyòtimani.*
> 3. *Xiuhcoyoltzitzilica in teōcuitlahuēhuētl.*
> 4. *Xiuhtlapallàcuilōlāmoxtli manca.*
> 5. *Nicchālchiuhcōzcamecaquēnmachtòtoma in nocuic.*
>
> 1. It is glowing with crimson color like the tlauhquechol bird.
> 2. And it is sparkling in the manner of the rainbow.
> 3. The silver drum sounds like cascabels of turquoise.
> 4. There was a book of annals written or painted in colors.
> 5. I go along untying my song in a thousand ways, like a string of precious stones.[29]

In Carochi's examples we recognize similarities of vocabulary and construction to the *cantares* excerpts we have examined, and indeed León-Portilla and Bierhorst have traced two of them to surviving *cantares*.[30] Moreover, the third and fifth of Carochi's compounds touch directly on the theme of song-performance so prominent in the *cantares*.

So also do other examples Carochi gave earlier in his chapter to illuminate the meaning of compounds; indeed he explicitly related these also to the *cantares*. This passage reveals both the extraordinary effort of cultural translation that went into Carochi's grammar and, I think, the limits of such effort. It needs to be quoted at length:

> It is very useful to know how to compound words with others, because compound words are in very frequent use, since nouns compounded with other [nouns] serve as genitives, are equivalent to the epithets of Latin, and render the style smoother and more sonorous. . . .

---

[29] Carochi, *Grammar*, trans. Lockhart, pp. 286–7.
[30] See Horacio Carochi, *Arte de la lengua mexicana con la declaración de los adverbios della*, ed. Miguel León-Portilla (Mexico City: Instituto de Investigaciones Filológicas, Universidad Nacional Autónoma de México, 1983), pp. xxviii–xxix; also Bierhorst, *Cantares mexicanos*, pp. 117–18.

Cantares mexicanos

> Nouns are also compounded with verbs. When the noun is compounded with a transitive verb and the latter has no other noun as object (which will be recognized by its having no mark of transitivity), the compounded noun will be the object, e.g. *nixōchitēmoa*, I seek flowers, and *nicxōchipèpena*, I choose or pick them. But if the verb should have another object outside the compound, and on the other hand does not govern two objects [i.e., direct and indirect], then the compounded noun will signify similarity with the object or the instrument applied to it [*el compuesto significa semejança, ò instrumento del caso paciente*]. E.g., *nicxōchitēmoa cuīcatl, nicxōchipèpena cuīcatl*, I seek and choose songs like roses [*cantares, como las rosas*]. ... A noun compounded with a verb, when the latter governs an object, also serves to specify and determine some part [*alguna parte*] of the noun object on which the action of the verb is exercised, e.g. *ōquiquechcotōnquè in ichtecqui*, they decapitated the thief. The noun *quechtli*, neck, compounded with the verb, denotes that the wound was in the neck. ...
>
> When the noun is compounded with a passive verb, either it will be nominative, or it will signify similarity or instrument, or specify a part of the object, as was explained. *Xōchitēmōlo*, flowers are sought. *Xōchitēmōlo in cuīcatl*, songs are sought like flowers [*como flores*]. ... A noun compounded with an intransitive verb either expresses similarity or specifies part of the subject noun, as in *quetzalilacatzihui, quetzalhuītōlihui, xōchicuepōni in nocuic*, my song goes along being intertwined and twisted in the manner of [*à manera de*] a quetzal plume and bursts out like [*como*] a flower. These are words from the *cantares* of the Indians; *ilacatzihui* and *huītōlihui* are for something to be twisted; the second adds, in the form of an arc.[31]

The semantic relation brought about by compounded nouns is, for Carochi as for us, the crux of the issue. However, his lexicon for describing this relation is limited. He is able to speak of relations of likeness (*semejança*) between the subject or object outside the compound and the noun agglutinated in it, and he translates these cases in a way that modern renderings of the *cantares* compounds have tended to follow: "... like a flower." He is also able to capture some of the metonymic aspect of these compounds in the classical sense of that trope: the relation of part to whole, as in the example of decapitating – i.e., "neck-wounding" – a thief.

But Carochi only glimpsed dimly the more general metonymy at work in the songs. This metonymy is not a connection of part to whole but rather the contact of proximate aspects of the world, in contrast to the relations across distance struck up in metaphor. Such metonymy seems to be mooted in Carochi's relations of likeness, but it calls for more straightforward expression than this. It entails a view of the world that attends to, even exalts, the borderline where likeness shades into identity – a borderline well known to premodern European thought, well known in different guises to Mexica thought, but pushed into obscurity by European analytic habits of mind that emerged in Carochi's own day. Carochi's analysis – his grammar as a whole, for that matter – exemplifies this new way of

---

[31] See Carochi, *Grammar*, trans. Lockhart, pp. 282–5. I have lightly adapted Lockhart's translation.

The Singing of the New World

Example 17: *Cantares mexicanos*, Song 4, f. 3r

Mexicaotoncuicatl		**A Mexica-Otomi Song**
Strophe 1		[1] I turquoise-sunray-polish it; I tzinitzcan-bird-feather-mount it; I recall the place where song originates. I zacuan-bird-arrange a good song, I the singer; I precious-turquoise-scatter it. In this way I produce here flower-blossomings, in this way I entertain the Ever-Present, the Ever-Near.
Nicchalchiuhtonameyopetlahuaya	1	
nictzinitzcanihuicaloaya niquilnamiquia	2	
nelhuayocuicatla nicçaquanhuipanaya yectli yan	3	
cuicatl nicuicani nicchalchiuhtlaçonenelo ic	4	
nichualnextia in xochicueponallotl ic	5	
nicelelquixtia in tloque in nahuaque.	6	

2
Çaquantlaçoihuiticaya tzinitzcan tlauhquechol ic   7
nicyaymatia nocuicatzin; teocuitlatzitzilin i   8
nocuic nitozmiahuatototl nõcuica cahuantimania   9
nicehuaya xochitzetzelolpã ixpan in tloque   10
nahuaque.   11

[2] With precious zacuan feathers, it is a tzinitzcan, a red quechol-bird: thus I order my dear song. A gold-jingle-bell is my song; I am a corn-flower-parrot; I sing! It is resounding; I raise it up, flower-shaken, there – before the Ever-Present, the Ever-Near.

3
Qualli cuicanelhuayotlo, teocuitlaquiquizcopa   12
nicehuaya ilh.ᶜ cuicatlo nictenquixtia   13
nitozmiahuatototl, chalchiuhtonameyotica   14
niccueponaltia yectli yan cuicatlo nicehuaya   15
xochitlenamaquiliztzicaya ic nitlaahuialia nicuicani   16
ixpan in tloque nahuaque.   17

[3] This song-origin is good. Like a gold conch trumpet I lift up an in-the-sky-song. I, corn-flower-parrot, declaim it; with turquoise-sunrays I make a good song burst into bloom. I raise it up by way of burnt flower-incense. Thus I the singer make things fragrant before the Ever-Present, the Ever-Near.

4
Teoquecholme nechnananquilia in nicuicani   18
coyolihcahuacaya yectli ya cuicatlan,   19
cozcapetlaticaya chachalchiuhquetzalitztonameyo   20
xopaleuhtimania xopanxochicuicatl   21
onilhuicaahuiaxtimanio xochitlenamactli   22
onmilintimani onayauhtonameyotimanio,   23
xochiahuachtitlan nihualcuicaya nicuicani etc.   24

[4] Divine quechols answer me, the singer; they jingle-bell-twitter in the place of good song. Like a mat of jewels, the green-season-flower-songs turquoise-jade-shine; they are glowing green. The flower-incense is sky-fragrance-spreading. It is blazing; it is mist-shining. Here in this flower-drizzle I the singer sing [before the Ever-Present, the Ever-Near.]

5
Nictlapalihmatia nicxoxochineloaya yectli yan   25
cuicatlan cozcapetlaticaya ett.ᵃ   26

[5] I color-design it; I flower-mix it together in the place of good song. Like a mat of jewels etc. [as strophe 4]

6
Nocontimaloaya nocontlamachtiao   27
xochiteyolquima cuicatlã poyomapoctli ic ye   28
auian ye noyollo, nihualyolcuecuechahuaya   29
nicihnecuia ahuiacaxocomiqui in noyolia   30
nicyhnecuia yectli ya xochitla netlamachtiloyan   31
xochiyeihuinti noyolia.   32

[6] I exalt, I enrich this flower-soul-delight in the song-place. My heart is pleased with the fuddling-flower-vapor. In it I soften my heart. I inhale it; my heart becomes sweetly drunk. I smell the good flowers in this place of joy; my heart gets flower-drunk [before the Ever-Present, the Ever-Near.]

Notes to Example 17

As Garibay stated (*Historia de la literatura náhuatl*, I, p. 263), the problem of capturing in translation the combinatory nuances of Nahuatl compounds is particularly pressing in this song, filled with rich, suggestive agglutinations. I have attempted to overcome this linguistic distance with a translation that distorts normal English usage more than most. I use hyphenated constructions to translate the many striking verbal phrases incorporating infixed nouns (e.g. line 1, *Nicchalchiuhtonameyopetlahua[ya]*, I turquoise-sunray-polish it) and also for a few compound nouns (e.g. line 12, *cuicanelhuayotl[o]*, song-origin). Noun compounds with relational postpositions, instead, are translated into normal English using adverbial or prepositional phrases: e.g. line 12, *teocuitlaquiquizcopa* = gold or silver + conch-shell trumpet + suffix indicating relation of like manner = "like a gold conch trumpet," and line 7, *çaquantlaçoihuitica[ya]* = zacuan-bird + something precious, rare + feather + suffix of instrumentality = "with precious zacuan feathers." For more standard translations – to which, as usual, I owe much – see, for Spanish, Garibay, ibid., I, pp. 263–4, and, for English, Bierhorst, *Cantares mexicanos*, pp. 139–41, and Daniel Brinton, *Ancient Nahuatl Poetry*, p. 65.

Lines 2, 3, 7, 9, etc.: I have retained Nahuatl loan words for the birds named in the song. Bierhorst, working mainly from Sahagún's *Florentine Codex* and Francisco Hernández's *Historia natural de Nueva España*, has identified the birds mentioned as follows: *quecholli*: generic name for several types of birds; *tlauhquecholli*: roseate spoonbill; *toztli*: parrot; *tzinitzcan*: trogon; *zacuan = zacuametl* (cf. Molina's *çacuantototl*) = troupial.

Line 3: Bierhorst reads *nelhuayocuicatla* as *nelhuayocuicatl* + vocable *a* (root-song, original song); I read it, along with Garibay, as an apocopated *nelhuayocuicatlan* (place of song's origin), in keeping with the *cuicatlan* of lines 19, 26, and 28.

Line 32: "Etc." is probably missing from the end of this line by scribal oversight; it seems doubtful that the refrain *ixpan in tloque nahuaque* would be dropped only in this, the final strophe, and I supply it in the translation.

---

knowing. Indeed it is a signal instance of the way Europeans' encounters with non-European languages contributed to a new, analytic understanding of language all told. Carochi can describe with an air of prescient modernity the grammatical aspects of the compounds; he can penetrate their meanings up to the limits permitted by his own discrimination and distinction of things. But he cannot describe a grammar of metonymies-collapsing-toward-identities.

Glimpsing this transformative proximity, on the other hand, helps to explain the *semantic inevitability* of the compounds concerning song in the *cantares*. Their insistent recourse to a small repertory of things that can be produced through song cuts deeper than a mere play of poetic image. The precious stones, feathers, metals, paintings, and flowers of the *cantares*, that is, should not be understood as the limited tropic repertory of Nahua ritual in its colonial afterlife, but rather as the upwelling in this latter-day ritual of perceived Nahua realities. It is not a question of songs being like flowers but simply of songs *being* flowers. A central task of the *cantares* singers seems to have been to exploit the capacities of their language to present vividly the making in song of these objects.

Whatever he does not see of indigenous metonymies, Carochi sees clearly enough the general connection of exaggerated agglutination to Nahua ritual utterance.[32] More

---

[32] For Carochi the connection to ritual seems not to come without its threatening aspect. He perceives it in his own day in the excessive Nahuatl speech about *"cosas sagradas"* – a phrase clearly intended to signify the

specifically, he sees the hypertrophic development of compounds as a hallmark of the *cantares* of a bygone time, of the "poetic language" of "*los antiguos*."[33] We have witnessed already a number of examples of such elaborate compounding, but we now need to appreciate this feature in its most elaborated form (see Example 17).

This song occurs near the beginning of the manuscript of the *Cantares mexicanos*, in a section (ff. 1r–7r) containing songs that stand stylistically somewhat apart. (We have already seen another excerpt in this style from the same folios; see Example 9.) Bierhorst has suggested calling the language of these first songs "missionary Nahuatl," since he finds it to be less idiomatic and more readily translatable than the Nahuatl of the later songs.[34] In the context of those other songs, these texts impart a studied tone, as if composed by someone at a small distance from the heart of the repertory preserved elsewhere in the manuscript; Bierhorst suggests a bilingual Indian singer rather than a non-Europeanized one. Moreover, these songs show other features that distinguish them: longer strophes than is customary, for example, and the absence, for the most part, of indications of vocable refrains. All these things together yield the impression that these are stylized songs, selfconscious exercises in the *cantares* style rather than expressions nearer to the indigenous sources of the tradition. This impression is only strengthened by the similarity of tone and diction between the very first song of the manuscript, which seems to have been composed with programmatic intent to begin the collection, and the ones, like Example 17, that follow it in ff. 1–7.

Song 4, then, may have been composed selfconsciously as an epitome of *cantares* themes and stylistic traits. Or, of course – given how little we know about the genesis of the *cantares* all told, let alone individual songs – these impressions may be mistaken, and the special features of song 4 simply an intensification bred from within the tradition.

In either case, the result is the same: The song is an exuberant celebration of the genesis, performance, and effects of a singing that burgeons in material form. The text expresses the contiguities of song and other materials through a dizzying accumulation of long compounds that begins with the first words and continues, with little slackening of pace,

---

Christian, not indigenous sacred, but nonetheless recalling the late sixteenth-century suspicions of the *cantares* themselves voiced by Sahagún and others; see above, pp. 23 and 57, and chap. 6 below.

[33] Carochi does not specify the era he intends here. Bierhorst (*Cantares mexicanos*, p. 47) presumes that he refers to prehispanic times and is quick to correct him, cautioning that such compounding occurs only in the *cantares* repertory and hence is to be dated from the second half of the sixteenth century. (For Bierhorst, indeed, it represents a "last wild burst of energy" in "classic Aztec diction.") But Carochi's imprecise "*antiguos*" does not necessarily point back before 1519; it more likely refers to the mid- and late sixteenth century. One strand of evidence might suggest that Carochi referred back only as far as the post-contact *cantares*. Carochi knew, in some version, portions of the accounts of indigenous society gathered in Sahagún's *Florentine Codex* (see Carochi, *Grammar*, ed. Lockhart, p. xii fn). It is not implausible, then, that he read in these materials the texts of twenty sacred songs preserved in the appendix to bk. 2, the so-called "Demons' Songs." Of all the Nahuatl songs that have come down to us, these make the most legitimate claim to an origin that pre-dates Spanish contact. They share some features with the cantares, particularly in their use of vocables and, occasionally, in theme; but they show nothing comparable to the most complex agglutinations of the *cantares*. A linguist of Carochi's caliber would not have needed long to see the differences between these songs and the *cantares* from which he drew his examples; if he knew Sahagún's songs, he surely would not have confused them with the *cantares*.

[34] Bierhorst, *Cantares mexicanos*, p. 47.

Cantares mexicanos

through to the end. Double- and triple-noun compounds, along with noun-noun-verb compounds, dominate the syntactic and semantic fabric. (These are mostly rendered as hyphenated constructions in the translation; see the notes to Example 17.) The lexicon of materials connected here to singing differs little from what we have already seen, with allowance for some greater emphasis on birds (to which we will attend below), fragrances, and the shining, glimmering play of light. The overall impact is of a wondrous *ne plus ultra*, drunk on its own verbal power to affirm the proximity of song to other rare and prized materials.

The first strophe alone presents a verbal exaltation of the singer's powers by means of an amassing of long compounds rarely matched elsewhere in the *cantares*. The opening words vividly set the tone: "Nicchalchiuhtonameyopetlahuaya nictzinitzcanihuicaloaya – I turquoise-sunray-polish it; I tzinitzcan-bird-feather-mount it." The referent of these compounds is the singer's song itself. It is somewhat unclear at first, though it probably would have been obvious to initiates of the tradition, accustomed to the singer announcing his actions (if more modestly) to begin a song. At any rate, it is clarified by the parallelism of the next long compound, in lines 3–4, now accompanied by the direct object governed by all these compounds: "nicçaquanhuipanaya yectli yan cuicatl nicuicani – I zacuan-bird-arrange a good song, I the singer." And the array of birds, feathers, precious stones, and shimmering light of this strophe is completed by the compound that follows immediately: "nicchalchiuhtlaçonenelo – I precious-turquoise-scatter it." Through all these mobile, incandescent materials are created the singer's song-flowers, alluded to at the close of the strophe.

At the same time, unexpectedly, this agglutinative song-magic reveals the limits of Nahuatl – perhaps of language all told – in displaying metonymic identities. The compounds are so laden with the materials connected to song, so very noun-heavy, that their verbal elements fade before their nominative ones. Whereas in the more measured passages from other *cantares* examined above the language works to present the process of song's transmutation into other materials, here the nominative emphasis leans toward the objective, leaving process to one side. The materials related to song seem to crystallize, resisting in this the very fluidity of the transformations they aim to convey. Whoever composed this song pushed to the utmost Nahuatl's potential to capture the connections of song to the world and, in the same effort, began to unmake it.

There is nevertheless a general message to be gleaned from the luxuriant compounds of song 4. The *ne plus ultra* they represent is after all only the asymptotic limit of expressive possibilities everywhere touched in the *cantares*. These songs altogether make up a repertory selfconsciously absorbed in the act of singing. They portray this act as a transformation of song into an array of other meaningful, precious materials; thus they affirm song's bonds to the world. Meanwhile the agglutinative structures of Nahuatl, as we have seen, themselves bind word to world, both in their semantic dimension – articulating perceived contiguities of things in the world – and in their syntactic independence – enabling the kind of outward-looking conceptual parataxis described above. It is hardly surprising, then, that the compounding capacities of Nahuatl underwent a hypertrophic development in the *cantares* the like of which is found nowhere else in the surviving corpus of alphabetized

Nahuatl. It is unsurprising that Nahuatl, as linguistic construction of the world, flexed its muscles in *this* way in *this* repertory.

The language of the *cantares* is above all a sung language, and this mode of vocalization seeps to the heart of its grammatical structuring precisely in the compounds devoted to song and its worldly entailments. The language folds over on itself, describing a process of singing that produces precious material substances, to be sure, but deriving from this theme itself the energies that propel its syntax. The metonymic circle connecting words to song, song to world, and world to words is an unbroken one – or, if you prefer, the illusion of such wholeness of words, song, and precious things is maintained in perfect integrity. (In the workings of culture the two choices do not differ in any important regard.) In this unbroken circle resides a deep, lasting expressive achievement of the *cantares*.

Birds and the ambivalence of paradise

The singer of the *cantares* brings into existence many things, but birds are not normally among them. Instead birds are most often singers themselves, inspiring, supplying, or echoing their human counterparts.

Birds appear frequently and with many functions in the *cantares*, as the examples above have suggested. In Example 17 they play several roles: Divine birds respond to the singer's song (strophe 4), the singer himself assumes the guise of some sort of parrot (strophes 2–3), and of course bird-feathers are prominent (strophes 1–2). In these first two strophes birds even seem at first blush to be produced by song in the manner of flowers and other natural materials (see especially lines 3 and 7–8). But the verbs here, *huipana* (compounded in *nicçaquanhuipanaya*) and *ihmati* (in *nicyaymatia*), weaken this impression. They convey a selfconscious action of ordering, arranging, or disposing – even, perhaps, composing – as if it were not birds themselves being produced but songs articulated in their manner (or perhaps in the manner of their songs).

Example 11 provides another straightforward instance of bird echoing human, and moreover producing song-flowers as it does so. In addition, like Example 17, this example seems also to present the singer himself as a bird. He descends from on high to take his place at the drum, only to loose, then, feather-songs. Where do these songs finally come from? Are they human, earthly songs, or birdsongs from the sky? Is there a distinction between the two? Meanwhile, Example 9 describes a reciprocal relation between human and avian singers: The singer not only lifts up his mournful songs to the sky but derives them thence, from a variety of birds there.

In such ways the presence of birds in the *cantares* repeatedly raises the question of the origins of human song. In song 4 in Example 17, the question finds its crux in two intriguing compounds, *nelhuayocuicatla[n?]* (line 3) and *cuicanelhuayotl[o]* (line 12). Here we recognize *cuicatl*, song, and *cuica-*, its combinatory stem. *Nelhuayotl*, according to Molina, is a word about origins; he glosses it as "principio, fundamento, o comienço." It also has a less abstract meaning, signifying the roots of a tree or plant, an alternative Molina gives in his Spanish to Nahuatl section (s.v. "Rayz de arbol o yerva"). In song 4 it is the abstract meaning that is emphasized. The compounds seem to refer to some first, primary, or original song. The singer brings to mind the place of song-origins, perhaps borrows his song from it – though this is not specified – and in any case is pleased.

In another song from this opening section of the manuscript, song 2, the compound *cuicanelhuayotl* recurs. The somewhat abstract usage suggested in song 4 – the notion of an originary song – is underscored here. Moreover, the singer explicitly locates the place of song's origin in the sky and describes it in some detail:

Example 18

Onihualcalac nicuicani nepapan xochitlalpan huel teellelquixtican tetlamachtican, oncan ahuachtonameyoquiauhtimani, oncan cuicuica in nepapan tlaçototome, oncuicatlaça in coyoltotl cahuantimani in intozquitzin in quellelquixtia in tloque in nahuaq̃ yehuan Dios *ohuaya ohuaya*	I the singer have entered the place of many flowers, the land itself of respite, the place of enjoyment. There it is raining shimmering sprinkles; there myriad precious birds sing and sing; there the bell-bird raises up a song. Their lovely voices are resounding as they entertain the Ever-Present, the Ever-Near – God. Ohuaya, ohuaya!
Oncan nicaqui in cuicanelhuayotl in nicuicani, tlacahco ahmo ītlp̃c in peuh yectli yan cuicatl tlaca'ço ompa in ilhuicatlytic hualcaquizti in conehua in tlaçocoyoltototl in quimehuilia in nepapan teoquecholme çacuantototl oncã tlacahço quiyectenehua in tloque in nahuaque *ohuaya ohuaya*. (f. 2r)	There I hear the original song, I the singer. By god, such good songs do not begin on earth! Ah, from up there in the sky resounds what the precious bell-bird raises up, what the varied divine quechols and zacuan-birds raise up. There, by god, they praise the Ever-Present, the Ever-Near. Ohuaya, ohuaya!

These strophes, the opening of a six-strophe song, present a full-fledged narrative of the descent of song, with birds the protagonists. The human singer visits a paradisiacal garden where birds sing to refresh god. There he hears the original song (or the song-origin, song-source, source-song, first-song, etc.). He knows it comes to him from heaven, or at any rate from the place in the sky where birds gather to entertain god, and it is imparted to him by those birds. By the end of this brief song, he affirms his own ability to re-create the heavenly tones:

Example 19

Ma xicaquin nocuic in tinocniuh xochihuehuetl ỹ nictzotzonaya ilhuicacuicatl in nicehuaya . . . (f. 2r)	Listen to my song, friend! I strike the flower-drum, I raise up the sky-song . . .

This narrative of the heavenly origins of song has a ring to it familiar to students of early modern European musical ontologies. The birds entertaining the Ever-Present, Ever-Near are not so far from hosts of angels intoning god's praises, while the notion of birds as the messengers bearing divine song to humans reaches back in Christian myth at least as far as the Carolingian fable in which a holy dove sang chant to Pope Gregory. The frank placing of the origins of song in the sky that begins strophe 2 of Example 18 calls to mind contemporaneous European ideas of song's sources, colored with popular Neoplatonism and its notions of immaterial, heavenly transcendence and god-sent poetic frenzy. In song 2 and the related song 4, in short, *cuicanelhuayotl* seems to conjure up a phylogeny for human singing too close to European ideas not to be suspected of their influence.

The same cannot be said of the one other appearance of the compound of *cuica* and *nelhuayotl* in the manuscript of the *cantares*.[35] It occurs near the end of song 44, a threnody, famous among students of the *cantares*, that opens a series of *teponazcuicatl*. Instead of exploiting the more abstract semantic possibilities of the compound, it plays on the palpable, botanical connotations of *nelhuayotl*:

Example 20

Nichocaya niquittoaya nicnotza noyollo ma niquittā cuicanelhuayotl *aya* ma nicyatlalaquiya ma icaya tlp̄c quimmā mochihua onnenemiz noyol Et [i.e., *ayyo*] (f. 27v)	I weep; I speak, I call out to my heart: "Let me see the song-root, aya, let me plant it; let it stand upon the earth. Someday it will be begotten; my heart will wander forth, ayyo!"

Here the singer plants the roots of his song in the earth to nurture them. He reaps what he has sown in the very next strophe: "itzmolini ye nocuic celia notlatollaquillo," he sings, "my song grows; my word-fruit sprouts." Like this instance, compounds elsewhere in the *cantares* binding *nelhuayotl* to words other than *cuicatl* seem to stress the material connotations of the word: *nelhuayoxochitl* (root-flower, ff. 61r, 67v), *imaquiznelhuayo* (his bracelet-root, f. 70v).[36]

The material bent of these uses of *nelhuayotl* reminds us of the Nahua mentality we discerned in chapter 2. It did not mark the distance, characteristic of European modes of thought, between worldly matter and a transcendent, immaterial sacred. Instead Nahuas seem to have perceived a fully materialized sacral reality, a divine presence immanent in worldly things ranging from maize to all the special substances linked to song in the *cantares*.

In a reading of Nahuatl texts that features both the *cantares* and Sahagún's *Psalmodia Christiana*, Louise Burkhart has described the paradisiacal garden that is the characteristic locale of this Nahua sacred materiality. Sunlit, shimmering, iridescent, enlivened by the tinkling of precious substances and the twittering of resplendent birds, lush with flowers and their overpowering fragrances – this is the garden invoked in *cantares* such as those cited in Examples 17, 18, and 22. The missionaries were quick to seize upon it as the Mexican equivalent of a familiar Christian paradise, but in doing so they misconstrued its nature. It was not so much "a place where one would want one's soul to spend eternity," Burkhart writes, as "a transformational aspect of the here and now, a sacred aspect of reality that one called into being by manipulating . . . garden imagery in ritual contexts, particularly through song." The singing of things in the *cantares* – things of the glittering, precious sort that crowded the indigenous garden paradise – probably always pointed toward this wholesale sacralization of the material world.[37]

---

[35] See Bierhorst's concordance to the *Cantares mexicanos*, s.v. *cuicanelhuayotl*, in *A Nahuatl–English Dictionary*.
[36] Ibid., s.v. *nelhuayotl*.
[37] Louise M. Burkhart, "Flowery Heaven: The Aesthetic of Paradise in Nahuatl Devotional Literature," *Res* 21 (1992), pp. 88–109.

Cantares mexicanos

It is tempting to think, then, that the contrast between the *cuicanelhuayotl* of songs 2 and 4 and that of song 44 confirms the suspicion that the heavenly phylogeny of song presented in the first of the *cantares* reflects European influence – tempting to think, in addition, that the abstract originary schemes of songs 2 and 4 provide further evidence to strengthen Bierhorst's hypothesis that these opening songs in the manuscript are stylized exercises composed under greater European influence than songs later in the collection. But, as usual, the richness of the *cantares* does not permit such straightforward disentangling of indigenous and European strains in them. The clear image of the sky as the source of songs occurs well beyond the opening section of the anthology:

Example 21

A yn ilhuicacitic ompa ye ya huitz in yectli yã xochitl yectli yan cuicatly ... (f. 10r)	Ah! from there in the sky come these good flowers and these good songs ...

The god of the Europeans, enjoying the singing of quechols and quetzals in a garden of vivid material presence, also resurfaces later in the manuscript. In Example 22 the divine birds themselves represent the holy spirit and are even transformed into angels through the use of Spanish loan words. All this sits alongside painted books and flower-vines sung into existence:

Example 22

In ye no ye tehuatl ye mocel titeotl tiyamochiuhtica *y yehuan* Tiox ye motlan monemiyan çan ca moquecholhuã amoxtli mocuic achi motlatol toconehua ye mochan *a ohuaya ohuaya*

Even now, also, are you being created, o only god. Next to you, god, in your abode are your quechols; your songs are painted books; in your home you lift up some few of your words, a ohuaya ohuaya.

Tiquetzaltototl timochiuhtihuitz spilito xanto çan tihualacico can tiquihuicatihuitz in moquecholhuan a yn ageloti xochimecatlo ỹ ye coyatotoma ỹcuic çã mitzõahuiltia ipalnemohuani *ohuaya* Et.ª
...

You are a quetzal-bird; you come being created, holy spirit. You arrive; you come bringing your quechols and angels. There are flower-vines. They unloose their songs. They entertain you, o giver of life. Ohuaya, ohuaya!
...

Ixquich moquechol *aya* yxquich tiquinnechicohua oncan ye mochana ya in papalotl y huitzitzilin a ontlachichinaya ma ahuiltinemi huehuetitlan ye nican *ohuaya ohuaya*

All your quechols, aya! you gather them all there at your home. Butterflies and hummingbirds are drinking their fill; may they be entertained here beside the huehuetl, ohuaya, ohuaya!

Çan niquinmahuiçohuaya a ilhuicac in chanequeõ a y Ageloti onxochicuicotocon ỹ chalchiuhtetzilacatl oncahuãtimani ye ichano y yehuan Tiox *a ohuaya ohuaya* (ff.62v–63r)

I marvel at these residents of the sky. The angels are flower-singing; the turquoise-gong is resounding in the house of him, god. A ohuaya, ohuaya!

Garibay wanted to believe that such Christian eruptions in the vocabulary of the *cantares* were after-the-fact interpolations in once pristine indigenous utterances; he edited them out. But Sahagún, as we have seen, recognized a compositional activity around him that produced songs, perhaps just such as Example 22, with Christian ingredients alongside indigenous ones: "And if... they sing some songs they have composed, which deal with the things of God and His saints, they are surrounded by many errors and heresies." Sahagún himself, moreover, essayed a more correct Christian–Nahuatl synthesis in his *Psalmodia Christiana*.

The *cantares* draw no clear borderlines between European and indigenous worlds, even where we perceive stylistic distinctions that might tempt us to insert them. The songs, as we saw above, arose within a performance tradition that must have been marked both by its unities and by its division of function between public, Christianized display and more private, indigenous expression. We cannot know the full story of the relations between this tradition and wholly indigenous expressive modes reaching back before European contact; doubtless they were deep and complex. We do know, however, that the *cantares* tradition flourished in the midst of a society irrevocably wrenched from its pre-contact state, a colonial society of which the expressive culture, whether leaning toward indigenous modes or away from them, was always marked by its position in between.

There are many differences of style and message to be discovered in the *cantares*; the distinction raised by the question of the origin of song between a model of heavenly transcendence and one of immanent sacred presence – between a supercelestial heaven and an earthly garden – is one of the more basic of them. None of these differences, however, can be cleanly aligned with sections of the *cantares* manuscript or even with individual songs. The repertory as a whole is inescapably colonized, whatever its success in either entertaining the attentive ears or evading the watchful eyes of the colonizers. At the same time it remains inescapably other in the face of European poetic norms and the sacred ontologies behind them. Garibay's editing obscures these most indubitable truths about the songs.

The birds, for their part, revel in the multiform colonial world around them. They can appear as an ethereal heavenly host or a ringing, singing, earthly din. They can supply human song or respond to it. They can be prototypical singers or follow in imitation. They can, like humans, chant flowers into being. And, just as they can assume the form of Christian angels, so they can materialize, perched on a tree in the sacred garden, as a long-dead indigenous culture-hero:

Example 23

Ya çan ca xiuhquechool tzinitzcan tlauhquechol oncan oncuicantla'tohuaya y xochitl a y paqui *hoo a ylilio a ylilililinco huiyao ayyaha ohuaya ohuaya.*

A oncaya ycaqui y xochinquahuitl y huehuetitlan a *ayahue* çã ye ytech onnemiya in quetzalinquechol ỹ tototl ypan mochiuhtinemio, ỹ neçahualcoyotzin o xochicuicuicatinemio y xochitl a yc paqui *hoo a ylilio a ylilililinco huiyao* etc. (f.19r)

There the turquoise quechol, the tzinitzcan, and the red quechol are song-trilling. With flowers they rejoice: hoo a ylilio a ylilililinco huiyao ayyaha ohuaya ohuaya!

There stands a flower-tree beside the drum, ayahue! In it are the quetzal-quechol, the bird; on it appears Nezahualcoyotzin.
He flower-sings on and on; with flowers he rejoices: hoo a ylilio a ylilililinco huiyao ayyaha ohuaya ohuaya!

Cantares mexicanos

Here the ubiquitous song-flowers overflow in a wash of liquid vocables. Whatever shape the birds take, it is wise not to imagine them at too great a distance from the precious, sacred material reality the *cantares* evoke.

Vocables: Varieties of meaning

The profusion of vocables in Example 23 – and these not restricted to the usual *ohuayas*, *huiyas*, and *ayas* – reopens the question of their use and meaning. "Meaning" here is a loaded word, purposefully provocative, for the almost universal position of scholars on vocables in the *cantares* is that they are, in effect, meaningless. This position cannot withstand careful scrutiny. The vocables fulfill a variety of functions in the *cantares*, ranging from the syntactic to the fully – if not specifically – semantic. In their semantic capacities they upset too-easy distinctions of lexical and non-lexical words in the songs, blurring the border between meaning and meaninglessness. They demonstrate also that meaning occurs at different hierarchic levels in songs like the *cantares*, sometimes inhering in phrases even while lacking in the individual words that form them. And they show, perhaps most clearly of all, the special surplus of meaningful impact that a sung *phonos* can carry, over and above the spoken or written word.

Karttunen and Lockhart have best gauged the importance of the vocables and described their functions.[38] Though they emphasize what they consider to be non-semantic uses of these words – for effects of rhythm, assonance, punctuation, and the like – they also see that a "quasi-lexical" category is necessary to capture in particular the exclamatory impact of many of them. This is clearest in the case of the vocable refrains that mark the ends of strophes, the most frequent of them the familiar repeated *ohuaya*. It is true also for self-standing vocables that infiltrate the main lexical portion of the strophe. These words, especially *huiya* and *aya*, seem most often to play a punctuating as well as an exclamatory role, dividing complete thoughts one from another. Their punctuation should probably be thought of as a more local version of the end-of-strophe punctuation provided by the refrains there.

Other, shorter non-lexical elements, most frequently *ya* and *a*, either stand alone or are infixed into sentence-words. Even when not infixed, they can be juxtaposed or elided with the lexical particles that are ubiquitous in Nahuatl, such as *in*, *ma*, *ye*, and *zan* (written *çan* in the manuscripts). Karttunen and Lockhart suggest that some of these lexical particles in the *cantares* are often used much as non-lexical ones. Their abundance in the songs, that is, tends to blur again the clear border we might expect between semantic and non-semantic words. Distance between meaning and non-meaning is narrowed from both the lexical and non-lexical sides of the divide.

These features are present in the passages quoted above. Since I have restricted my italicizing there to the main, independent vocables, here I reproduce Example 11, this time

---

[38] See Karttunen and Lockhart, "La estructura," pp. 23–8.

italicizing all the non-lexical or quasi-lexical elements, including infixed syllables, and bracketing the lexical particles that have minimal semantic impact:

Example 24

[Yn] tlaca'ce otemoc *aya* huehuetitlan [ye] nemi in cuicanitl *huia* [çan] quiquetzal*in*toma*ya* quexexeloa *aya* ycuic ipalnemoa quiy*a*nanquilia in coyoly*a*ntototl oncuicatinemi xochimana ma*n aya* toxoch *a ohuaya ohuaya*. (f. 9v)

By god! He has come down, aya! The singer is at the drum, huia! He quetzal-plume-looses them, he disperses, aya, the songs of the giver of life. The jingle-bell-bird answers – goes along singing, flower-spreading. May they, aya, be our flowers, ohuaya, ohuaya!

One verb with only the usual pronominal prefix (*quiyananquilia*), one compound of two nouns (*coyolyantototl*), and one noun-verb compound (*quiquetzalintomaya*) are all enriched with infixed and/or suffixed non-lexical syllables. Meanwhile, the punctuating function of *huia* and *aya* is clear at the beginning of the strophe, while it weakens somewhat in the subsequent *ayas*.[39]

The impact of the infixed particles is hard to gauge. They occur habitually, though not exclusively, between the prefix(es) and the stem of a verbal sentence-word (e.g., *quiyananquilia* in Example 24). In all probability they were prized, at least, for the assonant fullness they brought to the words thus enriched. Perhaps, if metrical structures are eventually discerned in these texts, they will be seen to play a role in them. The lexical particles used in close proximity to the vocable particles seem, in the *cantares* and in other texts such as the *huehuetlahtolli* or elders' speeches preserved in the *Florentine Codex*, to have been valued as an element of rhetorical elegancy; probably the vocable infixes and suffixes functioned in this way as well. In any case, they are paradoxically the vocables that seem to carry the least semantic weight even as they most closely resemble lexical elements in their use. They are not associated with any one affective context or another, and they seem to lack the exclamatory force of vocables that are not infixed, such as *huia* and *ohuaya*. Whatever their semantic and rhetorical status, they should probably be placed in a category somewhat distinct from these free-standing vocables.

The independent vocables carry a clearer semantic charge. The exclamatory function of "quasi-lexicals" such as *aya* and *huia* in Example 24 must have endowed them with substantial affective weight, a weight increased often by the effect their role as punctuation gives them of confirming or underscoring the thought they conclude. We have, of course, little specific idea how passages such as this one were sung; perhaps the vocable exclamations in them were given special rhythmic or melodic emphasis. Whatever the nature of their delivery, it is difficult to imagine their lack of a specific semantic content somehow undermining their phonic substantiality, or indeed creating any marked

---

[39] For other clear instances of vocables used to punctuate full thoughts, see Example 1 above, strophes 2, 7, and 8.

difference of affective impact between them and the more specifically semantic words around them.

The point can be generalized: It is hard to imagine any singing of vocables, all the way to nursery rhymes, that would contribute no significance to their context. In the first place, the distance they mark from the lexical words around them is itself a form of meaning; the phrase "nonsense syllables" is always a misnomer. In addition, the affecting *phonos* of singing, its surplus over speech, works to define a space of meaning whether or not this space is filled with determinate semantic content. Vocables, which seem always destined to be chanted or sung, seek out a liminal position between non-linguistic cry and semi-semantic word. The very fact that the most specifically meaningful capacity of language is sidestepped at the moment of their irruption adds to their impact, granting them power to encapsulate and deepen a song's most general import.

Such non-specific meaning can at times transcend the individual word, accruing instead across a whole series of vocables. In Example 23 the long vocable sequence ending each strophe is anything but an ordinary strophic refrain in the *cantares*. The vocables that precede the redoubled *ohuaya* ending, particularly the words *a ylilio a ylilililinco*, are rarely seen in the songs; their very distinctiveness indicates a special usage and significance. The lexical words that precede them spell it out: They are, in the first strophe, the flower-generating song of the birds, in the second the incessant song of Nezahualcoyotl, who materializes (as a bird, it would seem) among them. Here meaning is conjured from a twofold difference – difference between the vocables as a whole and the lexical words that introduce them, and difference between these particular vocables and the more normal *ohuayas* and *ayyahas* around them. It is likely as well that the trilling liquid *ylilis* add an onomatopoetic ingredient to this meaning, imitating a generic birdsong or even mimicking the song of a particular species.[40]

This is not the only instance in the *cantares* where extraordinary vocables present in words the act of singing. Song 52, a lengthy *xochicuicatl*, offers four examples, all of which seem to be birdsongs (see f. 34r–v, strophes beginning *Toztli huiliuh* . . . , *Nepapan in moquechol* . . . , *Tollan chalcon* . . . , and *Xochatl imanca* . . .). The last two of these, constituting parallel strophes, are especially explicit, as an excerpt from the second shows:

---

[40] A census of the uses in the *Cantares mexicanos* of these liquid vocables – *ilili*, *tilili*, and related forms – seems to reveal two topoi with which they are associated. First among these is the singing, twittering, or even shrieking of birds; the main examples occur in songs 17 (especially on f. 10r), 22 (17v), 25 (18v–19r; see Example 23), 26 (19r–v; see Example 26), 29 (20v), 45 (27v), 52 (34r), 72 (63v), and 79 (66v). The sky-songs of song 34 (see f. 22v) may be related to birdsongs; while the songs heard in song 90 (f. 81r) probably are those of the birds mentioned a few strophes earlier in the text. The second topos that elicits these vocables is the lullaby or children's song; sometimes mention of the Virgin Mary seems to evoke or be involved in this theme, probably for the obvious reason of her connection to the Christ child. See songs 32 (f. 22r), 55 (38r–v), 57 (40r–v), and 84 (72r–v). Perhaps instances of these vocables in songs 60 (46r), 61 (48r–v), and 80 (67v) also pertain to this theme.

Example 25

... ytec oncuicaya ytec ontlatoaya çan quetzaltototl *huiya aye aye ayanco* Et. [i.e.: *yanco yia yie ehuaya onco aye ahuaya ha ohuaya*] (f. 34v)

... inside sings, inside trills the quetzal: huiya aye aye ayanco yanco yia yie ehuaya onco aye ahuaya ha ohuaya

Elsewhere it seems to be human song that breaks out. Song 26 is closely related to song 25, which concludes with the birdsong strophes of Example 23. The singer of song 26 begins by announcing his arrival from the sky; he could well be the Nezahualcoyotl of the preceding song, singing still. If so, the question of whether this is birdsong or not might be a splitting of hairs, since Nezahualcoyotl seems to materialize as a bird or birdman. In any case, he presents his song at three or four points by means of extraordinarily elaborate and varied vocables. These are particularly noteworthy because they do not merely extend back from the strophe-ending vocable refrain (as in Examples 23 and 25) but erupt at the beginning or in the midst of lexical material. Here, for example, is the end of the penultimate strophe:

Example 26

... in nimitzcecemeltitihuitz *aya* in noconpolotihuitz in notlayocol *y ahuay huay yaho yyao ao yatatantilili* nihuelincuica *ay yohuiya.* (ff. 19r–v)

... I come entertaining you, aya! I am leaving behind my sadness: y ahuay huay yaho yyao ao yatatantilili! I sing well, ay yohuiya!

The singer announces he will entertain, then sings, then announces satisfaction at his act, and finally ends the strophe with a customary vocable refrain. His song uses again the extraordinary liquid consonants of song 25, perhaps marking him as the birdman Nezahualcoyotl after all.

More unequivocally human are the vocable outbreaks in the midst of song 53, an *icnocuicatl* or bereavement song. The many vocables that appear in the midst of lexical material in this song stand mostly within the common exclamatory (and sometimes punctuating) usage of such interjections. Here they seem to underscore the song's general tone of autumnal sadness. Several instances are less commonplace, however, and call for a more specific semantic interpretation:

Example 27

Ça nihualichoa *ya yoohui yahayon* nihuallayocoya ...

I weep: ya yoohui yahayon; I am sad ...

...

...

... yca nichocay *Yoyahuia yoyahui yehua* cano ximoaya *ohuaya*

... and so I weep, Yoyahuia yoyahui yehua, in the place where all are shorn, ohuaya!

Nichoca *yehua* nicnotlamatia çan nicelnamiqui ticcauhtehuazque yectli ya xochitl yectli yan cuicatl ... (f. 35r)

I weep, yehua! I know it, I ponder it: We will leave behind these good flowers, these good songs ...

Cantares mexicanos

The singer's weeping is presented three times in successive strophes. While the exclamatory *yehua* of the third instance falls squarely within normal vocable usage, the first two instances employ unusual vocables, different from the liquid birdsong of Example 23 but just as extraordinary, that seem intended to capture weeping onomatopoetically. Whether or not this is so, their general significance as outbursts of sung lamentation is clear.

Such irruptions of semantically charged vocables, as I have suggested, *present* songs (or, in the last case, sung weeping) of which the enactment is otherwise merely *described* by lexical words. But it is important not to circumscribe this function too narrowly within the normal categories it suggests – the deictics of linguists, for example, or the indexical signs of semioticians. The vocable songs do more than merely point in the manner of certain other word-signs. They show the texts of the *cantares* doubling over on themselves in a manner akin to the phantasmatic agglutinations we have already analyzed. The songs, as we have seen, again and again exploit and extend the rich grammatical possibilities of Nahuatl in order to describe sonorous acts producing precious, non-songish substances. At the same time, the texts can from time to time leave aside their normal specificity of lexical meaning in order to accrue, by means of unusual vocable sequences, another more general significance. At these moments they allow the song described itself to materialize. The performer of the *cantares*, who so often sang a song about his song, could also sing the song sung about.

These instances of vocable songs are special cases, to be sure, but we should not separate them off categorically from more commonplace vocables in the *cantares*. They give full voice to the significance that most (if not all) of the other vocables whisper. Example 27 makes the point as clearly as any: The first two outbreaks of sung weeping are presented through extraordinary means, while the third uses one of the most commonplace of vocables; but its significance is sharpened by the proximity of more distinctive signifying alternatives. *Yehua*, in this instance, is assimilated as synonym to the *ya yoohui yahayon* and *Yoyahuia yoyahui yehua* that precede it. The extraordinary vocable songs show that vocables in general in the *cantares* are the phonic crudescence of the song-material so often sung about. (It is a lesson with far-reaching consequences beyond the *cantares*.) The exclamatory function of the more normal *huiyas* and *ohuayas* is, finally, nothing other than the singer's meaning-laden affirmation that he is singing.

A drumming lesson

What happens, then, when the singer stops singing his song and starts singing the drum's beat? One brief, unique song among the *cantares* poses just this question (see Example 28). The four syllables indicating drum cadences, elsewhere reserved for headings at the beginnings of songs or their subsections, enter into the words itself of this song. While they do not supplant normal vocables entirely, they repeatedly interrupt the lexical body of the strophes, playing a role similar to that of the vocable songs.

The Singing of the New World

Example 28: *Cantares mexicanos*, song 49, f. 30v

Ytotocuic Totoquihuatzin Tlacopā tla'toani		**The Toto-Song of Totoquihuatzin, Ruler of Tlacopan**
Tiquiti tiquiti tiquiti		Tiquiti tiquiti tiquiti

Nictzotzonayan tohuehueuh xahuiaca annicuihua   1   I strike our drum; take pleasure, friends! Let it
ma ihtohuaya *aya* **toto toto tiquiti tiquiti** xochitl   2   speak, aya: **toto toto tiquiti tiquiti**. The
y huelic o ma ihtoa ichan in totoquihuatzi   3   flowers are fragrant! Let it speak in
totiquiti toti toto toto Et tiquiti tiquiti tlp̄c ma   4   Totoquihuatzin's home: **totiquiti toti! Toto**
ahuilihua *ohuayye ayaoo* **totiquiti toti** man   5   **toto tiquiti tiquiti**. On earth let there be
tahuiacā *ayio hiya* **tiquiti**   6   pleasure, ohuaye ayao: **totiquiti toti**. Let us rejoice, ayyo hiya: **tiquiti**.

Chalchiuhtli noyollo **toto Et** [i.e.: **toto tiquiti**   7   My heart is turquoise, **toto toto tiquiti tiquiti**;
tiquiti] teocuitlatl noxochiuh yca ninapanaya in   8   gold are my flowers. I adorn myself with many
nepapā xochitl i noxochiuh a niquitquitehuaz   9   flowers; someday I will carry off my flowers,
quenmanian *yyee* **totiquiti toti** tlon cuicatl *yyo*   10   departing, yyee: **totiquiti toti**. May there be a
huiya **tiquiti**. **Et** [i.e.: ?]   11   song there: yyo huiya: **tiquiti** [+ ?]

Can oc moyoolic a xoncuicaya **toto Et** [i.e.: **toto**   12   Still you are slow? Ah, sing! **toto toto tiquiti**
tiquiti tiquiti] nican nicmanaya poyomaxochitla   13   **tiquiti**. Here I lay out fuddling flowers and
amoxtlacuilola **totiquiti toti** nie **Et**. [i.e.: ?]   14   painted books: **totiquiti toti** [+ ?]

Notes: Here the sung drumming syllables are in boldface, other, normal vocables in italics. The syllables to be repeated indicated by "Et" (= Etc.) are in some cases clear, in others not; where decipherable, they are spelled out in brackets in the Nahuatl original, without brackets in the English translation.

Line 4: The significance of "Et" here is unclear; it seems to call for the completion of the formula *toto toto tiquiti tiquiti* from line 2; if so, it is superfluous, since the remainder of the formula is written out after it.
Line 10: The passage "yyee totiquiti toti tlon cuicatl yyo" is difficult; Garibay's and Bierhorst's readings differ radically. I follow Bierhorst in interpreting *yyee* and *yyo* as vocables, Garibay in reading *tlon* as an elision of *tla* or *tle* with *on*.
Line 11: The strophe-ending "Et" is unclear, since the *tiquiti* before it duplicates the complete ending of the first strophe. Could it indicate that all three strophes are to end with the repeated *tiquitis* of the percussion heading of the song?
Line 14: Again the strophe ending is unclear, both in "nie," which may be lexical material or not, and in the significance of "Et" (which might, however, be accounted for by the note to line 11).

    The generic designation itself of the song calls attention to this special feature. *Ytotocuic* is derived from *totocuicatl*, a word that appears once elsewhere in the *cantares*, but not with the same meaning it has here. There, at the head of song 90, it is a compound of *tototl*, bird, with *cuicatl* and means a song about birds or a birdsong. Here it is more fanciful: Its *toto-* prefix is taken not from *tototl* but from the percussion syllables themselves. A new type of song is invented, the toto-song, punning on the name of the prehispanic ruler Totoquihuatzin, whom it celebrates.
    Another joke: The particular syllable from which the song takes its name is nowhere found in the percussive cadence to which it is to be sung. On the other hand, this cadence – *tiquiti tiquiti tiquiti* – reappears in the text, at least in part. Its repeated unit *tiquiti* appears

within each of the strophes (if I have interpreted correctly the "Et" near the beginning of the second and third strophes) and concludes each of the first two strophes, functioning as the tail end of their shared vocable refrain. (I read *ayio hiya*, line 6, and *yyo huiya*, lines 10–11, as orthographic variants of the same vocables.) It seems probable that this refrain was meant to conclude the third strophe as well, though the "Et." at its end is less clear even than the other such indications in this song. The correspondence between these sung syllables in the text and the accompanimental cadence for the song as a whole is suggestive – of what, it is hard to say – while the recurrence of *tiquiti* at the ends of strophes might be evidence (of a weak sort) for something I proposed above: that the vocable refrains in the songs functioned to allow a strophe-ending synchronization of voice with drum cadence after the freer recitation of the body of the strophe.

The percussion cadences in the midst of the lexical material of the strophes pose their own puzzles, particularly in their clear sequential organization. *Toto toto tiquiti tiquiti* is the first cadence sung in each strophe, followed later by *totiquiti toti*; this sequence of cadences is repeated in the long first strophe and stated once in each of the shorter second and third ones. Why is the drum made to "speak" these syllables and not others? Why the repeating pattern? Surely it must be a sign of regularities of some sort extending between the song and its drummed accompanimental patterns – but of what sort? The singer encourages his companions, singing a drum-speech that must in some way chime with the patterns he is beating out on the drum.

We gain in this short song the tantalizing impression that we can glimpse the tradition of Mexica percussion pedagogy in action. But the impression strains the writing that conveys it. The singing of the drum syllables alienates them from the alphabetic realm and returns them to the world of oral teachings where they no doubt originated. In doing so it takes them from a place where (as we saw in chapter 2) they languish as an inadequate music writing to one where their native capacities can flourish. In the same motion it distances them from the only inscriptive technology that could, under the circumstances in which the *cantares* were sung and written, preserve them for us.

What results from this is, in the first place, another folding over of the song text on itself, like that of the vocable songs or the grandiose agglutinations. But something else happens too: the reassertion, in the aftermath of alphabetic writing, of the sovereign powers of indigenous Mexican practices. The drumming lesson of song 49 differs in this crucial way from Lévi-Strauss's famous writing lesson in *Tristes tropiques*. His was a parable of the powers of Western writing, both enabling and corrupting. This song instead presents a parable in which voice and drum alike escape the alphabetic regimen that presents them. On the one side is a story of the expansion ever farther of the sovereign control of the West; on the other the reassertion, within the very technologies by which that control extends its reach, of a different, autochthonous power.

The singing of the drum cadences subtly shifts another aspect of the song as well. In theme and presentation song 49 seems routine enough: It is the by now familiar communal experience, lightly lamenting the transitory nature of things, in which material riches (painted books and fragrant, golden flowers) are sung and drummed into being. In the *cantares*, singer and drummer are often enough the same person (cf. Examples 5, 11, and

The Singing of the New World

19 above) – so often, indeed, that we may presume that it was a common practice in this tradition for the singer to accompany himself. So it is with song 49; "I strike our drum," the singer begins.

The intrusion of drum syllables as sung vocables casts a new light on these familiar features. It brings about an additional conflation: Not only are singer and drummer one but also song and drumming. The presentational capacity of non-lexical syllables, which we saw in the case of vocable songs, here enables a shift from persona to song-act; the singer does not merely sing *of* his drumming but sings his drumming (just as the singers of the vocable songs sing their singing). Voice and drum are assimilated to one another. Song crystallizes as the hard, reverberant stuff of the *huehuetl* and *teponaztli* while, by the same token, the drums melt into the fluid, raining sung matter whose powers are everywhere manifest in the *cantares*.

This completes the full, metonymic circle of Nahua song. Voice and drum ease toward one another to assume their relation of intimate metonymic proximity, never overlapping completely but displaced by only the smallest discrepancy. From these nearly identical positions they look out around the circle of precious things they produce, showering them down to lighten the passing travail of the humans gathered to savor the songs.

What is the place, in all this, of the alphabet that steals upon the *cantares* as a European dream? It is doubly thwarted. It is inadequate to do more than hint at the powers of song and drum to produce glittering gemstones, hallucinogenic flowers, painted books, and all the rest – inadequate to record the material transactions envisioned in the performance of the *cantares*. And it can do little more than oppose the near-identity of song and drum in pursuing these creative labors. In placing such labors somewhere near the heart of the expressive world of the *cantares*, we begin to understand how far short of their own aspirations mere reading of their alphabetic traces must fall.

Epilogue: Zapotec *Cantares*, ca. 1700

In 1704–5, in the rugged back country of northeast Oaxaca state, Fray Angel Maldonado, newly installed as Bishop of Oaxaca, conducted a vigorous campaign to wipe out non-Christian practices among the native Zapotecs. Preserved in the Archivo General de Indias of Seville is one product of the campaign: a series of more than a hundred confiscated and otherwise collected manuscripts from the Villa Alta region. Most of these are calendars, recording for the Zapotec speakers of the region the months of the venerable 260-day ritual round marked throughout ancient Mesoamerica. Four of the manuscripts, however, record something different: songs in local Zapotec dialects.

These songs have only begun to garner from scholars the attention they deserve. Nancy Farriss has set about translating one of the manuscripts, while David Tavárez has rendered in Spanish a single song from another. In the essay where his translation appears, Tavárez has placed the songs in the context of the Christian mission in the Villa Alta region, energized by a local Indian uprising of 1700 and the trials and punishments that followed. He has distinguished in the manuscripts two groups of songs in distinct Zapotec dialects, the first showing no Christian influence, the second devoted to Christian doctrine and, he surmises, probably the work of Dominican friars. Especially to the point here, he has enumerated the similarities the Zapotec *cantares* bear to the Nahuatl *cantares* from more than a century before.[41]

These similarities are indeed striking – this much is clear even in advance of further translation. The Zapotec songs employ all the formal features of the Nahuatl *cantares* described at the beginning of this chapter. They are organized into strophes. The strophes tend to conclude with vocables, which repeat across a song to create a refrain. The refrains are not limited to the vocables, however. Just as in the Nahuatl *cantares*, they typically extend back into the strophe to include lexical in addition to the final non-lexical words. Again as in the earlier repertory, these lengthy refrains do not for the most part extend across whole songs. Instead they are what I have called "local" refrains, and they organize some of the Zapotec strophes of Calendario 100 in the paired arrangement familiar from the Nahuatl songs.

Two more congruencies with the Nahuatl *cantares* are more specific still. The first concerns the identity of the vocables themselves. Surprisingly, given the linguistic distance between Zapotec and Nahuatl – they are unrelated and classed by linguists in distinct language phyla, the Otomanguean and Uto-Aztecan respectively – many of the vocables most often employed in the Zapotec songs are close variants of those prevalent in the earlier repertory: *iyaoo, ayau, ayao* (cf. *ayao*); *hiya, hiyo* (cf. *huiya*); and *ohueya, ho huaye* (cf. *ohuaya*). Second, the syllabic percussion notation of the *Cantares mexicanos* and *Romances* manuscripts resurfaces in Calendarios 102–3, the manuscripts containing the Christianized songs. These record the percussion cadences in headings over each of the songs, like the Nahuatl manuscripts. To judge from the single cadence transcribed by Tavárez, the notation lived on in early eighteenth-century Oaxaca in a form little altered from that used in the Valley of Mexico more than a century earlier. The syllables are essentially the same, though a final -n is sometimes added to them (cf. in the seventeenth-century *tocontín*) and *gui* or *guin* are substituted for *qui*.

Tavárez has brought to light the account of a witness, a certain Mariana Martín, to idolatrous ceremonies in the Villa Alta area. The testimony relates events of 1718 – showing that Bishop Maldonado's efforts of 1704–5 were less than fully effective – and gives a glimpse, similar to Sahagún's *Florentine Codex* discussed above, of the circumstances in which the Zapotec songs were sung:

> In the month of May it is true that there was more idolatry at the aforementioned farm....
> The witness, observing what happened from her house, which is located on the crest of a hill above the farm, saw all the native leaders of the aforementioned village gather,

---

[41] Farriss's work is as yet unpublished; she generously brought these *cantares* to my attention and supplied me with a photocopy of one of the four manuscripts containing them (Archivo General de Indias, México 882, Calendario 100; the remaining manuscripts preserving the songs are Calendarios 101–3). She also drew my attention to David Tavárez, "De cantares Zapotecas a 'libros de demonio': La extirpación de discursos doctrinales híbridos en Villa Alta, Oaxaca, 1702–1704," *Acervos* 17 (2000), pp. 19–27, which seems to be the first published essay on the songs. Tavárez translates the first song from Calendario 102 and devotes his attention mainly to the Christian songs in Calendarios 102–3. What follows relies on his essay and on a preliminary perusal (but not translation) of Calendario 100.

> accompanied by Gaspar Baptista and Fabián Luis, natives of Betaza.... One of them began to play the *teponaztli* and another a tortoise shell, and both sang in the language of the Valley, in the ancient manner [*a lo antiguo*]. The most [the witness] could hear was that they said "the stars burn bright." She could not hear more on account of the distance; neither could she see what they were doing, though she guessed they would cut the throats of chickens and birds as a sacrifice, having seen them do this on another occasion. . . .[42]

Here we find many of the features I have suggested for private performances of the Nahuatl *cantares*. The Zapotec songs seem to have been sung by and for the native elite, in private (not to say clandestine) settings away from the ears and eyes of colonial authorities, using intimate performing forces. If the witness was right in her hunch, the Zapotec ritual even seems to have retained the avian augury that was a central feature of Sahagún's merchants' banquets.

The existence in itself of these Zapotec songs after 1700 comes as no surprise. Native traditions, more or less affected by European colonialism, have persisted and even thrived down to the present day in many areas of rural Mexico, after all. More arresting, instead, are the specific similarities between these songs and the earlier Nahuatl ones – their identical formal arrangements and the recurrence of vocables and percussion notation. It seems likely that these attest a single, widespread tradition of percussion songs that lasted at least well into the eighteenth century, with formal attributes and modes of presentation that changed little over the first centuries of Spanish colonialism, whatever the shifting languages it employed and Christian ideologies it at times embraced. The similarities suggest that in all these manuscripts, Nahuatl and Zapotec, we confront distinct, icebergish tips of a mostly submerged history of native song and ritual performance. The Zapotec songs reveal that the earlier Nahuatl repertory was not an isolated instance; they encourage us to wonder whether other, similar songs in other languages are not lying unread in archives of Mexico or Spain.

The general tradition of song glimpsed in these manuscripts was strong enough to cross ethnic and linguistic divides as well as large geographical and chronological distances. It looked back on some common and widely dispersed, no doubt prehispanic habits – of instrumentation and vocal presentation, at least, if not of other ritual specifics as well. At the same time it evolved in a colonial context that must not have been so very different at the rural frontier ca. 1700 than it was in the center of Spanish colonization ca. 1580. The Nahuatl *cantares* of the sixteenth century, these Zapotec songs suggest, did not represent a last gasp of prehispanic Aztec song, as they have so often been imagined to do. Instead they stood near the beginning of another tradition of song – descended from earlier traditions, to be sure, but forging its own meanings amid the tense, secretive, determined modes of colonized self-making.

---

[42] Tavárez, "De cantares Zapotecas," p. 19.

4

Musicoanthropophagy: The songs of cannibals

Orality, in the presence of cannibals, means something else. The mouths of eaters of human flesh have seemed categorically distinct from other human mouths since long before European contact with the Americas. From that moment of contact on, for five hundred years, chroniclers, travel writers, moralists, apologists, philosophers, and anthropologists have labored variously to solidify or to dismantle this distinction. The case in point around which these debates have revolved has been Tupinamba society of the Brazilian coast, met by Portuguese and French adventurers in the early and mid-sixteenth century. Here was a society whose anthropophagy European writers were hard pressed to attribute to beastiality pure and simple, whose killing and consumption of their enemies progressed according to so intricate a set of protocols as to strike even the most benighted foreign observer.

In the midst of these Tupinamba protocols, another term arose to stand alongside the Indians' opaque orality: oratory. The earliest reports of the Tupinamba linger over their speeches associated with their cannibalism; from the first, Tupinamba mouths fascinated not only for the flesh they devoured but for the words they disgorged. Later, the fascination did not abate. From Montaigne down through Rousseau and Goethe to today's scholars, the utterance as well as the consumption of the Tupinamba has continued to command attention – so much so that one of those scholars, Frank Lestringant, could take the retrieval of their "proud and cruel eloquence" as the primary task of a recent and important book.[1]

Along the path toward this dual exegesis of cannibal orality and oratory, however, a crucial ingredient has dropped by the wayside. Almost systematically, Tupinamba eloquence has been conceived as speech, poetry, signifier, or semantics. In the event, however, it was more than this; as the early accounts assert (and as modern ethnographies of Amazonian Indians reinforce), the ritual utterance of the Tupinamba was not so much speech as song. The force of this intoned, rhythmicized chant has been largely ignored in the attempt to explicate the meanings of cannibal words.

---

[1] Frank Lestringant, *Cannibals: The Discovery and Representation of the Cannibal from Columbus to Jules Verne*, trans. Rosemary Morris (Berkeley: University of California Press, 1997), p. 7.

The Singing of the New World

Feeling the resonances of this force involves delving past the meaningfulness of words in order to capture something of the sonorous, extra-semantic capacities of Tupinamba ritual chant. Here in the presence of a certain mode of vocal and corporeal excess, more than in the realm of the imperturbable word-sign, relations of Tupinamba ingestion and expression stand out. We need, in the end, to ask not only the first question about the Tupinamba that springs to our lips – why did they eat their enemies? – or even to stop with the question next in line – what do their sayings recorded by the Europeans reveal about their anthropophagy? – but to pursue such further questions as these: Why and how did they sing their cannibalistic rituals? What role did this song play in opening out the societal space for human flesh consumption? What model of personhood-in-the-world was created in this matrix of sung ritual and enemy-eating?

The exegesis that follows unfolds in three stages; they approach these questions successively closer as they move farther from narrow consideration of the significance of Tupinamba words. From Montaigne's familiar report of cannibals' songs and the (less familiar) economy these reflect, it shifts to the cannibals' cult of the maraca, an entryway to their metaphysics and its spiritual voices. It closes by considering the constellation of Tupinamba song, anthropophagy, and self.

Montaigne's cannibals' songs

For all he has to tell us about many other things, Montaigne rarely speaks of music. His sporadic references to harmony, singing, and musical instruments are brief and general, the most common of commonplaces in an era when the recounting of ancient musical lore came easy and the concept of harmony exercised a pervasive and complex fascination. He might, for instance, rehearse hurriedly the tale of Pythagoras and the drunken youths tamed by music, a story from Boethius repeated often throughout the Renaissance (see "Of names"). He might speak, in broad outline, of the harmonic union of contraries in the makeup of the world ("Of experience"). He might summarize by way of aside the belief of philosophers in a sounding harmony of the celestial spheres ("Of custom, and not easily changing an accepted law"). Or he might affirm the power of a singing voice or a church organ over his own hearing and the hearing of others ("Apology for Raymond Sebond"). He might even nod approvingly in the direction of sung popular poetry ("Of vain subtleties"), although for the most part his discussions of poetry and poetic effect have a decidedly bookish feel to them and seem to distance, in an un-Pleiadean manner, written verse from its sung delivery. Altogether it is enough to make us take Montaigne at his word when, in the essay "Of presumption," he confesses that, "Of music, either vocal, for which my voice is inept, or instrumental, they never succeeded in teaching me anything."[2]

In this circumstance "Of cannibals" emerges among the *Essais* as unique in the attention it pays to singing. The words of two songs comprise most of the ethnographic evidence Montaigne reports of his cannibals, that is, of the Tupinamba tribes met by Frenchmen in

---

[2] I cite these essays in the translation of Donald M. Frame, *The Complete Essays of Montaigne* (Stanford: Stanford University Press, 1965). For the passages referred to, see, respectively, pp. 202, 835, 78, 448, 227, and 486.

Musicoanthropophagy

the Bay of Rio in the 1550s. Moreover, Montaigne implicates these songs in what he takes to be the essential elements of Tupinamba social order. There is much to be pondered here about singing and society both.

Yet merely to note this importance of song is to strike out on a little-trodden path in interpreting "Of cannibals." Among the *Essais*, it has received far more than its proportionate share of attention, a body of commentary enlarged in recent years by the poststructuralist, new-historical, and revisionist readings of Michel de Certeau, Frank Lestringant, Stephen Greenblatt, David Quint, Philippe Desan, Carla Freccero, and others. But this impressive literature has lingered only infrequently over the cannibals' singing – so rarely, indeed, as to suggest a constitutive deafness to this aspect of Montaigne's text.

Scholars have listened acutely to other important issues, to be sure. "Of cannibals" has attracted comment for its ostensibly utopian picture of Tupinamba life, stressing a pristine intimacy with nature long lost to Europe's own; for its evasion of ethnocentrism in describing customs radically different from European ones; and for its use of these unfamiliar customs to reflect on the foibles and failings of a French society torn by violent religious strife. "Of cannibals" has emerged as one of the clearest expressions of a singular and attractive feature of Montaigne's thought: its insistent acknowledgment of the contingency and instability of his (and Europe's) knowledge, customs, and ethics. "It seems," Montaigne writes, that "we have no other test of truth and reason than the example and pattern of the opinions and customs of the country we live in."[3]

These themes are famously evident in Montaigne's evenhanded approach to the Brazilian Indians' eating of human flesh. Flying in the face of local views that saw in this practice the indelible mark of a primitive and bestial non-Europeanness, Montaigne compares, in resounding phrases, Tupinamba cannibalism with the savagery of the religious wars of his own France:

> I am not sorry that we notice the barbarous horror of such acts, but I am heartily sorry that, judging their faults rightly, we should be so blind to our own. I think there is more barbarity in eating a man alive than in eating him dead; and in tearing by tortures and the rack a body still full of feeling, in roasting a man bit by bit, in having him bitten and mangled by dogs and swine (as we have not only read but seen with fresh memory, not among ancient enemies, but among neighbors and fellow citizens, and what is worse, on the pretext of piety and religion), than in roasting and eating him after he is dead.[4]

---

[3] For "Of cannibals," essay 31 of the first book, see Montaigne, *Essais*, ed. Maurice Rat, 2 vols. (Paris: Garnier Frères, 1962), and also Frame's translation. For the passages quoted I use Frame's translation; for citation I give pagination from both Rat and Frame. For the present quotation see Rat, p. 234; Frame, p. 152. Another essay centrally concerned with this theme also adducing New World examples is bk. 1, essay 23, "Of custom, and not easily changing an accepted law."

[4] Rat, p. 239; Frame, p. 155. Jean de Léry, Montaigne's primary authority for information on the Tupinamba, expressed similar sentiments in his *Histoire d'un voyage fait en la terre du Brésil*; see the facsimile of the edition of Geneva, 1580, ed. Jean-Claude Morisot (Geneva: Librairie Droz, 1975), pp. 228–9; trans. by Janet Whatley as *History of a Voyage to the Land of Brazil, Otherwise Called America* (Berkeley: University of California Press, 1990), p. 132. In bk. 3, essay 6, "Of coaches," Montaigne again favorably compares New World societies with Europe,

Nevertheless Montaigne hardly regarded cannibalism as a European custom; so for him its carefully staged practice among the Tupinamba called for explanation. The explanation he provided links it with polygamy, the other most strikingly foreign custom of the Brazilians. Together these practices represent for Montaigne an Indian "ethical science" of utter simplicity and naturalness. It has two obligations only for Tupinamba men: valor in war and love for their wives. These two articles, Montaigne tells us, are preached to the men each day before breakfast by a tribal elder; they also form the message of the "priests and prophets" who descend from the mountains every so often to exhort the men "to virtue and their duty" (Rat, p. 237; Frame, p. 154).

Cannibalism expresses Indian valor by virtue of the steadfastness of captives in the face of being eaten. Prisoners taken in war are not killed and consumed immediately; instead they live freely, even for two or three months, among their captors. During this time their captors, Montaigne says,

> entertain them with threats of their coming death, of the torments they will have to suffer, the preparations that are being made for that purpose, the cutting up of their limbs, and the feast that will be made at their expense. All this is done for the sole purpose of extorting from their lips some weak or base word, or making them want to flee, so as to gain the advantage of having terrified them and broken down their firmness.

But this attempt to terrify the captive, this "demand ... that they confess and acknowledge their defeat," inevitably fails: "there is not one in a whole century who does not choose to die rather than relax a single bit," Montaigne tells us. In this stoic firmness, for Montaigne, lies the fulfillment of the Tupinamba obligation of valor. And in this fulfillment, in turn, lies the sole rationale for the Indians' warfare itself. In their vast and abundant territories, the Tupinamba and their allies and enemies fight not for the conquest of new land and material possessions, but only to exercise their "rivalry in valor."[5]

The valor and love required of Tupinamba men are both expressed, indirectly, by their wives in the structures of Tupinamba polygamy. Wives are not jealous of their husbands' other wives, Montaigne tells us, but instead "strive and scheme" to increase their number, since a large number of wives is given to the most powerful warriors and marks their valor. Moreover, the solicitude of Tupinamba wives for their husbands' other companions turns out to be, as Montaigne put it in the last redaction of the essay, "a properly matrimonial virtue ... of the highest order," for which he cites ancient precedent both Biblical and pagan (Rat, p. 243; Frame, p. 158). In the structure of the essay this solicitude seems to reflect back the steadfast love of their wives that Tupinamba ethics demanded of husbands.

---

lingering this time over the European greed, hypocrisy, and treachery involved in the conquests of Mexico and Peru.

[5] Rat, pp. 240–1; Frame, p. 156. Similar views of New World constancy and warfare conclude the essay preceding "Of cannibals," "Of moderation." There, borrowing material from Francisco López de Gómara chiefly concerning the Aztecs, Montaigne notes the resoluteness in the face of death of victims chosen for sacrifice (who, by the way, "se presentent à la boucherie" with song and dance, "chantans et dansans") and states that warfare in Mexico was fostered for the exercise of youthful warriors and to gain prisoners for sacrifice. See Gómara, *Historia de la conquista de Mexico*, ed. Juan Miralles Ostos (Mexico City: Editorial Porrúa, 1988), pp. 311, 315–16.

So runs, in outline form, Montaigne's analysis of Tupinamba ethics, and so the glimpse of Indian society that the secondary literature continues to gain from his essay. De Certeau, for example, takes up in considering "Of cannibals" important issues he had raised in an earlier essay, "Ethno-Graphy," especially the problematic escape of indigenous American voice and body from European texts (to which I will return). But meanwhile he affirms and extends Montaigne's ethics, writing that "cannibalism ... brings to light an ethic of faithfulness in war; and polygamy ... reveals a superior degree of conjugal fidelity."[6]

David Quint, for his part, represents a strain in readership of Montaigne's essay that interprets it primarily as a meditation on European society. He sees in Montaigne's analysis of cannibal valor an allegory concerning the Stoic obstinacy that marked, disastrously, the positions of Huguenot and Catholic nobles alike in French religious wars and that condemned European society to "consume itself" in the manner of New World cannibals. But, however Eurocentric Quint takes Montaigne's concerns in "Of cannibals" to be, he finds in them also insight into Tupinamba society. "It does not follow that *everything* gets lost in the translation," he writes, taking issue with the Europeanist interpretation of another writer, Gérard Defaux; and indeed he accepts as the starting point for his description of "cannibal culture" the dual logic of valor and love that Montaigne discerned.[7]

Philippe Desan, finally, in his book *Les Commerces de Montaigne*, perceives in "Of cannibals" the description of a Tupinamba economy – or better, as Desan puts it, a "non-economy" – that cannot be dissociated from Tupinamba society itself. In this "social and economic interdependence" (to which, again, I will return), with its "complex web of symbolic exchanges," the Indian subject is defined. But this subjectivity is nevertheless circumscribed in the same dual ethics accepted by de Certeau and Quint: "Two things are urged on the male members of the tribe: 'valor against the enemy and love for their wives.' ... Cannibal ethics rests only on these two cardinal principles."[8]

To question this modern acceptance of Montaigne's Tupinamba ethics is to gain some clearer impression of Indian culture at the moment Europeans came upon it. Quint is right to insist that Tupinamba customs do not utterly escape from Montaigne's text – or, to put the matter more generally, that indigenous American perceptions do not disappear in the immensely problematic process of their translation and transformation in the writing of early modern Europe. This writing instead presents, inevitably, residues of otherness as

---

[6] See Michel de Certeau, "Montaigne's 'Of Cannibals': The Savage 'I'," in *Heterologies: Discourse on the Other*, trans. Brian Massumi (Minneapolis: University of Minnesota Press, 1986), pp. 67–79, esp. p. 75; also "Ethno-Graphy: Speech, or the Space of the Other: Jean de Léry," in *The Writing of History*, trans. Tom Conley (New York: Columbia University Press, 1988), pp. 209–43.

[7] See David Quint, "A Reconsideration of Montaigne's 'Des cannibales'," *Modern Language Quarterly* 51 (1990), pp. 459–89; esp. pp. 487, 463, and 469–70. Défaux expresses his views in "Un Cannibale en haut de chausses: Montaigne, la différence et la logique de l'identité," *Modern Language Notes* 97 (1982), pp. 919–57.

[8] Philippe Desan, *Les Commerces de Montaigne: le discours économique des Essais* (Paris: A.-G. Nizet, 1992), chap. 6 and esp. pp. 191–3; this chapter and the following one, in which Desan argues that a distinction between use value and exchange value is adumbrated in Montaigne's views of New World and Old World attitudes toward gold, are reprinted as *Montaigne, les cannibales et les conquistadores* (Paris: A.-G. Nizet, 1994).

a kind of disturbance of its ostensive form and substance. The moments when we sense this residue, glimpsing through the text others who in part motivated it, arise especially at torsions in its expository attempt to fix American discourses and practices that resist it. Fissures open in Europe's writing, through which oracular others may be heard faintly to speak – or, in the event, to sing.

The problem with accepting Montaigne's dual Tupinamba ethics at face value is that, while we may thereby see more clearly the lessons for European society he would draw from the Brazilians, we might also smooth over the rifted surface of his writing. By bringing pressure to bear on his ethics, instead, we may hear more clearly Tupinamba voices from the 1500s. Beneath Montaigne's ethics, shot through with the values of his critique of Stoicism and with Christian conceptions of generosity and dutifulness, we uncover a different dynamic at work in Tupinamba society, not so much an *ethics* as an *economy*. (As we will see, it is a signal virtue of Desan's analysis to have cast in bright light the economic aspects of the Indians.) This economy may serve as cornerstone for a speculative historical ethnography of Tupinamba cannibalism and polygamy.

A sung economy

This Montaignian ethnography needs to take the form of a historical ethnomusicology, because in "Of cannibals" the fracture line along which it emerges is the demarcation between normal speech and song. Montaigne's cannibals, as I have noted, *sing*, and sing repeatedly; in fact they sing in connection with the two Brazilian customs so needful of European exegesis, the eating of human flesh and polygamy. Moreover, the Tupinamba repeatedly sing also in the two proto-ethnographic reports on which Montaigne relied most heavily, by Jean de Léry and André Thevet.[9]

From the moment of their first inscription, however, these Tupinamba songs have been overwhelmed by European practices superimposed on them. This familiarization of the songs has continued through the modern secondary literature on their sixteenth-century sources and is evident even in the writings of de Certeau – this notwithstanding the fact that he certainly comes closer than most writers to describing the conditions of hearing them in some other guise. It is he who evoked a Tupinamba song that "is *heard* but not understood, hence ravished from the body of productive work" – that is, ethnography – only to return, along the margins of ethnographic knowledge, in the form of "the figure of the other."[10] This marginal figure undoes comfortable Europeanisms in our ethnographies. In the present case, we will see, it undoes Montaigne's ethics of valor and love. Along

---

[9] See Léry, *Histoire*, trans. Whatley, *History*; André Thevet, *Les Singularitez de la France antarctique*, ed. Paul Gaffarel (Paris: Maisonneuve, 1878); also *Les Français en Amérique pendant la deuxième moitié du XVIe siècle: Le Brésil et les Brésiliens* (Paris: Presses Universitaires de France, 1953), for excerpts concerning Brazil from André Thevet's *Cosmographie universelle* of 1575 and other writings. For a collation of Montaigne's text with his sources see Bernard Weinberg, "Montaigne's Readings for *Des cannibales*," in *Renaissance and Other Studies in Honor of William Leon Wiley*, ed. George Bernard Daniel, Jr. (Chapel Hill: University of North Carolina Press, 1968), pp. 261–79.

[10] De Certeau, "Ethno-Graphy," p. 227.

the way we must not forget, as de Certeau sometimes forgets, that this Tupinamba figure defines the borders of our knowledge not so much by speaking as by singing.

The two Tupinamba song texts Montaigne reports concern the two practices that represent his dual ethics. The first is a song about cannibalism. The prisoners to be eaten, Montaigne says,

> are so far from giving in, in spite of all that is done to them, that on the contrary, during the two or three months that they are kept, they wear a gay expression; they urge their captors to hurry and put them to the test; they defy them, insult them, reproach them with their cowardice and the number of battles they have lost to the prisoners' own people.
>
> I have a song composed by a prisoner which contains this challenge, that they should all come boldly and gather to dine off him, for they will be eating at the same time their own fathers and grandfathers, who have served to feed and nourish his body. "These muscles," he says, "this flesh and these veins are your own, poor fools that you are. You do not recognize that the substance of your ancestors' limbs is still contained in them. Savor them well; you will find in them the taste of your own flesh."

"An idea," Montaigne adds, "that certainly does not smack of barbarity" (Rat, pp. 242–3; Frame, pp. 157–8).

Quickly Montaigne turns his attention to polygamy, specifically to the absence of jealousy among Tupinamba women and their striving to gain as many wives as they can for their husband. Again his primary evidence consists of the words of a song. "Lest it should be thought," Montaigne says,

> that all this is done through a simple and servile bondage to usage and through the pressure of the authority of their ancient customs, without reason or judgment, . . . I must cite some examples of their capacity. Besides the warlike song I have just quoted, I have another, a love song, which begins in this vein: "Adder, stay; stay, adder, that from the pattern of your coloring my sister may draw the fashion and the workmanship of a rich girdle that I may give to my love; so may your beauty and your pattern be forever preferred to all other serpents." This first couplet is the refrain of the song. Now I am familiar enough with poetry to be a judge of this: not only is there nothing barbarous in this fancy, but it is altogether Anacreontic. (Rat, pp. 243–4; Frame, p. 158)

For the first of these songs, the song of the prisoner to his captors, Montaigne modeled his text on the earlier accounts of Thevet and Léry. In *Les Singularitez de la France antarctique* and later in the *Cosmographie universelle* Thevet related the song in two slightly different versions. In the first the prisoner sings:

> "The Margageas our friends are valiant, strong, and powerful in war; they have taken and eaten a great number of our enemies, who will eat me some day when it pleases them; as for me, I have killed and eaten relatives and friends of him who holds me prisoner"; with many similar words.[11]

---

[11] Thevet, *Les Singularitez*, pp. 199–200; trans. modified from Quint, "A Reconsideration," p. 472. The longer version of this song from Thevet's *Cosmographie universelle* reads: "Ce pendant qu'il est ainsi estendu, ce pauvre captif s'esjouyt et chante telle ou semblable substance de parolles: Noz amis les Margageaz sont gens de bien,

The Singing of the New World

Figure 4.1 Tupinamba captive singing before his execution, from Léry, *Histoire d'un voyage* . . .

Léry, for his part, reports the episode not as a song but as a speech, made by the prisoner about to be killed after "he has sung and caroused for six or seven hours." (The fact that Léry does not specify that the speech itself is sung has its own revelations; I will return to them.) The prisoner, Léry relates,

> will boast of his past feats of prowess, saying to those who hold him bound: "I myself, who am valiant, first bound and tied your kinsmen." Then, exalting himself more and more, with a demeanor to match, he will turn from side to side and say to one, "I have eaten your father," and to another, "I have struck down and *boucané* [grilled] your brothers." He will add, "Of you Tupinamba that I have taken in war, I have eaten so many men and women and even children that I could not tell the number; and do not doubt that, to avenge my death, the Margaia, whose nation I belong to, will hereafter eat as many of you as they can catch."[12]

What seems to operate at the heart of all three versions of this song – what the Tupinamba words reported by Europeans seem to be about – is not so much an *ethics of valor* as an

---

fortz et puissants en guerre: ils ont prins et mangé plusieurs de voz parents noz ennemis, et de ceux qui me tiennent pour me faire mourir: mais il vengeront bien tost ma mort, et vous mangeront quand il leur plaira, et voz enfans aussi: quant à moy j'ay tué et mangé plusieurs amis de ce malin Aignan, qui me tient prisonnier. Je suis fort, je suis puissant: c'est moy qui ay mis en route plusieurs fois vous autres coüards, qui n'entendez rien à faire guerre, et plusieurs autres parolles disent-ils, qui monstre le peu de compte qu'ils ont de la mort, et que la crainte d'icelle ne peut en rien esbranler leur plus que brutale asseurance." See *Les Français en Amérique*, p. 198.

[12] Trans. Whatley, *History of a Voyage*, pp. 122–3; see Léry, *Histoire*, pp. 212–13.

economy of exchange. In "Of cannibals" this constitutes a first rift, a point where Montaigne's words seem to cut across the grain of the message he would have them impart. Desan, as I have suggested, has recognized this Tupinamba economics. He analyzed the differences between, on the one hand, a Tupinamba exchange that is utterly bound up in the practice and representation of Indian social relations and, on the other, the impinging European form of exchange, an international (and soon to be global) network of circulating capital that overreached individual societies and their practices and could not be strictly bound to them. Suggestively, Desan brought Marcel Mauss's classic analysis of gift exchange to bear on "Of cannibals," concluding that Tupinamba exchange, as a social relation, entailed complex reciprocal obligations, that in it individuals were subsumed to the collectivity of the tribe, and that the consumption of human flesh was the literal and regenerative assimilation of individual self into other.[13]

This juxtaposition of Tupinamba exchange and Mauss's analysis is worth pursuing farther than Desan takes it. Mauss realized that the gift-giving systems of what he called "archaic societies" embodied, in their most elaborate forms, fundamental social practices, defining the manners in which power and status were gained and held by their practitioners and the ways in which personhood itself was achieved.[14] Across wide cultural reaches in Mauss's comparative analysis, these systems repeat a number of basic features. First, Mauss notes the obligatory nature of systems of exchange. Built into the most complex and deep-seated of them, systems of "total prestation" like Northwest American potlatch or Trobriand kula, is a network of obligations not merely to repay gifts, but to give them and receive them as well. A larger social, natural, and spiritual order, extending not only through space but through time in the form of past and future generations, is stabilized by fulfillment of these obligations and undermined by their breach (pp. 39–43; also p. 14). Second: preeminently in the case of potlatch, Mauss finds that a deep rivalry and even antagonism may be an essential part of complex exchange systems. Potlatch can be conceived as a war and, in certain circumstances, carried out in a way that destroys exchanged goods instead of circulating them, thus "killing property," as some clans have it (p. 37 and n. 141).

Third, and perhaps most important, Mauss repeatedly underscores the fact that the things given in obligatory exchange systems are not purely material goods but rather materials bearing in them a part of the giver, things imbued with some spiritual essence of their origins and therefore animate. The gift, then, takes on extraordinary spiritual powers, powers that guarantee the reciprocity of the exchange: "One must give back to another person what is really part and parcel of his nature and substance, because to accept something from somebody is to accept some part of his spiritual essence, of his soul." Or again: "What imposes obligation in the present received and exchanged, is the fact that the thing received

---

[13] See Desan, *Les Commerces*, pp. 186–8. Desan's Maussian approach puts him in line with earlier Brazilian anthropologists who took a similar tack in interpreting Tupinamba warfare and cannibalism; see especially Florestan Fernandes, *A função social da guerra na sociedade tupinambá*, 2nd edn. (São Paulo: Livraria Pioneira Editôra, 1970).

[14] See Marcel Mauss, *The Gift: The Form and Reason for Exchange in Archaic Societies*, trans. W. D. Halls (New York: Norton, 1990); further references given in the text.

is not inactive.... Invested with life, often possessing individuality, it seeks to return to ... its 'place of origin' or to produce, on behalf of the clan and the native soil from which it sprang, an equivalent to replace it" (pp. 11–13; see also pp. 14, 20, 45–6).

The Tupinamba prisoner's song, in all its versions, seems clearly to reflect a form of exchange similar to those described by Mauss, one embodying all three features enumerated above. It differs from those systems in the simple, momentous fact that in Tupinamba exchange, *the gift is human flesh*; but the notion of exchange remains paramount. Thus Thevet's prisoner sings that his allies have captured and eaten many of his captors, who in turn will eat him. Léry's captive elaborates a full circulation whereby those who eat him avenge his own eating of their kin and will be eaten by his allies in order to avenge his death, while Montaigne's adds the conceit that by virtue of the exchange those feasting on him will savor their own flesh.[15]

In singing, the captive affirmed his place in an intergenerational and intertribal circulation of flesh taken in battle and later eaten. He was a gift to his captors; a gift that repayed the obligation entailed in his own consumption of an earlier gift from his captors; a gift that incurred a new debt in his captors and obliged them to pay, in the future, with their own flesh. The Brazilian warfare for which Montaigne could give no other rationale than "rivalry in valor" – for which he could find no material explanation in the desire to conquer lands and thereby increase possessions (Rat, p. 240; Frame, p. 156) – can be seen to have been, on one level, a precisely material exchange after all.

Not, however, a material exchange driven by material want: Montaigne, Thevet, and Léry all agree that the Tupinamba did not subsist on human flesh.[16] Their flesh exchange was instead a society-wide system of intercourse among proximate tribes, entailing elaborate ritualized treatment of captives taken. It played out, during the lengthy period leading up to the consumption of the captive, the stable course of Mauss's obligatory gift exchange. Not one captive in a whole century, Montaigne tells us, would give in to fear – thereby, we may add, disrupting or destroying the protocols of exchange.[17]

Moreover, flesh exchange structured the whole of Tupinamba society according to the honor and prestige due to those who take captives; remember the more numerous wives of powerful warriors. Indeed these individual captors were bound up in just the sort of reciprocal obligations Mauss would lead us to expect as we rethink their captives as gifts received. Montaigne tells us that he interviewed a powerful Brazilian warrior who was brought to Europe and asked him what he gained from his superior valor; "To march

---

[15] Quint ("A Reconsideration," pp. 472–3) suggests that the specific conceit of the Tupinamba tasting their own flesh in the exchange might be Montaigne's invention. In Léry's account the prisoner's speech is followed by further "contestations" that underscore the exchange-character of the ceremony; see *Histoire d'un voyage*, pp. 213–17; trans. Whatley, *History of a Voyage*, pp. 123–5.

[16] See Rat, p. 238; Frame, p. 155; and, for the relevant passages from Thevet and Léry, Weinberg, "Montaigne's Readings," p. 274.

[17] In his *Cosmographie universelle* Thevet raises the possibility that captives might try to escape but goes on to describe their mockery of his suggestion to them that he might assist them in doing so or that they might fear their impending death. Even women and children among the prisoners, Thevet tells us, did not flee when given the opportunity. See *Les Français en Amérique*, pp. 197–9.

foremost in war" was the answer (Rat, p. 245; Frame, p. 159). From a Maussian perspective the answer might be glossed: Abundance of gifts received obliges the receiver to repay with special generosity. The bravest warrior, having partaken of the most flesh of his enemies, goes first either to receive more gifts or to settle the debt with his own flesh.

Meanwhile, to turn to the second point borrowed from Mauss, the cannibals' exchange was framed in a violent antagonism of military raids. This must have served precise social needs, perhaps with larger seasonal and cosmogonic ramifications, that are lost to us. (Hans Staden, a German soldier held captive by the Tupinamba for nine months in 1554, suggests that his captors launched their raids to coincide with the ripening of certain fruits in November and spawning of certain fish in August; here we may glimpse a broad world-rhythm governing them.[18]) Montaigne's vocabulary was inadequate for such an activity. He could do no more than liken it to the eminently *anti*social practice of sixteenth-century European "warfare," though in the same breath he registered an awareness of the difference between the two practices by noting that Tupinamba warfare, unlike the European version, was "noble and generous, and as excusable and beautiful as this human disease can be" (Rat, p. 240; Frame, p. 156). Limned here is the contrast between a warfare that upholds complex ritual patterns – a kind of warfare tentatively described by Europeans elsewhere in the New World, for instance in the flower-wars to gain victims for sacrificial rites in central Mexico – and one that destroys them.

Finally (the third point from Mauss), the gift in Tupinamba flesh exchange was so far from being inert matter that it could *sing* its spirituality, sing of its capacity to return to its receivers something they had given earlier, sing of its desire to bring in turn some recompense back to its place of origin. This unending circulation of flesh between warring tribes is certainly the most salient theme in all the versions of the song.

The social modes of Mauss's "total prestation" seem then to be clearly reflected in Tupinamba flesh exchange – so clearly, indeed, that it encourages us to extend a play on words offered by Eduardo Viveiros de Castro (in an analysis of cannibalism to which we will return). Tupinamba practices are not merely a question of human predation on other humans, or even a merger of this with the linguistic predication of self in cannibal oratory, but a conjunction of these two with an encompassing network of social imbrications and obligations. All three terms together, then: predation, predication, and prestation.

But why did the gift sing? Why do Thevet and Montaigne, at least, write of songs rather than plain talk? This special vocalization opens a second rift in Montaigne's text, alongside the American economics that speaks from behind his European ethics. Montaigne himself did not call attention to it. Neither can Mauss help us here; succumbing momentarily to

---

[18] Hans Staden, *Warhafftige Historia unnd Beschreibung einer landtschafft der Wilden, Nacketen, Grimmigen, Menschfresser Leuthen in der Newen Welt America gelegen* (Marpurg, 1557), trans. Albert Tootal as *The Captivity of Hans Stade of Hesse, in A.D. 1547–1555, Among the Wild Tribes of Eastern Brazil* (Hakluyt Society, First Series 51, 1874; rpt. edn. New York: Burt Franklin, n.d.), pt. 1, chaps. 17, 41 (pp. 49, 96–7). On the ethnographic importance of Staden's work see Neil L. Whitehead, "Hans Staden and the Cultural Politics of Cannibalism," *Hispanic American Historical Review* 80 (2000), pp. 721–51; for the period of Staden's captivity see Donald W. Forsyth, "Three Cheers for Hans Staden: The Case for Brazilian Cannibalism," *Ethnohistory* 32.1 (1985), pp. 17–36.

modern European modes of thought, he omitted the songs and dances that characteristically accompany gift-giving from his analysis, separating them off from the exchanges of which they form a part and short-shrifting them as so many "aesthetic phenomena."[19] De Certeau instead, as I have noted, at least broaches this question. For him the songs in Tupinamba cannibalism and polygamy indicate an "economy of speech" for which the body is the price. The songs are "speech-acts" whose operation submits the self-interest of individual bodies, whether the captive's or the wife's, to the communal interest of the social body as a whole. (De Certeau goes so far as to say that "The song symbolizes the entire social body.") In the process, de Certeau says, the individual body "becomes a poem," by which he means that it takes on the autonomous power of an utterance that effaces its bodily place of origin.[20]

In this, the relation of Indian body to Indian song comes to mirror, for de Certeau, the relation of Tupinamba culture all told to European writing of it. In both cases the first term is an absent presence in the second, an originating and sustaining figure that disappears to the margins of what it engenders: "The savage ethic of speech opens the way for a Western ethic of writing. . . . If one cannot be a cannibal, there is still the option of lost-body writing."[21] We are back at de Certeau's ethnography, in which the figure of the other, banished to the margins, conditions and allows our writing and knowledge.

What particularly appeals in de Certeau's interpretation is his emphasis on the efficacy of the Tupinamba songs. For him these are not statements of fact but rather effective vocalizations that actively forge specific relations between Tupinamba individuals and society. They are performatives, not constatives, to follow through on de Certeau's intimation of speech-act theory. But calling them speech-acts obscures their true nature. Call them, instead, *song-acts*: performatives of a special kind, marked by enough heightening of elements of vocal production – intonation, rhythm, and timbre – and set off, in social circumstance and function, clearly enough from normal speech that Europeans could easily distinguish them from everyday Tupinamba discourse.

Can we find it convincing, however, that de Certeau discovers the same Derridean play of remainders that he saw at work in the European writing of Americans also *within* the indigenous situation itself, in the relation of Tupinamba body and song? In the Tupinamba context de Certeau's disappearance of the body from the utterance it sustains seems, on the face of it, too congruent to the larger interaction he perceives between Europeans and Brazilians not to be suspect. Instead, I think, we need a different perspective: one that does not rely on the hermeneutic notion of a poesy that escapes the control of its authors, one that might see these Indian songs and bodies as mutually implicated in the broad social patterns of flesh exchange I outlined above.

Here anthropologist Webb Keane's recent work in the Maussian tradition of exchange analysis, on Anakalangese ceremonial exchange in eastern Indonesia, seems especially suggestive. This exchange, Keane has maintained, fulfills its social functions by striking up a crucial interdependency of words and things. Each draws near to the other: Objects take on "sign-like qualities" and words "object-like qualities" in their mutual association in the ritual. When this relation is successfully forged, the value of material objects is defined by

---

[19] Mauss, *The Gift*, pp. 3, 38.   [20] See "Montaigne's 'Of Cannibals'," pp. 75–9.   [21] Ibid., p. 79.

conventional but flexible utterances. When it is not, the exchange might collapse into other, lower forms of transaction such as barter or sale. The successful exchange complex, made up of thingish words and wordly things, establishes connections that are both diachronic, reaching back to society's past and looking toward its future, and synchronic, shaping the present-day social matrix. "Valid speech performance," Keane writes, "places the speaker in a continuous lineage linking past to future, while successful exchange of objects makes one a node in a continuous chain of contemporaneous partners." In this way words uttered during exchanges are "critical to the value and efficacy of the exchanges they mediate."[22]

Something similar probably occurred in Tupinamba flesh exchange. There words sung back and forth between captive and captors – throughout the lengthy period of captivity, perhaps, but with a culminating increase of ritual pace as the time of the killing neared[23] – seem to have provided a crucial enunciation of the worth of the gift of flesh. To judge from the song texts, captives enacted this worth not by expressing an ethics of valor but by voicing an economic strength measured by past consumption of their captors' kin. The resistance of the captive to fear, so central to Montaigne's and Thevet's *contexts* for the song, seems not to enter into its *text* at all. It stands outside the reported words of the song as a European gloss on them, measuring in its distance from the song texts themselves the breadth of the rift they open.

In addition to expressing the power and strength of the captive as these are reflected in his past consumption of flesh-gifts from his enemies, the words of the song affirm also, especially in the fuller versions given by Thevet and Léry, an ongoing circulation of flesh originating in the past and continuing into the future. In this history of consumption that it embodies, the song asserts the captive's suitability to repay the earlier gift of his captors' kin's bodies; in the process it also binds the present consumers in a web of future obligatory exchange of their own flesh. In this way, rather than by registering a courage redolent of the recently revived European Stoicism that so shaped Montaigne's values, the song marks the object – the captive's body – as suitable for exchange, as worthy, and as appropriate for inclusion in the gift-giving cycle. It projects the significance of the exchange both into the past (as repayment made) and into the future (as debt incurred), stabilizing the whole system as an ongoing social interaction. In this interaction, Stoic courage is not a determining – perhaps not even a relevant – sentiment.

This economy of strength depended on the heightened medium of song, which marked off the captive's words from the other locutions around them. In some putative non-ritualized context, first, taunts such as the captive's might well have seemed to claim for him a certain strength, but they would no doubt have brought him a quick death as well. Their ritualized nature, reflected in many circumstances surrounding their utterance but inhering crucially in the fact that they were song-acts, not speech-acts, gained them their efficacy by insuring their singer's impunity. The validation of the captive's flesh as gift was enabled, then, not

---

[22] Webb Keane, "The Value of Words and the Meaning of Things in Eastern Indonesian Exchange," *Man* n.s. 29 (1994), pp.605–29; see pp. 605, 621.

[23] On the ceremonies of the day of the killing, evidence of this acceleration, see Léry, *Histoire*, chap. 15, and Thevet, *Les Singularitez*, chap. 40, and *Cosmographie universelle*, bk. 21, chap. 15 (chap. 14 of *Les Français en Amérique*).

only by his participation in an ongoing history conveyed in the meaning of his words but also by the sung medium that cleared a cultural space within which this history could be enunciated. The value of the captive was affirmed at a level of cultural practice marked by the sung medium his utterances deployed as well as at the level of the meanings his words circulated.

The sung delivery of the captive's challenge may have been basic to the exchange in another way as well. Whatever the features that marked it, for Thevet and the other Europeans, as song (features now irrecuperable in any precise way), these must have operated in the most general fashion as such features of chanting or singing operate in other times and places: as markers of the boundaries between normal and extraordinary discourse and thus as an index of a special utterance-efficacy they embody. But the specific power of these songs, as in all such cases, was of a kind determined in their own context.

In Tupinamba flesh exchange, bodily intonation and rhythmicization probably were the central features of an utterance that could take on Keane's "object-like qualities," a vocalization that could warrant the worth of a fleshly gift. In their emanation, at the same time, they must have revealed the semiotic qualities of the captive body, its more than material, sign-like presence, its conveyance into the exchange of a spirituality linking a societal (and cosmological) past, present, and future. Here body affirmed through song its metamaterial presence – its spirituality, in Mauss's terminology. Body was not at all banished to the margins by song, as de Certeau would have it. Just the opposite: It was brought by singing to the very heart of social circulation, affirmed by song to be at once palpably material and worthily supersubstantial. The boundaries separating voice from body and both from metaphysics were effaced.

Léry, I noted above, did not describe as song the cannibals' challenges just before the killing and roasting of the captive. Rather, I think, he *could not* describe them as song, because in structuring his narrative he put Tupinamba singing to other uses.

Léry reserved song in the *Histoire* to affirm his proximity to the Indians and the humanity they shared with him. Their singing was for him a source of wondrous communion with the Americans, as is clear from an important episode when he witnessed and was enraptured by an elaborate ceremony of chant, song, and dance. Léry took from his experience of Tupinamba song, first, a marvel and transport that he could not forget and that he tried to convey in European music writing even thirty years later; he took from it, second, a confirmation that some dim memory of God's Word persisted among the Americans.[24]

For Léry to have recognized the connection between Tupinamba song and cannibalism would have emphasized instead the cultural gulf between himself and the Americans. The

---

[24] Léry, *Histoire*, pp. 242–50; trans. Whatley, *History of a Voyage*, pp. 140–5; see also de Certeau, "Ethno-Graphy," pp. 212–15, and Stephen Greenblatt, *Marvelous Possessions: The Wonder of the New World* (Chicago: University of Chicago Press, 1991), pp. 16–19. Léry's musical notations of Tupinamba singing are not found in the first editions of his *Histoire* of 1578 and 1580; they first enter the edition of 1585; for more on them, see chap. 2 above.

only Europeans whom a staunch Huguenot such as he could conceive as near to cannibals were the hated Catholics who had massacred so many of his religious brethren. Léry, in short, could not have it both ways. He could not experience Tupinamba singing both as a narrowing and a widening of the cultural distance that confronted him in Brazil.

Significantly, Léry demonstrates to us that the intercultural communion-in-song he experienced could operate in both directions. In an incident at the end of the chapter where he relates his wonderment at Indian singing, the tables are turned. Now he narrates how, while walking through the forest with several Indians, he was moved by the natural beauty around him to sing Psalm 104. The Indians, then, were struck with sympathetic wonder at his song, which reminded them of the singing of a tribe allied with theirs. And, according to Léry, their communion with his singing allowed them to appreciate the truth of his psalm's words. When he explained their meaning to them they exclaimed, "Teh! O you *Mairs* (that is, Frenchmen) how fortunate you are to know so many secrets that are hidden from us poor wretches!"[25]

For Léry, then, singing occupied a cultural space distant from cannibalism. It fulfilled roles not congruent with its use in the Tupinamba exchange of flesh, and fulfilled them so compellingly that this use was suppressed. But not completely: Perhaps the Tupinamba connection of singing and flesh given as gift intrudes into the *Histoire* despite Léry's opposed inclinations. The lead Indian among those who followed him through the forest, having marveled at his psalm and its doctrinal message, closed this episode by saying, "Here, because you have sung so well," and offering Léry an *agouti* he had just killed.

Meanwhile, Montaigne also avoided the native efficacy of the Tupinamba songs, but in a different way than Léry: He turned them into poetry. The conceit of the captive's song, as we have heard, does not smack at all of barbarity to his ears. As for the second song he reports, it is in his modest judgment no less than Anacreontic. We have witnessed in chapter 1, in another European–American encounter, the effects of this mapping of the European ideology of poetry on to indigenous American song. It is, above all, a gesture of domestication of others' singing, one almost bound to obscure in it efficacies unfamiliar to Europeans. The songs Montaigne related were for him *chansons*, pleasant trifles. Their naive and rustic beauties, he elsewhere remarks, likened them to European popular songs or *villanelles* and enabled them to withstand comparison with the most artful poetry.[26] In this naturalness, the songs were redolent of a grace among the Indians that in the ethics of Montaigne's argument must have stood opposed, whatever his cultural relativism, to the "barbarous horror" of Tupinamba cannibalism. He, like Léry if for different reasons, could not hear songs instead as the very driving force of human flesh exchange.

---

[25] Léry, *Histoire*, pp. 257–9; trans. Whatley, *History of a Voyage*, p. 149.

[26] These features also allow Montaigne to incorporate the songs in his complex thoughts concerning the role of human nature in nobililty; see Kate van Orden, "Vernacular Culture and the Chanson in Paris, 1570–1580" (PhD dissertation, University of Chicago, 1996), chap. 6 and esp. pp. 400–8. Montaigne's likening of New World songs to *villanelles*, from the essay "Des vaines subtilitez" (1, 54), is quoted by van Orden on p. 407; see also Rat, p. 347; Frame, p. 227.

And what of Tupinamba polygamy and the song Montaigne cites in connection with it? The evidence here is entirely equivocal. The song is not attested elsewhere in European accounts; it is conceivable that it is nothing more than a fabrication by Montaigne, though this seems unlikely, given his generally close reliance on specific sources for the rest of his information. Any presumption that it reflects Tupinamba realities is riskier than such a leap concerning the first song.[27]

If we take the leap, however, the song might enter intriguingly into the Indians' economy of flesh. It seems to act as a kind of magical charm, bidding a serpent hold still so that its scale pattern might be duplicated on a woven sash or girdle (as Frame translates *cordon*) to be worn by a lover. It suggests a magical transference of flesh that accompanies sexual relations. Perhaps – if the lure of an encroaching Freudianism can be warded off in hazarding such a guess – it assimilates the serpent to the penis of the singer who presents the sash; the relation of snake and penis is certainly not unknown in indigenous American iconographies.[28] The serpent-girdle itself, created with the aid of a charm song, marks the value of the adder it resembles: "So may your beauty and your pattern be forever preferred to all other serpents." By the same token it distinguishes the lover who wears it. A gift validates flesh, facilitating a somatic, sexual meeting, by special means again involving song.

The broadening of the economy of flesh exchange to include non-human flesh that is involved in this interpretation of the song finds its analogy in the Indian's gift of an *agouti* to Léry for his psalm singing. In the one case a gift of song is reciprocated with a gift of flesh; in the other a seemingly totemic gift resembling (snake's) flesh and created through song accompanies a fleshly sexual exchange. Both cases, like the encompassing social and ritual system of anthropophagic flesh exchange in which they occur, present singing as a special enunciation connected to the circulation of flesh. One more extension of ideas of flesh exchange, ranging farther still than these, is signaled by Hans Staden. It did not involve singing, but it shows how far into the non-human world Tupinamba conceptions of cyclic flesh consumption could penetrate. Staden tells how "When one picks lice from the others, she eats the lice." He asked why they did this; "They said that they were their enemies, who eat their heads, and that they would be revenged on them."[29]

The girdle, meanwhile, must have had its own special significance. No early accounts shed much light on this, but perhaps it is related to the girdle of the present-day Araweté, a Tupi-Guarani people of the Xingu region of the Amazonian interior described by Eduardo Viveiros de Castro. Araweté girls are made to wear girdles covering their genitalia from

---

[27] Moreover, the gendering of Montaigne's presentation of the song is puzzling, as Carla Freccero has noted. His introducing of it seems to suggest that it was sung by a wife. However, its reference to the giving of the girdle to a female lover – "un riche cordon que je puisse donner à m'amie" (Rat, p. 244) – instead calls, in the context of heterosexual relations that the whole passage concerns, for a male singer. See Carla Freccero, "Cannibalism, Homophobia, Women: Montaigne's 'Des cannibales' and 'De l'amitié'" in *Women, "Race," and Writing in the Early Modern Period*, ed. Margo Hendricks and Patricia Parker (London: Routledge, 1994), pp. 73–83.

[28] For an example see Gordon Brotherston, *The Book of the Fourth World: Reading the Native Americas Through Their Literature* (Cambridge: Cambridge University Press, 1992), Figure 19.

[29] Staden, *The Captivity*, pt. 2, chap. 16 (p. 141).

the time of their first menstruation. The weaving of this garment is, as in Montaigne's song, a female task, undertaken by a close female relative. The girdle is a potent sexual emblem, a material representation of the "stretching" of its wearer's labia through sexual intercourse (an effect much commented upon in Araweté discourse) and their resulting assimilation to the penis. The girdle also marks its wearer's individuality; it is a woman's only possession that cannot be inherited but is buried with her at her death. In both of these "emblematic" functions Viveiros de Castro finds in the girdle a parallel to an attribute of adult Araweté males: the *aray* or shamanic rattle, to which we will return below.[30]

The female sexuality marked by the girdle provides, at the broadest level of Viveiros de Castro's analysis, a point of entry for Araweté women into the warlike and cannibalistic ideologies dominated otherwise by men. It is the arena where their societal roles come closest to mirroring those of the man-killing warrior.[31] (Another entry-point, this one with well-documented analogies among sixteenth-century Tupinamba, is the female preparation of the maize beer employed in war-dance celebrations.)

These analogies from a modern-day group are at least suggestive. In their light we might take the girdle of Montaigne's song to signify the female access through sexuality to the cycles of human flesh exchange that ordered Tupinamba society. This in turn – to pursue one step farther this most speculative of the speculations offered here – might reflect a gynocentric view in which polygamy all told was configured by Tupinamba women as an exchange among themselves of male flesh rather than as anything akin to Montaigne's wifely selflessness and fidelity. Again European categories might fade to irrelevancy in the face of Tupinamba flesh exchange.

That Tupinamba women could link in this way their husbands' flesh to the flesh of enemies consumed may seem implausible. But the possibility of just such a linkage is raised in one of the roles women played in ritual cannibalism itself. Léry describes this role, with melodramatic relish. He tells us that a male captive, but not a female one, was sometimes given a spouse, who would "treat him well and minister to all his needs" during the period of his captivity. (Children resulting from such unions, the chroniclers tell us, were sometimes raised in order later to be killed and eaten as enemies.) Then, as soon as the captive was killed, his wife would

> perform some slight mourning beside the body – and "slight mourning" is just what I mean. For as one says of the crocodile, that having killed a man, he then weeps just before eating him, so too after the woman has made some or another lamentation, and shed a few feigned tears over her dead husband, she will, if she can, be the first to eat of him.[32]

What scant and problematic evidence we have hints, then, at something close to the opposite of Montaigne's interpretation of Tupinamba polygamy. It suggests not a social

---

[30] Eduardo Viveiros de Castro, *From the Enemy's Point of View: Humanity and Divinity in an Amazonian Society*, trans. Catherine V. Howard (Chicago: University of Chicago Press, 1992), pp. 187–9, 200–1.
[31] Ibid., p. 274.   [32] Whatley, *History of a Voyage*, pp. 125–6; Léry, *Histoire*, p. 217.

order in which a man's intercourse with several women might arouse jealousy among them but one in which the union of one man with several women was conceived as a circulation of worthy flesh analogous in its structure to cannibalism. It suggests also that the flesh of captives could enter, if in strictly limited ways, into this sexual flesh exchange.

This distances from Léry's perspective the Tupinamba wife's tears over her slaughtered, enemy husband. Whatever their emotional valence, they were nothing so legible as Léry wished them to be – not "crocodile tears," but tears shed in a circumstance mystifyingly foreign to their European interpreter. An attempt to analyze the social purport of these tears might start from another ritual described in the *Histoire*, the greeting of a male guest in which women gather around, "spouting big tears" and "weeping their welcome."[33] But wherever they led, these spiraling acts of interpretation would look back on beginnings in Montaigne's second song – on beginnings, that is, in the eruption in European writing of another of the song-acts that seem to have been a vital part of the Tupinamba economy of flesh exchange.

The maraca's voice

To the humans who employ them, musical instruments pose a twofold, supplementary logic. They enhance and amplify native capacities for music-making, extending the organism technologically in the manner of so many prosthetic devices. At the same time they displace and replace these capacities, obscuring them behind the allure, variously imagined, of new, distinctive sonic resources.

The native capacities themselves are at root of two kinds: powers of body and of voice. The first comprise the various clappings, slappings, stompings, and snappings, characteristically human, of the body in rhythmic motion. The second include all the modes of heightened, non- or trans-speech vocalization that make up the primary theme of these essays; emanations from a mysterious bodily interior, they are habitually associated in societies the world over with spirits and metaphysics. Taxonomies of instruments offered by musicologists and ethnomusicologists converge back, finally, on this simple dichotomy: devices that supplement the body and those that supplement the voice. The phenomenon of musical instruments, then, entails an axis of supplementary extension/displacement that intersects obliquely with a second axis extending from voice to body.

Across several centuries, the elite music-making of the West – to pause briefly over an example far from indigenous Brazil – played out a particular instance of this supplementary doubleness in the special status accorded to instruments deemed best to approximate the voice in their timbres, flexibility, and expressive powers. This status was erected on vocal foundations, but it enabled the evolution of virtuosic performance capabilities outstripping the voice and rich instrumental repertoires that finally threatened to dislodge voice from the heart of the tradition. At every point in this history musical instruments were prized

---

[33] See Léry, *Histoire*, pp. 283–5; trans. Whatley, *History of a Voyage*, p. 164.

for their similarities to voice at the very moment they replaced it with their own, distinct capacities; at some points in it the instruments prized were less vocal prostheses than bodily ones.

Thus about 1600 the now defunct cornetto was praised for its vocal qualities, only to be replaced, by the late seventeenth century, by the violin. Champions of this instrument acclaimed its voice-like suppleness and expression through the eighteenth century. Paradoxically, however, the violin approximated the voice even as it shifted vocalism away from the mouth itself and formed the basis of a non-vocal orchestral tradition that grew ever more prominent. The 1800s saw the high-water mark of this symphonic, string-centered displacement of voice. At the same time, in keeping with the industrial temper of the times, vocal expressivity was discovered in a more recent musico-mechanical wonder even farther removed from the oral source of voice: the piano.

With the advent of sound recording, finally, the voice reclaimed some of its diminished preeminence; indeed recording technology in its infancy was not much good for anything *but* voice. As the technology matured, however, the two massive Western musical developments of late modernity, jazz and rock and roll, advanced their own characteristic surrogates for voice: the trumpet first and later the saxophone in jazz and the electric guitar in rhythm and blues and rock.

Such instrumental supplementarity brings about a special relation between the human organism and the musical machines it contrives – a prosthetic relation, as I have suggested, in which are simultaneously manifested the technological extension of human powers and a compensation for limitation, loss, or absence within them. The sounds of musical instruments, that is, both supply an immanent, somatic plenitude and mark its origin elsewhere than in the body. In the first aspect their function is, at least on the face of it, transparent. The second, instead, points beyond incarnate sonic origins. It poses an ever-near mystery of decipherment: What other-than-human presence is borne in these sounds? The instrumental displacement of voice can be seen to echo and amplify aboriginal mysteries attendant on voice itself.

A supplementary understanding of musical instruments confronts, in this way, the metaphysical contact they have been thought through human history to initiate, facilitate, or reveal. Again and again – from the Siberian shaman's drum to the Greek lyre, from South Asian gongs to West African drums, from Australian didjeridoos to Andean raftpipes – the alterity inhabiting their sounds has appeared to open an aural window on normally unperceived realms.

The Tupinamba certainly participated in this worldwide musical metatechnology, and they did so in ways that will return us to their vocalized economy of flesh exchange. The rattles that were basic to their ceremonial song and dance provided a bridge to spirit realms, with such clarity that few early observers of their society missed the fact.

Two different kinds of rattles feature in the accounts of these observers. The first consisted of dried *ahouai* nuts, strung in bands around dancers' calves or ankles so as to rattle when they jumped and stamped the ground. The second was the famous maraca, a hollow calabash gourd transfixed by a stick, filled with grains or pebbles, and painted and adorned with feathers. Both are pictured in well-known sixteenth-century representations

The Singing of the New World

Figure 4.2 Tupinamba dance with maracas, from Staden, *Warhafftige Historia* . . .

of Tupinamba dancing, from Staden's *Warhafftige Historia*, Léry's *Histoire*, and, elaborated from details of Léry's narrative, in Theodor de Bry's republication of the *Histoire* in his *Grand Voyages* (see Figures 4.2, 4.3, and 4.4). Both rattles also appear in Thevet's woodcut of the *ahouai* tree in his *Cosmographie universelle*, where in addition we see an Indian preparing the leg rattle (Figure 4.5).

The *ahouai* rattles are an especially clear instance of a prosthetic extension of the powers of the human body, translating rhythmic movement into sound and transforming the dull thud of feet stamped on the ground. In this sonic function they seem related to the purely bodily sounds that accompanied Tupinamba voices in story-telling, speechifying, and song. Such performance is captured vividly in Thevet's description of the oratory of chief Cunhambebe (or Quoniambec or Konyan Bebe) of the Tamoio, one of the tribes of the Tupinamba:

Musicoanthropophagy

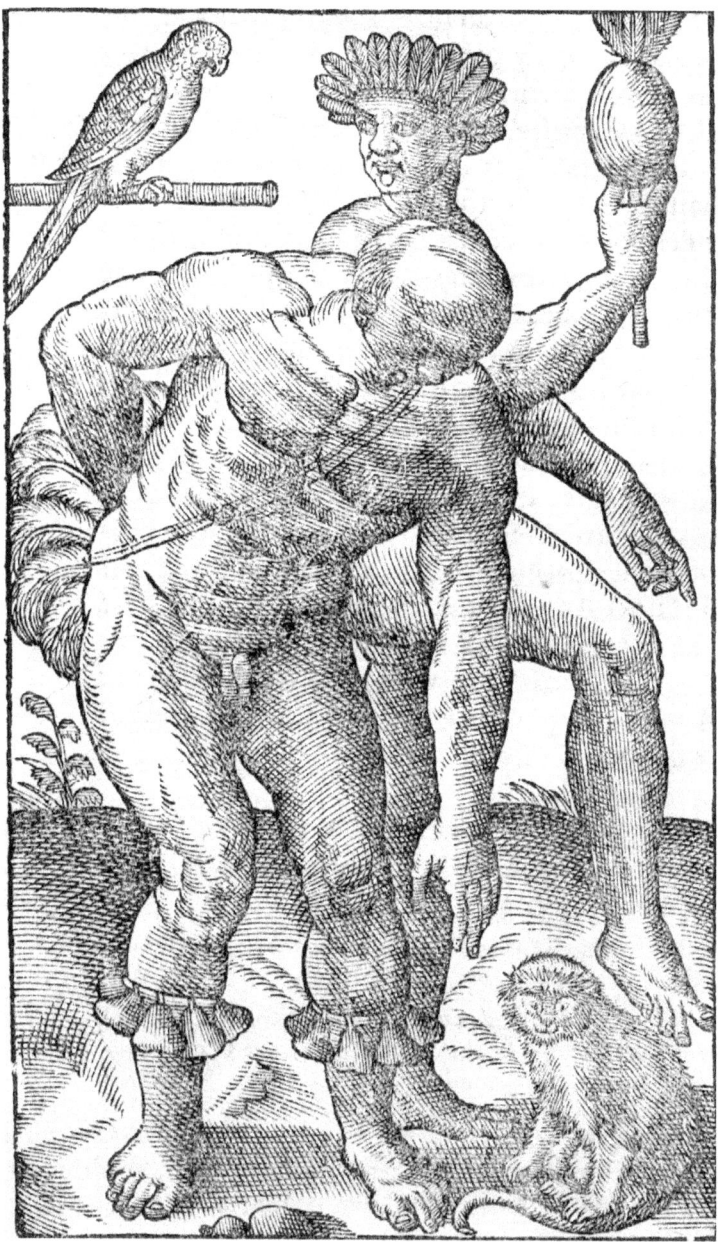

Figure 4.3 Tupinamba dance with maraca, from Léry, *Histoire d'un voyage* . . .

He would make a discourse and a harangue lasting two full hours, marching about quite naked, beating and slapping his chest and thighs, always interspersing it with menaces against his enemies the Peros (who were the Portuguese): "I have eaten so many of them, and of the Margageas also. I have killed so many of their women and children, . . ." and a thousand other boasts that this venerable king made while he walked about striking

113

The Singing of the New World

Figure 4.4 Tupinamba dance with maracas, from Léry, *Histoire d'un voyage* . . . , as translated in Theodore de Bry, *Dritte Buch Americae*.

his shoulders or thighs, with such gestures that there was scarcely a man who did not tremble hearing him speak with a voice so great, hideous, and terrible that you could hardly have heard had it thundered.[34]

Thevet offers a rare glimpse of the kind of heightened speech, involving emphatic bodily gesture – the sounding of the body – as well as voice, that Indian warriors must often have exploited. (Thevet's conceit that Cunhambebe's voice could have drowned out thunder may be suggestive of Indian responses to such performance; a thunder-spirit called Toupan occupied an important place in the Tupinamba spirit imaginary and was taken by the Europeans to be the closest equivalent the Indians knew to the Christian god.)

[34] Thevet, *La Cosmographie universelle*, in *Les Français en Amerique*, ed. Lussagnet, p. 92; translation adapted from John Hemming, *Red Gold: The Conquest of the Brazilian Indians, 1500–1760* (Cambridge: Harvard University Press, 1978), p. 124.

Musicoanthropophagy

Figure 4.5 *Ahouai* tree and rattles, from Thevet, *Lec Singularitez de la France antarctique*.

However close the leg rattles seemed to the slapping and pounding with which Cunhambebe accompanied his speech, they entered also directly into the rituals of cannibalism. Their specific function here is by no means made clear in the accounts, but Hans Staden, at least, gives intriguing particulars. Taken prisoner by the Tupinamba in 1554, he encountered the leg rattles immediately upon his arrival in his captors' village. There, during a period of ritual taunts and physical abuse by the women of the tribe, he was made to wear the rattles and dance to the measure of the women's songs:

115

The Singing of the New World

> They led me into the huts, where I had to lie in a hammock, whilst the women came and struck and pulled me before and behind, and threatened me how they would eat me.
>
> And the men were together in a hut, and drank the beverage which they call Kawi [*Caouïn*], and had with them their gods, called Tammerka, and they sang in praise of them, for their having so well prophesied that I should be captured by them. . . . Then they led me . . . to before the huts wherein the Tammerka their idols were, and made round about me a circle. . . . Two women were with me, and they tied to one of my legs strings of objects, which rattled. . . . Thereupon the womenkind all began together to sing, and to their time I was obliged to stamp with the leg to which they had tied the rattles, so that they rattled in harmony.[35]

This command performance with leg rattles offers another instance of bodies breaking forth in sound, analogous to the singing of Tupinamba captives in the period leading to their slaughter. Here again, in other words, an object seems to take on the semiotic qualities of a sign with more than physical attributes.

Whether this is true remains obscured in the vagueness of Staden's and other references to the leg rattles. About the metaphysical status of the Tupinamba maracas, on the other hand, there can be no doubt. The "Tammerka" idols or gods mentioned by Staden were the maracas themselves; his term is one of several corruptions in the early writings of the Tupi word *maracá*. A later episode in Staden's account reveals that the captives were made to dance to these too before their execution, to accompany the singing and ritual boasting that, as we have seen, established their place in the intergenerational cycling of flesh. Staden tells how the male captors and their prisoners

> . . . assembled together, and made a large ring, wherein stood the captives. Then the latter had all to sing and to rattle with the Tammaraka idols. Now when the prisoners had danced, they began to speak, one after the other, boastfully saying, "Yes, we went forth, as it beseems valiant men, to capture and to eat you, our enemies. . . ." "Yes," said the others, "you have already destroyed many of ours, and for this we will have our revenge of you."[36]

The fact that maracas are employed here instead of the leg rattles of Staden's own dance probably reflects the gender differences between the two episodes – male captors here, female taunters there – since Tupinamba women were forbidden from possessing maracas.

We probably glimpse here a deep dichotomy of function between the rattles. The early accounts do not pay special attention to the leg rattles or associate them with any extraordinary significance or power. The sparse information they provide suggests only that the rattles extended the sonic potency of the bodies of dancers who wore them, marking the kinship between their rhythmic motions and the singing around them ("they rattled in harmony" to the time of the women's songs). The several extended accounts concerning maracas, instead, do not fail to assert their much greater significance. We will see that they functioned not only as a sonic amplification and enhancement of bodily motion but as a displacement of the body in favor of voices of spirits or gods.

---

[35] Staden, *The Captivity*, pt. 1, chaps. 21–2 (pp. 60–1, 64).   [36] Ibid., pt. 1, chap. 43 (p. 103).

Musicoanthropophagy

Staden devoted most of his chapter on Indian beliefs to the maracas, and in it he described the voice they were thought to possess. "They believe," he began ingenuously, "in a thing which grows, like a pumpkin, about the size of a half-quart pot." He detailed the construction of the instruments, their use in song and dance, each man's possession of one, and the spiritual voices heard when they were made to sound. He dwelled in particular on this last topic and the consecration ceremony whereby the maracas were envoiced.

Tupinamba shamans or *paygi* (the more usual form of the word is *pagé*) came once a year to the village, acting as mediums for a spirit "from foreign places far off" and empowered to invest the maracas with a prayer-granting and prophetic voice. This they accomplished, after much "drinking, singing, and soothsaying," in a special, all-male ceremony in one of the longhouses. Each man, having painted his maraca red and ornamented it with feathers, planted it by its stick in the ground. The shaman took each instrument in turn and blew tobacco smoke over it. (De Bry's rendering of such fumigation can be seen in Figure 4.4, where *pagés* in the midst of a round dance employ long cane pipes.) Finally the *pagé* spoke to the maraca and received a response from its spirit. For Staden this consecration amounted to so much hocus-pocus, but this did not keep him from recognizing its sacred impact on the Indians:

> [The *pagé*] places the rattle close to his mouth, and rattles therewith, saying to it: "Nee kora, now speak, and make thyself heard, art thou therein?" Presently he speaks in a soft voice, and just a word or two, so that one cannot well perceive whether it is the rattle or he who speaks. And the other people believe that the rattle speaks; but the soothsayer does it himself. In such a manner he proceeds with all the rattles, one after the other: each one then believes that his rattle contains great power.... These are now their gods.

The consecrated maracas became, moreover, anthropophagic gods. The shamans commanded the men to go to war at the behest of the maraca spirits, who "desire to eat the flesh of slaves." After the ceremony each man constructed a hut for his enspirited rattle, where he cared for it and left it offerings of food, "calling it his dear son."[37]

Léry corroborates many of Staden's details in his own chapter on Tupinamba religion. In certain ceremonies, he writes, the Tupinamba played their maracas incessantly, "so that (as they said) the spirit might thereafter speak through these rattles." Like Staden, Léry tells of maracas planted in the ground in the middle of the Indians' longhouses, of their decoration with fine feathers and the offerings of food made to them. (He presumes that the *pagés* themselves consumed the food each night.) "They usually leave [the maracas] planted in the earth for two or three weeks," he concludes,

> always attended to in the same way; and they have a strange belief concerning these maracas (which they almost always have in hand): attributing a certain sanctity to them once this bewitchment has been accomplished, they say that whenever they make them sound, a spirit speaks to them.[38]

---

[37] For these quotations, ibid., pt. 2, chap. 22 (pp. 145–8).
[38] Léry, *Histoire d'un voyage*, pp. 245, 250; trans. Whatley, *History of a Voyage*, pp. 142, 145.

Thevet, finally, returns to the maraca and its spiritual nature several times in his writings. Along with Staden and Léry he describes its construction and decoration and tells how it was planted in the ground. He also dwells on the "mystère" of its voice, proclaiming this to be the speech of the great thunder-spirit Toupan:

> ... they make of it a certain mystery, the strangest imaginable ... , thinking (the poor idolators) that their Toupan speaks to them when they handle this fruit and make it sound, and that thereby all things are revealed to them and especially to their prophets. Thus they think and believe that there is some divinity there, and they worship no other material thing....[39]

Elsewhere Thevet is more specific concerning the revelations of the maraca's voice: "They believe their Toupan is there, for when their prophets come to them they make what is inside speak, hearing thus the secret of their enemies and (as they tell it) learning news from the spirits of their deceased friends."[40]

The maraca remained at the center of Tupinamba society long after the mid-sixteenth century, the time of these several accounts. It figures, for example, in the horrified reaction of the Capuchin Father Yves d'Évreux to Tupinamba revelry in the early seventeenth century:

> ... it is a very hideous spectacle to see these people in such assemblies and seems rather a witches' sabbath than an assembly of men. I found myself there only once, and only so as to be able to describe it, and I never again wanted to return. I saw some [Indians] lying in their hammocks to one side, vomiting with great force; others walking about, bereft of judgment on account of wine; others shouting; others making a thousand grimaces; others who danced to the sound of maracas; others who sang with cacophonous voice and tone; others who spiritedly drank and smoked so as to get drunk. And the worst that I found there was that the girls and women mixed helter-skelter [with the men], convincing me that Bacchus is rarely without Venus and that, to my mind, the French should do in this regard what the Portuguese have done, forbidding to the savages any such *Caouïnages*....[41]

---

[39] Thevet, *Les Singularitez*, pp. 276–7. Thevet is probably wrong in this last assertion. Other, somewhat later accounts tell of small idols in human form that the Indians also worshiped. Several accounts also relate that the same calabash gourds used for maracas were sometimes painted or incised with features of a human face. Staden does not speak of such idols but notes that the maracas themselves had a hole in the shape of a mouth carved in them, leading Alfred Métraux to propose an evolution in Tupinamba worship, under way at the moment the Europeans came, in which the calabash idols developed out of the enspirited maracas: "From a simple receptacle of the spirit, the maraca finished by becoming its material figuration" in the form of the idol. For calabash idols and the maraca in general see A. Métraux, *La Religion des Tupinamba et ses rapports avec celle des autres tribus Tupi-Guarani* (Paris: Ernest Leroux, 1928), pp. 72–8.

[40] Thevet, *Les Singularitez*, p. 224. For other, similar accounts of the maraca in Thevet's writings see *La Cosmographie universelle*, in *Les Français en Amerique*, ed. Lussagnet, pp. 117–18, and the passage from an unpublished manuscript reported in Père Yves d'Évreux, *Voyage dans le nord de Brésil fait durant les années 1613 et 1614*, ed. Ferdinand Denis (Leipzig: A. Franck, 1864), p. 419.

[41] D'Évreux, *Voyage*, pp. 258–9.

Musicoanthropophagy

By this time the sacred maraca had come to seem emblematic of native customs that needed to be controlled or extirpated in order for the Christian mission to succeed.[42] But the voice of the maraca continued to resound. Curt Nimuendajú, for example, a founding father of modern Brazilian ethnography, could still hear it in the early twentieth century among surviving Indian groups. For the Apapocúva-Guarani, he related, the magical force of the maraca remained strong and resided in its voice, while Sipaya shamans still used their maracas to summon spirits of the dead.[43]

This spiritual voice of the maraca, finally, raises a question concerning the sixteenth-century accounts of Staden and the rest. They are quick to note the metaphysical presence thought to inhabit the instrument and its central importance as the medium of shamanic prophecy and communications with gods or spirits; but at the same time they describe a very different use of the maraca in the communal songs and dances of warriors and the musical rituals leading up to the killing of prisoners. It seems that we are confronted here with two distinct employments of the maraca, perhaps even with two distinct maracas whose differences went unremarked or unnoticed by European observers. It is especially difficult to believe that Staden's "Tammerka" idols – decorated, fumigated, planted in the ground, nurtured, possessed of spirits, called "dear sons" – were one and the same as the rattles handed over to prisoners so that they could accompany their enforced song and dance. The seeming conflation here of two constellations of cultural practices gained iconic credibility, later, in De Bry's fanciful depiction of Tupinamba ceremony (Figure 4.4), where the decorated maracas and tobacco fumigations of the shamans are situated, without documentary corroboration, in the midst of a warriors' round dance.

The evidence of a recent consideration of rattles in a present-day Tupi-Guarani society, in Viveiros de Castro's ethnography of the Araweté, militates instead for the separation of Tupinamba shamanic and warrior rattles, for here we find two rattles distinct in form and function. We have already met the Araweté shamanic rattle or *aray* as an emblem of sexual identity possessed by all adult males of the group; it is also a primary material appurtenance of all men who become shamans. This rattle is not a transfixed calabash gourd, as Tupinamba rattles all seem to have been, but rather an elaborate construction of woven cane fibers carefully decorated with cotton string and bright feathers (the construction is socially determined, the weaving a female function, the decoration a male one). The *aray*'s muted sound provides the quiet backdrop to shamans' songs – or rather to the songs sung through shaman mediums by the spirits of deceased group members – and it is used

---

[42] The Brazilian historian Gilberto Freyre includes the maraca among aspects of Indian culture to be disempowered when he describes the indirect routes the Jesuits could take to undermine the native sacred imaginary: "Os jesuítas conservaram danças indígenas de meninos, fazendo entrar nelas uma figura cômica de diabo, evidentemente com o fim de desprestigiar pelo ridículo o complexo Jurupari [a spirit taken by the missionaries to represent the devil]. Desprestigiados o Jurupari, as máscaras e os maracás sagrados, estava destruído entre os indios um dos seus meios mais fortes de controle social: e vitorioso, até certo modo, o Cristianismo." Quoted from Amarilio Ferreira Jr. and Marisa Bittar, "Pluralidade lingüística, escola de bê-á-bá e teatro jesuítico no Brasil do século XVI," *Educaçao e sociedade* 25, no. 86 (April 2004).

[43] Nimuendajú is cited by Métraux, *La Religion*, p. 77.

to summon gods. It is not so much an instrument of musical accompaniment, then, as a sonorous "receptacle of spiritual forces," a container of invisible things and mysterious operative potencies – "a magical tool," in sum.[44] The parallels with the Tupinamba shaman's rattle, also a vehicle for spirit voices, elaborately constructed and decorated, and possessed by all the adult males of the group, are evident.

Evident also, however, are Tupinamba parallels to the other Araweté rattle, the *maraká'i* or dance rattle. This maraca is simpler than the *aray*, constructed like Tupinamba rattles from a gourd filled with seeds or beads. It is a warrior rattle, used to accompany the Araweté war-dance or *pirahe* (cf. Staden's term for Tupinamba dance, *aprasse*, from *aporacei*, to dance)[45] and the songs sung for it. Unlike the *aray*, the Araweté *maraká'i* possesses no specific spiritual or magical force.

It is impossible to conclude from sixteenth-century reports that the Tupinamba possessed, like the Araweté, two hand-rattles of radically different construction. Nevertheless something clearly redolent of the cultural dichotomies that mark Araweté rattle use today shaped two distinct sets of practices and ideologies determining the powers and uses of Tupinamba maracas. The evidence of the modern-day Araweté, in other words, speaks to the ideological and spiritual (if not precisely to the material) realities of the ancient Tupinamba, revealing differences read only between the lines of the early accounts.

The least we can conclude is that the Tupinamba maraca was a double object. It amplified the rhythms of the dancing body that shook it, in this way resembling the prosthetic leg rattles and even the stomping and body-slapping of other Tupinamba speech- and song-acts. At another moment, however, its rattling conveyed a voice from elsewhere, a potent oracle issuing commands, prophesying, or answering Indian prayers. This voice, conferred on the maraca through the power of a distant spirit summoned by the shaman medium, cannot be confused with the sounds produced by the Tupinamba themselves. It displaced the Indians' own bodies and voices, bringing to the center of their rites dead tribesmen or forest spirits or even the thunder-god Toupan. It impelled the flesh exchange central to their society, demanding war to satisfy its hunger and revealing enemy strategies to gain the upper hand.

Meanwhile a second mode of doubleness was superimposed on to this one. At the moment of displacing Tupinamba body and voice the maraca introduced – another voice. The rattle crossed the threshold between body and spirit world by means of an utterance that was at once lodged in the gourd and traceable only to supersensible realms. In this it revealed, with an impact probably not rivaled elsewhere in Tupinamba society, the super-substantial capacities of heightened voice. This double transit of the maraca, from body to spirit and from body to voice, captures once more the convergence of all three that brought singing near to the ideological heart of Tupinamba cannibalism.

---

[44] Viveiros de Castro, *From the Enemy's Point of View*, p. 221; for the shamans' songs, pp. 121–2.

[45] For Staden's *aprasse*, see *The Captivity*, pt. 1, chap. 22 (p. 62). On *pirahe* and its *maraká'i*, Viveiros de Castro, *From the Enemy's Point of View*, pp. 107–9; for the difference between warriors' and shamans' songs, pp. 116–17 and 125–9. Most of chap. 8 is devoted to textual analyses of a shaman's song and a warrior's song.

Self and song

We have isolated two Tupinamba experiences in this consideration of musico-anthropophagy: on the one hand, the flux of a cyclic economy of mortal flesh, extending undifferentiatedly into the past and foretelling an unchanging future; on the other hand, an access to the voices of the gods and spirits of the dead driving these cycles. In other words: immersion of the living self in the unending flow of flesh exchange and submission of that self to the voiced imperatives of a supersensible realm outside the social present. There would seem to be little room in this cosmology, this anti-eschatology, for a self stably asserted in the present-day human community.

Perceptions of something akin to this precariousness of the self have emerged from several recent analyses of Tupi-Guarani societies past and present. It stands behind Florestan Fernandes's classic interpretation of Tupinamba warfare, in which the killing of captives is compelled by the spirit voices in the maracas, while the consumption of them is an attempt to buttress through magic the communal autonomy of the cannibalizing group. Here the captive is a sacrificial victim in a cult of ancestors who demand, through shamans, revenge on those who killed and ate them. Eating the victim brings about a "mystical recuperation," a regaining of energies of the deceased ancestor transferred earlier to those other killers. Selfhood is defined communally, in the bellicose give and take of cycles of vengeance driven by voices from beyond.[46]

For the present-day Guarani, according to the ethnography of Hélène Clastres, a similar precariousness takes the form of an ambivalence constitutive of society all told. The space of human society is one of instability and impermanence suspended between two other realms: nature or animality, realm of decay and the flesh-eating jaguar; and the supernatural realm of immortality and the gods. Society is a liminal territory that is either surpassed in a solitary transmutation of the mortal self into the godly – Clastres traces this antisocial impulse back to the isolated existence led by sixteenth-century Tupi shamans – or fallen from into rottenness and beastiality. In either case a negation of the unstable social arena is at stake. The division of the cosmos into these three realms is of course not unique to Amazonian peoples, as Viveiros de Castro is quick to point out in glossing Clastres's account. Nevertheless, he agrees with her that the Tupi-Guarani case is distinguished by "the way in which it is hierarchically ordered: the focus is not on the central domain, *humanitas*, but on the other two, *feritas* and *divinitas*. Society is a space of dispersal and a time of transition, encompassed by that which is exterior to it."[47]

According to Clastres this dispersion of the social is reflected in Guarani sacred songs, the very grammar of which shifts their focus away from any lived present. The "beautiful words" of the songs – the verb forms and tenses themselves – locate "affirmation . . . only in the past and the future; the present is always the time of negation."[48] Here Clastres transposes the measure of Guarani social instability from an ontological

---

[46] Fernandes, *A função social*, pp. 316–31; for the maraca, pp. 75–7. Viveiros de Castro summarizes Fernandes's interpretation in *From the Enemy's Point of View*, pp. 274–6, 282–3.
[47] Viveiros de Castro, ibid., p. 29; see also pp. 267–70 discussing Clastres's views.
[48] Quoted ibid., p. 292; further references to Viveiros de Castro in the text.

axis (nature/society/supernature) to a temporal one (past/present/future). The ostensive meanings of Guarani songs, we might add, seem to recall those of the Tupinamba challenge songs of captive and captor, with their emphasis on past and future cycles of flesh exchange.

For Viveiros de Castro himself, finally, who devotes the long peroration of his Araweté ethnography to reflections on the Tupinamba, the ancient rites of verbal confrontation and killing did not negate the present. Instead they justified it as a time of vengeance, which itself constituted a background to Tupinamba social order of a categorical, Kantian sort – "universal, . . . necessary, and . . . independent of experience" (p. 278; also pp. 291–2). Nevertheless, here too selfhood found no firm ground. The affirmation of the vengeful present took place within a larger social order that dissolved individual autonomy in an incessant tacking toward the enemy other. Tupinamba society at a communal level took shape from this relation to the enemy; it was "a regime of generalized heteronomy" in "perpetual disequilibrium" (p. 283).

Such a society threatened to submerge the individual warrior in the general "ritual exchange of dead bodies," primary source of social differentiation among the Tupinamba. The warrior and his captive were equated, the first in his future as captive, the second in his past as captor, and their intoned verbal exchanges served to confound the two positions of killer and victim (p. 291). Even the warrior's dead, vengeful forebears entered into this equivocation of the self, at once killer/avenger and killed. The self was defined only, finally, by the fact of being someone's enemy; heteronomy thus came to be "the condition of autonomy" (pp. 284, 287).

What was consumed by the Tupinamba was not so crucially the flesh of the victim as the victim's status as enemy, his fleshly representation of the enmity defining a relationship (heteronomy) from which emerged Tupinamba identity (autonomy). This anthropophagy was thus symbolic (as Marshall Sahlins has affirmed all cannibalism to be). A *semiophagy*, it captured in its semantic play both the fragility of Tupinamba identity and the primary societal means of its establishment. Viveiros de Castro makes much of the fact, culled from the early reports, that the warrior did not partake along with the others in the flesh of his slaughtered victim. Instead he retired after the killing to the isolation of his longhouse, withdrawing from society like a shaman, to emerge days later having added the victim's name to his own (pp. 277–9, 286, 292).

The chanted challenges that led up to the slaughter of the captive enter for Viveiros de Castro into this semiophagy, one half of its "double schematism, verbal and cannibal" – that is, oratorical and oral. We have returned at last to the semantics of Tupinamba utterance we started with, except that we can now perceive in it new capacities. For the doubled rite marks off a place in time for warrior and enemy both. It produces from the convergence of uttering and eating a temporal articulation in the otherwise seamless revenge cycle where captor and captive selves emerge: "Far from being a . . . negation of becoming, the cannibal complex, through this agonistic exchange of words, brings forth time: the rite is the great Present" (p. 292).

Here Viveiros de Castro takes us to the verge of a deep explication of the impact of the cannibals' raised voices, only to pull up short. His view lingers within the precincts of familiar semantic exegesis, and it ends by impelling us back toward the selfless cycles of flesh exchange – the subject, after all, of the songs' words. In their meaningfulness, the songs' function was to celebrate, not resist, the undifferentiated past and future in which captive and captor took their place. The words chanted, like so much else in Tupinamba society, threatened to obliterate the very individuality that the prowess of the warriors, prisoner as well as captor, asserted. Semantics once again submerged self.

The self-making gesture of resistance came, instead, in the extra-semantic vocal presence of the songs. The features of rhythm and tone that set them apart from normal speech also marked in them the outbreak of autonomous voices in an articulated here and now. Considered not as signs within an elaborate semiosis but instead as acts in a congeries of cannibalistic rites, they appear as performative gestures short-circuiting the flow of time and exchange. They brought to a momentary halt the anti-eschatology of Tupinamba social cycles even as their semiosis impelled those cycles forward. In marking this stoppage they allowed warrior selves, both captor and captive, to emerge.

Here then is another power originating in the distance between normal speech and raised voice. These song-acts were not only conveyances of a meaning parallel to that of the spoken word but also a voiced social process in which semantics was suspended and self stabilized through chanted intersection with other. A heteronomy yielding autonomy, as Viveiros de Castro has it, perhaps – but by means of a channeling of the symbolic exchange of cannibalism through a special medium of utterance.

The raised voices of the Tupinamba and their enemies at the consummation of the ceremony functioned, finally, not merely to mark out a ritual space, and not even only to warrant the gift of flesh as worthy of its place in the ongoing exchange. In setting off the bodies that emitted them from the communal group around, these voices slowed the cycle to a momentary stop, opening an extratemporal niche for warrior selves. They were ambivalent in function, in their meanings inching forward the exchange while resisting it in their vocal superfluity. This second, supersemantic force of the songs profiled in brilliant clarity the contradictory self, at once made and unmade, around which Tupinamba society revolved. In its wake the killer moved off to social isolation, maintaining his new status, marking it with his new name, until it was time for him to "march foremost in war" in his turn. In its wake, meanwhile, the victim, having sacrificed body, name, and status to his killer, sank back into the stream of time and exchange – only to raise his voice again, through the maracas of his own group, to call out for the rift that would grant his descendants their own time-stopping moments of identity.

5

Inca singing at Cuzco

Whatever else it might do, human song signals a location in place and time. This function arches over the more specific uses to which song is customarily put: to join people in expressive communion, to convey in controlled circumstances passions stirring soul and body, to express local ideals of beauty, grace, or power (or – a peculiarly modern twist on the same impulse – to "entertain"), to enact dramatic depictions of human or divine actions, or to facilitate contact with the divine itself. The last of these is no doubt one of the most widespread uses of song, but it too forms, like the others, part of a broader picture. The sacred is, at root, an impulse to find oneself in a dwarfing cosmos, and song, marking humans' places in the world, comes to be the medium of choice of sacred utterance in countless societies – the anthropological evidence urges me to write *all* societies, casting aside customary cautions against universalism. The act of finding one's place in song ranges widely. It reaches out through the mundane landscape traversed in human lives to encompass the heavens – region of signifying motions at once ever- and never-changing – and invisible realms – metaphysical locales we perceive through sovereign powers of consciousness more than through the senses.

The impulse to locate oneself is not only spatial, however, but also temporal. The astonishing human capacity for memory seems to demand that we place ourselves in a succession of generations reaching back through the knowable past. Here again song is an expressive medium of first recourse the world over. "Knowable" is, however, a vague word, embracing many forms and degrees of awareness. Where memory of direct experience gives way to memories handed down from familiars and then to less attributable forms of recall, we find a border – between, as some societies have it, history and myth. At this border song comes again into close quarters with the sacred. At this border, also, the function of song-as-memory is richly equivocal. It so easily crosses from firsthand to less direct recall that in many circumstances it all but effaces the difference between the two.

Such workings of song are readily apparent in the world around us today, though they are typically disguised in the secular transience of style and gesture characteristic of a musical world dominated by recording and mass marketing. There is a paradox here: The preservation of sound through new technologies has brought about the immense proliferation of musics too numerous to become the backbone of tradition, musics that come and go with the rapidity of shifting market forces. Technologies of stable, precise recall have led to ever-replenished repertories and hence to forgetfulness. Nevertheless the underlying patterns remain. The identification of each new generation in twentieth-century America with specific styles of pop music, for example, is a clear instance of people marking through song their places in history.

These sung markings of place and time are all the more apparent in traditional societies, including those we have encountered in the preceding chapters. We see them behind the songs of the Tupinamba, serving to fix identities in the flux across generations of inter-clan exchange and warfare; and we see them in the case of the precolonial and early colonial Mexica, for whom song measured out a whole set of relations among the sacred materials basic to their society. Later we will perceive similar patterns in the revivalist songs of native South and North America under colonial rule.

The patterns emerge also, in vivid, sometimes surprising fashion, from the singing sponsored by the Inca empire. To see this we will start from more or less familiar sorts of song and work toward other, less recognizable ones. We will need to sketch in some detail, gradually and across the whole of this chapter, lineaments of Inca society at Cuzco. Meanwhile the songs we encounter will revise the sketch even as we make it, altering our picture of the Inca imaginary.

Introduction: Listening to Betanzos

To a casual observer of New World history, aware of the prominent place in it of the Inca empire, it may be startling to think that a major new manuscript chronicle on the Incas could appear at this late date. But that is exactly what happened in the early 1980s, when the Bartolomé March Foundation of Palma de Mallorca acquired a copy of Juan de Betanzos's *Suma y narración de los Yngas*. Betanzos's treatise had until then been known to scholars only in a fragmentary copy, containing the first quarter of the work, of which several editions had been published from the late nineteenth century on. The new manuscript preserved the complete work.[1]

Betanzos's *Suma y narración* is one of the earliest attempts we have at a systematic account of the pre-contact Incas; the Palma de Mallorca manuscript establishes that it was written across the years 1551–7. Even in its fragmentary form, the account was famous for its claims to authority as well as for its early date. Betanzos himself ranked among the most accomplished Spanish speakers of Quechua in the early colonial period. His Prologue suggests that he regarded his work on the *Suma* as one of translation and compilation more than anything else, a function that brought with it the obligation to "respect the

---

[1] See Juan de Betanzos, *Suma y narración de los Incas*, ed. María del Carmen Martín Rubio (Madrid: Atlas, 1987); trans. Roland Hamilton and Dana Buchanan as *Narrative of the Incas* (Austin: University of Texas Press, 1996). For quotations from the text I rely on this English translation except where otherwise noted; page citations to these editions are hereafter given in the text, with the Hamilton and Buchanan translation first. More general citations will also be given in the text, specifying part and chapter numbers.

The Singing of the New World

style and order of the speech of these natives" (p. 3; p. 7). Betanzos's emphasis on a fairly direct translation and transcription of oral accounts is borne out at numerous points in the work.

Moreover, Betanzos had unparalleled access to surviving members of the Inca elite and thereby to information about pre-contact society and the native perspective on the Spanish invasion. This came to him as a result of his marriage to Doña Angelina Yupanqui, also known as Cusi Rimay Ocllo. She was a favored niece of the last long-ruling Inca, Huayna Capac, was given in marriage at the age of ten to Atahuallpa (one of Huayna Capac's sons), then taken as hostage and later longterm mistress by Francisco Pizarro, only to marry Betanzos after Pizarro was murdered in 1541. She no doubt contributed her own testimony to the memories and events Betanzos narrated – how could it not have been remarkable? – and she certainly must have helped him gain access to "the oldest and most respected . . . among these natives," whom he cited as his informants (p. 3; p. 7).

Amid all the other information they conveyed, these informants gave Betanzos a striking impression of the role of songs in building and maintaining the political ideology of the Inca empire. This comes across in the early, long-familiar chapters of the *Suma* and, more clearly still, in the newly recovered portions.[2]

Betanzos's narrative accords preeminence in establishing the empire to Pachacuti Inca Yupanqui, the grandfather of Huayna Capac, great-grandfather of Atahuallpa and Huascar (who vied to control the realm as the Spaniards landed), and, according to most accounts, the ninth in the succession of Incas.[3] Already here we straddle the borderline between history and a less direct form of recall. Modern Inca scholarship remains divided as to the reality of the Inca kings named in the early accounts, especially those who came before Pachacuti. At the extremes of the dispute are those who accept most or all of the Incas as a factual dynastic succession, on the one hand, and, on the other, those who see the whole succession as a projection across time of leaders of clans in Cuzco at the moment the Spaniards arrived. (The dispute, then, arose as a reflection of disciplinary predilections, with synchronic structuralist anthropology pitted against historicist archaeology.) The moderate and these days prevalent view sees a historical succession of rulers in Cuzco reaching back

---

[2] Indeed the impact of song in Betanzos's *Suma y narración* is stronger and more frequent than in the other main early account of the Inca dynasty, Pedro de Cieza de León's *Crónica del Perú*, though he too notes the histories kept in song. See *The Incas of Pedro de Cieza de León*, trans. Harriet de Onis (Norman: University of Oklahoma Press, 1959), pp. 173, 187–8.

[3] Betanzos was not alone in according Pachacuti Yupanqui this important role. Cieza de León (see n. 2) agrees with him in general, if not in numerous particulars. Pedro Sarmiento de Gamboa, on the other hand, depicts Pachacuti in a less favorable light in his *Historia indica* of 1572; while the early seventeenth-century accounts of Garcilaso de la Vega and Fray Bernabé Cobo shift some achievements of his reign instead to his father, Viracocha Inca. See the editions of these writers' works cited below; also Sabine MacCormack, *Religion in the Andes: Vision and Imagination in Early Colonial Peru* (Princeton: Princeton University Press, 1991), pp. 111–12, and Geoffrey W. Conrad and Arthur A. Demarest, *Religion and Empire: The Dynamics of Aztec and Inca Expansionism* (Cambridge: Cambridge University Press, 1984), p. 144 n. 79. For a detailed comparison of the lives of Pachacuti by Betanzos and Sarmiento see Catherine Julien, *Reading Inca History* (Iowa City: University of Iowa Press, 2000), pp. 93–130.

to Pachacuti, if not to his father, Viracocha Inca, and grants him a significant role, if not one as grand as the accounts give him, in consolidating the empire and the city at its heart. In any case, we need not settle these questions or even take at face value lists of Pachacuti's achievements in order to understand the general import of Betanzos's *Suma*: It conveys one version of the fundamental mythopolitics of the Inca empire stumbled into by the Spaniards.[4]

According to Betanzos, Pachacuti's achievements were indeed impressive. He defeated the Chancas, a nearby group threatening the control, as yet limited, that the Incas under Viracocha Inca exercised over territories around Cuzco. He organized settlement, agriculture, and food storage in the city and its environs. He rebuilt the city itself, channeling the rivers that ran through it and constructing at its heart Coricancha, the "golden enclosure" or temple of the sun. He set out on expeditions of conquest that vastly expanded the lands and peoples under Inca control, especially toward the rich, fertile Collao to the southeast – what would become the Collasuyu quarter of the empire. He laid out the calendar, constructing large pillars on the horizons (in other sources they are called *sucancas*) to measure the seasonal motion of the sun and thus rationalize the time for planting. And he instituted the state religion and the major festivals to be observed across the year. (See pt. 1, chaps. 8–23.)

This religion, following on earlier Andean models, as archaeologists have shown, involved crucially the worship of the relics of previous Incas. According to Betanzos these relics were statues of the first seven Incas, which Pachacuti ordered fashioned, alongside the mummified remains of his father. Each of these Incas was assigned a household of *mamaconas*, cloistered women to worship them, and *yanaconas*, official retainers to serve them. The households were accorded livestock and land to farm outside Cuzco. The servants and their descendants were to care for their assigned Incas down through the generations, and Betanzos intimated that the relics were still hidden away in his own day and worshiped out of sight of the Spaniards (p. 80; p. 86).

Song had its central role to play in this system of ancestor worship. Pachacuti saw to this himself. He assigned a steward (*mayordomo*) to be in charge of the servants for each of the Incas. Then he

---

[4] Archaeologist John Howland Rowe has been a leading advocate of the view that at least part of the Inca lineage, perhaps back to the fifth Inca, Mayta Capac, was a true historical succession; anthropologist R. Tom Zuidema sees the whole lineage as something closer to a mythicized projection of social structures prevalent at the moment of Spanish contact. For a summary of the two positions and further literature see Gary Urton, *The History of a Myth: Pacariqtambo and the Origin of the Incas* (Austin: University of Texas Press, 1990), pp. 5–10; for a reconsideration of the whole issue, Brian S. Bauer, *The Development of the Inca State* (Austin: University of Texas Press, 1992). A rich recent analysis from a student of Rowe that accommodates both synchronic political agendas and a recognizable "Inca historical consciousness" in constructing dynastic history is Julien, *Reading Inca History*; see pp. 7–11 for a summary of her position. As an example of such political agendas, Julien (pp. 38–9) suggests that the lineage claims of Betanzos's wife led him to emphasize Pachacuti in his narrative. On this see also Susan A. Niles, *The Shape of Inca History: Narrative and Architecture in an Andean Empire* (Iowa City: University of Iowa Press, 1999), p. 18.

> ordered each one of these stewards to make songs which the *mamaconas* and *yanaconas* would sing in praise of the deeds done by each one of these lords in his day. These songs were ordinarily to be sung in an appropriate order by the servants of those statues whenever there were fiestas, starting first with the song, story, and praise of Manco Capac [the first Inca], and these *mamaconas* and servants would sing about each lord as they had succeeded one another up to that time. And that was the order that was followed from then on, so that in that manner they might keep the memory of them and of old-time things. (p. 79, trans. modified; p. 86)

Thus Betanzos remembers Pachacuti as having institutionalized the singing of the deeds and exploits of the Incas; thus Pachacuti "had his ancestors worshiped as gods and had them remembered." Betanzos concludes, cannily, that Pachacuti "did this because he understood that the same thing would be done for him after his days" (p. 80; p. 86).

Indeed the *Suma* highlights Pachacuti's efforts at self-promotion. Betanzos returns several times to the Inca's propaganda on behalf of his own exploits. This usually takes the form of song. Songs of Pachacuti's military prowess were, first, an important part of his campaigns, being composed to reflect the latest victory and then sung as part of the ritual humiliation of subjugated chieftains (pt. 1, chap. 19). Neither were these songs heard only by the victors and vanquished on the field of battle. In the first years after his defeat of the Chancas, Betanzos relates, Pachacuti called for a grand festival celebrating his patron the sun – and himself. In front of the gathered caciques from in and around Cuzco, accompanied by four golden drums, the women sang a song remembering Pachacuti's exploits during the war (p. 1, chap. 13).

Later in his reign, after long campaigns in eastern and northern territories, Pachacuti and his troops reentered Cuzco performing a review in song of the various wars they had waged: "When they came within sight of the city of Cuzco, he ordered the captains to assemble there all together with him and to enter the city singing, each one in order about the things that had happened on the expeditions that they had taken." The troops began with a song about Pachacuti's own defeat of the Soras to the west, then sang of other campaigns in the same quarter of Cuntisuyu, then recounted battles won in the rugged northern quarter of Antisuyu. Meanwhile the prisoners, paraded before the troops, were made "to cry and declare their guilt and crimes in a loud voice and how they were subjects and vassals of the son of the Sun and that no forces could resist him, starting first of all with the Soras and then the rest" (p. 89; p. 95).

In these episodes we witness Pachacuti constructing for the citizens of Cuzco the legacy of song that would later be passed on by his own *mamaconas* and servants. Even the strict ordering of the military songs, battle by battle, seems to mirror the careful, chronological sequence of the songs for previous Incas Pachacuti ordered sung at the fiestas. Song-as-memory here takes the form of precise, politico-military propaganda. Betanzos even gives the aged Pachacuti the last word in constructing his sung legacy, describing a swansong that he supposedly uttered with his last breath (pt. 1, chap. 32).

Betanzos returns to these historical songs several times later in the *Suma*. We learn, for example, that Topa Inca Yupanqui, son of Pachacuti, ordered such a sung history on the death of his brother Yamque Yupanqui, who had governed Cuzco while the Inca went off on military campaigns. When on his return Topa Inca learned of Yamque's death, he waited outside the city for the citizens to join him. "They were all dressed in mourning," Betanzos writes, ". . . crying in loud voices and playing their drums. As the Inca was coming with the rest of his people, the townspeople raised their voices much higher in crying than they had up to then, and they sang a song which contained all the deeds that lord [Yamque] had done while he lived" (p. 153; p. 166; translation modified). As for songs of military exploits, these could apparently be used for purposes of encouragement or intimidation even before the fact. When in 1536 the Indians laid siege to Spanish Cuzco, the warriors surrounding the city "sang their song about how they would kill the Christians" (p. 289; p. 299).

Most revealing of the political and social force conveyed in the sung histories of the Incas is an episode Betanzos recounts concerning Huayna Capac. Betanzos accords this Inca a role not unlike Pachacuti's, if less arresting in its dimensions. At the start of his reign Huayna Capac set about a thorough review of all the institutions of agriculture, tribute, and worship in and around Cuzco and of the infrastructure, as we would say, of the empire (pt. 1, chaps. 41–7). To begin this long initiative, lords of Cuzco fanned out to inspect storehouses, bridges and roads, irrigation systems, and so forth. Meanwhile, Huayna Capac himself undertook an inspection of the religious institutions within the city. After a thorough review of Coricancha, its servants, and its *mamaconas*, he began a lengthy tour, at once inspection and celebration, of the houses devoted to revering the statues of past Incas. He visited these houses, needless to say, in the order of their succession, enriching them wherever necessary with additional *mamaconas*, *yanaconas*, lands, and sources of tribute.

To inform himself of the conditions and requirements of each royal household, Huayna Capac listened to the songs of the Incas. He "ordered that, since he was looking into the things of these lords, the *mamaconas* and servants of each lord should sing his history and past deeds. Thus as he was visiting the statues and their houses, whenever he noticed anything lacking, he would provide it for them." Huayna Capac lingered especially long, more than two months in all, at the houses of his grandfather Pachacuti Yupanqui, his uncle Yamque Yupanqui, and his father Topa Inca Yupanqui. In each, Betanzos specifies, he listened to the songs of their exploits; afterward he held "great feasts and . . . sacrifices" (p. 166; p. 182; translation modified).

The purpose of this tour was, evidently, more than infrastructural improvements. It comes across in addition, first, as something like a selfconscious educational program. In it the songs provided a schooling for the young Inca Huayna Capac, a "mirror of princes" in which he might honor the past and spot the reflection of his own future exploits. Huayna Capac's tour in part represented the instructing obeisance of a young prince confronted with the pressures of rule and his larger-than-life ancestors. Only after his months spent communing in song with his ancestors did he set out from Cuzco on his own expeditions of conquest and expansion.

Huayna Capac's song-tour is noteworthy also for the glimpse it affords of the political uses of song in the Inca empire. The dynastic history of the Incas, as recent studies have argued, was not a static edifice passed down from the generation of Pachacuti or earlier but instead was an ideology of domination always under construction, a mobile, gathering cultural system of veneration of Incas past and present.[5] Its fluidity and elaboration continued through several generations, down through the rule of Huayna Capac, which endured almost until the coming of the Spaniards. This fluidity is signaled not only in the establishment itself of the households of former rulers by Pachacuti and his consolidation of the songs to be sung in their honor – politico-religious acts of compelling power, to be sure – but also in the tour of the households and celebration of these songs by his grandson Huayna Capac. Far from indicating a lack of historical awareness (much less confirming the unreality of the rulers memorialized in the songs), this ongoing elaboration is nothing other than historicity in its truest, perennial form: the ever-shifting construction of the past to meet the needs, imperatives, and desires of a present likewise in flux.

In Betanzos's account of Pachacuti we savor the product of such ongoing elaboration, episodes and exploits that feel dilated in the retelling (resinging!) to semi-mythic dimensions. Recollections of Huayna Capac's song-tour, on the other hand, were not handed down through several generations; it occurred no doubt during the life-spans, even perhaps the living memories, of some of Betanzos's informants. It reveals to us not the process by which Huayna Capac historicized his own exploits so much as his role in the ongoing historicizing of the Inca dynasty all told. It is powerfully suggestive, then, that the foremost medium of this intergenerational process, in the most direct account we have, is song.

The general sense we gain from Betanzos is of a slow consolidation of Inca rule, across ever-expanding territories, and of the state-sponsored institutions of religion and cult of ancestral Incas. This evolution was, the account suggests, not smooth but punctuated, with the two foremost leaps forward occurring under Pachacuti Yupanqui and his grandson Huayna Capac. Each of them relied on songs to solidify a sense of history, to institutionalize practices of worship, to aggrandize the position of former Incas in such worship, and to mark out a course for future development. This sung imperium may have reached its high point only with Huayna Capac; but the high point did not last even until the coming of Pizarro, since two of Huayna Capac's sons, Huascar and Atahuallpa, came to civil war about 1530. (Atahuallpa, with or without the blessing of his deceased father – the evidence is equivocal – was trying to set up a rival capital, a Cuzco of the north, in Quito.)

Nevertheless, the political functions of song shaped by Pachacuti and elaborated by Huayna Capac survived long enough for at least a few Spaniards to witness them. In early 1534 a celebration inaugurating Manco Inca, the puppet ruler installed by Pizarro after the deaths of Huascar and Atahuallpa, still maintained these roles of singing. The mummies and statues of former Incas were brought out into a square, and songs were sung memorializing each of them. "The songs," a follower of Pizarro recounts, "dealt with the conquests of each of these lords and with his goodness and bravery, giving thanks to the

---

[5] Both Julien, *Reading Inca History*, and Niles, *The Shape of Inca History*, have emphasized this aspect of Inca ideology, Julien through a painstaking attempt to glean the Inca narrative genres that stood behind the early Spanish chronicles, and Niles through a case study of the architectural legacy of Huayna Capac, the last long-reigning Inca.

Sun."[6] These must have been the very songs passed down in the royal households from the time of Pachacuti, the songs Huayna Capac had sought out for his princely education and promulgated. Their point was to affirm again Inca prowess, and their lessons in the exercise of political and military might were not lost on Manco Inca, though his efforts against the new, foreign invaders would ultimately be in vain.

These songs of bygone Incas outlived, in attenuated form, Manco Inca and resounded finally in circumstances more intimate than the ceremonies of the plazas and the rituals of the royal households. We can hear their echoes, in fact, in the words themselves of Betanzos's *Suma*.

Recent speculations concerning the relations between the early Spanish chroniclers of the Incas and their informants have often focused on the *quipucamayocs* or readers of the *quipus*, the intricate systems of knotted, colored strings the Incas used for writing and record-keeping. These *quipu*-readers, one general account confidently states, "were the principal sources from whom the Spaniards heard accounts of myths, dynastic genealogies and histories, and other stories of the Inca past." In this scenario the *quipucamayocs* would recite in Quechua from the *quipus*, and a bilingual informant (or *lengua*) would translate and dictate the recitation to a Spanish scribe.[7]

It is tempting to slot Betanzos into the role of *lengua* in such an account, given his Quechua expertise. We do not know, however, what role *quipus* may have played in the compilation of the *Suma*. Moreover, the exact role of the *quipu* in any such enterprise must remain vague, since we have not yet deciphered the semantic content *quipus* carried and since we have little information on the manner and content of the *quipucamayoc*'s recitation. It is not implausible to think that the *quipus* encoded something as elaborate as a song, and indeed several relatively early accounts of *quipus* suggest this was so; or perhaps the *quipus* coded a less elaborate semantics involving numerical, schematic, or even topological information.[8]

Obscured by the seductive fascination of the *quipus*, at any rate, is singing itself as a mode of remembrance and transmission. In this regard the *Suma y narración* is more suggestive

---

[6] False Estete [Miguel de Estete?], *Noticia del Perú*, ca. 1535; quoted from Julien, *Reading Inca History*, p. 163; trans. modified.

[7] Gary Urton, *Inca Myths* (Austin: University of Texas Press, and London: British Museum, 1999), p. 26.

[8] For a venturesome attempt to decipher *quipu* coding systems see Gary Urton, *Signs of the Inka Khipu: Binary Coding in the Andean Knotted-String Records* (Austin: University of Texas Press, 2003); securely grounded in present-day ethnographic detail, but hesitant to make claims concerning Inca *quipus*, is Frank Salomon, *The Cord Keepers: Khipus and Cultural Life in a Peruvian Village* (Durham, NC: Duke University Press, 2004), on which see below. Urton briefly entertains the notion of songs coded on *quipus* (p. 10). Two early accounts that mention the possibility are by Cieza de León (see *The Incas*, pp. 173, 187–8) and El Inca Garcilaso de la Vega, *Primera parte de los commentarios reales, que tratan de el origen de los Incas* (Madrid, 1723), bk. 2, chap. 27; trans. Harold V. Livermore as *Royal Commentaries of the Incas and General History of Peru* (Austin: University of Texas Press, 1966), p. 127; later in his account, however, Garcilaso is more cautious as to the recording capacities of the *quipus* (see bk. 6, chap. 9). For details of a fascinating if not wholly plausible poetic reading of a *quipu* published in 1750, the *Lettera apologetica* of Raimondo di Sangro, prince of Sansevero, see Jorge Cañizares-Esguerra, *How to Write the History of the New World* (Stanford: Stanford University Press, 2001), pp. 115–18 and plates 1–2. I will return below to Salomon's conclusions concerning *quipu* coding.

The Singing of the New World

than any other early source. Betanzos gives ample hints, in the newly uncovered portion of the work, that his informants sang to him. The first of these occurs when he describes the song Pachacuti Yupanqui sang at his death. He calls it "a song that is still sung today in his memory by his descendants," and he quotes, in Spanish translation, its text (p. 138, trans. modified; p. 149): "From the time I bloomed like a flower of the garden until now, I have given order and reason in this life and this world as far as my powers allowed; and now I am turned to earth." An even stronger suggestion concerns the song Pachacuti Yupanqui called for upon his defeat of the Soras. The Inca, Betanzos relates,

> ... ordered the wives of the lords of Cuzco to come out immediately and sing there, before him and those prisoners, a song that he had selected there, which said: "Ynga yupangue indin yocasola ymalca chinboleisola ymalca axcoley haguaya guaya haguaya guaya," which means "Inca Yupanqui, son of the Sun, defeated the Soras and put *borlas* on them" with that closing sing-song of "Hayaguaya," which is like the "tanarara" that we say. (p. 87, trans. modified; p. 93)[9]

It is hardly likely that the Inca elite Betanzos turned to for his information conveyed such specifics as these without performing the songs. By singing they would have conveyed the songs' words; in their singing he would have noticed the detail, in the song on the Soras, of concluding vocables and their similarity to the vocables of Spanish songs. (Suggestive in its own right is the fact that this second song was sung, in Pachacuti's time, by the wives of the lords. Could it have been passed along across several generations of noblewomen of Cuzco, to be repeated for Betanzos by the Inca princess he had married?)

Hints such as these, together with Betanzos's clear assertion of the indigenous oral testimony that stood back of his writing and his recurring emphasis of songs in the political ideology of the Inca elite, imply that singing was an important medium in the making of the *Suma y narración*. To put this more strongly: *We need to imagine the role of song in the political memory of the Incas as carried on in the written text of Betanzos.* How extensive this singing was in the making of the later portion of the *Suma*, devoted to cascading events after the Spaniards came, might well be doubted. But of the earlier portions, recounting the exploits of the Incas from Pachacuti Yupanqui through his son Topa Inca Yupanqui down to Huayna Capac, the evidence suggests that the role of historical songs was large. Even where he does not specify the fact, some of Betanzos's writing itself might well be nothing other than the words of songs translated and inscribed.

Betanzos's *Suma* is not merely the distanced inscription of Inca events by the conquering and colonizing hand. Instead this writing projects the tradition of an earlier singing into the colonial era. It stages the eruption into this tradition of the alphabet – the threatening disruption of singing by a writing foreign to it – at the same time as it nurtures and extends song by the very technology that threatens. In the confused forms of a society overcome by wrenching difference it offers yet another instance of an inscriptive impulse from the start unavoidably hybrid in nature: music writing.

---

[9] A *borla* was an Inca sash or tassel used, in this instance, to signify the Soras's subjugation. On this practice see Niles, *The Shape of Inca History*, pp. 42–3.

Inca singing at Cuzco

Singing at Cuzco, April 1535

Betanzos, at the very least, leaves us with ample evidence of the overweening importance of song in Inca politico-religious ritual. Of this ritual, of the Inca in full ceremonial regalia, only a few frail paragraphs survive as eyewitness and ear-witness testimony. The Spanish overturning of the Inca's social, religious, and cosmological order was that quick, at least regarding its public display. These slight paragraphs, nevertheless, corroborate the importance of song Betanzos asserts – indeed they underscore it in the most remarkable terms. At the same time they broaden our sense of Inca uses of song. If, to return to our beginning, the historical songs Betanzos describes served to locate Inca politico-religious power in a temporal succession of rulers and events, the songs of this other account, instead, plot the Inca's location, and by extension his subjects' and empire's, in a cosmic world order. They are not primarily songs of time but instead songs marking, with rich and provocative complexity, a sense of place.

The account in question comes in a chronicle whose long title begins *Relation of Many Occurrences in Peru*, the *Relación de muchas cosas acaescidas en el Piru*; the work is commonly known also, from other portions of its title, as the *Conquista y población del Perú*, *The Conquest and Colonization of Peru*, or simply as the *Destrucción del Perú*. The work dates from 1552 or slightly later. Its authorship is disputed, divided between two obscure clergymen among the first Spaniards in the Andes, Cristóbal de Molina and Bartolomé de Segovia.[10]

The passage recalls an indigenous festival celebrated at Cuzco in April 1535, eighteen months after the Spaniards first occupied the city. The festival was presided over by Manco Inca, a son of Huayna Capac we have already encountered. Francisco Pizarro had installed him at the end of 1533 to succeed the murdered Atahuallpa and his first successor, Topa Huallpa, who had succumbed to disease after two months in office.

Given its rarity, it is no surprise that this passage from the *Relación* forms a standard entry in the Inca dossier. One of the first to read it was Bartolomé de Las Casas, the great defender of the rights of indigenous Americans. He managed to see the text in Valladolid as early as the mid-1550s and quoted the whole passage more or less verbatim in his huge *Apologética historia*, from about 1559. Three centuries later William Prescott read the passage and alluded to it in his classic *Conquest of Peru* of 1847. In the twentieth century, references to the passage and editions of the *Relación* are legion. I have cited two editions of the work (see n. 10). John Hemming translated most of the passage in his fine updating of Prescott of

---

[10] I read the account in *Las crónicas de los Molinas*, ed. Francisco A. Loayza (Lima: Domingo Miranda, 1943), pp. 1–78; and in *Crónicas peruanas de interés indígena*, ed. Francisco Esteve Barba (Biblioteca de Autores Españoles, vol. 209; Madrid: Atlas, 1968), pp. 57–95. For the passage quoted here see pp. 50–3 (Loayza) and pp. 81–3 (Esteve Barba). On the question of the authorship of the account, see *Crónicas peruanas*, pp. xix–xx and the literature cited there. Esteve Barba considers Molina the more likely candidate, while others have argued in favor of Segovia. The evidence for either one is far from conclusive; for this reason I leave the question open here. This Molina, meanwhile, should not be confused with another, later clergyman in Cuzco, also named Cristóbal de Molina (and referred to in the plural in the title of Loayza's edition); he authored a famous and important *Relación de las fábulas y ritos de los Incas* of 1574–5, to which we will return below and in chap. 6. The earlier Molina is often distinguished as "el Almagrista" – he served with Diego de Almagro on campaigns in Chile – from the later one, "el Cuzqueño."

1970, *The Conquest of the Incas*. More recently still, finally, Sabine MacCormack discussed the passage at length in her important study *Religion in the Andes*.[11]

The passage describes a harvest festival:

> These things happened in April 1535 when in the Valley of Cuzco they harvested the maize and other crops. Each year after the harvest it was the custom of the rulers of Cuzco to make a great sacrifice to the sun and all the *huacas* or shrines of the city. This was done in them and through all the provinces and the whole kingdom. It was started by the Inca and consisted of eight days of giving thanks to the sun for the harvest just completed and praying to the sun for bountiful future crops....
>
> They brought out on to a plain at the entrance to Cuzco where the sun rises all the figures from the shrines, and they put the more important of these under rich and well wrought feathered awnings, which were a splendid sight. From rows of these awnings they made an avenue, with one row of awnings facing the other more than thirty paces away. In this avenue gathered all the rulers and lords of Cuzco, but no people of lower station. There were *orejones*, very richly dressed in cloaks and shirts of silver embroidery with bracelets and disks of fine shining gold on their heads.
>
> They formed two lines, each of more than three hundred lords. It was like a procession with one choir facing another, and they stood very quietly waiting for the sun to rise. When the sun was partly risen they began to intone a song with great order and harmony. While they sang each one tapped one of his feet, like our singers of polyphony, and as the sun rose they sang higher.
>
> A little way from these rows the Inca had his tent in an enclosure with a chair and a very fine bench. At the beginning of the singing he rose with great authority and put himself at the head of the lines and was the first to begin to sing; and as he did, so did the others. After he had stood for a little while he returned to his chair, where he remained conversing with those who came to him. On a few occasions, from time to time, he went and stood with his chorus for a while, and then he returned.
>
> Thus they sang from sunrise until the sun had set completely. And since until midday the sun was rising, their voices grew, and from midday on they diminished, carefully following the progress of the sun. All this time they made many offerings. On one side, on an embankment where there was a tree, there were Indians who did nothing but throw meat into a great fire where it was burned and consumed in the flames. To another side the Inca threw many llamas that the common and poor Indians scrambled for; this was a source of great diversion.
>
> At eight o'clock more than two hundred young women came out of Cuzco carrying large covered pitchers, each new and identical to the others, containing a great quantity of *chicha*. They came five at a time, in great order and harmony, each group awaiting its turn. They offered to the sun many baskets of an herb they eat, called in their language *coca*, which is a leaf rather like myrtle. And they observed many other ceremonies and offerings that would take long to recount.

---

[11] See Fray Bartolomé de Las Casas, *Apologética historia sumaria*, ed. Edmundo O'Gorman, 2 vols. (Mexico: Universidad Nacional Autónoma, 1967), I, pp. 238–9; William H. Prescott, *History of the Conquest of Mexico and History of the Conquest of Peru* (New York: Modern Library, n.d.), pp. 784–5; John Hemming, *The Conquest of the Incas* (New York: Harcourt Brace, 1970), pp. 172–4; MacCormack, *Religion*, pp. 74–9.

Inca singing at Cuzco

Let it suffice to say that, when in the afternoon the sun began to set they showed great sadness in their song and their bearing on account of its absence, and they worked to diminish greatly their voices. And when the sun set completely and disappeared from their sight they showed great wonder and, joining hands, prayed to it with deepest humility. Then they removed all the apparatus of the festival and took down the awnings, and everyone went home. They returned those figures and awful relics to their houses and shrines.

And thus in the same manner they celebrated for eight or nine days. And you should know that the figures of idols under those awnings were the past Incas who had ruled Cuzco. Each one was served by a crowd of men who all day long shooed away flies with certain fans made of swan feathers with tiny mirrors on them and by its *mamaconas*, who are like nuns; under each awning there were twelve or fifteen of them.

After all the festivals, in the last one they brought out many digging sticks, which in the old days used to be of gold; and after some rites the Inca took one and began to break the earth, and the other lords did the same. After this everyone in the empire also did the same. And if the Inca had not done this, no one would have dared to break the earth or to believe that it would produce crops.[12]

Many of the elements in this account are commonplace for students of Inca society, and some we have encountered already in Betanzos. The *mamaconas*, as we know, were virgin devotees belonging to the households of deceased Incas or to Coricancha, the temple of the sun. They were compared in early reports to priestesses, to Rome's Vestal Virgins, or, as in our text, to nuns. The *orejones* or "big ears," as the Spaniards called them, were the Inca lords themselves, marked by the gold spools they wore in their distended earlobes. The offerings here of meat and coca were a staple, as general, non-eyewitness accounts of Inca ritual suggest; while the consumption of *chicha* or maize beer was ubiquitous. (It was usually understood by the Spaniards to signal a debauched, even diabolical failing on the part of the Indians.) The agricultural significance of the festival and the Inca's role in insuring bountiful crops stand front and center here, as they seem to have done in other Inca rituals. This is no less than we would expect in a society not far removed from its subsistence origins, working a landscape that rendered farming challenging, even precarious. The *huacas* or shrines are everywhere remarked in colonial accounts of Inca ways, as are the statues or mummified remains of dead rulers – *mallquis*, in Quechua – that we have met in Betanzos. We will return to both.

Singing and dancing, activities that the Incas joined in the single Quechua word *taki*, were also a constant feature of their ritual. But our report gives arresting particulars about the *taki* of this festival – more arresting particulars, indeed, than any of the several other early discussions of it offer. These suggest that the songs of this festival mimicked the astronomical motions of the sun. What powers did the participants mean to activate through their performance? What capacities of *taki* are revealed in their expectations? Answering these questions will take us along a circuitous route, away from the song-act itself, out toward the broader Inca imaginary, then again to singing.

---

[12] For the Spanish original of this passage, see Appendix, pp. 202–3.

Dividing the realm, ordering the festival

Associated with the *taki* is the general ordering of the festival, and the author of the *Relación* dwells at some length on this. He describes two rows of awnings shading the *mallquis* and facing one another and, within them, two facing rows of Inca lords, each over three hundred strong. These provide a first entry into the indigenous world of the festival, for we can see in them a reflection of one of the most basic divisions of Inca society.

The rows of lords and *mallquis* must have represented ritually the physical and social division of Cuzco itself into two moieties: Hanan Cuzco, or upper Cuzco, and Hurin Cuzco, lower Cuzco. This was a division sanctioned in Inca history and myth, solidified in the social practices of the late imperial period if not indeed earlier, and, it seems, imposed by the Incas on each new town or village they subjugated. Hanan Cuzco was formed, according to Inca origin myths, by the first Inca, Manco Capac, while Hurin Cuzco was formed by his Coya or queen, Mama Ocllo; according to another, more historical account, Hurin Cuzco was the original settlement, the Hanan half being added by the sixth Inca, Inca Roca. Upper Cuzco took precedence over lower in certain ceremonial structures, but they were otherwise all but equal.[13]

In early accounts of Cuzco there is much direct if circumstantial evidence to suggest that the rows of Inca lords in the *Relación* represented the two moieties of the city. Writing in the seventeenth century of the division of Hanan and Hurin, Bernabé Cobo confirms that it was reflected in many rituals: in mock battles between representatives of the moieties, for instance, and in other competitions. More to the point here, the division was emphasized in all public festivals: "The people of one group did not mix with the people of the other one," Cobo writes of Hanan and Hurin, "and in the fiestas and public festivities, each group took great pains to distinguish themselves and perform better than their rivals in the inventions and festive dress that they came up with."[14] Cobo's evidence suggested to him that the nobles of Cuzco did not gather for any public display without identifying their attachment to one moiety or the other.

Other writers, earlier than Cobo and closer to the remnants of Inca society, also emphasized the division of Hanan and Hurin in describing ritual practices. Betanzos recounted a festival of mourning for Pachacuti in which "two squadrons of warriors came out, one with people from Hanan Cuzco and the other from Hurin Cuzco," to do battle; the warriors from Hanan Cuzco were the predetermined victors, "representing the wars the lord had in his life" (p. 136; p. 147). Cristóbal de Molina – not the possible author of the *Relación de*

---

[13] For a mythic account of the beginnings of the division, see Garcilaso, *Commentarios reales*, bk. 1, chap. 16; of the two halves he writes, "The distinction did not imply that the inhabitants of one half should excel those of the other in privileges and exemptions. All were equal like brothers, the children of one father and one mother" (*Royal Commentaries*, p. 44). For the more historical account, see Pedro Sarmiento de Gamboa, *Historia de los Incas* (Madrid: Miraguano, 1988), chap. 19; this second part of Sarmiento's *Historia indica* is trans. Clements Markham as *History of the Incas* (Cambridge: Cambridge University Press, 1907; rpt. New York: Dover, 1999).

[14] Bernabé Cobo, *Historia del nuevo mundo*, ed. F. Mateos (Biblioteca de Autores Españoles, vols. 91–2, Madrid: Atlas, 1964), 92, pp. 63, 113; trans. Roland Hamilton as *History of the Inca Empire* (Austin: University of Texas Press, 1979), pp. 106, 195–6.

muchas cosas, but the later, homonymous author of the *Relación de las fábulas y ritos de los Incas* – repeatedly alluded to the distinction of the "parcialidades" of Hanan and Hurin Cuzco, "each in its place," in describing the elaborate choreography of major Inca festivals. He recounted also a mock fight between representatives of the moieties and even a celebration, like ours, in which each moiety arranged its *mallquis* on opposite sides of a plaza.[15] The division could even have precise musical ramifications. Betanzos, describing the great December festival of Capac Inti Raimi, describes four golden drums employed in one of the *takis* sung then; Molina gives the *taki* a name (*coyo*), attributes it to Pachacuti Yupanqui, and specifies that the drums came "two from Hanan Cuzco and two from Hurin Cuzco."[16]

In the light of all this, there can be little doubt that the two rows of lords facing one another in the *Relación* were an expression of the affiliations with one moiety or the other manifest in many, if not all, Inca ceremonies.[17]

Nested within the major division of Cuzco into Hanan and Hurin moieties was another division fundamental to the social and ritual structures of the empire. Each half of Cuzco was subdivided into smaller barrios. These seem to have grown out of what the Incas called *ayllus*, a major organizing feature not only of Inca but of Andean society in general. This complex word carried many significances in the central Andes. In the valley of Cuzco and across the Inca empire, modern analysis suggests, it connoted an endogamous group tracing itself back to a single ancestor. It also had agricultural and sacred components: Each *ayllu* laid claim to tracts of land cultivated by its members, and each was responsible for the servicing and worship of specific sacred shrines or *huacas*.

By late imperial times, at least, the *ayllus* of Cuzco in particular had been allied with another social structure, even more consequential in Inca ritual life: the *panaca*. The *ayllus* and *panacas* seem to have been distinguished in social ranking. Whereas the *ayllus* were non-royal kinship groups, or perhaps kinship groups in general, the *panacas* comprised specifically the descendants of deceased Incas. Each *panaca* consisted of all the male descendants of a dead Inca except his successor. It was presided over by the *mallqui*, the relic of that ruler. A *panaca* functioned, in other words, as the court of a dead king.[18]

---

[15] Cristóbal de Molina, "El Cuzqueño," *Fábulas y ritos de los Incas*, in *Las crónicas de los Molinas*, ed. Loayza, second pagination, pp. 5–84; see pp. 56, 61.

[16] Betanzos, *Narrative*, trans. Hamilton and Buchanan, p. 63 (pt. 1, chap. 14); *Suma y narración*, p. 68; Molina, *Fábulas y ritos*, p. 58. These were no doubt the same four golden drums Pachacuti had used earlier, in the festival where his military exploits were sung (see above, p. 128). In describing this earlier festival, Betanzos too hints at the two moieties: "There in the square, they had the drums placed at intervals. Then they all, including those from both sections [*tantos a una parte como a otra*], joined hands. While the drums were played in the middle, they began to sing all together" (Betanzos, *Narrative*, p. 56; *Suma y narración*, p. 61).

[17] I am not the first to see in these rows of lords and *mallquis* a reflection of the moieties of Cuzco. R. Tom Zuidema came to the same conclusion some years ago and bolstered his hunch by comparison with early seventeenth-century reports of harvest festivals near Lake Titicaca where village moieties were similarly represented in festival organization. See R. Tom Zuidema, "The Moieties of Cuzco," in *The Attraction of Opposites: Thought and Society in the Dualistic Mode*, ed. David Maybury-Lewis and Uri Almagor (Ann Arbor: University of Michigan Press, 1989), pp. 255–75, esp. pp. 260, 266–8.

[18] On the *ayllu* in general see John Howland Rowe, "Inca Culture at the Time of the Spanish Conquest," in *Handbook of South American Indians*, ed. Julian H. Steward, 6 vols. (Washington: US Government Printing Office, 1946), II,

The *panacas* were the kinship groups associated with the households dedicated to the Incas, with their *mamaconas* and *yanaconas*, described by Betanzos. They functioned as the chief custodians of the ceremonies in honor of their respective Incas, including the songs of their exploits, and it was to these *panaca* households that Huayna Capac turned for the song-tour at the beginning of his rule. As we know also from Betanzos, the *panacas* held lands and other resources devoted to the *mallquis*; like the *ayllus*, moreover, they were responsible for the care and worship of specific *huacas* in and around Cuzco.

The history of the development of the *panacas* of Cuzco is a vexed question, one connected to the broader problem, mentioned above, of the historical reality all told of the full lineage of Inca kings related by the Indians to the early chroniclers. By the time of Huayna Capac, it seems clear, there were ten *panacas* divided between Hanan and Hurin Cuzco and dedicated to the Incas up through Huayna's father, Topa Yupanqui. Huayna's own *panaca* added an eleventh to the list, and Huascar, his son, may have added a twelfth.[19]

This extraordinary phenomenon of the *panacas* extended ancient Andean systems of ancestor worship in the direction of an imperial cult of kingship. Archaeological evidence suggests that something like it existed well before the Inca empire in the northern coastal empire of Chimu.[20] For the Spaniards it was a source of mixed wonderment, bemusement, and horror, especially since the Incas themselves treated the dead rulers much like the living, as is clear from accounts like this one, by Pedro Pizarro, of 1571:

> [The Incas] had the law and custom that when one of their rulers died, they embalmed him and wrapped him in many fine garments. They allotted these lords all the service that they had had in life, so that their mummies might be served in death as though they were still alive. . . . It was customary for the dead rulers to visit one another, and they held great dances and revelries. Sometimes the dead went to the houses of the living, and sometimes the living visited them.[21]

Pizarro and many other chroniclers also affirm that the *mallquis* – the statues or mummified remains of former Incas – always attended important festivals.[22] This returns us to the *Relación*: "They brought out . . . all the figures from the shrines," it reports, later specifying

---

pp. 183–330; esp. pp. 253–6; also Frank Salomon and George L. Urioste, *The Huarochirí Manuscript: A Testament of Ancient and Colonial Andean Religion* (Austin: University of Texas Press, 1991), pp. 21–3. On the *ayllus* and *panacas* of Cuzco see Brian S. Bauer, *The Sacred Landscape of the Inca: The Cusco Ceque System* (Austin: University of Texas Press, 1998), chap. 4 (esp. pp. 39–45), and Conrad and Demarest, *Religion and Empire*, pp. 97, 113–18.

[19] For comparison of the varying lists of *panacas* in the early sources see Julien, *Reading Inca History*, pp. 82–9.

[20] Conrad and Demarest, *Religion and Empire*, p. 113.

[21] Pedro Pizarro, *Relación del descubrimiento y conquista de los reinos del Perú*, ed. Juan Perez de Tudela Bueso (Biblioteca de Autores Españoles, vol. 168; Madrid: Atlas, 1965), pp. 159–242, p. 182; quoted from Conrad and Demarest, *Religion and Empire*, pp. 113–14. See also *inter alia* Molina, *Fábulas y ritos*, p. 58, describing Capac Raimi: "hacían reverencias . . . a todos los cuerpos embalsamados de los señores y señoras muertos; . . . los habían sacado a la plaza, para beber [chicha] con ellos, como si estuviesen vivos. . . ." On the place of deceased rulers in Inca ritual see MacCormack, *Religion*, pp. 68–71.

[22] For citations to this effect from Pizarro, Cieza de León, and Cobo, see Conrad and Demarest, *Religion and Empire*, pp. 113–14.

that these figures were the deceased Incas. What our witness saw, then, sitting under the two lines of awnings facing one another, attended by their crowds of male servants shooing away flies and by their priestesses or *mamaconas*, were the relics of the Incas of Hanan Cuzco facing those of Hurin Cuzco. What he saw in the two rows of living lords facing each other in front of these tents were the lords of the *panacas* of the upper moiety facing those of the *panacas* of the lower.

In addition to the *ayllus* and *panacas*, there was one more subdivision of the two moieties of Cuzco, one that extended out from the city to the farthest reaches of the empire to encompass, finally, the world as a whole. The Incas called their empire Tahuantinsuyu, the "four parts" or four provinces. (We have encountered three of these provinces already, in Betanzos's account of the wars of conquest of the Incas.) The four provinces met and indeed, in the theocratic terms of Inca dominion, originated in Cuzco, the centerpoint of the realm.[23] From this sacred center two of the realms, Chinchaysuyu and Antisuyu, reached out through Hanan Cuzco toward the northwest and northeast; two others, Cuntisuyu and Collasuyu, stretched from Hurin Cuzco to the southwest and southeast. Figure 5.1 shows a map of Inca Cuzco with the roads to the four provinces leading out from the city. Each pair of *suyus* was coordinated with specific *ayllus* and *panacas*; early accounts suggest that Cuntisuyu and Antisuyu were linked each to two *ayllus* and *panacas*, Chinchaysuyu and Collasuyu each to three.[24]

The shrines or *huacas* tended to by the various *ayllus* and *panacas* have been a central concern of Inca research over the past few decades. But they are by no means a new topic: Already in the sixteenth century they loomed large for missionaries bent on understanding the indigenous sacred topology so as to replace it with Christian sacraments. By the time Spanish missionaries began to investigate the system – its historical development before then is, of course, unclear – the *huacas* dotted the landscape throughout the valley of Cuzco and beyond with hundreds of places of sacred presence. They normally took the form of natural features of the landscape such as springs, caves, or rock outcroppings; of manmade altars or shrines as simple as piles of stones or complex as pillars and thrones carved out of living rock; and of idols placed within such shrines. They included several locales featured in Inca origin myths.

The Incas did not, it need hardly be said, consider haphazard the location of the *huacas*. But the way they conceived their arrangement says much about their relation to the divine. The *huacas* sat at intervals along forty-one more or less linear, imaginary rays, termed *ceques* by the Indians, extending out from Cuzco to the horizon all around. Three of the four provinces

---

[23] Garcilaso, *Commentarios reales*, bk. 2, chap. 11; *Royal Commentaries*, p. 93, elaborated this ideology of Cuzco's centrality with a probably fanciful etymology for the settlement's name: "They took as the central point [of the empire] the city of Cuzco, which in the private language of the Incas means 'the navel of the world'." Garcilaso seems here to transpose to the New World context the notion of Jerusalem as navel (*omphalos*) of the world, which reaches back to ancient times but was much circulated in medieval and early modern Europe. Other meanings for Cuzco, including "pile of stones" or "rock," are suggested in other sources; see John Hyslop, *Inca Settlement Planning* (Austin: University of Texas Press, 1990), p. 30.

[24] See R. Tom Zuidema, *Inca Civilization at Cuzco*, trans. Jean-Jacques Decoster (Austin: University of Texas Press, 1990), especially the charts on pp. 11 and 36; Bauer, *The Sacred Landscape*, chap. 4.

The Singing of the New World

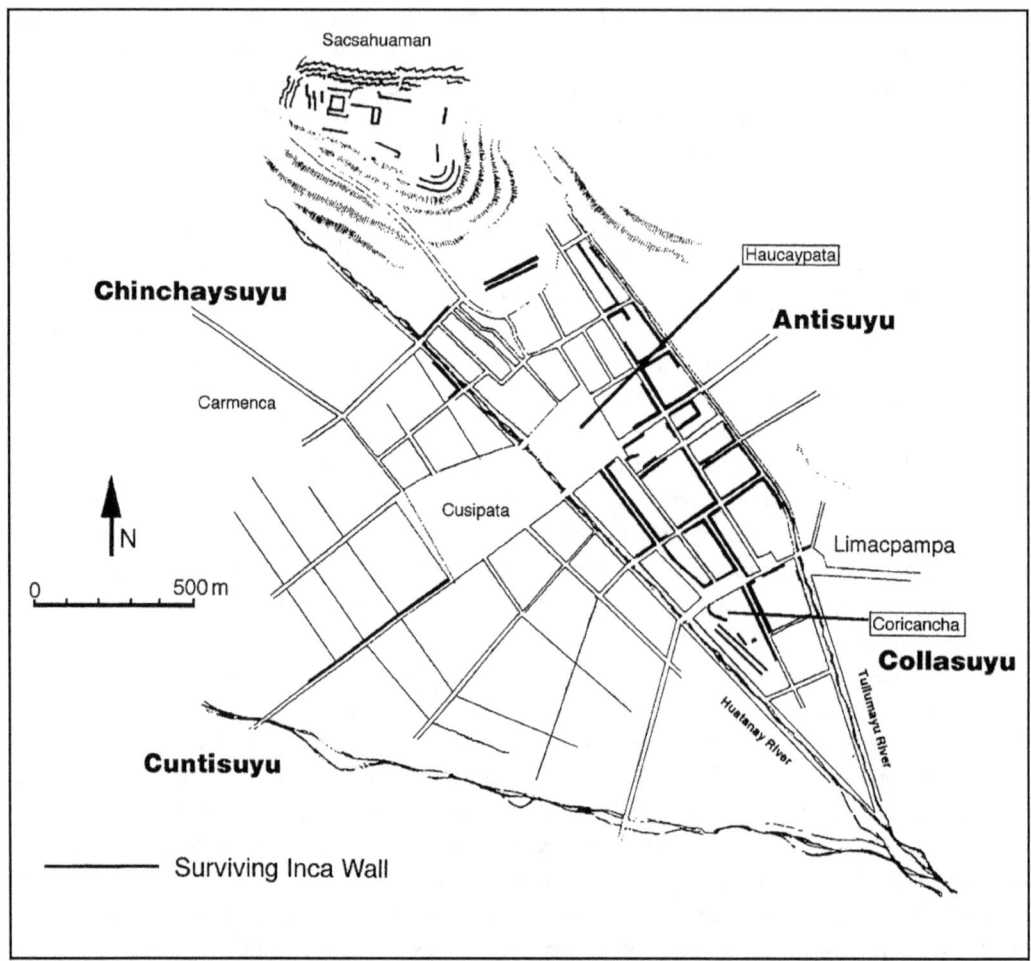

Figure 5.1   Inca Cuzco

of Tahuantinsuyu each had nine of these *ceques*, the fourth fourteen. Bernabé Cobo, basing his account on information gathered about 1570, enumerated all these *ceques* and the *huacas* along them in his *Historia del nuevo mundo*, completed in 1653.[25]

---

[25] Cobo's account, the crucial early testimony on the *ceques* and *huacas*, is the so-called *Relación de las huacas*; it comprises chaps. 13–16 of bk. 13 of his *Historia* (trans. Roland Hamilton and John Howland Rowe as *Inca Religion and Customs* [Austin: University of Texas Press, 1990], pp. 51–84). Cobo based his account on an earlier one, probably by Polo de Ondegardo, written between 1559 and 1572. For a good summary overview of the Andean phenomenon of *huacas* see Salomon and Urioste, *The Huarochirí Manuscript*, pp. 16–19. Bauer, *The Sacred Landscape*, provides the most comprehensive in-the-field reconstruction of the Cuzco *ceque* system; he shows that the *ceques* should not be imagined as true rays, since in many cases they were not even close to straight. For an earlier, classic structuralist interpretation whose findings remain at once foundational and controversial, R. Tom Zuidema, *The Ceque System of Cuzco: The Social Organization of the Capital of the Inca* (Leiden: E. J. Brill, 1964).

The sacred force of the *ceques* themselves, as distinct from the *huacas* along them, is hard to discern. There are hints that some of them related the earth to the heavens in complex ways involving astronomical and topological sightlines – sightlines for sunrise and sunset at important moments in the annual agricultural cycle, or for points where other astronomical features met the horizon in particular seasons. It is clear at least, from Cobo's account, that certain of the lines, viewed from central points in Cuzco, met the horizon where the sun rose or set at summer and winter solstice and at times for planting and harvesting. Some of the *huacas* marking these points on the horizon included the pillars or *sucancas*, erected according to Betanzos by Pachacuti Yupanqui as a huge solar clock.[26]

Whatever their precise valences, we may be sure that the *ceques* carried some sort of sacred force. They radiated out from Coricancha, the temple of the sun that was the heart of Inca worship and the heart of Cuzco (see Figure 5.1). The elaborate system of *ceques* and their hundreds of shrines bespeak the tremendous sacred force the Incas discovered in the landscape, in its features small and large, and in their own handiwork on it. The commitment of the kinship groups of Cuzco to the care of the *huacas* along the *ceques* indicates the degree to which Inca society was organized according to this sacral presence across the land. And the convergence of the *ceques* on Coricancha, finally, connected this presence through Cuzco to the mobile heavens above.

The calendrical role played by some of the *ceques* or *huacas*, in turn, emphasized the worship of the sun at the center of Inca ritual or, as one recent account has put it, the imperial cooption of solar cycles by which the Incas "took control of time itself." The *ceques* and *huacas* amounted to a topological representation of this solar divinity, the topology in and around Cuzco to a kind of circuitry conducting sacred forces out across the landscape from the sun temple – or, shifting the image, to the unfolding of a divine writing of the sun on the world.[27]

The sun played a particularly complex role in late imperial worship, one that seems to have been elaborated by the Incas on the foundations of sun worship in preceding and neighboring Andean religions. Many of these regional solar cults recognized more than one force or manifestation of the sun on earth.[28] Just so, Cobo suggests in his *Historia*, Inca

---

[26] The interpretation of the lines as marking many other, more subtle astronomical motions has been highly – occasionally even fancifully – developed, especially by R. Tom Zuidema, Anthony F. Aveni, and Gary Urton; for summaries see Aveni, *Skywatchers of Ancient Mexico* (Austin: University of Texas Press, 1980), pp. 294–306, and, more generally still, Aveni, *Empires of Time: Calendars, Clocks, and Cultures* (rev. edn., Boulder: University Press of Colorado, 2002), chap. 8. While accepting some findings of these researches, Bauer, *The Sacred Landscape*, p. 160, sounds a note of caution, maintaining that "the application of the ceque system for astronomical observation was limited to those specific references that are presented within the folios of Cobo's manuscript." For a full exposition of this restrained and sensible approach see Brian S. Bauer and David S. P. Dearborn, *Astronomy and Empire in the Ancient Andes* (Austin: University of Texas Press, 1995).

[27] The best summary statement in the early sources of the organization and importance of the *huacas* and *ceques*, including their dependence on Coricancha, is Cobo, *Historia*, bk. 13, chaps. 12–13 (*Inca Religion*, pp. 47–51). For the Incas' control of time see Bauer and Dearborn, *Astronomy and Empire*, chap. 7, esp. pp. 155–6.

[28] See Guillermo Cock C. and Mary Eileen Doyle, "Del culto solar a la clandestinidad de Inti y Punchao," *Historia y cultura* (Lima), 12 (1992), pp. 51–73.

worship distinguished three solar manifestations.[29] Two of these were associated with the solstices: Churi-Inti, or Child-Sun, was celebrated at the winter solstice, while its strengthening into Apu-Inti, Lord-Sun, was commemorated at the summer solstice together with the coming into maturity of all the new, young lords.

Apu-Inti, Cobo also suggests, represented "the sun itself" – the sun as a whole, so to speak – and was associated with the creator god Viracocha. Churi-Inti, Child-Sun, instead stood for "the day" – the sun manifested in its diurnal cycle. This in turn associated Churi-Inti also with Punchao, a golden platter in the temple of Coricancha whose name means "day." This famous effigy, melted down as a conquistador's plunder soon after the Spaniards arrived, depicted a face with rays around it. Cobo tells, in a chapter on the *mamaconas* of Coricancha, that it was hung so as to shine with the sun's first rays and that the *mamaconas* nourished it with special foods and solemn songs as it was newly illuminated each morning. Thus they marked the sun's daily beginning in childhood and nurtured its growth.[30]

Inti-Guauqui or Brother-Sun, finally, was the third aspect of the sun-deity. Cobo suggests that, while Apu-Inti was the sun itself and Churi-Inti its narrower manifestation as day, this third aspect expressed the sun's "power to grow things"; Demarest relates this to a golden statue in Coricancha in which were placed the ashes of the hearts of former Incas.[31] Inti-Guauqui's manifestation of the sun's beneficence on earth thus seems to have embraced not only the agricultural fertility on which the society depended but also the ancestry of the kings themselves in the sun, their deriving of their powers from this kinship, and their role in nurturing the resources of the empire.

Together these three aspects of Inti reveal that tight and intertwined bonds came to connect, by late imperial times, a number of basic elements of the Inca sacred imaginary: the sun, its annual and diurnal cycles, cultivation of foodstuffs and particularly maize, the nurturing of generations of lords, the Inca cult of ancestors, and the powers of the ruling Inca himself.

Naming the festival

In a culture so intent upon the sacred relation between landscape, heavens, and social order, the location of important festivals was carefully determined. The after-the-fact information we have on Inca festivals rarely fails to suggest that each was associated with a specific locale in or near Cuzco, and the festival described in the *Relación* is no exception. The author places it on "a plain at the entrance to Cuzco where the sun rises."

---

[29] See Arthur A. Demarest, *Viracocha: The Nature and Antiquity of the Andean High God* (Cambridge, MA: Peabody Museum, 1981), pp. 17–31; Conrad and Demarest, *Religion and Empire*, pp. 107–9; Cobo, *Historia*, 92, pp. 157–9; *Inca Religion*, pp. 25–7.

[30] Cobo, *Historia*, 92, pp. 157, 232–3; *Inca Religion*, pp. 26, 174. The association of Inti with the sun as a whole and Punchao with day is confirmed by early Quechua dictionaries; see Cock and Doyle, "Del culto solar," p. 65. Cock and Doyle show also that the distinctions of these solar manifestations lived on in regional solar cults long after the Incas; they present evidence that in some of these regional cults Inti was connected with potato cultivation, Punchao with maize; see pp. 62–6. Cock and Doyle discuss latter-day Punchao effigies on pp. 59–62.

[31] Cobo, *Historia*, 92, pp. 157–8; *Inca Religion*, pp. 26–7; Demarest, *Viracocha*, p. 23.

Inca singing at Cuzco

Only one main road led out from Inca Cuzco toward the dawn. It was the road into one of the four realms of Tahuantinsuyu, the Collasuyu Road (see Figure 5.1). This road took its name from the Collao, the fertile region stretching to the southeast from Cuzco toward Lake Titicaca. The Collao had special, mythic significance as the Incas' place of origin. According to some accounts it was on an island in the lake that the creator god Viracocha first brought forth the sun and the moon; the Incas maintained an important shrine there. According to other origin stories the sun created the first Inca, Manco Capac, and his queen Mama Ocllo on this island; afterward they sought refuge in a cave, Pacarictambo, also located in the Collao, finally emerging from it to found Cuzco. Still other versions have four brothers and four sisters, among them Manco Capac and Mama Ocllo, emerging from Pacarictambo.[32]

At the head of the Collasuyu Road, near its entrance into Cuzco, was an open area that survives as a plaza today. The Incas called it Rimacpampa, the "talking field" (the Spaniards corrupted this to Limacpampa or Limapampa; see Figure 5.1). Several early writers, including Molina, Garcilaso, and Cobo, affirmed its importance as a site of various rituals; and Cobo, in his enumeration of the *ceques* and *huacas*, specified that a maize festival reminiscent of the one described in the *Relación* was celebrated here: "The second *ceque* [of the Collasuyu Road]," he wrote, ". . . had eight *guacas*. The first was a flat place called Limapampa . . . ; there they held the festival when they harvested the maize so that it would last and not rot." Sabine MacCormack has concluded that the Rimacpampa was the site of the festival of the *Relación*, and there can be little doubt that she is right.[33]

If the location of the festival is clear, however, its name is not. For at least a century and a half the festival has routinely been identified with Inti Raimi, a sun festival mentioned by many of the early chroniclers and one of the three major celebrations of the Inca calendar. (We have encountered one of the other two: the Capac Inti Raimi or "great sun festival" of December; the third was Citua, a purification festival of September.) This identification has only the most general evidence to support it, namely, the solar and agricultural themes of the ritual of the *Relación*. These hardly cinch the case in an empire close to its agricultural foundation and ruled by divine descendants of the sun. Most Inca festivals devoted themselves in some manner to sun worship and prayers or thanks for bountiful crops. The identification reaches back at least as far as Prescott's *Conquest of Peru* in 1847, and later writers have followed Prescott's lead. To name a few: John Hemming, in *The Conquest of the Incas*, agrees that the *Relación* describes "the great annual feast of Inti Raymi." Sabine MacCormack analyzes the account, in *Religion in the Andes*, with sensitivity and even poignancy as "the last Inti Raimi." And, finally, I followed the trend in naming it thus when I translated the passage for inclusion in an anthology of writings on music.[34]

---

[32] For these origin stories see *inter alia* Garcilaso, *Commentarios reales*, bk. 1, chaps. 15 and 18; Sarmiento, *Historia*, chap. 7. For analyses of these myths, Zuidema, *Inca Civilization*, chap. 1; Urton, *The History of a Myth*, chap. 2; Constance Classen, *Inca Cosmology and the Human Body* (Salt Lake City: University of Utah Press, 1993), chaps. 3–4; and Julien, *Reading Inca History*, chap. 8.

[33] See Cobo, *Historia*, 92, p. 179; *Inca Religion*, p. 71; MacCormack, *Religion*, p. 161. For Molina and Garcilaso on the Rimacpampa, see Bauer, *The Sacred Landscape*, pp. 98–100.

[34] See the citations in n. 11 above; also Gary Tomlinson, ed., *Strunk's Source Readings in Music History*, general ed. Leo Treitler (New York: Norton, 1998), III: *The Renaissance*, pp. 221–3. Prescott does not precisely identify the

The April date of the festival suggests, however, that all of us were wrong – seduced, it would seem, by the temptation to match a rare firsthand account of Inca ritual to one of the great festivals treated in numerous later accounts. The early chroniclers of Inca ritual place Inti Raimi in June, not April. Several locate it rather approximately in this month. Others are more specific, placing it near the end of June and identifying it as a celebration of the winter solstice. Some pair this festival with its counterpart at the summer solstice of December, the Capac Inti Raimi. Only Molina places it as early as May; but all three of the major festivals come in his account a month earlier than in the other accounts, with Citua in August and Capac Inti Raimi in November, suggesting that his chronology is shifted a month early in relation to the Gregorian calendar.[35]

Modern interpreters have found more and more conclusive the matching of the Inti Raimi and Capac Inti Raimi festivals, the dual cornerstones of Inca solar worship, to the winter and summer solstices.[36] The evidence here is often difficult to weigh, given the propensity to astronomical imprecision of both the chroniclers and their informants. Garcilaso de la Vega is rare among early accounts in specifically mentioning the solstice; in his *Royal Commentaries of the Incas* of 1609 he places Inti Raimi "after the June solstice."[37] Cobo, Molina, and Fray Martín de Murúa are more typical. Cobo places the performance of part of the Inti Raimi on a hill called Mantocalla; earlier, in specifying a temple on this hill as a *huaca* along one of the *ceques*, he reported that the natives "said that the sun descended many times to sleep" there. The reference seems to be to sightlines from Cuzco through Mantocalla and to the effect observed along them, at the winter solstice, of the azimuth movement of the sun stopping as it reached its most northerly point and reversed its course along the ecliptic.[38]

Molina is similarly indirect – and, it would seem, unaware of the astronomical import of his information, given his locating of Inti Raimi in May. He says that the Indians "began to count the year" more or less halfway through this month. Later he enumerates the points

---

festival as Inti Raimi, but rather simply as "Raymi, held at the period of summer solstice"; thus he seems to confuse Inti Raimi with Capac Inti Raimi, mislocating in December the account from the *Relación*. Two authors who discuss the festival of the *Relación* but are careful not to call it Inti Raimi are Bauer and Dearborn; see *Astronomy and Empire*, pp. 22–3.

[35] We might wonder whether the author of the *Relación* simply misremembered by two months the timing of the festival. Given the many other circumstances which, as we will see, he remembered correctly, such a slip seems highly unlikely. Moreover, astronomical evidence also points to the April date of the festival. The dawn azimuth at Cuzco in April coincides closely to the direction pointed by the Collasuyu Road. The Inca could have looked down the avenue of mummies and shrines and lords along this road to watch the sun appearing above the distant hills. Any time much later than April would have shifted the dawn azimuth significantly to the north, away from the Collasuyu Road.

[36] This is a complex subject that spirals out to the broader question of the Incas' awareness of solstitial movement. The evidence for this awareness is overwhelming and by now accepted by most scholars, even those more cautious than Aveni and Zuidema (see n. 26 above). For a summary overview with citations of relevant literature, see Demarest, *Viracocha*, pp. 26–30; also Bauer and Dearborn, *Astronomy and Empire*, pp. 153–4 and passim.

[37] Garcilaso, *Commentarios reales*, bk. 6, chap. 20; *Royal Commentaries*, p. 356.

[38] Cobo, *Historia*, 92, pp. 176, 216; *Inca Religion*, pp. 65, 142. Such an observation is, of course, basic to original conceptualizations of the solstice the world over and gives us the term itself (cf. Latin *sol*, sun, + *sistere*, to cause to stand; to stop).

where Inti Raimi sacrifices were made outside Cuzco and says, "The reason they followed this road in this month was that they said that the sun was born there."[39] Both facts, again, suggest indigenous astronomical observations and the timing of Inti Raimi to coincide with the winter solstice. Murúa, writing about 1590, is less specific, but seems to link all the feasts Pachacuti Yupanqui supposedly instituted to the summer solstice: ". . . he ordered that many feasts and sacrifices be held, and made the year begin in December, which is when the sun reaches the end of its road. . . ."[40]

Guaman Poma de Ayala, meanwhile, in his famous manuscript, the *Nueva crónica y buen gobierno*, written about 1600, seems to have pictured, ingeniously, both Inti Raimi and Capac Inti Raimi festivals as solstice celebrations. (See Figures 5.2 and 5.3.) In his June Inti Raimi the Inca offers maize beer or *chicha* to a small, childish version of the sun. (The caption at the feet of the Inca says, "he drinks with the sun in the festival of the sun"; note the decidedly Christian demon who conveys the beer heavenward.) In his Capac Inti Raimi in December, instead, a seemingly less imploring Inca holds colloquy with a large, mature, and bearded sun. Guaman Poma depicts the maturation of the sun across the year, from its childhood at the winter solstice to its adulthood at the beginning of summer.

From all this evidence and more, modern commentators have concluded that the two great sun festivals of the Incas were timed to the solstices. In the face of this, we can match to Inti Raimi the April festival described in the *Relación* only by assuming either that a society intent upon marking the solstice in its rituals haphazardly observed the festival two months early or that the author of the *Relación* misremembered a June observance as occurring in April. If the first assumption is on the face of it implausible, the second is also unlikely, given the fine-grained detail the author of the *Relación* provides and its correlation with other evidence we have concerning Inca ritual. (We have witnessed some of this detail above and will return to it below.)

Fixing the festival of the *Relación* in April at the Rimacpampa, on the other hand, exposes one anomaly of the account. The witness remembers the festival as occurring *after* the harvest. April in the central Andes, however, is too early for a post-harvest celebration. Early accounts of Inca ways place the harvest season in May or, more broadly, from late April into June, and the modern harvest season begins in early May. In this regard, at least, the author of the *Relación* seems to have misremembered the timing of the festival; we will suggest below why he might have done so.

Despite this anomaly, we will see that there are strong reasons to accept our author's recollected dating of the festival in April and thin grounds to support the more recent, repeated assertion that the festival was Inti Raimi. But if it wasn't Inti Raimi, what was it?

The festivals assigned to April in a few later, general accounts of Inca ceremonial do not precisely resemble the celebration described in the *Relación*; in fact there is no other

---

[39] Molina, *Fábulas y ritos*, pp. 25, 27.
[40] Trans. R. Tom Zuidema, "The Lion in the City: Royal Symbols of Transition in Cuzco," in *Animal Myths and Metaphors in South America*, ed. Gary Urton (Salt Lake City: University of Utah Press, 1985), pp. 183–250; see p. 216.

The Singing of the New World

Figure 5.2 Iunio / Haucai Cusqui: June sun festival, from Guaman Poma, *Nueva corónica* . . .

Inca singing at Cuzco

Figure 5.3 Dezienbre / Capac Inti Raimi: December sun festival, from Guaman Poma, *Nueva corónica* . . .

The Singing of the New World

description of an Inca festival anywhere in these sources that does. Nevertheless, several of these sources shed bright light on the account of the *Relación*.

Guaman Poma's entry for April, in a section of the *Nueva crónica* devoted to the Inca ritual calendar, assigns to that month the Inca Raimi, the festival of the Inca. At first sight the rites of the Inca Raimi seem to have little to do with the festival of the *Relación*. Guaman Poma describes, for example, fascinating song-acts: The Inca sang at length with a sanctified llama – which sang back, holding its own part – and was joined by the queen and princesses in a type of long song called *aravi*. He also sang a song imitating the sound of the rushing streams that flowed through Cuzco. If, however, these bear little resemblance to the assembled lords of the *Relación*, raising hymns to the sun, the illustration Guaman Poma provided for this festival brings us closer. (See Figure 5.4.) Singing is depicted here, but we see no llamas or streams. Instead the Inca sings directly to the sun, just as in the *Relación*. He is accompanied by princesses playing the *tinya*, the hand-held, stick-beaten drum still found today in the Andes.[41]

Another seeming incongruity between Guaman Poma's festival and that of the *Relación* turns out to be illusory. Guaman Poma specifies that the llama-song of Inca Raimi was sung in a plaza called Aucaypata. There was in Inca and early colonial times a famous square of this name near the heart of Hanan Cuzco, northwest of Coricancha and Rimacpampa. (See Figure 5.1; the square corresponds to the largest plaza in modern-day Cuzco, the Plaza de Armas.) Readers of Guaman Poma have not to my knowledge doubted that this was the square he meant for the llama-song. Molina, however, offers another possibility. Describing maize-planting rituals, he writes that the common people "came to drink and dance at Aucaypata, where the Spaniards now call Limacpampa, which is below Santo Domingo," the cathedral built on the foundations of Coricancha. Molina's remark reveals that there were two ritual plazas the Incas called Aucaypata. This is not altogether surprising, since the Quechua word itself means "terrace of pleasure" or "plaza of rejoicing," which might characterize in general many ritual sites. Modern scholars have seen in the redundancy yet another expression of the all-important moieties of Cuzco: Rimacpampa served as the Aucaypata of Hurin Cuzco, corresponding to the larger Aucaypata of Hanan Cuzco. Guaman Poma, in assigning his Inca Raimi to Aucaypata, could well have been locating it in the Rimacpampa.[42]

Still other elements in Guaman Poma's description correspond neatly to the details of the *Relación*. He wrote:

> In this month, they offered some colored llamas [i.e. *carneros*, sheep] to the already mentioned *huacas* or idols, gods of the commoners, which were scattered throughout the realm; they performed many ceremonies with them. And the Inca held a very great festival; he invited the *señores* and the lords and the rest of the leaders as well as the poor Indians and they ate and sang and danced in the public square.... In this month the food

---

[41] Felipe Guaman Poma de Ayala, *Nueva crónica y buen gobierno*, ed. John V. Murra, Rolena Adorno, and Jorge L. Urioste, 3 vols. (Madrid: Historia 16, 1987), pp. 234–5; also 318–21.

[42] Molina, *Fábulas y ritos*, p. 29; see Hyslop, *Inca Settlement Planning*, p. 99; Zuidema, "The Inca Calendar," p. 236; MacCormack, *Religion*, p. 161 n. 9.

Figure 5.4 Abril / Camai Inca Raimi: April Inca festival, from Guaman Poma, *Nueva corónica* . . .

> [i.e. crop] is full-grown and the people eat and drink and satiate themselves at the expense of the Inca. . . . The whole realm celebrates in this month of April the *Inca Raimi* and they pierce the ears of [the noblemen]. . . . they hold a great festival and invite everyone, rich or poor.[43]

Here are gathered together all the lords of our festival, here are its offerings of meat, here is the largesse offered to poor Indians, here is the celebration of the mature harvest. Here also, of course, are public singing and dancing – though as I have said these are ingredients of almost every Inca celebration mentioned in the chronicles.

None of this is identical to what the eyewitness of the *Relación* saw, of course, and we need always to remember that Guaman Poma constructed his account of Inca ways many decades after they were disrupted and their public observance suppressed. Nevertheless enough elements in his account ring true to our festival to encourage us to call it not *Inti* but *Inca* Raimi – the festival of the Inca.

What Guaman Poma does not say is that the Inca Raimi was a celebration *after* the harvest. Instead his festival celebrates the maturity of the crops; it seems to mark the commencement of harvest, not its completion. This is confirmed by the next pages of his manuscript, where he designates May, not April, as the month of harvest (*aymoray*) and of storing the crops. His illustration for that month shows the workers carrying sacks of foodstuffs to the storehouses of the empire. According to Guaman Poma, then, Inca Raimi was not a commemoration of a harvest already collected but the kick-off celebration leading up to the reaping of the sun's bounty. Such celebrations, ending with the beginning of harvest, are widespread in the Andes to this day.[44]

Cobo and Molina (one of Cobo's several sources) describe rituals leading up to the harvest that seem to coincide with both Guaman Poma's Inca Raimi and the festival of the *Relación*, though neither author mentions the Inca Raimi by name. Cobo describes a festival in April with sacrifices and a sanctified llama – undoubtedly, as MacCormack has inferred, the singing animal Guaman Poma reports. The sacrifices were made in anticipation of the harvest, like Guaman Poma's, "so that the maize seeds would develop"; they celebrated the mature crop, not the completion of its gathering. As for the harvest itself, both writers associate it with "a song called *aravi*," and both mention the small sacks in which it was carried that Guaman Poma pictured. Molina places the harvest in April, in keeping with the shift of his whole calendar a month forward, but Cobo corrects the timing and shifts it to May.[45]

---

[43] Guaman Poma, *Nueva crónica*, p. 234.

[44] Often these Christianized celebrations come under the name of Cruz Velakuy or Fiesta de las Cruces; for an analysis of this rite in modern-day Pacariqtambo, south of Cuzco, see Urton, *The History of a Myth*, esp. pp. 107–19. In Pacariqtambo and elsewhere Cruz Velakuy occurs on May 3, after which the harvest begins. For a recording of instrumental music played on raftpipes for Cruz Velakuy in the Ayacucho region, southwest of Cuzco, see *Traditional Music of Peru 6: The Ayacucho Region* (Smithsonian Folkways Recordings CD 40449), bd. 8.

[45] Cobo, *Historia*, 92, p. 214; *Inca Religion*, pp. 139–40; Molina, *Fábulas y ritos*, pp. 66–7. For the identification of the llama in Cobo's April festival with that in Guaman Poma see MacCormack, *Religion*, pp. 173–5. Molina describes a series of sacrifices in May that MacCormack likens to the singing of our festival in its following of the sun's course from east to west (p. 167). MacCormack is no doubt right in noting the astronomical significance of these

Inca singing at Cuzco

If in these particulars Cobo and Molina describe a festival that recalls Guaman Poma's Inca Raimi, in another element shared by their accounts they mirror an important ritual event of the *Relación*. They describe the beginning of harvest itself in a similar way. The new, young lords (whose coming of age had been marked in the previous December's Capac Inti Raimi) went out to a field or *chacara* called Sausero to collect the maize there. On the first day, the new lords collected it alone (a pointing up, probably, of the symbolic congruency between the recently matured crops of maize and of lords); after that all the other people of Cuzco pitched in. Here Cobo diverges from Molina. "A little later," he writes – how much later he does not specify – "all the lords and important people of Cuzco, accompanied by a large number of other people, went to the same *chacara* with their plows, and they plowed the field."[46]

Sausero was not, clearly, just any field, but another important ritual site. Elsewhere in his *Historia* Cobo tells us that it "belonged to the sun." The Inca marked it by special ceremonies throughout the year: ". . . at sowing time, the king himself went and plowed [it] a little. What was harvested from it was for sacrifices of the Sun. The day when the Inca went to do this was a solemn festival of all the lords of Cuzco." Cobo also specifies the location of Sausero in the *ceque* system extending out from Coricancha. It was the third *huaca* on the second *ceque* of the Collasuyu quarter.[47] The first *huaca* along this *ceque* was none other than Rimacpampa, the site of the days of singing described in the *Relación*. Sausero lay approximately a mile to the southeast.[48]

The association of Sausero with Rimacpampa along the same *ceque* is, to say the least, suggestive. Positively provocative is the fact that the eyewitness account of the *Relación* ends with a precise correspondence to Cobo: The Inca and the other lords took out their digging sticks and ritually broke the earth. The implication is clear, and has been grasped by MacCormack: Cobo's *chacara* of the sun and the unnamed scene of groundbreaking in the *Relación* were one and the same.[49] After the singing at Rimacpampa, the festival closed when the Inca went with the lords to Sausero for the groundbreaking recalled by both Cobo and the author of the *Relación*.

The festival, then, seems to have traced its way along the near *huacas* of the second *ceque* of the Collasuyu quarter: from Rimacpampa, the first, to Sausero, the third. Indeed, with hints from Cobo, MacCormack has found the second *huaca* of this *ceque* also, reading between

---

sacrifices, which moved from a place to the east of Cuzco at dawn, to Coricancha at noon, and then out of the city to the west at dusk. These would be in keeping with the correlation, proposed above, of the winter solstice sun with the Child-Sun Churi Inti, the effigy Punchao, and the sun's diurnal motion. There is, however, no evidence in the festival of the *Relación* of such sojourns for sacrificial purposes; the eight days of singing and sacrifice took place in and near the avenue of *mallquis* on Collasuyu Road, as we will see. Moreover, Molina's account assigns the sacrifices to May, which must be shifted forward to June. They probably were part of Inti Raimi – hence, again, connected to the solstice – and not "performed during [the] same days" as the solar singing of April, as MacCormack suggests.

[46] Cobo, *Historia*, 92, p. 215; *Inca Religion*, p. 140; Molina, *Fábulas y ritos*, pp. 66–7.
[47] Cobo, *Historia*, 92, pp. 216, 179; *Inca Religion*, pp. 144, 71.
[48] For the location of Sausero in relation to Rimacpampa see Bauer, *The Sacred Landscape*, p. 99 Map 7.2.
[49] MacCormack, *Religion*, p. 161.

the lines of the *Relación*. Cobo reports that it was called Raquiancalla, "a small hill . . . on which there are many idols of all four *suyus*. Here a celebrated festival was held which lasted ten days, and the usual things were offered." This hill was in the same *chacara* as the Rimacpampa, Cobo also relates, hence close to where the Inca and the lords and *mallquis* were arranged. It must correspond to the "embankment where there was a tree" of the *Relación*, where celebrants threw offerings of meat into a great fire.[50] The "eight or nine days" recalled in the *Relación* even match approximately the ten days of the "celebrated" but unnamed festival cited by Cobo.

The web of inference grows thick: The rituals described in the *Relación* ended, at some point "after all the festivals" – that is, after the eight or nine days of singing and sacrifice – when the Inca went to Sausero and broke the earth. This groundbreaking occurred after the ritual harvesting of Sausero, *chacara* of the sun, by the new knights and others. No account specifies when it took place in relation to the harvesting of all the crops of the empire; however, since it seems to have come at the end of a pre-harvest festival, its most likely timing would be between the ritual harvesting of Sausero and the general harvest. The groundbreaking occurred, in any case, sometime after the celebrations described by Cobo, Molina, and Guaman Poma. These all seem to be versions of the same festival described in the *Relación*. This festival was not Inti Raimi. Instead it took place in April, two months or so before the solstice celebration. It was a kicking-off celebration, of a sort still celebrated today in the Andes, for the general harvest that would follow and culminate, around the solstice, in Inti Raimi.

So the author of the *Relación* misremembered neither the time of the festival he saw nor the locales where it was celebrated; these all fit precisely to the first three *huacas* of the second Collasuyu *ceque*. What he seems to have confused, instead, is the fact that it was not a celebration of a harvest already completed but one to inaugurate that harvest. This confusion might well have resulted from the fact that the ritual harvesting of Sausero took place within the span of the various celebrations he described. And it might have resulted, more generally, from the fact that the pre-harvest celebrations he witnessed were the start of a two-month period, from April to the June solstice, that marked the successful end of the agricultural cycle and incorporated in its midst the reaping itself of the crops.

Only Guaman Poma gave the pre-harvest festival a name: Inca Raimi. Indeed the Inca was central to the celebration. Without his enactment, leading the groundbreaking, of his sovereign nurturing power, the *Relación* tells us, no one would have believed that the earth would again bring forth crops. Likewise, we shall see that his singing to the sun, described in the *Relación* and pictured by Guaman Poma, was crucial.

It would have been the third manifestation of the multiplex sun-god, Inti-Guauqui, Brother-Sun, neither the child of the winter solstice nor the lord of the summer one, that the Inca and lords invoked here. This aspect of the sun, we have seen, bound together several basic tenets of Inca worship. It manifested the sun's divine generative powers, especially as revealed in a plentiful harvest. It affirmed the Inca's ancestry in

---

[50] Cobo, *Historia*, 92, p. 179; *Inca Religion*, p. 71; MacCormack, *Religion*, pp. 161–2.

the sun and the close bond between celestial deity and the succession of earthly divine kings he represented. And it channeled the sun's generative power through its earthly avatar.

All three of these were fundamental elements in the festival our witness saw. It involved the harvest and the Inca's primary role in rendering the earth fertile, and it gathered all the previous Incas together with the living Inca in repeated observance of the sun's diurnal course. It placed the sun at the sacred nexus of agricultural bounty, the history of Inca imperial dominion, and the present-day powers of the living Inca. The Inca Raimi, affirmation of the ruler's connection not to the solstitial suns, child or adult, but to the brother-sun, generator of bounty, fits the occasion neatly.[51]

Realpolitik

It is an old habit, bred within European colonialism, to deny to others the historical flux we ourselves experience. Over against an expanding, flexible, always mobile sense of self we imagine remote others dully repeating static patterns of ritual and myth. In a reflection of this old pattern, general accounts of the Inca empire have tended to overestimate the venerable stability of its major celebrations. The earliest accounts provide much evidence for a different view. They date these rituals back only as far as Pachacuti Yupanqui, three generations before the advent of the Spaniards, and they recount many particular circumstances that would have offered opportunities to revise and overhaul the rites. Betanzos's description of Huayna Capac's review of religious institutions at the start of his reign is one example; it leaves room for the fluid evolution of Inca ritual right up to the eve of the Spanish invasion. Even the ritual assertion of the Inca's relation to the sun, as I have already suggested, was not handed down from the earliest Incas but instead was a work in progress into the sixteenth century and perhaps even when the Spaniards arrived.[52]

The early accounts also repeatedly describe the performance of more or less ad hoc festivals, festivals to commemorate a victory in war, the completion of a civic building project, or other communal events. While it seems unquestionable from the sources that there was a regular pre-harvest festival celebrated in April, we have little evidence as to

---

[51] The lack of specification of Inca Raimi in most later accounts of Inca ritual is probably explained by a tendency in these to conglomerate in retrospect the pre-harvest rites, harvest itself, and the solstice festival of Inti Raimi after harvest. This creates the impression of a huge festival that extends, improbably, straight through the work of harvest itself, rather than distinguishing separate festivals celebrating its beginning and end. The confusion is related to that of the author of the *Relación* in remembering the Inca Raimi as a post-harvest event. A case in point is offered by Betanzos (*Narrative*, trans. Hamilton and Buchanan, pp. 65–6; *Suma y narración*, p. 72). He describes a festival of May and June celebrated at the Rimacpampa, featuring the new *orejones* from the previous December and involving all the other lords, multiple sacrifices, etc. This fiesta, he writes, "would start at the beginning of the maize harvest and it would last until the end of June." Rather than a sixty-day festival extending straight through the harvest, it seems more likely that the historical reality Betanzos aims to describe comprised Inca Raimi, celebrated in late April, the ritual breaking of ground at Sausero and harvest itself in May, and the Inti Raimi of June.

[52] This is a fundamental argument of Julien, *Reading Inca History*; see pp. 296–7.

how regular the particulars of this observance might have been. They certainly might well have responded, like those ad hoc celebrations, to the vicissitudes of rulership, empire, and indeed divine beneficence.

In April 1535 there would have been ample reason for Manco Inca to celebrate a particularly grand Inca Raimi. Manco was a by then teenage son of Huayna Capac, the ruler whose other sons Huascar and Atahuallpa had been waging civil war when Pizarro happened into the empire. In late 1533 Manco was only too happy to cast his lot with the Spaniards, since in executing Atahuallpa a few months before they had rid him of his main rival to the Inca throne – a rival, indeed, who had sought to kill Manco Inca when he systematically massacred the family and followers of Huascar. The Spaniards, for their part, felt fortunate to have under their control a malleable but genuine Inca, a young man new to power whom the indigenous population owed allegiance and regarded as divine. Pizarro permitted Manco to be crowned Inca in Cuzco in December 1533, a month after the Spaniards first occupied the city.

This arrangement of mutual advantage quickly deteriorated, however. Factions among the Indians were leery of accepting Manco's legitimacy. Factions among the growing population of Spaniards in Cuzco resented Manco's power and wealth and began harassing him, extorting gold from him and forcing him to relinquish his wives to them as concubines. These injuries increased with each passing month in late 1534 and early 1535. They destabilized relations on all sides, not only souring Manco's dealings with the Spaniards but also revealing a weakness that redoubled the wariness of Indians not solidly allied to him. Meanwhile the Spaniards were struggling among themselves. The followers of Pizarro and those of Diego de Almagro came to the verge of civil war in Cuzco in May 1535, one month after the Inca Raimi of the *Relación*.

In the midst of all this, the survival of Manco's rule – his survival at all – was precarious enough that mid-1535 would find him at one moment fleeing his own palace in the middle of the night for fear of an attempt on his life and at another arranging to have Spanish assassins kill one of his chief native rivals. The months around April were months when Manco was stinging under the insults of the Spaniards, weakened by them in the eyes of other Indians, and desperately trying to consolidate his power. Only a few months later he would answer the injuries and continue the consolidation by determining to rebel against the foreigners and cast them out altogether.[53]

The Inca Raimi of April 1535 took place against this backdrop of political and social turmoil. We must understand its ceremony, on one level, as adroit political spin: the spectacular, public, ritual assertion of Manco's power to govern Cuzco and the broader empire of Tahuantinsuyu – of his *temporal* power, if we may delineate for a moment European categories we will want quickly to blur. The lengthy singing and dancing, the gathering of large numbers of ostensibly loyal *orejones*, the grand sacrifices, and the ostentatious largesse to the poor were all demonstrations of Manco's stature, no doubt compelling for the Indian participants and witnesses but directed also toward the European newcomers.

---

[53] For the preceding paragraphs see Hemming, *The Conquest*, chap. 9, and Prescott, *History of the Conquest*, chaps. 8–10.

Imagine the sheer effort required – at any point, but especially in an unstable, threatening time – to organize and execute the ceremonies the author of the *Relación* watched. Imagine also his position: With what emotions and thoughts did he follow for eight or nine days the extraordinary display?

The sources allow us to speculate more specifically still about the internal (that is, indigenous) political agenda Manco was playing out. His predecessor Huascar was the last prehispanic Inca to rule in Cuzco, since Atahuallpa never reached the city after defeating his brother but was instead captured by the Spaniards. More than one account tells that Huascar wished to dismantle the *panaca* system, the courts of the dead Incas. There was ample reason for him to do so. The *panacas* relied on a system of split inheritance, retaining all the dead Inca's material resources for his *mallqui* and *panaca*, passing on to each new Inca nothing but rulership itself, and thus requiring of each new Inca that he conquer and consolidate new resources for himself.[54] Pedro Pizarro reports just such a motive: Huascar, he writes, "annoyed one day with these dead [Incas], said that he ought to order them all buried and take from them all they had . . . because [the dead] had all that was best in the country." Betanzos, whose depiction of Huascar is anything but sympathetic, reports the issue not as a project but as a *fait accompli*: "When he became lord, he went out into the square and declared that henceforth the lands of coca and maize production that had been owned by the Sun and the bodies of the dead rulers, including those of his father, Huayna Capac, would be taken from them. All these he took for himself, saying that neither the Sun nor the dead nor his father who was now dead ate."

As we might expect, this threat to the *panaca* system encountered stiff resistance from the lords who controlled the dead Incas' wealth. Pizarro continues: "The greater part of the chief people were on the side of [the dead] . . . and they began to hate Huascar, and they say that the captains whom he sent against Atabalipa [i.e., Atahuallpa] let themselves be conquered and that others deserted and passed over to him." Betanzos writes that Huascar's "action horrified the lords. And they were saddened because they had permitted him to become lord."[55]

Cobo, finally, echoes Pizarro and Betanzos but also views the whole situation, from his more distant vantage point, in general terms:

> Huascar had lost the support of his vassals because he treated them harshly. . . . He seldom let himself be seen by his subjects; he did not go out to eat in public in the plaza, as the Incas had been accustomed to do; he was lax in observing the veneration of the dead bodies of his ancestors and of the nobility that was to guard and serve these bodies; and for this reason his captains allowed themselves to be defeated by Atauhualpa and others came to Atauhualpa's side.[56]

---

[54] See Niles, *The Shape of Inca History*, p. 74; also Conrad and Demarest, *Religion and Empire*, p. 136. Conrad and Demarest consider this system of split inheritance the primary force at first driving and finally exhausting Inca imperial expansion.

[55] Pedro Pizarro quoted from Conrad and Demarest, *Religion and Empire*, pp. 136–7 (see Pizarro, *Relación*, p. 183); Betanzos, *Suma y narración*, p. 207; *Narrative*, p. 189.

[56] Cobo, *Historia*, 92, p. 96; *History of the Inca Empire*, p. 166.

The Singing of the New World

Manco Inca, despite his youth, seems to have learned much in watching Huascar fall. In all the regards Cobo mentions, the festival of the *Relación* suggests clearly that he was intent on not repeating his predecessor's mistakes. In it he formally celebrated the mummies, recognized appropriately the *orejones*, appeared magnanimously before his subjects, and ate and drank in public. The Inca Raimi of 1535, on this level, aimed to consolidate Manco's power by reassuring the lords and impressing the commoners; it probably aimed to reassure them, more specifically, that he was not the threat to the *panaca* system Huascar had been.

In the tightrope-walk of *Realpolitik* the Inca Raimi no doubt also aimed beyond the Indians at the Spaniards. Its sumptuous, extravagant display of indigenous resources and manpower could not help but seem to them an implicit warning. The numbers of ritual participants alone rivaled the total population of Spaniards in Cuzco in April 1535. In the back of his mind, at a moment when his own people could not seem to unify in the face of the Indians, the author of the *Relación* probably saw in this festival a reminder that his life hung in the balance. Only eleven months later more than 100,000 native troops gathered by Manco would lay siege to Spanish Cuzco, singing from outside the walls their intent to massacre the foreigners within.

We circle back now toward the songs of our festival. In political terms, the Inca Raimi of 1535 reminds us of the more familiar rituals a century later of another Sun King, Louis XIV of France. He too needed warily to guard his power and his claims to divine legitimacy; he too did so in part through his participation in spectacular, elaborate displays of song and dance. The force of Manco Inca's *taki* was at this level little different from the force deployed at Versailles when Louis XIV danced in Lully's *tragédie-ballets*.

This parallel is particularly compelling since both monarchs stood in close relation to the sun. With this difference, however: In Louis XIV's Europe, no matter how firmly the divine legitimacy of kings was asserted, no one believed that the king was directly descended from a solar god. Louis's relation to the sun was symbolic – endowed, to be sure, with all the rich, premodern potency symbolism could carry in the European seventeenth century, but not presented or conceived as a real ancestral relation.

Manco Inca's asserted ancestry in the sun made his power different. It was not akin to a European ruler's temporal power, set apart from his divine legitimacy. Bauer and Dearborn have maintained that Inca rule and power depended on the king's ritual exalting of the sun over all other divine phenomena of the Andean world. This took the form, even, of the coopting of time itself, as Inca rulers imposed a solar calendar of worship and practice on older lunar ones.[57] In the most basic sense the Inca's divine powers were identified with his temporal ones, measured out in the repeated cycles of days and seasons and fulfilled in the annual rounds of sowing, cultivating, and harvest. These powers were warranted by his descent from the sun.

Warranted, but also circumscribed. The Inca's power depended, first, upon an always uncertain cosmological largesse. His empire was a complex administrative and ritual structure overlaid on many simpler agrarian societies (of which the Incas themselves had at first

---

[57] Bauer and Dearborn, *Astronomy and Empire*, chaps. 1 and 7.

Inca singing at Cuzco

been one). In such societies, especially high in the Andes, the sun looms large in mythic structures in part because subsistence depends on it so palpably and even tenuously. In Inca society specifically, the annual course of the sun was carefully watched in order to time crop plantings at different altitudes; the coming of the rains in September or October, conversely, was a time of pestilence and of a great cleansing ritual, Citua, to ward it off.[58]

The Inca's power was circumscribed also by the whole lineage of previous Incas. They did not cede their powers upon their deaths but extended them in their continuing relation to the sun, in their participation in rituals and daily affairs of Cuzco, in the actions of the lords in charge of the *panacas*, and in their control, ultimately, of the valuable resources Huascar wished to wrest from them. They too channeled the sun's divinity on earth. They too attended the Inca Raimi, and native ideologies suggest we would do well to think of it as a celebration of all the rulers rather than merely the living one.

Much was at stake in Manco Inca's singing to the sun in 1535. Its many religio-political valences made of it a richly overdetermined activity. It no doubt ranked among the most imposing and significant of the countless songs sung in Inca rituals – how could it not, this huge song-act, extending over a week and fashioned so as to mark and enhance the king's astronomical kinship? The *taki* patterned itself after the very cycles that defined the Inca's power. Each day it traced in its waxing the increasing strength of the sun but also of the Inca. Each day the sun's waning led to the diminishment of these powers and to contrite acts in which the witness sensed the despair of loss and humble prayer for its recuperation. In its mimesis of the sun's own growing and diminishing force, this song marked both the grandeur and fragility of the Inca's power. This must have seemed an especially acute dichotomy at this moment, when doubts about this power were raised by the deaths of Huascar and Atahuallpa and the continuing challenge the Spaniards posed.

In rehearsing the cosmological bond of all the Incas with the sun, meanwhile, the song likewise showed the Inca's power to be shared out among his ancestors. It reaffirmed the place in the empire's sacral structures not only of Manco Inca but of the dead Incas of the other *panacas*. It was not his song alone, but shared with hundreds of lords – all descended, like him, from the sun – and with the dead rulers they served. The lords were heard to sing with the Inca. (The fact that their singing disappeared from the later drawing of Guaman Poma – see again Figure 5.4 – might reflect a conception of absolute kingship shaped as much by European as by Andean notions.) Can we doubt, also, in this daily course of ritual song, that the Indians heard the mummies themselves sing, even if these voices of the *mallquis* were lost on Spanish ears?

How solar song worked

This complex expression of the Inca's power – celestial and earthly, absolute and shared, irresistible yet constrained from all sides – was achieved in a song and dance that were not symbolic in the manner of the mythic allegories Louis XIV danced. Instead the *taki*,

---

[58] Two detailed accounts of Citua are Cobo, *Historia*, 92, pp. 217–19; *Inca Religion*, 145–8; and Garcilaso, *Commentarios reales*, bk. 7, chaps. 6–7; *Royal Commentaries*, pp. 413–17. See also Guaman Poma, *Nueva crónica*, pp. 244–5.

following the sun's course, bypassed the semiotic dualism of the symbol and *embodied* the sacred power. In this way it was akin to the system of *ceques*, by which divinity was plotted out, written across the landscape (as I have suggested), and the physical organization of the *panacas* of Cuzco, entrusted with the care of the *huacas* into which this divinity flowed. But with this difference: The embodiment of divinity in solar song was not a fixed structure. It took the form of an energized, musical flux, of concerted motions of voice and body by which the celebrants themselves traced a cosmic relation.

This mobile *taki* reflected a daily movement of the sun that stood, as we have seen, in microcosmic relation to its macrocosmic, annual, solstitial motion. Such a relation between universal and local phenomena was characteristic of Inca representations. It is evident also in fixed aspects of Inca social order: in the reflection within Cuzco of the four realms of the cosmos as a whole, in the division of Hanan and Hurin moieties the Incas imposed not only on new settlements but on larger stretches of territory, and, in a manner mixing synchronic and diachronic experiences, in the embodiment of Inca imperial history in the *panacas*.[59]

More specifically, the equating of each day's dawning sun with the Child-Sun of the winter solstice seems to have been a basic gesture of Inca worship. Recall that Punchao, the golden image of the Child-Sun in Coricancha, was nourished with food and celebrated with hymns when the morning sun's rays struck it. Diurnal and annual motions of the sun both expressed a mutability of sacred powers that at once consoled and threatened Inca society; the sun's diurnal and annual waning, in particular, needed to be assuaged in the empire's ritual practices.

The diurnal growth and ebb of the solar singing of the Inca Raimi connected out to the broader waxing and waning of solar powers from solstice to solstice – an annual motion that could not in its entirety be sung. It connected to the confident, coming-of-age celebrations of Capac Inti Raimi, to the beseeching prayer of Inti Raimi, to the forlorn cleansing rites of Citua. And, like the breaking of arable land with sanctified hand-plows, it framed in ritual gesture the Inca's role in channeling the sun's generative energies. The *taki* of the Inca Raimi can be seen to encompass in its rhythms the most basic needs and fears expressed in Inca ritual and life.

If the microcosmic reflection of macrocosm in the solar *taki* is redolent in this way of other gestures of the Inca sacred imaginary, in another aspect the song shows its deep-seated connection to Inca expressive modes all told. The transformation of the movement of the sun into the flux of *taki* was a replication of a pattern from one realm in another, distinct one. The conducting of sacred force between them (we may speculate) depended upon this human act of duplication. The patterned similarity itself (we may be confident) – the diurnal motion on the one hand and the slow rising and falling of the song on the other – was schematic and geometrical.

This tendency toward abstract schematism characterized most of the modes we know of Inca writing, painting, and textile design. The traces that preserve it take several forms: the

---

[59] For the extension of the Cuzco moieties to the whole valley of Cuzco, see Zuidema, "The Moieties," p. 256; on Cuzco's microcosmic reflection of the empire as a whole, see Garcilaso, *Commentarios reales*, bk. 7, chap. 9; *Royal Commentaries*, pp. 421–2.

knotted writing system of the *quipu*; the designs incised on sacred drinking vessels or *keros*; the patterns woven in ceremonial tunics, belts, and other textiles; and, in one late instance, related designs carried over into an otherwise alphabetic manuscript. The textile designs in particular were called *tocapu*; they can be seen, in Guaman Poma's renderings, on the tunics of the Incas in Figures 5.2–5.5.[60]

Art historian Tom Cummins has described all these graphic modes, analyzed the abstract, geometrical patterning characteristic of them, and pointed up the wide chasm between them and European alphabetic writing and representational depiction. According to Cummins, the designs derived their meaning from their ability schematically to present general truths of Inca mythic history. The myths were written, in other words, by means of patterns that do not strike up the iconic relation typical in European pictorialism between signifier and worldly signified, and certainly do not show the close connection of writing symbols to speech that characterizes phonetic writing. Rather they create a relation of basic, intrinsic arrangement of elements connecting one realm or medium to another.[61]

Anthropologist Frank Salomon has extended this kind of thinking in his recent, rich ethnography of the surviving *quipu* culture of a village in the highlands east of Lima.[62] For Salomon the *quipus* of Tupicocha exemplify a kind of writing loosed entirely from speech-acts. They are predicated on and record no vocalization and hence are radically non-logocentric and non-phonocentric, unlike most inscriptive technologies historians of writing consider. Instead the *quipus* record social patterns themselves, patterns of communal labor commitments and their fulfillment among the *ayllus* of the village. Moreover, by virtue of their alterability, as knots along the pendant strands were untied and retied in new configurations, these *quipus* became ongoing performative representations of the shifting social relations they recorded. Salomon is cautious about extending such findings back to the distant Inca past. Nevertheless the formal, schematic coding of social patterns in his Tupicochan *quipus* seems in general to bear a close kinship to the geometrical patterning of myth in the Inca graphic modes discussed by Cummins.

---

[60] For color reproductions of spectacular preserved tunics with such *tocapu*, see Elena Phipps, Johanna Hecht, Cristina Esteras Martín, et al., *The Colonial Andes: Tapestries and Silverwork, 1530–1830* (exhibition catalogue, New York: The Metropolitan Museum of Art, 2004), pp. 153–9, 167–75, and passim.

[61] Tom Cummins, "Representation in the Sixteenth Century and the Colonial Image of the Inca," in *Writing without Words: Alternative Literacies in Mesoamerica and the Andes*, ed. Elizabeth Hill Boone and Walter D. Mignolo (Durham, NC: Duke University Press, 1994), pp. 188–219. One other medium Cummins mentions, painted boards, we know only through scattered remarks in early sources; no surviving instances have been identified. On the importance of such boards as genealogical records for the *panacas* see Julien, *Reading Inca History*, pp. 12, 57–8, 89. The paintings on these boards seem often to have shared in the schematism of other Inca graphic designs; see Cummins, "Representation," pp. 198–9. They were not, however, always non-representational, as he suggests. Betanzos tells of an offering Huayna Capac made at Coricancha in which he burned "a small bundle of firewood the servants of the Sun brought. This wood was carved, of four edges, and on it were painted birds, butterflies, and other things that he found pleasing" (*Narrative*, trans. Hamilton and Buchanan, pp. 165–6; *Suma y narración*, pp. 181–2). What interests here, in addition to the possibility of representational images in Inca painting, is the efficacy conceived to be unleashed in the sacrificial burning of such images.

[62] Salomon, *The Cord Keepers*.

Significantly, when Cummins considers the use of such graphic designs in ritual performance, he speculates that their general, abstract, mytho-historical meaning would have been specified and made less abstract – pinned down, in other words, to worldly things and events – especially in the bodily gestures of dance and in the words of songs. The *keros* and textiles, he writes,

> . . . were brought out together in later ceremonies[,] and . . . their physical presence and their designs were capable of suggesting a specific type of Inca "historical" event. However, [they] . . . could only convey the type of event in general[,] so that . . . the specific content . . . was conveyed by the songs and dances that were performed at the time of their appearance.

The *keros* and textiles, Cummins continues, had a prompting function that was "quasi-linguistic," one that needed to be filled out by the "texts to be sung" that accompanied them.[63]

This might well have been the role fulfilled by some sorts of Inca song. Certainly, at least, many Inca songs proferred words with semantic messages related to those of normal speech. The mytho-historical recitations Huayna Capac listened to in his tour of the *panacas* probably functioned in this way. And some of the songs Guaman Poma reports did so as well, though the semantic intent of the sung words he records for them is sometimes obscure.[64] The words of these and many other Inca songs seem to have signified, often enough, in ways roughly familiar to us from many manners of European and other song.

The solar singing of the Inca Raimi, on the other hand, points to the existence of a much less scrutable Inca vocalization. To miss this other possibility and accept the role Cummins accords to singing is to make Inca song conform to Western expressive molds at the very moment of breaking those molds in order to decipher Inca graphism. The solar song suggests that the abstraction whereby Inca myth, cosmogony, or societal structure was captured in graphic design could function the same way in *taki*. The Inca's derivation of power from, and dependency on, the sun seems to have been presented schematically *in the design itself* of each day's singing and choreography; what was sung, simply but also ineffably, was the movement of the sun. The *taki*, in this view, was nothing other than the pattern of heavenly force, waxing and waning in regular cycles, brought to earth in movements of voice and body. It was a performative enactment – in this perhaps akin to Salomon's *quipus* – of societal arrangements reaching from the earth to the heavens. It manifested a general relation between general events, requiring no specific, logocentric semantics for its meaning to be palpable and its force to be felt. It struck up an unmediated connection of similitude between the Inca and his lords and the *mallquis*, on the one hand, and the cosmic order on which they relied, on the other.

If this is right, then we need to conclude that Inca singing could share with modes of Inca graphism its way of encountering the world. The same cannot be said of European singing vis-à-vis European writing. Put another way, we seem to encounter in this Inca singing, at the far fringes of European perceptions in the early modern period, a mode of categorical

---

[63] Cummins, "Representation," p. 207. [64] See Guaman Poma, *Nueva crónica*, pp. 314–30.

Inca singing at Cuzco

musical formalism. Unlike many modern Western formalisms, however, it makes no claim to absolution from the world. Instead it poses itself precisely as a human replication of and immersion in the deep-set patterns of world-design.

This description remains incomplete, however, for it does not take account of the crucial regard in which solar *taki* diverged from other kinds of Inca graphism: its movement. Unlike the static designs Cummins considers, unlike even the somewhat flexible inscriptions of Salomon's *quipus*, *taki* could shift with the moment-to-moment motions of the cosmos around it. Its special capacity, in all likelihood, was its ability to move along with cosmic motions. It transferred mobile geometric patterns into other mobile patterns.

Such dynamism is in keeping with the multiplex, changing nature of the Inca pantheon. Demarest describes the shifting aspects of Inca divinity. He argues that a universal sky-god, revealing itself in different aspects from one moment to the next, expressed a fundamental truth of Inca relations to the cosmos that the Spaniards were hard pressed to appreciate. This truth was at odds with the ancient Mediterranean pantheons, as framed in and handed down by late antiquity, that they were predisposed to map on to Andean religion:

> ...unlike the chroniclers' classical, "pagan" models, pre-Columbian religions emphasized the *movements and transformations of astronomical phenomena*, not merely the deification of specific heavenly bodies. Thus, in ... Inca ... conceptions, the *movements* of the sun (daily and solstitial), the *recurrent appearances* of phenomena such as Venus, and the *partitioning* of the universe by astronomical movements were of even more importance than the celestial bodies themselves. . . . This emphasis on movement and transformation was reflected in the dynamic and fluid nature of the pre-Columbian high gods....[65]

To judge by the solar singing of the Inca Raimi of 1535, *taki* was an ideal ritual means of channeling the powers of a cosmos and of a divinity thus conceived. The singing of our festival replicated in its motions the diurnal growing and waning of a sun that also grew and diminished across the year. In doing so it traced a rhythm fundamental to the Inca imaginary, a rhythm that encompassed the history of the Inca's forebears projected as a shared power in the present, the agricultural life-cycle the empire depended upon, even the changeable powers of the Inca himself. No wonder the Spanish witness sensed sadness and humility in the celebrants' demeanor each day when the sun disappeared beneath the western horizon.

This conception of the solar *taki* as a generalized, cosmological ritual rhythm raises the issue of its words. The notion of hundreds of lords singing "with great order and harmony" eight days' worth of words, no matter how repetitious, seems improbable. But perhaps, again here, pressure needs to be brought to bear on customary ways of thinking, in this case our idea of song conveying a specific "text."

Remember that Guaman Poma, in addition to the generically familiar song texts whose words he reproduced, reported other, less familiar song-acts in his account of April rituals. The Inca, he wrote, "sang the song of the llamas, *Red [puca] llama*, and the song of the rivers

---
[65] Demarest, *Viracocha*, pp. 72–3; original emphasis.

The Singing of the New World

[and] that sound they make. These are the natural, proper songs of the Inca; like the llama he sings and says 'yn' for a very long time and with a beat."[66] Later, in his small section on Inca songs, Guaman Poma provided a drawing of the Inca singing *Puca llama* in the Inca Raimi (see Figure 5.5) and gave more particulars concerning its performance:

> They sing the *Puca llama* to the tone of the llama. [The Inca] pronounces thus: With a very slow measure, for half an hour he says "y, y, y," to the tone of the llama. The Inca begins like the llama; he says and goes on saying "yn." He takes this tone and, beginning there, he says very many of his songs. The queens and princesses respond; they sing very sweetly with a high voice.[67]

For long stretches, at least, the Inca's part of the exchange did not consist of lyrics as we think of them but rather of imitation of the llama's whining *yyynnn*.

Guaman Poma offers no description of the ruler's singing the sound of the rivers. But his phrase referring to this song – "song of the rivers [and] that sound they make" (*cantar de los rríos aquel sonido que haze*) – is suggestive. It leads us to imagine an intonation setting aside the verbal semantics of speech and familiar song texts in favor of a mimetic capturing of the sound of rushing water. The analogy to the working of the solar *taki* and the llama song seems close. Suggestive also is Guaman Poma's specification that both the llama song and the river song were "natural" and "proper" to the Inca, as if communing in song with the extra-human world of natural forces were his special predilection.

Guaman Poma's illustration for the April Inca Raimi, we remember, shows the Inca singing neither with a llama nor with a river, but with the sun (see Figure 5.4). What sound, in the ears and minds of the Incas, did the sun make on its daily course through the heavens? Whatever it was, it probably was this sound that their song festival aimed to reproduce. Words in our conception of them might have been largely or wholly irrelevant in this song, as they were in the Inca's exchange with the llama and, probably, in his rushing water songs.

We confront here, finally, the possibility of a song fully divorced from the spoken language around it – a vocalization whose inevitable *phono*centrism in no way involved it in a customarily kindred *logo*centrism. The prospect is of an Andean expressive mode, like Salomon's *quipus*, with no basis in or reliance on speech; but in this case, startlingly, it is the voice itself that flourishes in this non-grammatical, non-semantic space.

Two more glimpses of indigenous singing, from the early seventeenth and the twentieth centuries, support this idea. In a treatise of 1621 reporting on lingering practices of Inca idolatry, the Jesuit missionary Pablo José de Arriaga recalled a town in the *altiplano* where the Indians still celebrated the three main indigenous festivals in order to honor the old

---

[66] Guaman Poma, *Nueva crónica*, p. 234.
[67] Ibid., pp. 234, 320: "... *puca llama* al tono del carnero cantan. Dize ací: Con conpás muy poco a poco, media ora dize: 'Y, y, y', al tono del carnero. Comiensa el Ynga como el carnero; dize y está diziendo 'yn'. Lleva ese tono y dallí comensando, va disiendo sus coplas muy muchas. Responde las *coyas* y *ñustas*. Cantan a bos alta muy suauemente." Guaman Poma's illustration of the song shows not only queens and princesses but lords joining in with the Inca.

Inca singing at Cuzco

Figure 5.5 Fiesta de los Ingas / Varicza Aravi del / Inga canta co[n] su puca llama: Inca singing with sacred llama, from Guaman Poma, *Nueva corónica* . . .

The Singing of the New World

gods with dancing, musical instruments, and singing. "When they sing these *cantares*," Arriaga wrote,

> which are about many follies from their ancient times, they invoke the name of the *huaca*, raising their voices; and, saying a single verse, they either lift their hands or turn around, according to local custom. And their ordinary way [of singing] is not to pronounce all at once the name of the *huaca* but instead to interpolate the voice between the syllables [of the name] without articulating any syllable.[68]

Here Arriaga seems to be struggling to describe the singing of vocables, a phenomenon familiar to us from the Nahuatl *cantares* both in its complexities and in the tendency of commentators to underestimate them. The particular vocalizing he describes seems to have dominated the singing of lengthy festivals, and it may well shed light on one aspect of a solar song that could last for a day and be repeated over and over for a week. It might also underscore the possibility that such a song could gain its significance from the broad and incantatory design of long invocation instead of from the more determinate semantics of ordinary language.

Just such a featuring of signifying design over linguistic semantics, finally, characterizes shamanic songs that survive today in the river valleys north of Cuzco leading down the eastern slopes of the Andes to the Amazonian basin. The Shipibo-Conibo people there produce pottery and embroidered and painted cloth covered with intricate, geometric filigree designs. These are representations of designs from the spirit world – they are all thought to be ultimately derived from the skin of a great snake or world-anaconda called Ronin – and they are the material remnants of designs once much more widespread in the society, decorating houses, boats, tools, and faces and bodies alike.

It is, however, the immaterial remnants of such designs that interest us here. These are conveyed to shamans as visions from the spirit world. In a synaesthetic conversion, a shaman sings songs whose melodic designs present in sound one or more of the patterns he has seen in visions. Such songs form together a corpus of medicinal design-melodies used to cure illness. The holistic application of a design-song to the patient brings about the cure; the words of the song, ad hoc and improvised, are thought to play no important role. An almost extinct dance tradition, meanwhile, in which signifying designs are traced on the ground by moving bodies, may once have been connected also to the designs of the spirit realm.[69]

Here we recognize a conjuncture of cultural practices we have discerned also in the solar singing of the Inca. Both Shipibo shamans' cures and Inca rites construct a sung connection to metaphysical powers whose force does not reside in the modes of meaning of spoken language. Instead its source is the relation of patterns between song and the cosmic or spiritual designs it reenacts. It is certainly an insecure speculation that

---

[68] Pablo José de Arriaga, *Extirpación de la idolatría del Pirú*, in *Crónicas peruanas de interés indígena*, ed. Esteve Barba, pp. 191–277; see pp. 213–14.

[69] See Angelika Gebhart-Sayer, "The Geometric Designs of the Shipibo-Conibo in Ritual Context," *Journal of Latin American Lore* 11 (1985), pp. 143–75; for some transcribed melodies, Theodore D. Lucas, "Songs of the Shipibo of the Upper Amazon," *Anuario Interamericano de Investigación Musical* 7 (1971), pp. 59–81.

Inca singing at Cuzco

would arch over half a millennium of profound social change – not to mention regional and ethnic differences present from the start – to posit cultural ties. Nevertheless, the temptation is great to imagine that we glimpse in Shipibo shamans' songs the remnants of a musical formalism that antedated the rise to power of the Incas and from which the geometric, nonlinguistic powers of their ritual song might long ago have been extrapolated.

Singing Cuzco

The eminent archaeologist John Rowe long ago warned us that in thinking of Inca Cuzco as a city, thus following the lead of the first Spaniards who entered it, we might load on to it an inappropriate European baggage. Rowe describes Cuzco instead as a ceremonial center – something of the sort we have learned also to discern, if on greatly varying scales, in the great center Teotihuacan in the valley of Mexico or the Mixtec center of Monte Alban in the highlands near Oaxaca.[70] Later writers, among them R. Tom Zuidema, Brian Bauer, and John Hyslop, have built on Rowe's insight.[71]

From Coricancha at the heart of Cuzco, as we have seen, radiated out not only the *ceques* with their hundreds of shrines but also the roads to the four corners of the world. I have suggested that we think of this arrangement of *huacas* as a writing of sacred powers of the cosmos across the landscape itself, a writing that could be reflected in smaller graphic designs of the sort Cummins and Salomon have discussed. But the solar *taki* makes it clear – in case it was not clear already from the *ceques* and *huacas* themselves – that this writing of the sacred was no inert geographical inscription. Instead it pulsed with living energy.

In the embodied solar cycle of the *taki* described in the *Relación*, in other words, the sacred energy flowed through the flesh and blood of the celebrants themselves. This is not surprising since, as Rowe and later writers have pointed out, the population of Cuzco itself was a *ceremonial* population to match its ceremonial settlement. By late imperial times, if not earlier, it was controlled for dynastic and religious ends. Residency in the central district seems to have been reserved for the royal households or *panacas*, no doubt with their retainers and servants; the non-royal *ayllus* were arrayed around the center; while Indians less closely tied to the Inca lived farther from Coricancha.[72] The ceremonies in Cuzco, in their ritual organization (such as the Hanan/Hurin division with which we began), affirmed the

---

[70] John Howland Rowe, "What Kind of a Settlement Was Inca Cuzco?," *Ñawpa Pacha* 5 (1967), pp. 59–77.
[71] See *inter alia* Zuidema, *Inca Civilization*; Bauer, *The Development of the Inca State*, esp. chap. 2; and Hyslop, *Inca Settlement Planning*, chap. 2.
[72] Moreover, the population in and around Cuzco seems to have been a carefully regulated microcosm of the empire as a whole. It comprised not only the Incas of the *panacas* and the lords of the *ayllus* but also important leaders from all corners of the realm since, by requirement of the Inca, the chief nobility from every province had to live in Cuzco for a portion of the year. In the countryside around the center, probably arrayed in the particular quarters of the empire from which each of these leaders came, were support settlements of their own countrymen. See Rowe, "What Kind of Settlement," p. 62; Hyslop, *Inca Settlement Planning*, pp. 62–4.

microcosmic sacrality of the settlement by emphasizing the dynamism of its living, sacred topology.[73]

The center from which all the energy flowed was not only the unmoving, stone enclosure of Coricancha but also the Inca himself, the chief earthly medium of the sun's bounty. It was in this capacity more than any other that he led all the major rituals across the year. The divine energy of the sun, driving the agricultural cycle on which the society depended, seems to have been channeled by means of ritual through the Inca, to be dispersed out through the *huacas*, the topoi of divinity on earth, and into the landscape. Indeed, as we have seen, this harnessing in human form of solar powers, more and more clearly marked in Inca ritual from Pachacuti on down, was the Incas' chief claim differentiating them from other indigenous rulers and religions. The writing of the sacred on earth took the form, at least in part, of the ruler's gestures, actions, and utterances.

The solar *taki* of the Inca and his minions in 1535 was the final major demonstration – the only one recorded in much detail by the Spaniards – of this web of sacred powers radiating out from Cuzco and the Inca. In it, it seems more than plausible to suggest, we witness song deployed not merely as a celebration of the sacred, not as a representation of it, not even as a magical mimesis of it. We witness instead song extended out in its dynamic designs as the cosmic rhythm itself whereby higher powers reached the Inca, the *mallquis*, the *orejones*, the *huacas*, the crops, and perhaps – though they could not know it – even the Spaniards. We witness song as a vital, mobile inscription of these powers on the world. But if this is so, must we not recognize in this Inca Raimi a music writing unnoticed by those Spaniards who witnessed the festival and unsuspected by all those since who have conspired, even in passing, to hear its echoes?

The moment of hesitancy in Tom Cummins's work on Inca graphism – the retreat in his argument from an estranging conception of writing to a recognizable, modern view of words and music – is, from another vantage point, a familiar recourse to the logocentric metaphysics Derrida labored in his early works to make visible. In the operation of this metaphysics writing always remains at one remove from the human subject in the world – a static, lifeless inscribing of human expression rather than expression in its full and present immediacy. For its fulfillment, in this conception, writing wants speech.

The abstraction of Inca graphism Cummins describes smacks, at the moment he introduces song and dance as compensatory gestures, of this sort of writing-as-absence. It is a capacity of Inca expression marked by insufficiency. It requires first-person, living utterance – the songs with their conventional semantics – to revive it, to draw it back from the land of dead inscription. Singing, in this view, is a version of a speech always alive and therefore unlike writing; it is the body of which abstract writing is merely the shadow.

The *taki* of the Inca Raimi of 1535 suggests instead that singing may have occupied a place in Inca expression encompassed within a broader writing of the world. This singing

---

[73] This point recalls Sabine MacCormack's important reminder (*Religion*, p. 113) that Andean *huacas* could be animate beings, and indeed humans, as well as things we consider inanimate; see also Salomon and Urioste, *The Huarochirí Manuscript*, p. 19. This versatility of the indigenous notion of *huaca* was underscored for the Spaniards in the *Taki onqoy* episodes of the 1560s; see chap. 6 below.

Inca singing at Cuzco

was not a compensation for the non-presence of writing, but instead a mode itself of human designation of the divine on the world. In this it was like the *ceques*, like the *huacas*, like Coricancha, like the plastic presentations within this temple of the various aspects of the sun, like all the microcosmic reflections that structured Cuzco as the larger cosmos. The sonorous waves and embodied motions of this *taki* distinguished it, no doubt, from some of these other landmarks of the Inca sacred imaginary. But this difference did not pull *taki* outside the circle of Inca graphism; if anything, instead, it shifted the position of the circle so as to make singing its centerpoint. It made of *taki* a mobile writing, full of presence, of the designs signaled more statically elsewhere in the circuitry of Inca society, ritual, and cosmos.

As a marking out of a human habitation, of a place and time in the world defined by mytho-historical trajectories and sacred energies, it is hard to imagine a singing more compelling than this one must have been.

6

Fear of singing

> The zoo used to contain not just the animals, but also a music pavilion and, occasionally, exhibitions of exotic tribes, Samoans and Senegalese. But the only sound that penetrated to them from the distant pavilion was the sound of the kettledrum. Whether it be the memory of this, or simply the condensation of what has long been forgotten – even today, when I hear the kettledrum it brings back the memory of Tamasese, the tribal chief. And at the same time I recall that the heads of Tamasese's prisoners were used as drums, or perhaps they were the cauldrons in which the savages cooked human flesh. Is the drum the successor of human sacrifice or does it still sound the command to kill? In our music it resounds as an archaic survival. It is the legacy of violence in art, the violence which lies at the base of all art's order. While as a spiritualized activity art strips violence of its power, it continues to practise it. Freedom and domination commingle inseparably in art. Its integral form, the triumph of its autonomy, is what also casts a spell on the listener, leaves no one out and subjects everyone to its speechless performance. It is only necessary to listen to the humane Beethoven from outside, from a sufficiently great distance, and nothing remains but the terror aroused by Tamasese. But perhaps all humaneness does is to keep the consciousness of terror alive, the consciousness of all that can never be made good.[1]

It is difficult to tease apart, in this passage by Theodor Adorno, the layers of Euro-chauvinism and blinkered fantasy about others, of sad, ironic wisdom about Europe itself, even of vestigial hopefulness – almost as difficult, indeed, as it is to analyze our ambivalences in reading it today. Adorno's is a convoluted parable, at once celebrating the grand European *fin de siècle* at the expense of savages and pointing an accusing finger at Europe's own savagery.

If, on the one hand, the passage beckons us to contemplate it, it is not only because the brutality Adorno commemorated – his words come from 1951 – is with us still. It beckons also with its recognition that a familiar, comforting humaneness, the humaneness of Beethoven, is shadowed by atavistic terror. And it beckons, on a specifically musical level, in naming an art of hearing-at-a-distance that has been too rarely assayed by musicians

---

[1] Theodor Adorno, *Quasi una fantasia*, trans. Rodney Livingstone (London: Verso, 1992), pp. 33–4.

Fear of singing

and critics. (Musicologists have tended to hear only up close. When one of them, Susan McClary, heard Beethoven from an Adornian distance in the 1980s and said so in print, she was castigated for heterodoxy by other scholars and journalists.)

If also the passage repels with its apparatus of skull cauldrons and cannibalism – one more European fancy of others' savagery – it is because Adorno hesitated in the face of the proposition that humaneness might be found in equal measure in Beethoven and Tamasese. This diffidence is not unimportant. It allows formulations ostensibly like Adorno's to slide toward another vantage point from which music comes to seem equally the cipher of European refinement and others' barbarity. Music not our own becomes the fearsome, wild cry in the darkness. *The natives are restless tonight*.

It is not only Europeans, however, who are seized by fear at the sound of savage music. The essential richness of Adorno's *minimum moralium* lies in the role it accords Tamasese. Though he inspired terror in the child Adorno, the music in the parable casts him in the part of terrified listener, not musician. *He* heard the primal drum from the distance; it was not his own drum but its modern descendant that resounded from the pavilion where the acme of cultivated Europe, the symphony orchestra, played. Tamasese listened from a space Europe had fashioned, equivalent to the cages of the animals around him. Savagery is in the ear of the beholder.

During the period of first contact between Europeans and Native Americans, the fear of others' singing, dancing, and playing of musical instruments was everywhere writ large. A rough anthology of citations reflecting this fact is easily culled from narratives of exploration and conquest. It starts at the very beginning, in one of the letters Columbus wrote of his voyages to the Indies:

> When this canoe arrived, it hailed us from a great distance, and neither I nor anyone else could understand them. However, I ordered signs to be made to them that they should approach, and in this way more than two hours passed, and if they came a little nearer, they at once sheered off again. . . . And I greatly desired to have speech with them and it seemed to me that I had nothing that could be shown to them now which would induce them to come nearer. But I caused to be brought up to the castle of the poop a little drum, that they might play it, and some young men to dance, believing that they would draw nearer to see the festivity. And as soon as they observed the playing and dancing, they all dropped their oars and laid hand on their bows and strung them, and each one of them took up his shield, and they began to shoot arrows. I immediately stopped the playing and dancing, and then ordered some crossbows to be discharged.[2]

Here the Indians of Trinidad interpreted as hostile acts impromptu blandishments meant to allure. We have little means of judging exactly why they did so. Perhaps they were accustomed to threatening musical displays in their meetings with Arawaks or Caribs

---

[2] Christopher Columbus, *Narrative* of the third voyage to the Indies [1498], trans. Cecil Jane, *The Four Voyages of Columbus* (New York: Dover, 1988), pp. 14–16. I have altered Jane's translation of *tanborín* as "tambourine" to the more faithful "little drum."

The Singing of the New World

from neighboring islands; in all likelihood they knew well parallel rituals of intimidating gift exchange with other indigenous groups.

It is true, at any rate, that in their first meetings Indians and Europeans alike often employed singing, dancing, and playing as shows of strength meant to intimidate. Thus Martin Frobisher, in his second search for a northern passage in 1577, encountered Inuits on the shore who

> mustered themselves in our sight uppon the toppe of a hill, to the number of twentie in a rancke, all holdyng handes over theyr heads, and dauncing, with greate noyse and songs togither, wee supposed they made thys daunce and shew for us to understand, that we might take vew of theyr whole companyes and force, meaninge belike, that we should doe the same. And thus they continued uppon the hyll toppes untyll nighte, when hearinge a peece of oure greate ordinance, whiche thundered in the hollownesse of the hygh hylles, made unto them so fearefull a noyse, that they hadde no greate wyll to tarrie long after. And this was done, more to make them knowe oure force, than to do them anye hurte at all.[3]

Other musical shows of force were more reciprocal than this and marked ostensibly peaceable meetings with an undercurrent of menace. René de Laudonnière, on his ill-starred attempt to establish a French foothold on the Florida coast in 1564, first met the local chief Saturiba and a large group of his warriors on terms amicable enough; but the underlying wariness of the Frenchmen was redoubled by an impressive noise of pipes:

> Chief Saturiba came with seven or eight hundred handsome, strong, and well-built men, the best-trained and swiftest of his tribe, all armed as if on the warpath. In the van marched fifty youths with javelins and spears; behind these, and next to the chief, came twenty pipers making the wildest kind of noise, without any harmony or rhythm, each blowing with all his might as if to see who could blow the loudest. Their instruments were thick reeds, like organ pipes or whistles, with only two openings. They blew into the top hole, while the sound came out the other end.

Not long after, Saturiba returned to find the French fortifications almost complete. This time the Europeans were in a position to repay the earlier intimidation. They turned back his force of over a thousand warriors, allowing him to enter the walls with only a small party:

> Saturiba was disappointed, but he disguised his feelings well. He selected twenty of his followers, and with these he entered the fort, where he was shown everything. The sound of drums and trumpets and the reports of the brass cannon, which we fired in his presence, frightened him vastly. When he was told that all his men had run away, he could readily believe it, since he himself would gladly have been somewhere else. . . . after this, the natives believed us to be far more powerful than we actually were.[4]

---

[3] Richard Collinson, ed., *The Three Voyages of Martin Frobisher, in Search of a Passage to Cathaia and India by the North-West* (London: Hakluyt Society, 1867), p. 149.

[4] Jacques Le Moyne de Morgues, *Brevis narratio* of the French expedition to Florida of 1564 [ca. 1585], trans. Stefan Lorant, in *The New World: The First Pictures of America*, rev. edn. (New York: Duell, Sloane and Pearce, 1965), pp. 38–42.

Fear of singing

As in Frobisher's meeting with the Inuits, cannon fire trumped native music-making. But in each case music – singing with dancing, or piping, or trumpets and drums – was deployed in exactly the same spirit as artillery displays. Its terrors were thought to be useful by Europeans and Native Americans alike.

These terrors were especially marked in situations of outright conflict. The early accounts of warfare between Europeans and Native Americans abound in references to music either frightening or intended to frighten. Given that the narratives are almost always by Europeans, it is no surprise that the fearsome music reported is usually the Indians'. Again the topos reaches back to the earliest voyages to the Indies, to Columbus's fourth voyage of 1502–3. Diego Mendez, left by Columbus on the coast of the isthmus of Panama with a small party of men, faced repeated assaults accompanied by war-cries and music. He repulsed them with light (but impressive) artillery:

> Just as the admiral had got out to sea, and while I remained on land with some twenty men, . . . suddenly there came upon me many natives, so that there were more than four hundred men armed with bows and arrows and slings. They spread across the mountain opposite, and they gave a shriek and then another and again another, and, thanks be to God, they thus gave me time to prepare for the battle and to make ready a defence against them. . . . In addition to all this, the Indians did not cease to come to attack us, every moment sounding trumpets and small drums and making loud cries, believing that they had us at their mercy. The defence which we had against these people consisted in two very good brass falconets and much powder and ball, with which we so terrified them that they did not dare to come up to us.[5]

We are left in doubt as to the nature of the Indians' shrieks, but their repetition (*una grita y otra y luego otra*) suggests some kind of organized chant. The suggestion seems to be confirmed by the Indians' later "loud cries" (*alaridos*), since these were accompanied by instruments. The ritual war-chants were reduced to furious howls, then, in Mendez's frightened apprehension (or faded memory: his account was not written until 1536).

A whole miniature study of Europeans' fear of native song at wartime could be based on the accounts of the back-and-forth battle for the Mexica capital, Tenochtitlan. In his third letter on the campaign (1523), relating a moment when the Spaniards' hopes were at low ebb, Hernán Cortés captured the horrifying circumstances in which they listened for hours to Mexica ritual music:

> Once they had gained their victory, the people of the city, in order to terrify the alguacil mayor and Pedro de Alvarado, took all the Spaniards they had captured dead or alive to Tlatelulco, which is the market, and on some high towers which are there sacrificed them naked, opening their chests and tearing out their hearts as an offering to the idols. The Spaniards of Alvarado's camp could see this clearly from where they were fighting, and recognized those who were being sacrificed as Christians by their white naked

---

[5] Diego Mendez, *An Account* of incidents on Columbus's fourth voyage [1536], trans. Cecil Jane, in *The Four Voyages*, pp. 120–2.

> bodies.... All during that day and the following night the enemy celebrated with drums and trumpets so loudly it seemed as if the world was coming to an end.[6]

Bernal Díaz, writing some forty years later, still vividly recalled the same scene; he adds the hint of a Satanism that was usually not far (as we have repeatedly seen) from Europeans' imaginings of native ritual:

> As we were retreating, we heard the sound of trumpets from the great *cue* of Huichilobos and Tezcatlipoca, which dominates the whole city, and the beating of a drum, a very sad sound as of some devilish instrument, which could be heard six miles away; and with it came the noise of many kettle-drums, conches, horns, and whistles. At that moment, as we afterwards learnt, they were offering the hearts and blood of ten of our comrades to these two idols.[7]

Even when the Spaniards moved brutally on the offensive, as we hear from Cortés, they were haunted by the unnerving song-ceremonies of their enemies:

> As soon as the foot soldiers arrived, they, together with our allies, who numbered more than seventy thousand men, began to run toward the town [of Matalcingo], where the enemy turned and faced them.... so fierce was the attack that the defenders were... forced to retreat to . . . [a] fortress on the hill, which was very steep and almost impregnable. The town was burned and sacked in a very short time, but as it was late and as the men were very tired, for they had fought all day, the alguacil mayor decided not to attack the fortress. The enemy spent most of that night howling and beating drums and blowing trumpets.[8]

Arguably the most eloquent testimony to the fear aroused in the Spaniards by Mexica musical ritual is an implicit one. It comes from accounts of the infamous slaughter of Indian nobles during the celebration of Toxcatl, the festival of Huitzilopochtli (Díaz's "Huichilobos"), in May 1520. Pedro de Alvarado, second in command of Cortés's forces, had been left with a small group in Tenochtitlan while Cortés marched out to meet the opposing Spanish force of Pánfilo de Narváez. After agreeing to the celebration of the festival, Alvarado took the Indians by surprise, slaughtering most of them.

The motivation for this act must have seemed compelling to Alvarado, as its dangers had to have been foreseeable; in the event it led to a Mexica uprising and the ouster (temporary, as it turned out) of the Spaniards from the city. Alvarado apparently suspected – whether from good intelligence or treacherous, or out of a general anxiety at his vulnerability, will never be known – that the feast was a signal for an uprising already planned. He determined to strike first. However, the details themselves of two Nahuatl narratives of the massacre, from the *Florentine Codex* of Sahagún and the *Codex Aubin*, suggest another, more proximate motivation:

---

[6] Hernán Cortés, *The Third Letter* concerning the conquest of Mexico [1523], in Hernán Cortés, *Letters from Mexico*, trans. and ed. Anthony Pagden (New Haven: Yale University Press, 1986), pp. 241.
[7] Bernal Díaz, *The Conquest of New Spain* [1560s], trans. J. M. Cohen (London: Penguin, 1963), p. 381.
[8] Cortés, *Letters from Mexico*, pp. 245–6.

Fear of singing

> And . . . when already the feast was being observed, when already there was dancing, when already there was singing, when already there was song with dance, the singing resounded like waves breaking. When it was already time, when the moment was opportune for the Spaniards to slay them, thereupon they came forth. They were arrayed for battle. They came everywhere to block each of the ways leading out. . . . No one could go out. . . . Thereupon they surrounded the dancers. Thereupon they went among the drums. Then they struck the drummer's arms; they severed both his hands; then they struck his neck. Far off did his neck [and head] go to fall. Then they all pierced the people with iron lances and they struck them each with iron swords. . . . And the blood of the brave warriors ran like water.
>
> Then the songs and dances began. A young captain wearing a lip plug guided the dancers; he was Cuatlazol, from Tolnahuac. But the songs had hardly begun when the Christians came out of the palace. They entered the patio and stationed four guards at each entrance. Then they attacked the captain who was guiding the dance. One of the Spaniards struck the idol in the face, and others attacked the three men who were playing the drums. After that there was a general slaughter until the patio was heaped with corpses.[9]

Each account specifies, if with varying detail, that the Spaniards targeted the musicians and struck them first. It is as if frightening energies were loosed in the ritual music, energies that needed to be quelled before any other threats could be put down. The Nahuatl itself of the first version, from the *Florentine Codex*, seems to take pains to emphasize the force of the song and dance, both in the elegant, burgeoning repetitions with which it begins and in the frequentative verbal form, redolent of the special vocabulary of the *Cantares mexicanos*, it employs to capture the resounding ("like waves breaking") of the song: *in cujcatl, iuhqujn xaxamacatimanj*. If the native informants themselves tried thus to convey in words such song, we might well imagine that its impact on the Spanish witnesses, who probably heard it as the sonic excrescence of demonic idolatry and perhaps as the electrifying call for their murder, was profound.

In fact, European eyewitness accounts of indigenous American ritual, sung, danced, and drummed, make up the largest category of testimony to the fear of singing. A much-discussed example comes from Jean de Léry's *History* of his time among the Tupinamba of Brazil:

> The next morning very early, . . . we saw the savages . . . arriving from all directions, . . . and suspecting that they would do something extraordinary, I urged my companions to stay with me to see this mystery, and they agreed. . . . They . . . ordered us to confine

---

[9] For the first account see Fray Bernardino de Sahagún, comp., *The Florentine Codex*, trans. Arthur J. O. Anderson and Charles E. Dibble, 12 vols. (Santa Fe and Salt Lake City: School of American Research and University of Utah Press, 1975), XIII, pp. 55–6; for the second, Miguel León-Portilla, *The Broken Spears: The Aztec Account of the Conquest of Mexico*, trans. Lysander Kemp, rev. edn. (Boston: Beacon Press, 1992), p. 81; León-Portilla translates it from *Historia de la nación mexicana: Reproducción a todo color del Codice de 1576 (Codice Aubin)*, ed. and trans. Charles E. Dibble (Madrid: Porrua, 1963), p. 83. The event seems to be pictured in the sixteenth-century Codex Azcatitlan; there the *huehuetl* and *teponzatli* players are prominent, and the *huehuetl* player is shown drumming even though his hands are already severed. See *Codex Azcatitlan*, ed. Michel Graulich and Robert H. Barlow (Paris: Bibliothèque nationale de France, 1995), facsimile volume, f. 23r.

> ourselves to the house where the women were. While we were having our breakfast, with no idea as yet what they intended to do, we began to hear in the men's house (not thirty feet from where we stood) a very low murmur, like the muttering of someone reciting his hours. Upon hearing this, the women (about two hundred of them) all stood up and clustered together, listening intently. The men little by little raised their voices and were distinctly heard singing all together and repeating this syllable of exhortation, *He, he, he, he*; the women, to our amazement, answered them from their side, and with a trembling voice, reiterating that same interjection *He, he, he, he*, let out such cries for more than a quarter of an hour that as we watched them we were utterly disconcerted (*ne sçavions quelle contenance tenir*). Not only did they howl, but also, leaping violently into the air, they made their breasts shake and they foamed at the mouth. . . .[10]

As we saw in chapter 2, Léry dwelled long on the memory of this singing, attempting in later editions of his *Histoire* to capture it in European music writing and analyzing the force behind it as an instance of demonic possession, with terminology borrowed from Jean Bodin.

The observation of such ritual usually took place in a situation where the Europeans were vastly outnumbered by the Indians, as were Léry and his party. The disparity must only have increased the discomfiture of the interlopers. The account of Owen Griffin among the Abenaki Indians of Maine in 1605 comes to us at second hand, in the words of James Rosier, also on the voyage; and there is no intimation in it of the emotional impact of the ceremony Griffin witnessed. But imagine his situation: alone among the Indians; exchanged – as guest? hostage? – for three of them who slept on board the English ship; witnessing hours of chant, dance, and beating of sticks and rocks, the aim of which he could not have known:

> At our coming away, we would haue had those two that supped with vs, to go abord and sleepe, as they had promised: but it appeared their company would not suffer them [to do so]. Then Owen Griffin . . . went with them in their Canoa, and 3 of them staied aborde vs. . . . Owen Griffin, which lay on the shore, reported vnto me their maner, and (as I may terme them) the ceremonies of their idolatry: which they performe thus. One among them (the eldest of the Company, as he iudged) riseth right vp, the other sitting still, and looking about, suddenly cried with a loud voice, Baugh, Waugh: then the women fall downe, and lie vpon the ground, and the men all together answering the same, fall a stamping round about the fire with both feet, as hard as they can making the ground shake, with sundry out-cries, and change of voice and sound. Many take the fire-sticks and thrust them into the earth, and then rest awhile: of a sudden beginning as before, they continue so stamping, till the yonger sort fetched from the shore many stones, of which euery man tooke one, and first beat vpon them with their fire sticks, then with

---

[10] Jean de Léry, *History of a Voyage to the Land of Brazil, Otherwise Called America* [1585], trans. Janet Whatley (Berkeley: University of California Press, 1990), pp. 140–1. For the French original see Jean de Léry, *Histoire d'un voyage fait en la terre du Brésil*, facsimile rpt. of the 1580 edition, ed. Jean-Claude Morisot (Geneva: Droz, 1975), p. 242.

the stones beat the earth with all their strength. And in this maner (as he reported) they continued aboue two houres.[11]

Native American ritual could pack a fearsome punch even when its object was clear and its powers were marshaled in aid of the Europeans involved. Lionel Wafer, stranded on the shore of Panama in 1681, asked his Cuna hosts whether they expected any European ships to arrive:

> They told us they knew not but would enquire; and therefore they sent for one of the Conjurers, who immediately went to work to raise the Devil . . . for they are very expert and skilful in their sort of Diabolical Conjurations. We were in the house with them, and they first began to work with making a Partition with Hammocks, that the *Pawawers*, for so they call these Conjurers, might be by themselves. They continued some time at their Exercise, and we could hear them make most hideous Yellings and Shrieks; imitating the Voices of all their kind of Birds and Beasts. With their own Noise, they join'd that of several Stones struck together, and of Conch-shells, and of a sorry sort of Drums made of hollow Bamboes, which they beat upon: making a jarring Noise also with Strings fasten'd to the larger Bones of Beasts: And every now and then they would make a dreadful Exclamation, and clattering all of a sudden, would as suddenly make a Pause and a profound Silence. . . . The Oracle . . . was to this Effect: That the 10th Day from that time there would arrive two Ships; . . . That one of us should die soon after; . . . which fell out exactly according to the Prediction.

The ceremony itself was clearly unnerving for its European witnesses, all the more so, no doubt, when it resulted in a fatal prognostication. Wafer's account of efficacious diabolical conjuration, meanwhile, conveyed this power also to his readers. In the preface to the second edition of his book he felt the need to defend its veracity against "several of the most eminent Men of the Nation" who "seem'd very much startled" by it.[12]

Scenes and songs of apostasy

These incidents – their number could with ease be doubled from New World sources, then doubled again from accounts of European travels in Africa and Asia[13] – commemorate the powers of raised voices. In the travel narratives we do not often hear of instances where Indians or Europeans were frightened by exchanges of everyday speech, no matter how mutually incomprehensible these often were. Across huge cultural distances, that is, the burden of speech as communication was clear and unthreatening, even when what it said

---

[11] James Rosier, *A True Relation* of George Waymouth's voyage to Virginia [1605], quoted from *The English New England Voyages, 1602–1608*, ed. David B. Quinn and Alison M. Quinn (London: The Hakluyt Society, 1983), pp. 277–8.

[12] Lionel Wafer, *A New Voyage and Description of the Isthmus of America* [1699], quoted from Frank Harrison, *Time, Place and Music* (Amsterdam: Frits Knuf, 1973), pp. 89–90.

[13] For a sensitive consideration of accounts, similar to those here, of musical encounters from southern Africa, see David Smith, "Colonial Encounters through the Prism of Music," *International Review of the Aesthetics and Sociology of Music* 33 (2002), pp. 31–55.

was neither the one nor the other. Heightened utterance, instead, showed a special capacity to threaten. In setting itself apart from normal talk it entered a realm expansive enough to embrace recitations, invocations, incantations, chants, song – and sometimes whispers, howls, and shrieks as well. The customary accompaniment of such utterance by musical instruments and extraordinary bodily movement and gesture only increased its distance from everyday speech.

This distance was ample enough to accommodate a whole metaphysics. The special qualities of song and its corollary forms of utterance were experienced, in a cognitive step that growing evidence suggests is hardwired like the capacity for language itself, as a gaining of access to special realms not open to speech alone. In encounters of difference as dramatic as those between Europeans and Americans these realms loomed especially in the marshaling of song in organized, determinate rites – ceremonies of the sort that made Léry and Owen Griffin shudder and Alvarado and the Trinidadians attack. The real threat was not singing *per se* but what everyone involved knew to be conjured in its difference from speech. At the heart of ritual, the altered behavior of voice and body constituted the unmistakable sign of a frightening, unassuageable otherness.

Throughout the Spanish colonies in America the missionaries charged with Christianizing the Indians paid implicit homage to the metaphysical powers of song, and this in two ways. First, they recognized it as a foremost element of the teaching they needed to bring to the Indians to convert them – as, in other words, a potent force in conveying their own metaphysics. Church schools throughout early Latin America placed teaching of singing (of Gregorian chant and church polyphony) alongside reading and writing as high priorities. The importance of music in celebrating Catholic services was everywhere recognized. Pedro Sanchez de Aguilar, reporting in the early seventeenth century on lingering idolatry in the Yucatán, affirmed the commonplace when he wrote that "It is necessary that the divine offices be celebrated with music and instruments," that is, "with trumpets and cymbals, with the great melody of many voices and organs, flutes, and all types of music, as is proper for so great and venerated a sacrifice. . . ." Hearing such music, he added, ". . . the Indians marvel, are attracted, and are provoked to devotion. . . ."[14]

Second, the friars drew attention time and again to the insidious force of indigenous ceremony. Indeed, by the early seventeenth century a whole literature had sprung up concerned with the problematic persistence of such ceremony.[15] In it singing, drumming, and dancing were often enough named explicitly; more often still they were implicitly present, understood to be the medium of the drunken rites and orgies of the natives. Everywhere in New Spain, it seemed, the Spaniards could rest assured that the old gods were truly dead

---

[14] Pedro Sanchez de Aguilar, *Informe contra idolorum cultores del obispado de Yucatan*, in Jacinto de la Serna, *Tratado de las idolatrias, supersticiones, dioses, ritos, hechicerias y otras costumbres gentilicas de las razas aborigenes de Mexico*, 2 vols., 2nd edn. (Mexico: Ediciones Fuente Cultural, 1953), II, p. 312.

[15] For examples of this literature from Mexico, see Hernando Ruiz de Alarcón, *Treatise on the Heathen Superstitions That Today Live Among the Indians Native to This New Spain, 1629*, trans. J. Richard Andrews and Ross Hassig (Norman: University of Oklahoma Press, 1984), and Serna, *Tratado de las idolatrias*; from Peru, Pablo José de Arriaga, *Extirpación de la idolatría del Pirú*, in *Crónicas peruanas de interés indígena*, ed. Francisco Esteve Barba (Biblioteca de Autores Españoles, vol. 29; Madrid: Atlas, 1968), pp. 191–277.

only when they silenced the voices that invoked them. Conversely, where these voices were raised again (or raised still), the friars' deepest fears and most dogged efforts of cultural extermination were set in motion.

This literature concerning native idolatry arose as a response of missionaries to an earlier, broad evolution in the dynamic of conversion. Across the first decades of colonization and evangelization a similar course of this evolution was played out in different local situations throughout the Spanish colonies. It was linked to the consolidation of relations between colonizers and colonized and in particular to the contrasting, intermingled religious conceptions of these groups: the shifting efforts at conversion by the one, the complex of resistance and adaptation practiced by the other.

On the Spanish side this evolution traced in general outline a course from initial optimism, to confidence that the process of evangelization was taking hold, to, finally, the crushing discovery of native backsliding and persistent idolatry. Fernando Cervantes has recently analyzed the ideological forces behind these shifts. For him the gathering pessimism in the mission of New Spain reflects religious currents imported from a Europe riven by Church schism and doctrinal reevaluation. From the midst of this Reformation turmoil a new conception of the devil emerged. The maleficent devil of the late Middle Ages (signally, for Cervantes, the devil of the *Malleus maleficarum*, the infamous "hammer" of witches first published in 1486) had posed a tractable evil, one that expressed itself in local, unsystematic offenses and was finally impotent in the face of God and Church. The early modern devil that replaced this figure posed a direr threat. He ruled over a kind of counterfeit church, aping in his own rites the ceremonies of God and luring those he duped into a systematic idolatry and apostasy. This was the devil of the late sixteenth-century witches' Sabbath.

Increasingly across the sixteenth century, European observers of New World religious rites came to see in these the counterfeit church of Satan. A paganism that had in the first years of contact seemed a relatively innocent perversion, one that would be quickly eradicated through the sacred power of Christian sacraments, especially mass baptisms and communion, came more and more to seem the entrenched liturgy of the devil. Fray Bartolomé de Las Casas, writing in the 1550s and –60s, found demons and devils aplenty in indigenous American deeds, but explained them as the naturalistic products of a fallen human imagination. José de Acosta, writing a few decades later, saw behind all pagan religion the supernatural threat of an institutionalized, Satanic idolatry.[16]

The role of singing and related envoicings in these developments may appear at first glance to have been a peripheral one, but it was not. Heightened utterance had always resounded at the heart of Christian worship, a fact marked in Spanish evangelization by the importance, noted above, accorded to the teaching of Christian song. In an analogous way, it resounded also in the rites of indigenous Americans. The Spanish observers could

---

[16] Fernando Cervantes, *The Devil in the New World: The Impact of Diabolism in New Spain* (New Haven: Yale University Press, 1994), chap. 1. For an important musicological exploration of some similar issues in early European encounters with Native North Americans, see Olivia Ashley Bloechl, "Sounding Savagery: Native American Song and the Frontiers of Early Modern Music" (PhD dissertation, University of Pennsylvania, 2002), esp. chaps. 3–4.

hardly have ignored or minimized the force of such song, familiar as it was from their own parallel religious experience. As they came increasingly to imagine indigenous ceremony as the diabolical mirror image of their own rites, the powers of its singing grew proportionately. The analogy itself between European and American systems of worship demanded an ever-clearer distinction of good singing (and ceremony) from bad. Ultimately, when ceremonies of song and dance thought to have been eradicated by the force of evangelization were found to be celebrated still in all their native force, the most basic doubts about evangelization arose among the missionaries. The ceremonies of the natives, rediscovered by the Spaniards, led to the crash; Spanish disenchantment in the New World was a product of lingering indigenous enchantment. It grew from a song that could not be silenced.

Bernardino de Sahagún left testimony as eloquent as any to this history as it unfolded in the valley of Mexico. It comes in his excursus in the *Florentine Codex* entitled *Relación del autor digna de ser notada*, which we exploited in chapter 3 for the clues it gives to the performance of the Nahuatl *cantares*.[17] This miniature treatise of 1576 is a cry from the heart of the aged Franciscan, faced with the failure of the college for Indians he had helped to found four decades earlier at Tlatelolco and, worse still, the decline of the Christian mission in general. In a rambling exposition Sahagún attributed this decline to several causes: to the insidious moral effects of the mild Mexican climate (pp. 75, 77), to the repeated plagues that struck down so many (pp. 84–5), and of course to the licentious drunkenness of the natives (p. 75).

Sahagún's diagnosis, however, did not stop at these commonplaces. He went on to assign blame for the failure to the Spaniards themselves. He looked back with admiration to prehispanic Mexica teaching practices in which children were educated in state schools away from their parents, seeing in them the proper antidote to the effects of climate and to natural tendencies toward licentiousness; he faulted the old system only for the pagan idolatry it embraced (p. 77). He told how the early Franciscan initiative to educate the Indians had patterned itself after the the old ways, raising the boys in the Franciscans' own houses. But this regimen, steeped in Christian tenderness, had not enforced the same rigors as the ancient one, so the students began to slide toward lascivious practices and had to be sent back to live with their parents (pp. 77–8). The Christian adaptation of the ancient ways collapsed, and no system of education remained that could steer the natives away from immodesty and idolatry.

Beneath this sincere critique of Spanish methods lay one more level in Sahagún's diagnosis: a deep-rooted sense of betrayal by his Indian charges. The early optimism as to their capabilities in learning all they were taught – "There is no art they do not have the capacity to learn and practice," he proclaimed near the beginning of the *Relación* (p. 74) – had disappeared, displaced over the years not so much by a changed sense of the Indians' abilities as by the imputation to them of an incorrigible deceitfulness.

---

[17] For the passage see Fray Bernardino de Sahagún, *Florentine Codex*, I, pp. 74–85; page references below will be given in the text.

Fear of singing

The Indians, according to Sahagún, had managed to convince the Spaniards that the old idolatry was dead, when in reality it was still practiced. He recounted how, with an aim similar to the first educational arrangements, married couples early on had been settled near the monasteries, so they could attend mass every day – "a very good way to free them from the infection of idolatry and other evil practices which they could contract through association with their parents." This practice lasted only a short time, however, since the young couples convinced the Franciscans "that all idolatry, with all its ceremonies and rituals, was already so forgotten and abhorred that there was no reason to have this caution, since all were baptized and servants of the true God." But in this the monks had been deceived, Sahagún now knew: "And this was very false, as since then we have witnessed very clearly. Not even now do there cease to be many dregs of idolatry and drunkenness and many evil practices. . . . Now it is almost hopeless to correct" (p. 79).

Meanwhile, the boys trained early on in Christian ways had once helped to root out the idolatry of their elders. Eventually they were stymied in their efforts by punishments they received from the other Indians. These at first were sometimes severe – some child informants were even killed by their parents, Sahagún reports. But now they were niggling, insidious, and doubly effective: ". . . they punish evilly, deceitfully, and slyly, keeping after [informants] in their private tasks, and inflicting other vexations on them which the sufferers neither can complain of nor are able to remedy" (p. 81).

It is clear from these examples of Indian duplicity that it was most of all the pagan ceremonies, once thought to have been eradicated, that marked for Sahagún the natives' betrayal. "The idolatrous rituals which were held at night, and the orgies and celebrations which they secretly performed . . . in honor of the idols" had been brought to an end with the help of native informants – or so it had seemed. Then the Spaniards eased their surveillance, "because nothing which was worthy of punishment appeared publicly," and the ceremonies sprang up again (p. 80).

The ceremonies were marked above all by singing and dancing in honor of the old gods, and so they brought these acts to the heart of Sahagún's *Relación*. Song, indeed, is mentioned again and again in this miniature treatise. It plays the dual role we have already described, for there are two modes of singing: one the blazon of the Indians' capacity to adopt European ways, the other the sorry measure of Indian deceit and missionary failure.

Of the first Sahagún wrote frequently. Singing "of plainsong and polyphony" (*de canto llano, de canto de organo*) and with it the playing of instruments figure in the list of disciplines the Indians are capable of mastering that begins the treatise; they come just before high academic pursuits of grammar, logic, rhetoric, astrology, and theology (p. 74). After beginning thus Sahagún called attention to instruction in Christian singing every time he referred to the educational efforts of the Franciscans: "they . . . come of a morning to the schools to learn to read and write and sing"; "there is no one in the schools . . . who correctly teaches reading and writing and singing nor the other musical things"; "there we taught them to read and write and sing"; "after we came to this land to implant the Faith, we assembled the boys in our houses . . . [and] began to teach them to read, write, and sing" (pp. 78–9, 82). The singing of the divine Catholic word, along with the reading and writing of the European alphabet, made up the core of Sahagún's

The Singing of the New World

educational program for the Indians – itself a striking testimony to the powers he heard in such song.

A different kind of singing, however, with powers originating elsewhere, intruded at the impassioned culmination of Sahagún's complaint. Nowadays, he writes, the Indians

> ... sing when they wish and celebrate their feasts as they wish and sing the ancient songs they were wont to sing in the days of their idolatry – not all of them but many of them. And no one understands what they say as their songs are very obscure. And if, after their conversion here, they sing some songs they have composed, which deal with the things of God and His saints, they are surrounded by many errors and heresies. And even in the dances and *areitos* many of their ancient superstitions and idolatrous rituals are practiced, especially where no one resides who understands them. ... This continues; every day it grows worse. (p. 81)

These obscure, suspect *cantares* were diametrically opposed to the Catholic songs taught at the college of Tlatelolco. Their power to undermine Christian values stemmed not merely from the duplicity the Indians manifested in maintaining them but especially from the terrifying entity looming behind them. Sahagún made this diabolical presence amply clear in the brief introduction he provided to the Nahuatl "demons' songs" transcribed (but not translated) elsewhere in the *Florentine Codex*:

> It is a very ancient practice of our adversary, the devil, to seek hiding places in order to perform his works, consistent with the Holy Gospel which says, "He who does evil detests the light." ... our enemy planted, in this land, a forest or a thorny thicket filled with very dense brambles, to perform his works therefrom. ... This forest or brambled thorny thicket is the songs which, in this land, he contrived to be prepared and utilized in his service and for his divine worship – his songs of praise, in the temples as well as beyond them. These songs contain so much guile that they say anything and proclaim that which he commands. ... And they are sung to him without anyone being able to understand what they are about except those who are natives and versed in this language, so that all he desires is sung with impunity – be it of war or peace, of praises to himself, or of scorn of Jesus Christ – without being understood by the rest.[18]

Here the *cantares* occupy a place analogous to Christian plainchant in a liturgy guided by and celebrating the devil; the imputing of institutional diabolism to the Indians described by Cervantes is stimulated in full force by native song.

Singing was thus divided between the two sides of Sahagún's Manichean cosmos. It could not pose itself as a neutral force, but conveyed either the word of God or the blandishments of Satan. No wonder it figured so centrally in Sahagún's gloomy and fearful complaint on the state of Mexico in 1576.[19]

---

[18] Sahagún, *Florentine Codex*, I, p. 58; trans. modified.

[19] Writing also played a dual role in Sahagún's divided cosmos, if one seemingly less threatening than singing. He mentioned writing alongside singing each time he referred to the educational program for the Indians (see above); then, as in the case of singing, he turned to writing of a different sort near the end of the *Relación*: "This people ... communicated with one another by means of representations and paintings. And all their ancient

Fear of singing

The history Sahagún traced in the *Relación* was one of intense optimism – in the Indians' capacities and docile nature, in the Franciscans' effective conversion measures – giving way across several decades in the mid-1500s to equally intense disillusionment. The roles of singing in this history were central ones, both as educational cornerstone and, later, as revelation of diabolism and native backsliding. We have little evidence with which to reconstruct the Indians' side of this history, but it is important to note that Sahagún's version of it was, in all likelihood, as much a product of his fond hopes as a reflection of reality – fond hopes for the early and thorough conversion of the Indians that cast later realizations in that much harsher a light. The history of indigenous worship, viewed from the Indians' side, probably entailed an unbroken practice of their ceremonies, more and more out of view of the Spaniards and involving selective adoption of Christian gestures, rather than any wholesale stoppage and later resurgence of them.[20] The combined history of colonizers and colonized, in this case, would have involved two trajectories: the continuous, gradually shifting performance of ancient rites in the midst of newly imported Christian practices on the part of the Mexica, and the overreaching optimism of the Franciscans at the start of their mission, doomed to selective blindness and final, angry collapse.

This kind of continuous, evolving indigenous perception of the sacred, with its adoption of and adaptation to Christian elements, has been described for the Yucatec Maya by Nancy Farriss. In its midst, she notes, indigenous sung ceremony survived and even thrived: "Pre-Columbian songs and dances were incorporated into the Christian round of fiestas, and the great wooden drum, the *tunkul*, was still being used to accompany the dances, as well as summon people to mass, throughout the colonial period."[21] In the sixteenth century the missionaries adopted a wavering, ambivalent stance toward the native songs and dances. Often enough they praised them for the skill and synchrony they displayed, as when Diego de Landa, writing in the 1560s, described Maya dances that were "very manly and worth seeing."[22] In 1588, meanwhile, an "ancient dance" was performed to applause in front of the visiting Franciscan Commissary:

> customs and books they had about them were painted . . . in such a way that they knew and had records of the things their ancestors had done and had left in their annals. . . . Most of these books and writings were burned when the other idolatrous things were destroyed. But many remained hidden, for we have seen them. And, even now, they are kept; through them we have understood their ancient customs" (p. 82). It is probably revealing of the special force of performed song that Sahagún's reaction to the native books seems so much more dispassionate – so much less caught up in a sense of betrayal – than his reaction to the singing of *cantares*.

[20] For a description of the climate in which these native ceremonies carried on and analysis of the deep differences with Christianity they manifested even as they adapted many of its traits, see Cervantes, *The Devil in the New World*, chap. 2.

[21] Nancy M. Farriss, *Maya Society under Colonial Rule: The Collective Enterprise of Survival* (Princeton: Princeton University Press, 1984), chaps. 10–11; for the quotation, p. 320; the *tunkul* mentioned by Farriss is the equivalent of the Mexica log-drum *teponaztli*.

[22] *Landa's Relación de las cosas de Yucatan*, trans. Alfred M. Tozzer (Cambridge, MA: Peabody Museum, 1941), p. 93; see Fray Diego de Landa, *Relación de las cosas de Yucatan*, ed. Angel María Garibay K. (Mexico: Porrua, 1966), p. 39.

The Singing of the New World

> The Indians brought out to welcome him a strange device and it was: litter-like frames and upon them a tower round and narrow, in the manner of a pulpit, of more then two *varas* in height, covered from top to bottom with pieces of painted cotton, with two flags on top, one on each side. In this pulpit, visible from the waist up, was an Indian very well and nicely dressed, who with rattles of the country in one hand, and with a feather fan in the other, facing the Father Commissary, without ceasing made gestures and whistled to the beat of a *teponaztli* that another Indian near the litter was playing among many who sang to the same sound, making much noise and giving shrill whistles; six Indians carried this litter and tower on their shoulders, and even these also went dancing and singing, doing steps and the same dancing tricks as the others, to the sound of the same *teponaztli* . . .[23]

The darker side of native ceremony was, however, never far from the friars' vigilant minds. The litter-dance performed for the Commissary calls to mind – and may have descended from – a pre-contact dance described by Landa:

> . . . for the celebration of this festival, they made a great arch of wood in the court, filling it on the top and on the sides with firewood, leaving in it doors for going in and out. After this most of the men took bundles of sticks, long and very dry, tied together, and a singer, mounted on the top of the wood, sang and made a noise with one of their drums. All danced below him with great order and devotion, going in and out through the doors of that arch of wood. . . .[24]

But while the Commissary enjoyed the performance of 1588, Landa, stepping back from his earlier praise of other native dances, saw in this one a diabolical rite: It was part of an observance to ward off drought and famine that involved statues of demons made at the behest of Satan (*"Obligábales el demonio, para remedio de estas miserias, [a] hacer cuatro demonios . . ."*). Suspicions like this one concerning native song and dance were voiced early in the Yucatán. Though the mission there did not get under way until the mid-1540s, already by 1552 a judge sent from the *audiencia* of Guatemala was disturbed to find that the native Maya chiefs still preached "their rites and ancient ceremonies" in public gatherings and openly held feasts where "dirty things of their pagan days" were sung to accompany drunken dancing.[25]

This wavering on native performances is typical of missionaries throughout early Latin America. It bespeaks in the first place their pragmatic coming to grips with the ineradicable presence of native song and dance. It also suggests that in optimistic moments they believed that Christian conversion could be achieved in a happy syncretism with native cultural patterns dissociated from their original diabolism. Such moments, however, had their pessimistic counterpart: the gloomy, panicky realization that the connections of native rituals to the devil could never be fully severed.

---

[23] Antonio de Ciudad Real, *Relación de las cosas que sucedieron al R. P. Comisario General Fray Alonso Ponce*, trans. by Inga Clendinnen in *Ambivalent Conquests: Maya and Spaniard in Yucatan, 1517–1570* (Cambridge: Cambridge University Press, 1987), pp. 159–60.

[24] *Landa's Relación*, trans. Tozzer, pp. 148–9; Landa, *Relación*, p. 69.

[25] Quoted in Clendinnen, *Ambivalent Conquests*, pp. 57–8.

Fear of singing

In the midst of the immense and uncertain labors of conversion in the Yucatán, it wanted only the right stimulus to arouse anguished pessimism similar to Sahagún's. This came, more dramatically than in Mexico, in May 1562, when idols and human skulls were discovered in a cave near the village of Mani. For complex reasons – involving power struggles between the friars, secular clergy, and lay settlers; the remoteness of the region from the centers of New Spanish authority, which lent its mission a special sense of frontier vulnerability; and the nature of the relics themselves, redolent of old patterns of human sacrifice – the effect of the discovery was electric. The response of the shocked Franciscans rose immediately to the level of hysteria and revealed through horrific deed the same anger at betrayal found in Sahagún's *Relación*.

The friars, led by Landa, resorted to torture. They rounded up thousands of Indians and coerced confessions of idolatry from them; over 150 died from the interrogation alone, others killed themselves at the approach of the friars rather than face the ordeal, and many more were left maimed and crippled.[26] Some of this testimony related practices that confirmed the Franciscans' worst fears: The surviving documents from several of the villages tell over and over again tales of the sacrifice of children, of their hearts torn still beating from their chests and offered to demonic idols, even of their crucifixion, before the very altars the Christians had built and consecrated, and sacrificial dumping in local *cenotes*.[27] How many of these blood-chilling incidents really occurred remains a matter of debate among historians. Some of them, at least, were probably the product of Franciscan suggestion and Indian eagerness to appease the torturers.[28]

The Yucatec crisis of 1562 had the effect of stiffening the local friars' resistance to native ceremony of all sorts, but it was not explicitly linked, as was Sahagún's complaint, to song. This does not mean, however, that song and the fearsome, heightened utterance of which it is a primary manifestation had no role to play in the testimonies extracted from the natives. Instead its role was an implicit one. Many of the accounts of human sacrifice relate also the invocations to Satan that accompanied the heart-offerings:

> Antonio Pech and Diego Tzotz cut open the children with a knife and pulled out their hearts and gave them to the *ah-kin* [chief] Francisco Uicab. The said *ah-kin* held them up high and burned them and offered them to the idols that were there. And he said to the idols, speaking with them, "Powerful Señor god, we offer you these hearts and we sacrifice to you these children so that you will give health to our governor," speaking of the governor Juan Cocom.[29]

---

[26] See Clendinnen, *Ambivalent Conquests*, chap. 6, for a general account of the crisis; for the Indian deaths and suicides, pp. 75–6.

[27] Much of the documentation concerning the idolatry, including reports of testimony extracted under torture, is gathered in Frances V. Scholes and Eleanor B. Adams, *Don Diego Quijada, Alcalde Mayor de Yucatán, 1561–1565*, 2 vols. (Mexico: Porrua, 1938), I, pp. 24–232; see esp. documents 12 and 13, pp. 71–134.

[28] See Clendinnen, *Ambivalent Conquests*, chaps. 8 and 12; Farriss, *Maya Society*, p. 291.

[29] Scholes and Adams, *Don Diego Quijada*, pp. 76–7; other examples on pp. 88, 101, 115, 123, 127, and 155; for similar invocations not involving human sacrifice see pp. 62–3.

One of the testimonies also records words recited by a chief, officiating at a sacrifice, to a victim about to die. "Strengthen yourself and console yourself," he is reported to have pronounced, "for we are doing you no evil; neither are we sending you to a bad place or to hell, but instead to the heavens and to glory in the customary way of our ancestors." Inga Clendinnen has heard in these words the echoes of an outright song preserved elsewhere; it perhaps recalls in turn words sung in pre-contact days to captive warriors about to be sacrificed.[30]

If these roles of heightened utterance do not add up to the centrality Sahagún accorded *cantares* in his complaint about native idolatry, the testimonies of 1562 nevertheless focused the Yucatec friars' attention with new clarity on native rites that habitually involved singing, invocation, dancing, drumming, and drinking. It attuned them to their own fears of ritual song and its corollaries so that, after this watershed year, their watchfulness was redoubled, their Sahaguntine pessimism provoked. Singing as such was no doubt not their main concern as they hung up and whipped another native to wrest from him unsettling confessions. But they knew that the heart of darkness they discovered in his words, so unimaginably different (as they thought) from their own behavior, was entered into as effectively as any other way through special uses of voice.

The very decade of the 1560s that marked the collapse of the friars' confidence in the Yucatán saw, in the Viceroyalty of Peru, another crisis linked to indigenous ceremony and song. In Huamanga in the central Andes west of Cuzco, in 1564 or 1565, a native movement was discovered that the clerical authorities would come to conceive as a full-fledged, millenarian revival of indigenous ceremony bent on destroying the Spaniards and their religion and restoring the old Inca ways. It traveled under the Quechua name *taki onqoy*, song-dance sickness; sometimes it was referred to also as *ayra*, a word whose meaning remains unclear but which probably likewise referred to singing and dancing.[31]

The most comprehensive account we have of the *taki onqoy* comes from a text we met in chapter 5, Cristóbal de Molina's *Relación de las fábulas y ritos de los Incas*, written a few years after the events in 1574 or 1575. Molina reported the testimony of Luis de Olvera (or Olivera), a *padre* who, while serving in the parish of Parinacochas, was among the first Spaniards to discover the sect. Molina left no doubt that the movement aimed to revive the sacred *huacas* of olden times and destroy the Spaniards in the bargain. The Indians

---

[30] For the speech to the victim, Scholes and Adams, *Don Diego Quijada*, p. 106. The whole passage is translated in Clendinnen, *Ambivalent Conquests*, pp. 195–200; on its similarities with the pre-contact song see pp. 176–7; and for the words of the song itself, Alfredo Barrera Vázquez, *El libro de los cantares de Dzitbalché* (Mexico: Instituto Nacional de Antropología e Historia, 1965), p. 26.

[31] For various interpretations of *ayra* see Ranulfo Cavero, *Los dioses vencidos: Una lectura antropológica del Taki Onqoy* (Ayacucho, Peru: Universidad Nacional de San Cristóbal de Huamanga, 2001), pp. 196–7, 199, 205; one of the most plausible connections of the word is to the *ayrihua*, a harvest song and dance mentioned by Pablo José de Arriaga in his *Extirpación de la idolatría del Pirú*, pp. 191–277; see p. 213.

believed that all the *huacas* of the realm, all those that the Christians had torn down and burned, were resurrected, and that they had formed two sides, the first joined with the *huaca* of Pachacamac, the other with the *huaca* Titicaca. [They believed] that all the *huacas* flew through the air, commanding [the Indians] to do battle against God and defeat him, [saying] that already his defeat was near; and that when the Marqués [Pizarro] entered this land, God had defeated the *huacas* and the Spaniards the Indians, but that now the world was overturning; and that God and the Spaniards would be left defeated this time, and all the Spaniards killed, and their cities flooded; and that the sea would rise and drown them so that no memory of them remained.[32]

The division of the revived *huacas* into two camps, allied to the major Andean sacred sites of Pachacamac (on the coast northwest of Cuzco) and the Island of the Sun in Lake Titicaca (to the southeast of Cuzco), conjures up the image of dual centers of sacred force arrayed on opposite sides of the primary area of diffusion of the *taki onqoy*, the area around Huamanga to the west and southwest of Cuzco. The detail lends an indigenous authenticity to Molina's report, since it seems to reflect the moiety organization that characterized not merely Inca rites and social organization but central Andean societies in general.[33]

We may be less confident, on the other hand, about another suggestion offered by Molina: that the whole movement was fostered by the Inca Titu Cusi, hidden still in the forests of Vilcabamba. "No one was able to find out who had begun this business," the *Relación* states, "but it was suspected and charged that it was invented by the sorcerers that the Incas had at Vilcabamba" (p. 78). Scholars have in recent years tended to agree that, whatever the *taki onqoy* was, it originated as a local manifestation of pan-Andean religious rites rather than as a conspiracy organized from on high by the exiled Inca.[34]

According to Olvera and Molina, various practices marked the *taki onqoy*. Its preachers spread through the villages and countryside, proclaiming the return of the *huacas* and the need for the Indians to give them sustenance. While they fed the *huacas* with traditional celebrations and offerings, the Indians themselves had to turn away from all Spanish practices, avoiding the houses of the colonizers and even renouncing their Christian names. They needed also to abstain from sex and to fast, eating no salt, chilis, or corn – both practices recalling pre-contact purification rites.

One other development, however, was not anticipated in the ancient patterns: The *huacas*, the preachers said, ". . . no longer put themselves in the rocks and clouds and streams,

---

[32] Cristóbal de Molina, *Fábulas y ritos de los Incas*, in *Las crónicas de los Molinas*, ed. Francisco A. Loayza (Lima: Domingo Miranda, 1943), second pagination, pp. 5–84; see esp. pp. 78–84; for this quotation, pp. 79–80; further references in the text.

[33] On these moieties see chap. 5 above, pp. 136–9; on the division of the *taki onqoy huacas* into two camps as a reflection of such moieties, Cavero, *Los dioses vencidos*, p. 180, and the literature cited there.

[34] See Rafael Varón Gabai, "Las raíces andinas de un fenómeno colonial," in *El retorno de las huacas: Estudios y documentos sobre el Taki Onqoy, siglo XVI*, ed. Luis Millones (Lima: Instituto de Estudios Peruanos, 1990), pp. 331–405; also Steve J. Stern, *Peru's Indian Peoples and the Challenge of Spanish Conquest: Huamanga to 1640* (Madison: University of Wisconsin Press, 1982), chap. 3. A decade after Molina one other writer, Cristóbal de Albornoz (on whom see below), also mooted the connection between the *taki onqoy* and Vilcabamba; see Cavero, *Los dioses vencidos*, p. 55.

but instead incorporated themselves now in the Indians and made them speak."³⁵ The movement as a whole seems to have been, in other words, a possession cult, and the actions of its devotees involved sorts of behavior typical of possessed individuals the world over:

> And thus it was that many Indians trembled and rolled around on the ground; others shouted taunts [*tiraban de pedradas*: hollered obscenities?] as if possessed by demons [*como endemoniados*], grimacing, and then fell silent. If they fearfully approached such a one and asked him what he had and what he felt, he responded that such-and-such a *huaca* had entered his body. Then they took him in their arms and carried him to a designated place where they made him a room with straw and blankets. Then they painted [his face] red, and the Indians entered to worship him. . . . (pp. 80–1)

This burgeoning of ritualized spirit possession seems to place the *taki onqoy* among those sects I. M. Lewis has called "peripheral" possession cults, "thinly disguised protest movements" that arise in the midst of some more dominant religious authority and empower in some measure their practitioners. Certainly the desperate situation in the 1560s of the Indians in the area of Huamanga – they were increasingly victims of famine, disease, and the *encomenderos* who demanded ever larger commitments of labor and payments from them – rendered them ripe for such a development.³⁶

At the same time, the *taki onqoy* answered to indigenous patterns that reached far beyond a local reaction to the hardship of the 1560s. In Cuzco and its environs, the Spaniards encountered a complex world of religious syncretisms involving three strands: the state religion of the Incas; local religious rites that pre-dated and coexisted with Inca institutions; and the pan-Andean worship of a few major sacred sites and their *huacas*. In all likelihood the *taki onqoy* had little direct connection with the state rites persisting at Vilcabamba; nevertheless it seems to have reflected patterns of some of the most important Inca celebrations, in particular the purification rite of Citua. To these patterns it added a rich mixture of local rites influenced in some measure, if only a reactionary one, by Christian importations and emphasizing, as revival movements in stressful periods often do, spirit possession. All this it combined with the larger, pan-Andean reliance on the *huacas* of Titicaca and Pachacamac.³⁷

The village fortunate enough to have a man possessed by a *huaca* in its midst "held fiestas for two or three days, dancing and drinking and staying up at night without sleep and invoking the *huaca* that he represented and said was in his body" (p. 81). Molina presented these festivals as after-the-fact celebrations of possession already achieved, although modern interpreters have also seen them, in line with other, better-documented possession

---

[35] Molina, *Fábulas*, p. 80. Huacas lodged in rocks and streams are characteristic of Andean sacred practices, but *huacas* in clouds are not; Molina's *nubes* is probably a mistake either in his recounting of Olvera's information or in the transmission of the *Relación*. Olvera's own later testimony about the *taki onqoy* (see below) uses almost exactly the same wording but substitutes the more appropriate *árboles* (trees) for *nubes*. See *El retorno de las huacas*, ed. Millones, p. 178.

[36] I. M. Lewis, *Ecstatic Religion: A Study of Shamanism and Spirit Possession*, 2nd edn. (London: Routledge, 1989), p. 27. For the situation of the Indians in these years, see Varon, "El Taki Onqoy," pp. 380–405; for the 1560s as a particularly troubled time, Cavero, *Los dioses vencidos*, p. 134, and esp. Stern, *Peru's Indian Peoples*, chaps. 2–3.

[37] See Cavero, *Los dioses vencidos*, pp. 36, 168, 191, 195ff.; Stern, *Peru's Indian Peoples*, chap. 3.

Fear of singing

rituals, as trance-inducing exertions.[38] In either case, these festivals brought communal singing and dancing to the heart of the *taki onqoy*. They probably were the chief reason that Molina, in introducing Olvera's account, called the whole movement "a kind of song" (*una manera de canto, el cual llamaban taquihongoy;* p. 78). Or perhaps he responded simply to the name *taki onqoy*, since *taki* was the primary Quechua word used in Inca times to denote singing, or even to the oracular pronouncements of the possessed *taki onqocs*. Whatever his reason, the remainder of the account in the *Relación* gives few hints as to the nature of this singing. Do we hear it dimly in the ritual that the *huaca*, speaking through its human medium, instructed its devotees to perform?

> Those possessed people demanded in the villages that, if someone had any remains of the burned *huacas* or some piece of stone from them, he should cover his head with a blanket in front of the village, and pour *chicha* on the stone and rub it with white maize flour, and then raise his voice, invoking the *huaca*, and lift himself up, with the stone in his hand, saying to the village: "You see here your refuge, and you see here what it can do for you, giving you health, and children, and fertile fields; put it in its place, where it was in the time of the Inca." And thus the sorcerers did, with many sacrifices.... (p. 82)

Here, as in the Yucatán, we find ourselves in the presence at least of a powerful invocation.

Aside from Molina's *Relación*, the chief sources giving extensive information about the *taki onqoy* are three *informaciones de servicios* concerning Cristóbal de Albornoz, recorded in 1570, 1577, and 1584. Albornoz had arrived in Cuzco in 1567. In his first years there, he had traveled to the parishes south and west of the city and taken an aggressive lead in the extirpation of the *taki onqoy* idolatry, uncovering and destroying hundreds of *huacas*. The *informaciones* later collected were, in effect, job recommendations – series of testimonials from influential Spaniards gathered at the instigation of Albornoz himself in hope of career advancement. They extolled his services to Church and crown and were devised to be presented as formal testimony to the Council of the Indies.[39]

As witnesses to the *taki onqoy*, the *informaciones* are valuable chiefly in view of the scarcity of other accounts. (Admittedly they are valuable also because some of the testimony in them seems well informed: Molina and Olvera themselves appear among the witnesses.) In general, however, as sources on Indian practices they are more dubious and compromised than most Spanish writings. In the first place, their aim was not so much to report the doings of the natives as to praise those of Albornoz. Moreover, they took the form of interrogations in which each testifier answered the same series of questions, with the result that the testimony often did little more than echo the wording of the question asked.

What makes the *informaciones* most suspect as accounts of native practices is, however, something else: They trace, across the fourteen years of their production, an evolution of thinking about the *taki onqoy* that seems to have little to do with observation of indigenous

---

[38] For discussion of possession songs and dances, see Cavero, *Los dioses vencidos*, pp. 182–6, 203–7.

[39] The *informaciones* collected by Cristóbal de Albornoz and related documents are gathered in *El retorno de las huacas*, ed. Millones, pp. 41–308; further page references will be given in the text. For the date of Albornoz's arrival in Cuzco see Pedro M. Guibovich Pérez's introduction to *El retorno*, "Nota preliminar al personaje histórico y los documentos," pp. 24–5.

practices on the ground outside Cuzco. This evolution instead seems to capture the growth of the Spaniards' own ideas about the movement, and thus it plots a course through a sacred imaginary more Spanish than Andean.[40] Along the way it reveals a crystalizing of the Europeans' fear of indigenous song around certain specific issues.

The testimony in the first *información* of 1570, recorded close to the heart of *taki onqoy* country in Huamanga, depicted the movement, with relative simplicity, as an apostasy in which converted natives denied God and his sacraments (especially confession), turned away from his churches, and revived the old *huacas* and the ceremonies in their honor. It named some of the major *huacas* allied to the revival – Titicaca, Tiahuanuco, Pachacamac, Tambutoco, and a few others – and mentioned the belief that these had defeated the Christian god (pp. 64, 93). But there was no explicit (and scant implicit) sense in this testimony that the movement aimed to destroy all things Spanish or kill the Spaniards.

Only a few of the witnesses in this *información* departed from the wording offered in the question itself about the *taki onqoy*. One who did was Gerónimo Martín, a priest in one of the outlying *repartimientos* and an expert in native language and affairs. He described the consequences the preachers foretold for those who did not worship the *huacas*: "... if they didn't adore the said *huacas* and do the said ceremonies and sacrifices preached to them, they would die, they would go about with their heads on the ground and feet in the air, others would turn into *guanacos*, deer, *vicuñas*, and other animals, and they would lapse into idiocy..." (p. 130). Another priest, Pedro Barriga Corro of Huamanga, introduced the name of one of the chief preachers of the sect, Juan Chono, reported bits of the speeches of the preachers, and affirmed that they spoke in their houses to the *huacas* and that "the *huacas* responded to them" (p. 147) in the fashion of oracles. All this seems to stay close to the kind of practices of indigenous worship we might expect to have lingered on throughout the Andes, especially in areas far from the newly established or ever more hispanized cities. All this, moreover, reflects a Spanish reaction to such practices that is relatively temperate: another patch where the work of evangelization had not fully penetrated, another episode of native backsliding to be chastised.

In the second *información*, recorded seven years later at Cuzco, the *taki onqoy* took on a different, more threatening profile. Here it resembled in most particulars the movement described in Molina's *Relación* – not surprisingly, since the most informative of the witnesses was Molina's source himself, Luis de Olvera. In contrast to the *taki onqoy* of the first *información*, now the movement came to seem murderous to the Spaniards. (There is, however, no mention of plots emanating from Vilcabamba.) Now also, recalling the *Relación* but not the first *información*, the *taki onqoy* displayed the trappings of a possession cult. In wording similar at numerous points to his account that Molina had reproduced, Olvera told how the *huacas* invaded the bodies of the Indians, how those Indians trembled as they were

---

[40] Cavero, *Los dioses vencidos*, p. 24, has noted this shifting emphasis: "Las distintas *Informaciones*, conforme va pasando el tiempo, se presentan más contaminadas con la percepción occidental y judeo cristiana." On the general topic of Spanish interpretations of the Andean sacred imaginary in the sixteenth century see Sabine MacCormack, *Religion in the Andes: Vision and Imagination in Early Colonial Peru* (Princeton: Princeton University Press, 1991); for the *taki onqoy* in particular see pp. 181–6.

Fear of singing

possessed and spoke with the voice of the *huaca*, how their faces were painted, and how they were placed in closed spaces where they were worshiped (p. 178). Most of this account of Olvera was echoed, almost verbatim, later on by another witness, Cristóbal Ximénez (p. 191). Molina himself also testified, and for his part added to the details found in his *Relación*. He related now that the principal preachers of the apostasy were two men and a woman. They told the Indians, he added – fleshing out the mention in the *Relación* of *huacas* that flew through the air – "that it was not God who gave them food, but one who flew through the air in a kind of basket" (p. 181).

As it had in Molina's *Relación* two or three years earlier, the *taki onqoy* reflected here, ten years after the events, practices feared in Europe, especially the devil's possession of unwary souls – remember the phrase *como endemoniados* from the *Relación* – and the nocturnal flights of witches. The two nearly contemporary and closely related documents mark the second stage in a process that seems to constrain ever more narrowly Andean practices within a European metaphysical imaginary. This is a process we witnessed, in a separate case, in chapter 2: The differences between the first and second *informaciones* reproduce almost precisely the shift in Jean de Léry's discussion of Tupinamba ritual in his *Histoire*, from a lay vocabulary of fearful wonderment in the first edition to the technical apparatus of Jean Bodin's demonology in later ones.

The third and final stage in this describing of the *taki onqoy* was reached in the last *información*, dictated in 1584, two full decades after the discovery of the movement. One new detail redolent again of European witchcraft emerged in these relatively short testimonies. Molina testified once more, naming among the leading preachers of the sect the same Juan Chono mentioned already in the first *información* (Molina called him Joan Chocne or Chocna). Molina added that Chono had told his Indian followers that he was accompanied by an invisible familiar: ". . . Don Joan Chocna said that he brought with him someone they could not see, who told him these things [he said], and that this one gave them their food and sustenance . . ." (p. 225).

But the major change in the portrayal of the *taki onqoy* came in the phrasing of the question about it. This offered wording, repeated in the answers of several of the witnesses, that cast the movement in a new, dimmer light:

> Item: whether they know that the said canon Cristóbal de Albornoz was the first who brought to light . . . the sect and apostasy called Taqui Ongo, in which the Indians, already baptized, gave themselves over to dancing and shaking, going round and round; and in that dance they invoked the devil [*ynbocaban al demonio*] and his *huacas* and idols, and in the dance they rejected and abjured the true faith of Jesus Christ and of all the teachings they had received from the Christians and priests that had come into this realm. . . . (p. 205)

From a grassroots revival of *huacas*, to a demonic possession ritual, and finally to an orgiastic, Satanic rite: Across the fourteen years of the *informaciones*, the questioners and witnesses transformed the *taki onqoy* into the round dance and chant of the witches' Sabbath, conjuring the dark lord himself. Just as in Mexico and the Yucatán, native ceremony in the

Andes assumed a more and more explicit diabolical form in the perfervid imaginations of Spaniards wearied by the rigors and setbacks of evangelization.

In this the *taki onqoy* took its place as an Andean variant of the larger evolution we have traced in Spanish views on native song, dance, and ceremony. The Peruvian historian Juan Carlos Estenssoro Fuchs has discerned in the 1560s and 1570s the emergence of a new, uncompromising stance in the Andes toward indigenous ceremony and its *takis*. During the first decades of evangelization, optimistic, assimilationist models had prevailed. The Spaniards looked on as native ceremonies were incorporated in Catholic services; festive dance-songs called *hayllis* were sung in the cathedral of Cuzco, and Inti Raimi ceremonies were transplanted into Corpus Christi processions. By the 1560s, however, views were strenuously divided. Some, especially among the Dominicans, continued to maintain that the answer to the problem of indigenous ceremony was to assimilate it to Christian practices while separating it absolutely from its original, diabolical associations; others, including the investigator of Andean religion Juan Polo de Ondegardo, urged a general extirpation. The arrival of Francisco de Toledo as the new Viceroy of Peru in late 1569, followed by the founding of a tribunal of the Inquisition in Lima in 1571, helped tilt the balance toward harsher measures. At the Third Ecclesiastical Council of Lima of 1583, native celebrations in general were prohibited.[41]

It would be convenient to see this shift as a reaction to the alarm brought about by the discovery of the *taki onqoy*. But the change of views on this movement evident across the three *informaciones* of Albornoz and the fact that these documents span the very years from Toledo's arrival to the Third Council suggest that this is too easy an explanation. In place of its one-way causality, the evidence we have calls for a model of mutual evolution, in which the *taki onqoy* aroused new suspicions regarding native ceremony at the same time as it was transformed – produced, we might even say, in the form in which the scant documentation brings it to us – by a more and more pessimistic and fearful Spanish imagining of indigenous deed. What began in all probability as a local, peripheral possession cult, in the midst of indigenous hardship and native *huaca* worship that had never lapsed, evolved into a diabolical Sabbath. But the evolution seems to have taken place above all in the anxious minds of Spanish observers.

A new form of fear

The chronological coincidence of these three outbursts of Indian nativism and Spanish suspicion concerning it – in the valley of Mexico, the Yucatán, and the Andes – is almost exact: All three reflect experiences of the 1560s and 1570s. Together they reveal, at least, the widespread undermining of the missionaries' earlier confidence in the steady and

---

[41] Juan Carlos Estenssoro Fuchs, "Los bailes de los indios y el proyecto colonial," *Revista andina* 10 (1992), pp. 353–89; esp. pp. 360–7. For Estenssoro's further discussion of this topic in an excellent general analysis of evangelization in Peru, see Juan Carlos Estenssoro Fuchs, *Del paganismo a la santidad: La incorporación de los Indios del Perú al catolicismo, 1532–1750*, trans. Gabriela Ramos (Lima: Instituto Francés de Estudios Americanos, 2003), chap. 2.

unperturbed progress of evangelization of the Indians. At most, as I have suggested, their coincidence betokens a more general shift of the colonizers' and Indians' perceptions at this moment.[42]

On the part of the Indians, this shift probably had to do with a dawning awareness that the foreigners in their midst represented not a transient tremor but a permanent, seismic alteration of their cultural landscape. Undoubtedly, for both Indians and Europeans, the shift involved a deepening appreciation of the differences separating the two groups. In the fear the Spanish friars felt at the witnessing or even the mere reports of indigenous song and ceremony we sense recognition of the yawning gap that lay open between them and the Indians. In their moves to comprehend this song and ceremony within familiar structures of the European sacred imaginary we see their aggressive effort to close the gap.

European colonizers would repeat this dual move, recognizing and disavowing difference, in countless meetings with others over the next several centuries. In *Orientalism* Edward Said discerned something similar as a common thread in European encounters in Asia:

> What gives the immense number of encounters some unity . . . is . . . vacillation. . . . Something patently foreign and distant acquires . . . a status more rather than less familiar. One tends to stop judging things either as completely novel or as completely well-known; a new median category emerges, a category that allows one to see new things . . . as versions of a previously known thing. In essence such a category is not so much a way of receiving new information as it is a method of controlling what seems to be a threat to some established view of things.

Homi Bhabha has taken Said's median category as the jumping-off point for an analysis of racial and sexual stereotypes in colonial societies. These, he argues, amount to something more complex than mere vicious misrepresentations promulgated by the colonizers. They exemplify a systematic pattern of ambivalence characteristic of colonial discourse in which a confronting of difference is countered by its masking and psychic accommodation. From this flux, this recognition and disavowal of difference, arise, in colonizers and colonized alike, kinds of subjectivization specific to colonial societies.

This subject-forming flux is not unrelated, for Bhabha, to the most basic interplay of self and other in which psyches take shape. He considers this from both Freudian and Lacanian perspectives, that is, as a function of early sexual differentiation reflected later in the fetish and of the mirror stage, the initial step of the self toward recognition of its identity and distinction from others. At this time the subject coalesces as a product of both alienation and identification: the child's recognition of sexual difference and fetishistic denial of it, the child's simultaneous separation from and desire for its image in the mirror.

---

[42] The synchrony extends beyond Spanish to Portuguese America. In the Bahia region of Brazil the 1560s witnessed the rise of another messianic, nativist movement, which came to be called *Santidade*. Like the *taki onqoy* this movement prophesied an end to European rule and a deliverance of the Indians from disease and hardship. It involved rites, modeled in some features after Christian ceremony, in which "the priests and congregation . . . intoned their prayers in a language nobody understood." See John Hemming, *Red Gold: The Conquest of the Brazilian Indians, 1500–1760* (Cambridge: Harvard University Press, 1978), pp. 143, 156–8.

The stereotypes in colonial discourse incorporate a related tacking between aggression and pleasure, derision and desire, separation and narcissistic merger. They construct colonized and colonizer in relation to one another as at once radically other and wholly familiar (again, Said's median category), since they gesture toward difference but absorb it in the reactivation of a primal scene of wholeness and sameness.[43]

The two terms in this intersubjective relation – the sheer other and the utopic, undivided self – fix the poles of an incalculable, fearful difference and a desirous assimilation of it. These polar oppositions are however not distinct, dissociated subject positions. Instead they are bound together in the stereotype, hindering the more fluid interactions of differing subject positions of non-colonial societies. The stereotype remains unstable because the dynamic of difference and its effacement is continually disturbed by renewed assertions of difference. The play of different identities in colonial situations is in this way an exaggerated version of identity interactions in less confrontational circumstances.[44]

This theoretical model seems to capture, in general terms at least, the stage of colonial discourse reached in New Spain and Peru by the 1560s. The revivals of indigenous ceremony and song perceived by the Spaniards in Mexico, the Yucatán, and the Andes were probably not organized uprisings at all, and perhaps not even revivals, but rather persistent local practices adapted and answering to the worsening hardship of Indian life in these decades. The Spaniards were brought to perceive them as murderous conspiracies and devil worship because of the collapse of the utopic visions of evangelization they had earlier entertained, a collapse needing only small shifts in native practices for its onset and registered in the disenchantment, sense of betrayal, and anger of the missionaries. (This perspective is not exclusive of other views, but rather coextensive with them: If the Spaniards' panicky reactions and harsh reprisals reflect the emergence of the new view of native diabolism that Cervantes has analyzed, they are also commensurate with the dissipation of a desired, illusory psychic ideal.)

The collapse of Spanish confidence seems to have been new in its day. There is little trace, at any rate, of such widely dispersed and institutionalized fears in earlier decades of New World evangelization. They represent a crisis of the Christian mission in Spanish America about 1570 that seems to have entertained, for the first time, the prospect that the Indians might never be saved through conversion. The dawning of this possibility helps to explain the pessimism – despair, even – that spread through the mission in these years.

In giving palpable form to this new fear, the crisis assumes a broad, even epochal significance in the history of European colonialism. The idea of the failure of conversion must have challenged the friars' most basic presumptions concerning time and history. Johannes Fabian has described the sense of history involved in Europe's early modern global expansion as an incorporative, Christian temporal order that held out a future of salvation for all peoples – *eschatological time,* as we might call it, recognizing its teleological orientation

---

[43] Homi K. Bhabha, "The Other Question: Stereotype, Discrimination, and the Discourse of Colonialism," in *The Location of Culture* (London: Routledge, 1994), pp. 66–84; see esp. pp. 73–84 and, for Said, p. 73.

[44] Colonial identities, Bhabha writes, are "played out – like all fantasies of originality and origination – in the face and space of the disruption and threat from the heterogeneity of other positions." Ibid., p. 77.

toward an ultimate salvation. In Fabian's view this conception of time gradually ceded ground before the advance of a new, secular order. Secular time arrayed human history along a graded, evolutionary scale, effectively fragmenting it, since contemporary peoples could be located with ostensive scientific neutrality at different, disconnected points along it. "Primitives" in a world increasingly controlled by Europeans came to be seen to be playing out their own, separate evolutions rather than awaiting, within a single temporal fold, the saving grace Europe brought. As Fabian put it, the "pagan . . . always *already* marked for salvation" gave way to the "savage . . . *not yet* ready for civilization."[45]

Fabian located the advent of the new temporality in a generalized "Enlightenment thought," and undoubtedly the eighteenth century of Vico, Rousseau, and the rest is the moment of its first culmination. (Vico's model of independent providential histories for all societies provides an especially clear instance of the new temporal order conceived within an overarching Christianity.[46]) The true nascence of the new order, however, can be discerned two centuries earlier, in the late sixteenth-century crisis of evangelization marked throughout the Spanish colonies. What was left in the wake of this disillusionment was certainly not a full-blown secular temporality; neither, of course, did it involve a wholesale decline of Christian tenets or any retreat of Christian missionaries. What was left instead was a new set of uncompromising imperatives guiding the mission, including new strictures aimed at indigenous expressive cultures. Left also was something less tractable but of far-reaching consequence: a tension between Europe's evangelizing efforts and a growing, unsettling awareness that irredeemable cultural difference might exist in the world. This was the impact on European mentalities, no doubt unsettling at deep levels, of the first decades of colonization.

At this time the fear of singing entered a new phase. Singing, chanting, and other raisings of the voice, along with their corollaries, dance and music-making, had a large role to play in opening out the new prospect of incorrigible difference. The heightened voices of the Indians were time and again heard by the Spaniards as a primary symptom of a dangerous, unassuageable otherness – heard, as I suggested above, as a locus of foreign metaphysical powers. Their special significance was redoubled by the extraordinary movements of Indian bodies, whether in organized, ritual dance or in the uncontrolled trembling of the possessed, and by the prosthetic extension of voice through the use of drums, trumpets, and other musical instruments.

Here the colonial dynamic of difference explored by Bhabha converges on the metaphysics of voice. Raised voices broach, in all societies and in ways recognizable across gaping cultural divides, an order of meaning distinct from that of normal speech. Singing, chanting, invocation, and so forth come to signify in part through their surplus over speech.

---

[45] Johannes Fabian, *Time and the Other: How Anthropology Makes Its Object* (New York: Columbia University Press, 1983), pp. 26–7.

[46] For this model, the important role of singing in it, and its eighteenth-century application to Mexican society see Gary Tomlinson, "Vico's Songs: Detours at the Origins of (Ethno)Musicology," *The Musical Quarterly* 83 (1999), pp. 344–77.

Their effects cannot be pinned down and plotted through the signifying modes of the language they exceed, and this helps to explain why song traditions the world over exploit the non-lexical words (or vocables) I dwelled on in chapters 3 and 5. In song, language itself is twisted by a torque of surplus vocalization away from its modes of meaning in speech.

Because of this generalized, non-speech significance, heightened vocalization conveys much of its meaning in the manner of a binary code, yielding only two possibilities: comforting, communal sameness or discomfiting otherness. In the confrontation of divergent identities characteristic of colonial society, then, discomfiture grows into threat. Amid perceptions of ungraspable difference of the kind that nurture the colonial stereotype, the always audible gap between speech and raised voice widens, the mysteries of surplus signification are deepened, and the fear of singing burgeons.

There is this difference, however, between song and stereotype: The stereotype is a symptom of the psychic mechanism that moves to control threatening difference, and in this it shows a kinship to all the measures the friars took across the late sixteenth century to manage and limit Indian ceremony. Heightened voice, instead, is itself productive of the threat, inscrutable but bound to be heard and understood too well.

This difference signals once more the special place of ritual utterance and its many appurtenances in contact scenes and colonial societies. We may clarify it by comparison with another of the constitutive elements of Bhabha's colonial discourse. For him part of the apparatus producing colonial subjects is the colonizers' surveillance, which exercises a "scopic" power over the colonized. This gaze effectively objectifies the colonial subject, at the same time offering an image in which is affirmed the wholeness of the viewer's identity; from this dynamic comes its power. But this specular construction of identity is, like the stereotype, easily undone. It depends on the colonized subject's consent in not gazing back. The gazing subject recognizes itself in a condition of continual risk that the objectified other might turn the tables. As long as the gaze is not returned, the colonizer's surveillance approaches the empowered condition of voyeurism.[47]

Listening to others sing does not hold out the promise of the control and empowerment of voyeurism; instead it offers the ambivalences of eavesdropping. Eavesdropping has in certain recent accounts been regarded as a kind of auditory voyeurism and thus assimilated to Lacanian theories of the gaze and its powers.[48] This can obscure important differences between the two phenomena. In eavesdropping there is no possibility of the unchallenging

---

[47] See Bhabha, "The Other Question," pp. 76–7. This Lacan-derived theory of the gaze, first brought into general cultural theory especially in film studies, has been extended to music by a number of scholars, with compelling results in the area of feminist and gender studies. See especially two writings by Lawrence Kramer: *Music as Cultural Practice, 1800–1900* (Berkeley: University of California Press, 1990), chap. 4 and esp. pp. 111–12; and "Culture and Musical Hermeneutics: The Salome Complex," *Cambridge Opera Journal* 2 (1990), pp. 269–94, esp. pp. 272–3.

[48] This is one implication of Kaja Silverman's consideration of the female voice in cinema; see *The Acoustic Mirror: The Female Voice in Psychoanalysis and Cinema* (Bloomington: Indiana University Press, 1988), pp. 55–63. For an adaptation of these views to musicological ends, Rose Theresa, "Spectacle and Enchantment: Envisioning Opera in Late Nineteenth-Century Paris" (PhD dissertation, University of Pennsylvania, 2000), esp. pp. 235ff. and 389ff.

Fear of singing

passivity on which the voyeur's power depends. The overheard necessarily assumes the form of a sonic intrusion from elsewhere. The confrontation that is possible in the returned gaze of the scopic dynamic here becomes inevitable. Where the gaze might operate to reassure and empower the viewer with illusory self-integration – with the narcissistic sense of undivided self and world without difference – the listener instead is always faced by an othering utterance. The eavesdropper, it is said, never hears good of himself. What is unsaid is that he *cannot* do so, if hearing good means attaining the comfort of a psychodynamic wholeness. Such solace, transiently proffered by the eye, is always out of earshot.

The colonial aural dynamic might then be conceived in relation to the Lacanian "object voice" described by Mladen Dolar, a voice at once bearing plenitude of self-presence and the unassuageable otherness of the Real. For Dolar the musical voice poses this ambivalence in acute form, though at the same time he works to retain a force domesticating the voice's otherness in the "aesthetic pleasure" music gives. By broadening his category beyond music to all heightened vocalization we come close to the otherness ever inhabiting voice – and to the special fears it has provoked in confrontational situations of encounter, conquest, and colonization.[49]

These fears, to turn the matter around, are nothing but a focusing of the peculiar force that voice exerts above and beyond its capacity to carry specific linguistic meaning. Gilles Deleuze and Felix Guattari, in their ontology highlighting instability and transformation rather than being and identity, recognize this special force. The name they give to transformation – of human subjects also – is deterritorialization; and among human acts music and the voice from which it springs are second to none in their power to deterritorialize. "Perhaps," they add, "this trait explains the collective fascination exerted by music, and even the potentiality of [its] 'fascist' danger . . . : music (drums, trumpets) draws people and armies into a race that can go all the way to the abyss (much more so than banners and flags, which are paintings . . .)."[50]

We have found our way back to the psychic violence of music – to Tamasese, the tribal chief on display in Adorno's recollected zoo, frightened by the rumble of the timpani from the distant orchestral pavilion. Perhaps, indeed, the back-and-forth convolutions we noted in Adorno's narrative are inescapable, reflecting the ambivalent dynamic of overheard sounds that cannot but undo the comfort of an empowered, stable self.

All the scenes that began this chapter, when they do not describe outright sonic aggression, are instances of terrifying eavesdropping; think of Cortés and Díaz listening in on Mexica ritual, or Owen Griffin left among the Abenaki, or the Trinidadians hearing the music from Columbus's ship. Likewise, Spanish alarms at Indian apostasy in central Mexico, the Yucatán, and the Andes all were set off by the overhearing – direct or imagined,

---

[49] See Mladen Dolar, "The Object Voice," in *Gaze and Voice as Love Objects*, ed. Renata Salecl and Slavoj Žižek (Durham, NC: Duke University Press, 1996), pp. 7–31; p. 14: "There is, . . . inside the narcissistic and autoaffective dimension of the voice, something that threatens to disrupt it – the voice that affects one at the most intimate level, but which one cannot master and over which one has no power or control"; also pp. 10, 16–28.

[50] Gilles Deleuze and Felix Guattari, *A Thousand Plateaus: Capitalism and Schizophrenia*, trans. Brian Massumi (Minneapolis: University of Minnesota Press, 1987), p. 302.

through reports of the Indians themselves – of native ceremony involving singing, invocation, and drumming. In these cases the integrated selves the Europeans had laboriously constructed in the face of dramatic difference, the stable subjectivities they achieved by objectification of the Indians, were undone by Indian actions. The Europeans' most primal fears of a world they could neither comprehend nor control were confirmed by the aggressive sonic excess of Indian ritual utterance. And was this not an inevitable confirmation, in conditions of exacerbated difference and through heightened voice, of a terror of transformation the Europeans had always already known?

The afterlife of fearsome song

Michel de Certeau posed a related question in respect to the difference between writing and speech: "Would it be too much to recognize already in the gap between what is seen and heard the distinction between two functionings of the savage world in relation to the [European] language that deals with it? Either as an *object* of a discourse that constructs schemes and pictures, or as a *distortion*, a rapture, but also a calling of this discourse?"[51] In a language itself almost rapturous, de Certeau reveals the most basic absence – of living vocality – that haunts modern historiographic and ethnographic projects.

We need to take a step beyond de Certeau, calibrating more finely the gauge by which we measure this absence. Within the utterance that for him unsettled European discourse concerning the New World, we must discriminate speech from all its heightened alternatives. (Here again I broach, as I did in chapters 1 and 2, the Derridean but un-Derridean possibility of song as a third term in an epochal metaphysics, positioned on the other side of speech from writing.) Raised voices, far more than speech, disrupted the European imaginary in which the colonizers struggled to locate the colonized. Writing, de Certeau argued, facilitated the fixing of Indians within European discourse, while speech threatened their escape from it. But this is incomplete; speech remained a largely tractable force in the dynamic of seizure and escape. It was song, especially, that made good the natives' flight.

A history of European colonialism could be written as the story of negotiations of the space between speaking and singing. This history, in addition to chapters on the fear of song in the early modern period and the reaction-formations it inspired, would need to pause over the eighteenth century and take account of a watershed there in European responses to the singing of the rest of the world. This was the consolidation, by about 1800, of a category of modern, elite European artistic attainment predicated on newly reimagined powers of instrument-playing; call it Music. The novel ideology that gave rise to this category exalted the non-songish, sovereign powers represented especially by the European orchestra and celebrated the European cultural preeminence that was seen to have uncovered them. The ideology was nurtured by the same thinking that in this period divided history from anthropology and set these disciplines on their modern, parallel courses. It worked, like other ideologies, to universalize and naturalize the human doings within its range by

---

[51] Michel de Certeau, "Ethno-Graphy: Speech, or the Space of the Other: Jean de Léry," in *The Writing of History*, trans. Tom Conley (New York: Columbia University Press, 1988), pp. 208–43; p. 236.

Fear of singing

rendering invisible (in this case, inaudible) those outside it. In musical terms, the ideology separated an elite European instrumentalism from the songs and chants of the rest of the world. In this it distanced European musical refinements from the colonial terrors that were especially pressing in others' raised voices.[52]

But if the history imagined here would need to chronicle this much, it would need also to record the failure of this opening of ideological divides to silence the voices of others and the otherness of voice. For the difference registered in song, like the difference that inspired the colonial stereotype, could never be confidently managed. Again and again it leaked through the sound-barriers constructed to muffle it. It echoed even in the midst of the European instrumental triumph: in the revival of Gregorian chant, for example, captured and controlled by Solemnes doctrines even as it burgeoned; in autochthonous currents within elite music-making that ran counter to Germanic instrumentalism, especially Italian opera, exported to exert Europe-wide impact; in, at the dawn of the twentieth century, technologies of recorded sound, which at first could negotiate successfully only the most brazenly powerful of voices, like Caruso's, and later fostered novel categories of vocal emotionalism and promoted them in the new, expansive cultural niche of recorded popular song.

These internal eruptions of vocalism were quiet, however, compared with the more unsettling singing that could still be overheard at the expanding margins of control of Europe and, by now, the United States. There the fear of singing lived on in a form little altered since the sixteenth century; eavesdropping and its terrors lingered. In words that harken clearly back to much earlier reports, for example, a US Army general described the beginning of an uneasy council between the Cavalry and the Sahaptini (Nez Perce) Indians in May 1877, on the eve of the outbreak of the Nez Perce War:

> A long rank of men, followed by women and children, . . . all were mounted on Indian ponies as various in color as the dress of the riders. These picturesque people, after keeping us waiting long enough for effect, came in sight from up the valley from the direction of their temporary camp just above the company gardens. They drew near to the hollow square of the post and in front of the small company to be interviewed. Then they struck up their song. They were not armed except with a few tomahawk pipes that could be smoked with the peaceful tobacco or penetrate the skull bone of an enemy, at the will of the holder. Yet somehow this wild sound produced a strange effect. It made one feel glad that there were but fifty of them, and not five hundred. It was shrill and searching; sad, like a wail, and yet defiant in its close. The Indians swept around outside the fence and made the entire circuit, still keeping up the song as they rode. The buildings broke the refrain into irregular bubblings of sound until the ceremony was completed.[53]

The passage has an almost lyrical manner of capturing the Indians' song, different from most of the sixteenth-century reports we have read; a distinctly modern, proto-Adornian

---

[52] For more on these topics see Gary Tomlinson, "Musicology, Anthropology, History," in *Il saggiatore musicale* 8 (2001), pp. 21–37.

[53] Gen. O. O. Howard, *Nez Percé Joseph: An Account of . . . His War, His Pursuit, and Capture* [1881], quoted from James Mooney, *The Ghost-Dance Religion and Wounded Knee* (New York: Dover, 1973 [1896]), p. 713.

nostalgia for the scenic savage has set in. Otherwise the hearing of the Indians' songs it relates differs in no substantial way from the experiences of Léry, Cortés, and the others.

The famous ghost-songs of Native North Americans about 1890 offer the most telling case-in-point of the persistent fear of Indian song. They frightened white settlers and the reservation agents of the US government in almost exactly the same manner the *taki onqoy* had alarmed the Spaniards three centuries earlier. The panic they aroused helped to precipitate the last of the many horrific episodes that make up the final chapter of the government's controlling and destruction of indigenous Americans: the massacre of Sioux Indians at Wounded Knee on December 29, 1890.

James Mooney, from the Bureau of American Ethnology in Washington, had set off to conduct ethnographic research on the movement in the weeks just before the massacre. His travels and interviews would take up much of the next three years, and in 1896 he published the lengthy and extraordinary study that resulted, "The Ghost-Dance Religion and the Sioux Outbreak of 1890."

The religion Mooney described was neither a single rite nor a unified conspiracy of different Indian groups or nations. Instead, like the *taki onqoy*, it was a loose messianic movement revolving around a millenarian prophecy. It celebrated the visions of Wovoka, a Paiute Indian of Nevada, which held out the prospect of a reuniting of the Indians with their dead ancestors and a restoration of all the old ways in a land of health, peace, and plentiful game. Such a prospect gripped many groups of Plains Indians, whose situation was in some cases fully as desperate as that of native Andeans in 1560. They had been repeatedly wronged by the unlawful incursion of whites onto their territories, by the wasteful depletion (by whites) of their resources, especially the buffalo, and by a federal government willing to turn a blind eye on all this as well as broken treaties and unfulfilled promises.

The celebrations associated with Wovoka's prophecies, like the prophecies themselves, again recall the *taki onqoy*. They took the form of long, taxing dances which came to involve hundreds or even thousands of participants. These extreme exertions caused many dancers to fall into trances, during which they experienced vivid visions of ancestors and deceased friends and the utopic world to come. And, of course, the dancing moved in time to the singing of the songs that have come to be called ghost-songs. The repertory of these songs, discussed and partially transcribed by Mooney (pp. 953–1103), was like the movement itself no unified thing, but grew and changed as it spread from group to group.

Ghost-dance ceremonies sprang up quickly through the late 1880s. Wovoka himself was believed by some groups to be Christ resurrected. His visions, as they spread from nation to nation, were transformed in various ways, expressing sometimes peaceful coexistence with whites, sometimes hostility toward them. But even among the most disaffected Sioux, in the months leading up to the massacre, the US agent overseeing the reservation discerned no intention of violence to the whites around them.[54]

---

[54] A facsimile edition of Mooney's report is James Mooney, *The Ghost-Dance Religion*. For Wovoka's prophecies, chap. 9; for the spread of the movement and its features, chaps. 10–14. On the causes of the Indian wars in these years, Mooney, writing of the Nez Perce War, minces no words: "As is generally the case with Indian wars, it originated in the unauthorized intrusion of lawless whites on lands which the Indians

Fear of singing

As the ghost-dance celebrations spread, the whites near them grew ever more alarmed. Rumor ran high that the ceremonies signaled the start of a general Indian uprising, as in Tenochtitlan watched over nervously by Pedro de Alvarado 370 years before. At the Sioux reservations, where the first ceremonies sprang up early in 1890, the agents in charge were by August sending reservation police to break them up, with only partial success. By October one agent (particularly inept according to Mooney) "reported that more than half of his 6,000 Indians were dancing, and that they were entirely beyond the control of the police, and suggested that it would be necessary to call out the military." On November 17, finally, the War Department, acting on an order from President Harrison, issued the command for troops to move into the area (pp. 846–50).

Many whites witnessed ghost-dance ceremonies – probably many more than ever witnessed indigenous ceremonies in sixteenth-century Spanish colonies. Nevertheless, no careful consideration of their significance was ordered before troops were sent in to stop them. The threat of the ghost-dance was magnified by a general lack of firsthand knowledge, and Mooney's after-the-fact research was the first to illuminate the movement in any bright way.

This does not mean, however, that we lack altogether accounts that bespeak the fearsome spectacle the ceremony involved. A government agent who witnessed a Shoshone and Paiute ghost-dance, for example, reported that

> Fully one thousand people took part in the dance. While the best of order prevailed, the excitement was very great as morning approached. When the dancers were worn out mentally and physically, the medicine-men would shout that they could see the faces of departed friends and relatives moving about the circle. No pen can paint the picture of wild excitement that ensued. All shouted in a chorus, Christ has come, and then danced and sung until they fell in a confused and exhausted mass on the ground.... (p. 806)

Meanwhile a white schoolteacher wrote of the celebration she witnessed at White Clay Creek, near Wounded Knee, which involved three or four hundred dancers in a circle. "After walking about a few times, chanting, 'Father, I come,'" she wrote, "they stopped marching, but remained in the circle, and set up the most fearful, heart-piercing wails I ever heard – crying, moaning, groaning, and shrieking out their grief, and naming over their departed friends and relatives...." Later, after invoking the Great Spirit to allow them to speak with these dead people, they began in a state of "intense excitement" to sing a song over and over, "until first one and then another would break from the ring and stagger away and fall down" in a vision trance. "They kept up dancing until fully 100 persons were

---

claimed as theirs by virtue of occupancy from time immemorial" (p. 712). On the mismanagement and malfeasance leading up to the Sioux outbreak, see pp. 824–8, 845. As to the onesided nature of the "outbreak" itself, the views recorded in January 1891 by V. T. McGillycuddy, agent among the Sioux in question until 1886, are resonant: "Up to date there has been neither a Sioux outbreak or war. No citizen in Nebraska or Dakota has been killed, molested, or can show the scratch of a pin, and no property has been destroyed off the reservation" (p. 888). The deaths resulting from the month-long hostilities, among Indians and US soldiers, are tallied by Mooney on p. 891. Further citations from Mooney in the text.

lying unconscious. Then they stopped and seated themselves in a circle, and as each one recovered from his trance he was brought to the center of the ring to relate his experience" (pp. 916–17). In the ghost-dance, as in the *taki onqoy*, the ceremonies of the Yucatán, and the Mexican *cantares* celebrations, Europeans and their descendants came face to face with a metaphysics that seemed incalculable.

It says much that history could repeat itself in this way across the three centuries separating the *taki onqoy* from the ghost-dance movement. At a moment when the Amerindian threat to Europeans and their descendants was nearly extinguished, when the victors were busily writing their histories and beginning to capture Native Americans in the modern discourse of ethnography – as in the many photographs they took – the frisson of terror at native ceremony was very much alive.

To put it this way, however, might suggest that the fear of singing would soon fade before the modern human sciences. This would be the mistake of a scientism that has too often relegated the atavistic force of the song of others to a past or to prehistory, rather than recognizing its continued strength down to the present day. It would be the hubris that can deny, only a century after Freud (and two after Kant), the mysteries that linger in our notions of the psyche and the intersubjective collisions that shape it. And it would betray a deafness to the powers that singing, favored haunt of these mysteries, has refused to relinquish.

While he was putting finishing touches on "The Ghost-Dance Religion," Mooney welcomed to Washington a well-connected young German historian of Florentine painting, Aby Warburg. Warburg was at this moment distracted from his Renaissance studies, succumbing to a fascination with Native American rites that would take him on his own ethnographic journey to the American Southwest. Mooney fired his imagination with tales of Hopi snake-dances with live rattlesnakes.

Warburg, however, was no ordinary art historian. Richly trained by early German mythographers in comparative views of society rooted in Vico, armed with a Nietzschean sense of the laborious, precarious negotiation in all societies of Dionysiac impulses, and something of a Dionysiac visionary himself, he saw in the Hopi ceremony neither a fearsome past to be expunged nor a subject for a nascent scientific ethnography. Instead he saw an implicit critique of the Euro-American present and future. It took him almost thirty years, and experiences of his own psychosis and the technological horrors of a new kind of warfare, to articulate this vision in a lecture of 1923. But when finally he did so, his words countered the prevailing winds of modernism with a prescience that is stunning even now:

> The American of today is no longer afraid of the rattlesnake. He kills it; in any case, he does not worship it. It now faces extermination. The lightning imprisoned in wire – captured electricity – has produced a culture with no use for paganism. What has replaced it? Natural forces are no longer seen in anthropomorphic or biomorphic guise, but rather as infinite waves obedient to the human touch. With these waves, the culture of the machine age destroys what the natural sciences, born of myth, so arduously achieved: the space for devotion, which evolved in turn into the space required for reflection....

Fear of singing

> Telegram and telephone destroy the cosmos. Mythical and symbolic thinking strive to form spiritual bonds between humanity and the surrounding world, shaping distance into the space required for devotion and reflection: the distance undone by the instantaneous electric connection.[55]

In Warburg's journey to the American frontier, at the infancy of modernist ethnography – and not even five years beyond a massacre redolent of the ugliest acts of an earlier colonialism – possibilities surpassing modernity came into view.

The song that was everywhere the chief medium of the devotions described by Warburg was not a prehistory on the wane, but a vocation transformed within modernity into symbolic reflection – a *musicology* in the truest sense of the word. If the survival of such reflection was in doubt, this was not incentive to memorialize old, passing orders but a call to struggle to maintain it in the face of its technological predators. The ceremonies of the Hopis, Warburg seems to say, are *our* ceremonies as well; they are ceremonies limning through the veil of their foreignness a mode of reflecting on the world not overmatched by modern machines – the human sciences all told, perhaps. In striving to hear the uncanny otherness of the songs of these ceremonies, we listen for the calling of those who constitute us and the clamor of a difference that will not be assuaged. Listening thus holds sundry terrors, as Warburg recognized just as well as Adorno. Over against it, terrifying in its own right, is the unvarying drone of the machine.

---

[55] See Aby M. Warburg, *Images from the Region of the Pueblo Indians of North America*, trans. Michael P. Steinberg (Ithaca: Cornell University Press, 1995), p. 54; for Warburg's meeting with Mooney, p. 61. For Warburg's Vichian mythography, see Gary Tomlinson, "Five Pictures of Pathos," in *Reading the Early Modern Passions: Essays in the Cultural History of Emotion*, ed. Gail Kern Paster, Katherine Rowe, and Mary Floyd-Wilson (Philadelphia: University of Pennsylvania Press, 2004), pp. 192–214.

APPENDIX

Excerpt from the *Relación de muchas cosas acaescidas en el Piru*

From Francisco Esteve Barba, ed., *Crónicas peruanas de interés indígena* (Biblioteca de Autores Españoles, vol. 209, Madrid: Atlas, 1968), pp. 81–3.

Acaecieron estas cosas en el mes de Abril de 1535, cuando en el valle del Cuzco se cogían los maíces y sementeras, en la qual cosecha los señores del Cuzco tenían costumbre hacer cada año un gran sacrificio al Sol y a todas las huacas y adoratorios del Cuzco, por ellos y por todas sus provincias y reinos, los cuales comenzó el Inga a hacer y duraron ocho días arreo dando las gracias al Sol por la cosecha pasada y suplicándole que en las sementeras por venir, les diese buenos frutos . . .

Sacaban en un llano, que es a la salida del Cuzco, hacia donde sale el Sol en amaneciendo, todos los bultos de los adoratorios del Cuzco, y los de más autoridad ponían debajo de toldos de pluma muy ricos y bien obrados, que parecían muy bien, y hacían de esta toldería una calle, que distaban la una toldería de la otra un gran tiro de herrón, en la cual distancia se hacía una calle muy ancha de más de 30 pasos, y en esta calle se ponían todos los señores y principales del Cuzco, sin intervenir señor alguno de otra generación; y éstos todos eran orejones muy ricamente vestidos con mantas y camisetas ricas de argentería y brazaletes y patenas en las cabezas, de oro fino y muy relumbrantes, los cuales hacían dos filas que cada una tenía más de trescientos señores; y en manera de procesión los unos del un coro y los otros del otro, estaban muy callando y esperando a que saliese el Sol, y aún no había bien salido cuando así como comenzaban ellos a entonar con gran orden y concierto con canto, entonándole con menear cada uno de ellos un pie, como cantores del canto de órgano, y como el Sol iba saliendo, más alto entonaban su canto. El Inga tenía su tienda en un cercado con una silla y escaño muy rico apartado un poco de la fila de éstos, y al entonar, levantábase con gran autoridad y poníase en el principio de todos y era el primero que comenzaba el canto, y como él hacía, hacían todos, y ya que había estado un poco, volvíase a su silla y allí se estaba negociando con los que venían a él, y algunas veces, de rato en rato, iba a su coro y estaba un poco, y luego, se tornaba; y así se estaban estos cantando desde que salía el Sol hasta que se encubría del todo, y como hasta el medio día el Sol iba saliendo, ellos iban acrecentando las voces, y de medio día abajo las iban menguando, teniendo gran cuenta con lo que el Sol caminaba; y en todo este tiempo le hacían grandes ofrecimientos; en una parte, en un terraplén donde estaba un árbol, estaban indios que en un gran fuego no hacían sino echar carnes y quemarlas allí y consumirlas en el fuego, y en una mandaba el Inga echar cantidad de ovejas a los indios comunes y pobres a la rebatiña, lo qual era cosa de gran pasatiempo. A las ocho del día, salían del Cuzco más de doscientas mujeres mozas cada una con su cántaro nuevo grande de más de arroba y media de chicha, embarrado con su tapadera, los cuales todos eran nuevos y un mismo

Appendix

embarramiento, y venían de cinco en cinco y con mucha orden y concierto, esperando de trecho en trecho; ofrecían aquellas al Sol muchos cestos de una yerba que ellos comen que se llama *coca*, en su lengua, que es la hoja a manera de arrayán; y tenían otras muchas ceremonias y ofrecimientos que sería largo de contar; basta que ya, quando a la tarde el Sol se quería cubrir, ellos, en el canto y en sus personas, mostraban gran tristeza por su ausencia y enflaquecían de industria mucho las voces, y ya cuando del todo se entraba el Sol que se desaparecía a la vista de ellos, hacían una gran admiración, y, puestas las manos, le adoraban con profundísima humildad y alzaban luego todo el aparato de la fiesta y se quitaba la toldería y cada uno se iba a su casa y tornaban aquellos bultos y reliquias pésimas a sus casas y adoratorios, y así por la misma orden, vinieron ocho o nueve días arreo. Y es de saber que aquellos bultos de ídolos que tenían en aquellos toldos, eran de los Ingas pasados que habían señoreado el Cuzco; cada uno tenía allí gran servicio de hombres que todo el día les estaban mosqueando con unos aventadores de plumas de cisnes de espejuelos y sus *mamaconas*, que son como beatas; en cada toldo había como doce o quince. Pasadas todas las fiestas, en la última llevaban muchos arados de mano, los cuales antiguamente eran de oro, y hechos los oficios, tomaba el Inga un arado y comenzaba con él a romper la tierra, y lo mismo los demás señores para que de allí adelante en todo su señorío hiciesen lo mismo; y siempre que el inga no hiciese esto no había ya quien osase romper la tierra ni pensaban que produjese . . .

WORKS CITED

Abbate, Carolyn, "Opera; Or, the Envoicing of Women," in *Musicology and Difference: Gender and Sexuality in Music Scholarship*, ed. Ruth A. Solie, Berkeley: University of California Press, 1993, pp. 225–58.
Unsung Voices: Opera and Musical Narrative in the Nineteenth Century, Princeton: Princeton University Press, 1991.
Adorno, Theodor, *Quasi una fantasia*, trans. Rodney Livingstone, London: Verso, 1992.
Andrews, J. Richard, *Introduction to Classical Nahuatl*, Austin: University of Texas Press, 1975.
Archivo General de Indias, México 882, Calendario 100.
Arriaga, Pablo José de, *Extirpación de la idolatría del Pirú*, in *Crónicas peruanas de interés indígena*, ed. Francisco Esteve Barba, Madrid: Atlas, 1968, pp. 191–277.
Austin, Alfredo López, *The Human Body and Ideology: Concepts of the Ancient Nahuas*, trans. Thelma Ortiz de Montellano and Bernard Ortiz de Montellano, 2 vols., Salt Lake City: University of Utah Press, 1988.
Aveni, Anthony, *Empires of Time: Calendars, Clocks, and Cultures*, rev. edn., Boulder: University Press of Colorado, 2002.
Skywatchers of Ancient Mexico, Austin: University of Texas Press, 1980.
Barrera Vázquez, Alfredo, *El libro de los cantares de Dzitbalché*, Mexico: Instituto Nacional de Antropología e Historia, 1965.
Bauer, Brian S., *The Development of the Inca State*, Austin: University of Texas Press, 1992.
The Sacred Landscape of the Inca: The Cusco Ceque System, Austin: University of Texas Press, 1998.
Bauer, Brian S., and David S. P. Dearborn, *Astronomy and Empire in the Ancient Andes*, Austin: University of Texas Press, 1995.
Bautista, Juan, *Cómo te confundes? Acaso no somos conquistados? Anales de Juan Bautista*, ed. Luis Reyes García, Mexico: Ciesas, 2001.
Betanzos, Juan de, *Narrative of the Incas*, trans. Roland Hamilton and Dana Buchanan, Austin: University of Texas Press, 1996.
Suma y narración de los Incas, ed. María del Carmen Martín Rubio, Madrid: Atlas, 1987.
Bhabha, Homi K., "The Other Question: Stereotype, Discrimination, and the Discourse of Colonialism," in *The Location of Culture*, London: Routledge, 1994, pp. 66–84.
Bierhorst, John, *Cantares mexicanos: Songs of the Aztecs*, Stanford: Stanford University Press, 1985.
A Nahuatl–English Dictionary and Concordance to the Cantares mexicanos, with an Analytical Transcription and Grammatical Notes, Stanford: Stanford University Press, 1985.

Works cited

Bloechl, Olivia Ashley, "Sounding Savagery: Native American Song and the Frontiers of Early Modern Music," PhD dissertation, University of Pennsylvania, 2002.

Boone, Elizabeth Hill, and Walter D. Mignolo, eds., *Writing without Words: Alternative Literacies in Mesoamerica and the Andes*, Durham, NC: Duke University Press, 1994.

Boturini, Lorenzo Benaducci, *Idea de una nueva historia general de la America septentrional* (Madrid, 1746), facsimile edn., Paris: Genet, 1933.

Brinton, Daniel G., *Ancient Nahuatl Poetry, Containing the Nahuatl Text of XXVII Ancient Mexican Songs* (Philadelphia, 1890), rpt., New York: AMS Press, 1969.

Brotherston, Gordon, *Book of the Fourth World: Reading the Native Americas through Their Literature*, Cambridge: Cambridge University Press, 1992.

"Nezahualcóyotl's 'Lamentaciones' and Their Nahuatl Origins: The Westernization of Ephemerality," *Estudios de Cultura Náhuatl* 10 (1972), pp. 393–408.

"Towards a Grammatology of America: Lévi-Strauss, Derrida and the Native New World Text," in *Literature, Politics and Theory: Papers from the Essex Conference 1976–84*, ed. Francis Barker, Peter Hulme, Margaret Iversen, and Diana Loxley, London: Methuen, 1986, pp. 190–209.

Burkhart, Louise M., "Flowery Heaven: The Aesthetic of Paradise in Nahuatl Devotional Literature," *Res* 21 (1992), pp. 88–109.

Cáceres, Abraham, "*In xochitl, in cuicatl:* Hallucinogens and Music in Mesoamerican Amerindian Thought," PhD dissertation, Indiana University, 1984.

Cañizares-Esguerra, Jorge, *How to Write the History of the New World*, Stanford: Stanford University Press, 2001.

Cantares mexicanos, ed. José G. Moreno de Alba and Miguel León-Portilla, facsimile edn., Mexico: Instituto de Investigaciones Bibliográficas, 1994.

[Carli, Gian Ricardo], *Lettere americane*, 2 vols., Cosmopoli, 1780.

Carochi, Horacio, *Grammar of the Mexican Language with an Explanation of Its Adverbs* (1645), ed. and trans. James Lockhart, Stanford: Stanford University Press, 2001.

Carrasco, David, *Religions of Mesoamerica: Cosmovision and Ceremonial Centers*, San Francisco: Harper, 1990.

Cavero, Ranulfo, *Los dioses vencidos: Una lectura antropológica del Taki Onqoy*, Ayacucho, Peru: Universidad Nacional de San Cristóbal de Huamanga, 2001.

Certeau, Michel de, "Ethno-Graphy: Speech, or the Space of the Other: Jean de Léry," in *The Writing of History*, trans. Tom Conley, New York: Columbia University Press, 1988, pp. 209–43.

"Montaigne's 'Of Cannibals': The Savage 'I'," in *Heterologies: Discourse on the Other*, trans. Brian Massumi, Minneapolis: University of Minnesota Press, 1986, pp. 67–79.

Cervantes, Fernando, *The Devil in the New World: The Impact of Diabolism in New Spain*, New Haven: Yale University Press, 1994.

Cheyfitz, Eric, *The Poetics of Imperialism: Translation and Colonization from "The Tempest" to "Tarzan,"* New York: Oxford University Press, 1991.

Cieza de León, Pedro de, *The Incas of Pedro de Cieza de León*, trans. Harriet de Onis, Norman: University of Oklahoma Press, 1959.

Classen, Constance, *Inca Cosmology and the Human Body*, Salt Lake City: University of Utah Press, 1993.

Clendinnen, Inga, *Aztecs*, Cambridge: Cambridge University Press, 1991.

Cobo, Bernabé, *Historia del nuevo mundo*, ed. F. Mateos, Biblioteca de Autores Españoles, vols. 91–2, Madrid: Atlas, 1964.

Inca Religion and Customs, trans. Roland Hamilton and John Howland Rowe, Austin: University of Texas Press, 1990.

Works cited

Cock C., Guillermo, and Mary Eileen Doyle, "Del culto solar a la clandestinidad de Inti y Punchao," *Historia y cultura* (Lima), 12 (1992), pp. 51–73.
Codex Azcatitlan, ed. Michel Graulich and Robert H. Barlow, Paris: Bibliothèque nationale de France, 1995.
Collinson, Richard, ed., *The Three Voyages of Martin Frobisher, in Search of a Passage to Cathaia and India by the North-West*, London: Hakluyt Society, 1867.
Columbus, Christopher, *Narrative* of the third voyage to the Indies [1498], trans. Cecil Jane, *The Four Voyages of Columbus*, New York: Dover, 1988.
Conrad, Geoffrey W., and Arthur A. Demarest, *Religion and Empire: The Dynamics of Aztec and Inca Expansionism*, Cambridge: Cambridge University Press, 1984.
Cortés, Hernán, *Letters from Mexico*, trans. and ed. Anthony Pagden, New Haven: Yale University Press, 1986.
Crónicas peruanas de interés indígena, ed. Francisco Esteve Barba, Biblioteca de Autores Españoles, vol. 209, Madrid: Atlas, 1968.
Cummins, Tom, "Representation in the Sixteenth Century and the Colonial Image of the Inca," in *Writing without Words: Alternative Literacies in Mesoamerica and the Andes*, ed. Elizabeth Hill Boone and Walter D. Mignolo, Durham, NC: Duke University Press, 1994, pp. 188–219.
Damrosch, David, "The Aesthetics of Conquest: Aztec Poetry Before and After Cortés," *Representations* 33 (1991), pp. 101–20.
de Man, Paul, "The Rhetoric of Blindness: Jacques Derrida's Reading of Rousseau," in *Blindness and Insight: Essays in the Rhetoric of Contemporary Criticism*, 2nd edn, Minneapolis: University of Minnesota Press, 1983, pp. 102–41.
Défaux, Gérard, "Un Cannibale en haut de chausses: Montaigne, la différence et la logique de l'identité," *Modern Language Notes* 97 (1982), pp. 919–57.
Deleuze, Gilles, and Felix Guattari, *A Thousand Plateaus: Capitalism and Schizophrenia*, trans. Brian Massumi, Minneapolis: University of Minnesota Press, 1987.
Demarest, Arthur A., *Viracocha: The Nature and Antiquity of the Andean High God*, Cambridge, MA: Peabody Museum, 1981.
Derrida, Jacques, *Of Grammatology*, trans. Gayatri Chakravorty Spivak, Baltimore: Johns Hopkins University Press, 1976.
Desan, Philippe, *Les Commerces de Montaigne: le discours économique des Essais*, Paris: A.-G. Nizet, 1992.
Montaigne, les Cannibales et les Conquistadores, Paris: A.-G. Nizet, 1994.
Díaz, Bernal, *The Conquest of New Spain*, trans. J. M. Cohen, London: Penguin, 1963.
Dolar, Mladen, "The Object Voice," in *Gaze and Voice as Love Objects*, ed. Renata Salecl and Slavoj Žižek, Durham, NC: Duke University Press, 1996.
Durán, Fray Diego, *Book of the Gods and Rites and The Ancient Calendar*, trans. Fernando Horcasitas and Doris Heyden, Norman: University of Oklahoma Press, 1971.
Estenssoro Fuchs, Juan Carlos, *Del paganismo a la santidad: La incorporación de los indios del Perú al catolicismo, 1532–1750*, trans. Gabriela Ramos, Lima: Instituto Francés de Estudios Americanos, 2003.
"Los bailes de los indios y el proyecto colonial," *Revista andina* 10 (1992), pp. 353–89.
Évreux, Père Yves d', *Voyage dans le nord de Brésil fait durant les années 1613 et 1614*, ed. Ferdinand Denis, Leipzig: A. Franck, 1864.
Fabian, Johannes, *Time and the Other: How Anthropology Makes Its Object*, New York: Columbia University Press, 1983.

Works cited

Farriss, Nancy M., *Maya Society under Colonial Rule: The Collective Enterprise of Survival*, Princeton: Princeton University Press, 1984.
Fernandes, Florestan, *A função social da guerra na sociedade tupinambá*, 2nd edn., São Paulo: Livraria Pioneira Editôra, 1970.
Ferreira Jr., Amarilio, and Marisa Bittar, "Pluralidade lingüística, escola de bê-á-bá e teatro jesuítico no Brasil do século XVI," *Educaçao e Sociedade* 25 (April 2004).
Forsyth, Donald W., "Three Cheers for Hans Staden: The Case for Brazilian Cannibalism," *Ethnohistory* 32. 1 (1985), pp. 17–36.
Foucault, Michel, *The Order of Things: An Archaeology of the Human Sciences*, New York: Vintage Books, 1970.
Freccero, Carla, "Cannibalism, Homophobia, Women: Montaigne's 'Des cannibales' and 'De l'amitié,'" in *Women, "Race," and Writing in the Early Modern Period*, ed. Margo Hendricks and Patricia Parker, London: Routledge, 1994, pp. 73–83.
Fuller, Mary C., "Ralegh's Fugitive Gold: Reference and Deferral in *The Discoverie of Guiana*," *Representations* 33 (1991), pp. 42–64.
Furst, Jill Leslie McKeever, *The Natural History of the Soul in Ancient Mexico*, New Haven: Yale University Press, 1995.
Garibay K., Angel María, *Historia de la literatura náhuatl*, 2 vols., Mexico: Editorial Porrua, 1953–4.
  Poesía náhuatl, 3 vols., 2nd edn., Mexico City: Universidad Nacional Autónoma, 1993.
Gebhart-Sayer, Angelika, "The Geometric Designs of the Shipibo-Conibo in Ritual Context," *Journal of Latin American Lore* 11 (1985), pp. 143–75.
Gómara, Francisco López de, *Historia de la conquista de Mexico*, ed. Juan Miralles Ostos, Mexico City: Editorial Porrúa, 1988.
Goody, Jack, *The Interface between the Written and the Oral*, Cambridge: Cambridge University Press, 1987.
Granados y Gálvez, Joseph Joaquín, *Tardes americanas: Gobierno gentil y católico: breve y particular noticia de toda la historia indiana*, Mexico, 1778.
Greenblatt, Stephen, *Marvelous Possessions: The Wonder of the New World*, Chicago: University of Chicago Press, 1991.
Gruzinski, Serge, *La Colonisation de l'imaginaire: Sociétés indigènes et occidentalisation dans le Mexique espagnol, XVIe–XVIIIe siècle*, Paris: Gallimard, 1988; trans. Eileen Corrigan as *The Conquest of Mexico: The Incorporation of Indian Societies into the Western World, 16th–18th Centuries*, Cambridge: Polity Press, 1993.
  Man-Gods in the Mexican Highlands: Indian Power and Colonial Society, 1520–1800, trans. Eileen Corrigan, Stanford: Stanford University Press, 1989.
Guaman Poma de Ayala, Felipe, *Nueva crónica y buen gobierno*, ed. John V. Murra, Rolena Adorno, and Jorge L. Urioste, 3 vols., Madrid: Historia 16, 1987.
Harcourt, R. and M., *La Musique des Incas et ses survivances*, 2 vols., Paris: Paul Geuthner, 1925.
Harrison, Frank, ed., *Time, Place and Music*, Amsterdam: Frits Knuf, 1973.
Hemming, John, *The Conquest of the Incas*, New York: Harcourt Brace, 1970.
  Red Gold: The Conquest of the Brazilian Indians, 1500–1760, Cambridge, MA: Harvard University Press, 1978.
Hill, Jane H., and Bruce Mannheim, "Language and World View," *Annual Review of Anthropology* 21 (1992), pp. 381–406.
Historia de la nación mexicana: Reproducción a todo color del Codice de 1576 (Codice Aubin), ed. and trans. Charles E. Dibble, Madrid: Porrúa, 1963.

Works cited

Hosler, Dorothy, *The Sounds and Colors of Power: The Sacred Metallurgical Technology of Ancient West Mexico*, Cambridge, MA: MIT Press, 1994.

Hyslop, John, *Inca Settlement Planning*, Austin: University of Texas Press, 1990.

Julien, Catherine, *Reading Inca History*, Iowa City: University of Iowa Press, 2000.

Karttunen, Frances, *An Analytical Dictionary of Nahuatl*, Norman: University of Oklahoma Press, 1992.

Karttunen, Frances and James Lockhart, "La estructura de la poesía náhuatl vista por sus variantes," *Estudios de cultura náhuatl* 14 (1980), pp. 15–64.

Keane, Webb, "The Value of Words and the Meaning of Things in Eastern Indonesian Exchange," *Man* n.s. 29 (1994), pp. 605–29.

Keen, Benjamin, *The Aztec Image in Western Thought*, New Brunswick: Rutgers University Press, 1971.

Kennedy, Jean, *Isle of Devils: Bermuda under the Somers Island Company, 1609–1685*, Hamilton, Bermuda: Collins, 1971.

King, Mark B. "Hearing the Echoes of Verbal Art in Mixtec Writing," in *Writing without Words: Alternative Literacies in Mesoamerica and the Andes*, ed. Elizabeth Hill Boone and Walter D. Mignolo, Durham, NC: Duke University Press, 1994, pp. 102–36.

Kramer, Lawrence, "Culture and Musical Hermeneutics: The Salome Complex," *Cambridge Opera Journal* 2 (1990), pp. 269–94.

Music as Cultural Practice, 1800–1900, Berkeley: University of California Press, 1990.

Landa, Fray Diego de, *Landa's Relación de las cosas de Yucatan*, trans. Alfred M. Tozzer, Cambridge, MA: Peabody Museum, 1941.

Relación de las cosas de Yucatan, ed. Angel María Garibay K., Mexico: Porrúa, 1966.

Las Casas, Fray Bartolomé de, *Apologética historia sumaria*, ed. Edmundo O'Gorman, 2 vols., Mexico: Universidad Nacional Autónoma, 1967.

Le Moyne de Morgues, Jacques, *Brevis narratio* of the French expedition to Florida of 1564 [ca. 1585], trans. Stefan Lorant, in *The New World: The First Pictures of America*, rev. edn., New York: Duell, Sloane and Pearce, 1965, pp. 38–42.

Leander, Birgitta, *In xochitl in cuicatl: flor y canto, la poesía de los Aztecas*, Mexico: Instituto Nacional Indigenista, 1972.

Léon-Portilla, Miguel, *The Aztec Image of Self and Society: An Introduction to Nahua Culture*, ed. J. Jorge Klor de Alva, Salt Lake City: University of Utah Press, 1992.

Aztec Thought and Culture, trans. Jack Emory Davis, Norman: University of Oklahoma Press, 1963.

The Broken Spears: The Aztec Account of the Conquest of Mexico, trans. Lysander Kemp, rev. edn., Boston: Beacon Press, 1992.

"Cuícatl y tlahtolli: Las formas de expresión en náhuatl," *Estudios de cultura náhuatl* 16 (1983), pp. 13–108.

Fifteen Poets of the Aztec World, Norman: University of Oklahoma Press, 1992.

Léry, Jean de, *Histoire d'un voyage fait en la terre du Brésil*, facsimile of the 1580 edn., ed. Jean-Claude Morisot, Geneva: Droz, 1975.

History of a Voyage to the Land of Brazil, Otherwise Called America, trans. Janet Whatley, Berkeley and Los Angeles: University of California Press, 1990.

Lestringant, Frank, *Cannibals: The Discovery and Representation of the Cannibal from Columbus to Jules Verne*, trans. Rosemary Morris, Berkeley: University of California Press, 1997.

"The Philosopher's Breviary: Jean de Léry in the Enlightenment," *Representations* 33 (1991), pp. 200–11.

Lewis, I. M., *Ecstatic Religion: A Study of Shamanism and Spirit Possession*, 2nd edn., London: Routledge, 1989.

Works cited

Lockhart, James, "Care, Ingenuity, and Irresponsibility: The Bierhorst Edition of the Cantares Mexicanos," *Reviews in Anthropology* 16 (1991), pp. 119–32.
  The Nahuas after the Conquest: A Social and Cultural History of the Indians of Central Mexico, Sixteenth through Eighteenth Centuries, Stanford: Stanford University Press, 1992.
  Nahuatl as Written: Lessons in Older Written Nahuatl, with Copious Examples and Texts, Stanford: Stanford University Press, 2001.
Lucas, Theodore D., "Songs of the Shipibo of the Upper Amazon," *Anuario Interamericano de Investigación Musical* 7 (1971), pp. 59–81.
MacCormack, Sabine, *Religion in the Andes: Vision and Imagination in Early Colonial Peru*, Princeton: Princeton University Press, 1991.
Marcus, Joyce, *Mesoamerican Writing Systems: Propaganda, Myth, and History in Four Ancient Civilizations*, Princeton: Princeton University Press, 1992.
Martí, Samuel, *Canto, danza y música precortesianos*, Mexico: Fondo de Cultura Económica, 1961.
Mauss, Marcel, *The Gift: The Form and Reason for Exchange in Archaic Societies*, trans. W. D. Halls, New York: Norton, 1990.
Mendez, Diego, *An Account* of incidents on Columbus's fourth voyage [1536], trans. Cecil Jane, in *The Four Voyages of Columbus*, New York: Dover, 1988.
Métraux, Alfred, *La Religion des Tupinamba et ses rapports avec celle des autres tribus Tupi-Guarani*, Paris: Ernest Leroux, 1928.
Miller, Arthur G., *The Mural Painting of Teotihuacán*, Washington, DC: 1973.
Millones, Luis, ed., *El retorno de las huacas: Estudios y documentos sobre el Taki Onqoy, siglo XVI*, Lima: Instituto de Estudios Peruanos, 1990.
Molina, Alonso de, *Vocabulario en lengua castellana y mexicana*, Mexico, 1571; facsimile edn., Madrid: Ediciones Cultura Hispanica, 1944.
Molina, Cristóbal de, "el Cuzqueño," *Fábulas y ritos de los Incas*, in *Las crónicas de los Molinas*, ed. Francisco A. Loayza, Lima: Domingo Miranda, 1943, second pagination, pp. 5–84.
Molina, Cristóbal de, "el Cuzqueño," and Cristóbal de Molina "el Almagrista," *Las crónicas de los Molinas*, ed. Francisco A. Loayza, Lima: Domingo Miranda, 1943.
Monaghan, John, "The Text in the Body, the Body in the Text: The Embodied Sign in Mixtec Writing," in *Writing without Words: Alternative Literacies in Mesoamerica and the Andes*, ed. Elizabeth Hill Boone and Walter D. Mignolo, Durham, NC: Duke University Press, 1994, pp. 87–101.
Montaigne, Michel de, *The Complete Essays of Montaigne*, trans. Donald M. Frame, Stanford: Stanford University Press, 1965.
  Essais, ed. Maurice Rat, 2 vols., Paris: Garnier Frères, 1962.
Mooney, James, *The Ghost-Dance Religion and Wounded Knee* [1896], 2nd edn., New York: Dover, 1973.
Motolinía, Fray Toribio de, *Memoriales de Fray Toribio de Motolinía*, ed. Luis García Pimentel, Mexico: published by the editor, 1903.
Neubauer, John, *The Emancipation of Music from Language: Departure from Mimesis in Eighteenth-Century Aesthetics*, New Haven: Yale University Press, 1986.
Niles, Susan A., *The Shape of Inca History: Narrative and Architecture in an Andean Empire*, Iowa City: University of Iowa Press, 1999.
Olsen, Dale A., *Music of El Dorado: The Ethnomusicology of Ancient South American Cultures*, Gainesville: University Press of Florida, 2002.
Ong, Walter J., *The Presence of the Word: Some Prolegomena for a Cultural and Religious History*, Minneapolis: University of Minnesota Press, 1981.
  Ramus: Method and the Decay of Dialogue, Cambridge, MA: Harvard University Press, 1958.

Works cited

Pérez de Ribas, Andrés, *Historia de los triumphos de nuestra santa fee . . . en las missiones de la provincia de Nueva-España*, Madrid: Alsonso de Paredes, 1645.

Phipps, Elena, Johanna Hecht, Cristina Esteras Martín, et al., *The Colonial Andes: Tapestries and Silverwork, 1530–1830*, exhibition catalogue, New York: The Metropolitan Museum of Art, 2004.

Pizarro, Pedro, *Relación del descubrimiento y conquista de los reinos del Perú*, ed. Juan Perez de Tudela Bueso, Biblioteca de Autores Españoles, vol. 168, Madrid: Atlas, 1965.

Pohl, John M. D., "Mexican Codices, Maps, and Lienzos as Social Contracts," in *Writing without Words: Alternative Literacies in Mesoamerica and the Andes*, ed. Elizabeth Hill Boone and Walter D. Mignolo, Durham, NC: Duke University Press, 1994, pp. 137–60.

Pozos, Luis Alveláis, *Los cantos de Nezahualcóyotl*, Toluca: Instituto Mexiquense de Cultura, 1989.

Prescott, William H., *History of the Conquest of Mexico and History of the Conquest of Peru*, New York: Modern Library, n.d.

Quint, David, "A Reconsideration of Montaigne's 'Des cannibales'," *Modern Language Quarterly* 51 (1990), pp. 459–89.

Quiroga, Vasco de, *La Utopía en América*, ed. Paz Serrano Gassent, Madrid: Historia 16, 1992.

Rosier, James, *A True Relation* of George Waymouth's voyage to Virginia [1605], in *The English New England Voyages, 1602–1608*, ed. David B. Quinn and Alison M. Quinn, London: The Hakluyt Society, 1983, pp. 248–311.

Rousseau, Jean-Jacques, *A Complete Dictionary of Music*, trans. William Waring, London: J. French, 1779.

Dictionnaire de musique [Paris, 1768], facsimile edn., Hildesheim: G. Olms, 1969.

Essai sur l'origine des langues, ed. Charles Porset, Bordeaux: Guy Ducros, 1970.

The First and Second Discourses Together with the Replies to Critics and Essay on the Origin of Languages, trans. Victor Gourevitch, New York: Harper, 1986.

Rowe, John Howland, "Inca Culture at the Time of the Spanish Conquest," in *Handbook of South American Indians*, ed. Julian H. Steward, 6 vols., Washington: US Government Printing Office, 1946, II, pp. 183–330.

"What Kind of a Settlement Was Inca Cuzco?", *Ñawpa Pacha* 5 (1967), pp. 59–77.

Ruiz de Alarcón, Hernando, *Treatise on the Heathen Superstitions That Today Live Among the Indians Native to This New Spain, 1629*, trans. J. Richard Andrews and Ross Hassig, Norman, Oklahoma: University of Oklahoma Press, 1984.

Sahagún, Fray Bernardino de, *Bernardino de Sahagún's Psalmodia Christiana*, trans. Arthur J. O. Anderson, Salt Lake City: University of Utah Press, 1993.

Florentine Codex: General History of the Things of New Spain, ed. and trans. Arthur J. O. Anderson and Charles E. Dibble, 13 vols., Santa Fe and Salt Lake City: School of American Research and University of Utah Press, 1950–82.

Historia general de las cosas de Nueva España, ed. Angel María Garibay K., Mexico: Editorial Porrúa, 1956.

Salomon, Frank, *The Cord Keepers: Khipus and Cultural Life in a Peruvian Village*, Durham, NC: Duke University Press, 2004.

Salomon, Frank, and George L. Urioste, *The Huarochirí Manuscript: A Testament of Ancient and Colonial Andean Religion*, Austin: University of Texas Press, 1991.

Sanchez de Aguilar, Pedro, *Informe contra idolorum cultores del obispado de Yucatan*, in Jacinto de la Serna, *Tratado de las idolatrias, supersticiones, dioses, ritos, hechicerias y otras costumbres gentilicas de las razas aborigenes de Mexico*, 2 vols., 2nd edn., Mexico: Ediciones Fuente Cultural, 1953.

Works cited

Sarmiento de Gamboa, Pedro, *Historia de los Incas*, Madrid: Miraguano, 1988.
 History of the Incas, trans. Clements Markham [1907], rpt. edn., New York: Dover, 1999.
Scholes, Frances V., and Eleanor B. Adams, *Don Diego Quijada, Alcalde Mayor de Yucatán, 1561–1565*, 2 vols., Mexico: Porrúa, 1938.
Segala, Amos, *Literatura náhuatl*, Mexico City: Grijalbo, 1990.
Serna, Jacinto de la, *Tratado de las idolatrias, supersticiones, dioses, ritos, hechicerias y otras costumbres gentilicas de las razas aborigenes de Mexico*, ed. Don Francisco del Paso y Troncoso, 2 vols., 2nd edn., Mexico: Ediciones Fuente Cultural, 1953.
Silverman, Kaja, *The Acoustic Mirror: The Female Voice in Psychoanalysis and Cinema*, Bloomington: Indiana University Press, 1988.
Smith, David, "Colonial Encounters through the Prism of Music," *International Review of the Aesthetics and Sociology of Music* 33 (2002), pp. 31–55.
Soustelle, Jacques, *Daily Life of the Aztecs on the Eve of the Spanish Conquest*, trans. Patrick O'Brian, Stanford: Stanford University Press, 1961.
Staden, Hans, *The Captivity of Hans Stade of Hesse, in A.D. 1547–1555, Among the Wild Tribes of Eastern Brazil*, trans. Albert Tootal, Hakluyt Society, First Series 51, 1874, rpt. edn., New York: Burt Franklin, n.d.
Stern, Steve J., *Peru's Indian Peoples and the Challenge of Spanish Conquest: Huamanga to 1640*, Madison: University of Wisconsin Press, 1982.
Stevenson, Robert, *Music in Aztec and Inca Territory*, Berkeley: University of California Press, 1968.
Sullivan, Thelma D., *Compendium of Nahuatl Grammar*, trans. Thelma D. Sullivan and Neville Stiles, Salt Lake City: University of Utah Press, 1988.
Tambiah, S. J., *Magic, Science, Religion, and the Scope of Rationality*, Cambridge: Cambridge University Press, 1990.
Tavárez, David, "De cantares Zapotecas a 'libros de demonio': La extirpación de discursos doctrinales híbridos en Villa Alta, Oaxaca, 1702–1704," *Acervos* 17 (2000), pp. 19–27.
Theresa, Rose, "Spectacle and Enchantment: Envisioning Opera in Late Nineteenth-Century Paris," PhD dissertation, University of Pennsylvania, 2000.
Thevet, André, *Les Français en Amérique pendant la deuxième moitié du XVIe siècle: Le Brésil et les Brésiliens*, Paris: Presses Universitaires de France, 1953.
 Les Singularitez de la France antarctique, ed. Paul Gaffarel, Paris: Maisonneuve, 1878.
Tomlinson, Gary, "Five Pictures of Pathos," in *Reading the Early Modern Passions: Essays in the Cultural History of Emotion*, ed. Gail Kern Paster, Katherine Rowe, and Mary Floyd-Wilson, Philadelphia: University of Pennsylvania Press, 2004, pp. 192–214.
 Metaphysical Song: An Essay on Opera, Princeton: Princeton University Press, 1999.
 Music in Renaissance Magic: Toward a Historiography of Others, Chicago: University of Chicago Press, 1993.
 "Musicology, Anthropology, History," *Il saggiatore musicale* 8 (2001), pp. 21–37.
 ed., *Strunk's Source Readings in Music History*, general ed. Leo Treitler, III: *The Renaissance*, New York: Norton, 1998.
 "Vico's Songs: Detours at the Origins of (Ethno)Musicology," *The Musical Quarterly* 83 (1999), pp. 344–77.
Torquemada, Juan de, *Monarchia indiana* [1615], facsimile rpt. of the 1723 edn., Mexico: Salvador Chavez Hayhoe, 1943.
Treitler, Leo, "The Early History of Music Writing in the West," *Journal of the American Musicological Society* 35 (1982), pp. 237–79.

Works cited

"Reading and Singing: On the Genesis of Occidental Music-Writing," *Early Music History* 4 (1984), pp. 135–208.

Urton, Gary, *The History of a Myth: Pacariqtambo and the Origin of the Incas*, Austin: University of Texas Press, 1990.

Inca Myths, Austin: University of Texas Press, 1999.

Signs of the Inka Khipu: Binary Coding in the Andean Knotted-String Records, Austin: University of Texas Press, 2003.

van Orden, Kate, "Vernacular Culture and the Chanson in Paris, 1570–1580," PhD dissertation, University of Chicago, 1996.

Varón Gabai, Rafael, "Las raíces andinas de un fenómeno colonial," in *El retorno de las huacas: Estudios y documentos sobre el Taki Onqoy, siglo XVI*, ed. Luis Millones, Lima: Instituto de Estudios Peruanos, 1990, pp. 331–405.

Vega, El Inca Garcilaso de la, *Primera parte de los commentarios reales, que tratan de el origen de los Incas, Reies, que fueron del Perù*, Madrid: Rodriguez Franco, 1723.

Royal Commentaries of the Incas and General History of Peru, trans. Harold V. Livermore, Austin: University of Texas Press, 1966.

Viveiros de Castro, Eduardo, *From the Enemy's Point of View: Humanity and Divinity in an Amazonian Society*, trans. Catherine V. Howard, Chicago: University of Chicago Press, 1992.

Warburg, Aby M., *Images from the Region of the Pueblo Indians of North America*, trans. Michael P. Steinberg, Ithaca: Cornell University Press, 1995.

Weinberg, Bernard, "Montaigne's Readings for *Des cannibales*," in *Renaissance and Other Studies in Honor of William Leon Wiley*, ed. George Bernard Daniel, Jr., Chapel Hill: University of North Carolina Press, 1968, pp. 261–79.

Whitehead, Neil L., "Hans Staden and the Cultural Politics of Cannibalism," *Hispanic American Historical Review* 80 (2000), pp. 721–51.

Wilkinson, Henry C., *The Adventurers of Bermuda: A History of the Island from Its Discovery until the Dissolution of the Somers Island Company in 1684*, London: Oxford University Press, 1958.

Zuidema, R. Tom, *The Ceque System of Cuzco: The Social Organization of the Capital of the Inca*, Leiden: E. J. Brill, 1964.

Inca Civilization at Cuzco, trans. Jean-Jacques Decoster, Austin: University of Texas Press, 1990.

"The Lion in the City: Royal Symbols of Transition in Cuzco," in *Animal Myths and Metaphors in South America*, ed. Gary Urton, Salt Lake City: University of Utah Press, 1985.

"The Moieties of Cuzco," in *The Attraction of Opposites: Thought and Society in the Dualistic Mode*, ed. David Maybury-Lewis and Uri Almagor, Ann Arbor: University of Michigan Press, 1989.

INDEX

Abbate, Carolyn 48
Acosta, José de 177
Adorno, Theodor W. 168–9, 195, 201
Africa, music of 175
agglutination, as basis of language 29–30, 75–8
Aguilar, Pedro Sanchez de 176
ahouai, see leg rattles, Tupinamba use of
Albornoz, Cristóbal de 187, 190
Almagro, Diego de 154
alphabet 132
    limitations 17
alphabetization (of Nahuatl language/songs) 21–2, 28, 46
    impact on song 28–30, 32–4, 44–5, 50
    song's escape from confines of 89, 90
Alvarado, Pedro de 171–2, 176, 199
Anales de Juan Bautista 59–60
ancestor worship, Inca practice of 127–8, 138–9, 157
Anderson, Arthur J. O. 60
Andrews, J. Richard 29–30
Arawaté people 108–9, 119–20, 122
Arriaga, Pablo José de 162–4
Atahuallpa 126, 130–2, 133, 154, 155, 157
Aubin, J.-M.-A. 19
Austin, Alfredo López 34
ayllus (Inca social groups) 137
Aztecs, *see* Mexica

banquets, songs performed at 59
Basso, Ellen B. 5

Bauer, Brian S. 127, 140, 141, 156, 165
Bautista, Juan, *see Anales de Juan Bautista*
Beethoven, Ludwig van 168–9
Benavente, Toribio de, *see* Motolinía
bereavement, songs of 86–7
Bermuda 1–2
    European myths 2–3
Bermúdez, Juan de 1
Betanzos, Juan de, *Suma y narración de los Yngas* 125–6, 132, 136–7, 141, 153, 155
    sources 126, 131–2
Bhabha, Homi 191–2, 193, 194
Bierhorst, John 26, 27, 51, 53, 54, 56, 57, 60, 71, 72, 75–6, 81, 88
birds, as theme of song 78–83, 85, 86
    singer represented as 78
    See also quetzal plumes
Bloechl, Olivia Ashley 177
Bodin, Jean 46–8, 174, 189
body:
    (parts), references in *cantares* 65, 68
    relationship with (cannibal) song 104, 106
Boone, Elizabeth Hill 9, 10
Boturini Benaducci, Lorenzo 22, 23, 24–5
Brinton, Daniel G. 51, 75
Brotherston, Gordon 9, 10, 108
Bry, Theodor de 112, 117, 119
Burkhart, Louise 80
butterflies, mentioned in song 69

Cáceres, Abraham 39
cahow (grey and white petrel) 2–3
Camargo, Diego Muñoz 21
Cañizares-Esguerra, José 18

213

Index

cannibalism:
   ethics/customs of 96, 102–3
   European attitudes to 93, 106–7 (*see also* Montaigne);
      role of song 103–4,105–6,122–3
   slayer's abstention from feast 122, 123
   songs by victims of 99–100, 101, 102–3, 105–6
   See also Tupinamba
cantares 11, 164
   accompaniment 56–7 (*see also* drums, drumming)
   circumstances of performance 57, 61, 91–2;
      dichotomy of 60–1; noted in manuscript
   conceptual structure 61–2
   continuity of tradition 92
   dating 76
   divisions, *see* strophic divisions
   European commentaries/interpretations 22–7, 31, 32–4, 72–6, 80
   formal features 54–5, 91
   fusing of European and indigenous cultures 82
   genres 58, 62–3, 65, 88
   as "ghost-songs" 26
   length 55, 56
   links with other writings/ceremonies 173, 200
      (*see also* Zapotec people)
   metaphor, use of 23–5
   non-vocal elements 34–5 (*see also* drums, drumming; percussion)
   oral transmission 44
   poetic meter 55–6, 84
   recurring themes 62, 64, 76–8
   repetition, use of 55
   Spanish-organized public performances 59–61
   strophic divisions 54–5; length 55
   stylistic/thematic diversity 82–3
   supraperformative analysis 50–1
   surviving manuscript collection 28, 42–3, 51
   suspected anti-Catholicism 57–8, 180
   transcription 28–30, 32–4
Carli, Gian Ricardo 19
Carochi, Horacio 72–6
Carrasco, Davíd 25
Caruso, Enrico 197
"casting-out song" 60
Catholicism, *see* Christianity
Cavero, Ranulfo 188
ceques (Inca lines) 139–41
   religious significance 141, 151–2, 158, 165
Certeau, Michel de 45–6, 95, 97, 98–9, 104, 106, 196
Cervantes, Fernando 48, 177, 192
Chávez, Carlos 22

Cheyfitz, Eric 27
children's songs 60, 85
Chono, Juan 188, 189
Christianity
   alleged punishment for practicing 179
   attempts to stamp out opposition 90, 178–90
   impact on harvest festivals 150
   Indian attitudes to 191
   influence on *cantares* 58, 59–61, 70, 81–2
   role of music in 176, 177–8, 179–80
   view of Mexica culture 48
Cieza de Léon, Pedro de 126
Classen, Constance 34
Clastres, Hélène 121–2
Clavigero, Francisco Javier 19
Clendinnen, Inga 30–1, 32, 34, 40–1, 42, 184
Cobo, Bernabé 136, 140, 141–2, 143, 144, 150–2, 155
Cock C., Guillermo 142
Codex Aubin 172–3
Codex Azcatitlan 173
Codex Borbonicus 35, 42, 45, 64
codices 69–70
Columbus, Christopher 169–70, 171, 195
compound words, use of 66, 71, 72–8; *see also* agglutination, as basis of language
Condillac, Etienne Bonnot de 16, 24
connections, role in Mexica thought 40, 42
Conquest and Colonization of Peru, see Relación de muchas cosas acaescidas en el Piru
Conquista y población del Peru, see Relación de muchas cosas acaescidas en el Piru
conversion (religious), evolution in dynamic of 177
Corro, Pedro Barriga 188
Cortés, Hernán 171–2, 195, 198
Cummins, Tom 7, 159, 160, 161, 166
Cuna people 175
Cunhambebe, Chief 112–15
Cuzco:
   festival locations in/near 142–3, 148
   as Inca cultural/theocratic centre 139, 165, 166
   physical/social divisions 136, 137, 158, 165–6, 185

Damrosch, David 25
de Man, Paul 12
Dearborn, David 156
Defaux, Gérard 97
Deleuze, Gilles 195
Demarest, Arthur A. 142, 161
demonic possession, native song/ritual equated with 46–8, 174, 177, 180, 182–4, 189–90

214

Index

Derrida, Jacques 3, 10, 11, 12–13, 15, 16, 19–20, 34, 104, 166, 196
   De la grammatologie 11–13, 46
Desan, Philippe 95, 97, 98, 101
Destrucción del Perú see Relación de muchas cosas acaescidas en el Piru
Díaz, Bernal 172, 195
diphrasis 24, 40
Dolar, Mladen 195
Dominicans 190
Doyle, Mary Eileen 142
drums, drumming 43–4, 56, 87–90, 181–2
   oral pedagogy 44, 89
   played by singer 58, 89–90
   references in words of song 66
   relationship with voice 56–7, 90
   song genre defined by 63
   surviving examples 34–5
   See also percussion cadences
Durán, Diego 20, 23

eavesdropping 194–6
Eguiara y Eguren, Juan José de 19, 21
Enlightenment 193
ephemerality, as theme of song 65, 89–90
eschatology 41
Esteve Barba, Francisco 133
Europeans:
   encounters with native cultures 11
   history of colonialism 192–3
   military conflicts with indigenous peoples 171–3
   responses to native song 169–73, 174–5
   see also Christianity; Spanish
Évreux, Yves d', Father 118

Fabian, Johannes 192–3
Farriss, Nancy 90, 91, 181
fear, induced by music/song 168–75, 193–4, 195–6, 197–200
feathers, *see* quetzal plumes
Fernandes, Florestan 121
flowers, relationship with song 39–40, 63, 64–7, 68–9, 82–3
   associated vocabulary 65–6
Foucault, Michel 30
Frame, Donald M. 108
Freccero, Carla 95, 108
Freud, Sigmund 191–2, 200
Freyre, Gilberto 119
Frobisher, Martin 170

Fuchs, Juan Carlos Estenssoro 48, 190
Fuller, Mary C. 30

Gante, Fray Pedro de 60
Garcilaso de la Vega, El Inca 131, 136, 139, 143, 144
Garibay K., Angel María 22, 24, 26–7, 32–3, 39–40, 51, 53, 55–6, 60, 63, 71, 75, 81, 82, 88
gaze, theories of 194, 195
ghost songs 198–200
   cantares as 8
gift exchange 101–3, 104–6, 107
girdle, wearing of 108–9
Goethe, Johann Wolfgang von 93
Gómara, Francisco López de 21, 96
Goody, Jack 29
Granados y Gálvez, Joseph Joaquín de 21
Greenblatt, Stephen 45, 95
Gregorian chant 45, 176, 197
   fabled origins 79
Griffin, Owen 174–5, 176, 195
Gruzinski, Serge 9, 29, 30, 33–4, 39, 41, 48
   La Colonisation de l'imaginaire 33
Guaman Poma de Ayala, Felipe 145, 148, 157, 159, 160, 161–2
Guarani peoples 121–2
Guattari, Félix 195
Guss, David M. 5

hallucinogens 58
Harcourt, R. and M. d', *La Musique des Incas et ses survivances* 4
Harrison, Benjamin, President 199
harvest, celebrations of 134–5, 145, 150–1, 152, 153, 184
Hegel, Friedrich 11
Hemming, John 133–4, 143
Hernández, Francisco 75
hieroglyphs, compared with Mexican pictographs 18–19
history, as focus of study 5
Hopi snake-dances 200–1
Hosler, Dorothy 67–8
Howard, O. O., General 197
huacas (Inca shrines) 139–41, 166, 186
   geographical arrangement 139–41, 165
   planned revival (alleged) 184–5, 188
   possession of individuals (alleged) 185–7, 189
Huascar (brother of Atahuallpa) 126, 130, 138, 154, 155–6, 157
Huayna Capac 126, 130–1, 132, 138, 154, 155, 160
   tour of inspection 129–30, 153

215

Index

human sacrifice, allegations of 183
   equated with Satanism 183–4
Hyslop, John 165

Inca 6
   art 159; schematism 158–60
   (celebration of) military prowess 128–9, 132, 153–4
   festivals 134–5, 136–7, 138–9, 142–57; ad hoc 153–4; dates 144, 150; historical longevity 153; locations 142–3, 148, 151–2; names 143–53
   garments 132
   history 126–30, 153–7
   manuscript chronicles 125–32
   physical/social divisions, *see ayllus*; Cuzco; *panacas*
   politico-religious ritual 133–5
   provinces 139
   relations with Spaniards 156, 166
   religion 141–2, 161, 186; *see also* ancestor worship, Inca practice of; *ceques*; harvest, celebrations of; *huacas*; sun, role in Inca worship
   songs 125, 127–32, 156, 157–8, 160–5, 166–7
   Spanish responses to 135, 184–90
   writing/record-keeping system 131
Inca Raimi, festival of 148–53, 158, 160, 166
   celebrations 154–7, 161, 166–7
India, musical traditions 44
Indonesia 104–5
informaciones de servicios 187–8, 190
   wording of questions 189
Inquisition 190
instruments, musical
   metaphysical significance 111, 193
   as supplementary to bodily resources 110–11
   Western 110–11
   See also drums, drumming; leg rattles, Tupinamba use of; maracas
Inti Raimi, festival of 143–4, 145
Ixtlilxochitl, Fernando de Alva 23, 24–5

Julien, Catherine 127–30

Kant, Immanuel 122, 200
Karttunen, Frances 54, 55–6, 61, 71, 83
Keane, Webb 104–5, 106
Keen, Benjamin 18
King, Mark B. 9
Kircher, Athanasius 19

Lacan, Jacques 3, 12–13, 46, 191–2, 194–5
Landa, Diego de 181–2, 183

language:
   literal/figurative, duality of 41
   origins 15
   relativist view of 62
Las Casas, Bartolomé de 133, 177
Laudonnière, René de 170–1
Leander, Birgitta 24–5
leg rattles, Tupinamba use of 111–16
   role in cannibalistic ritual 115–16
Léon-Portilla, Miguel 19, 24, 25, 39–40, 51, 54, 55–6, 61, 64, 72
Léry, Jean de 45–8, 95–6, 98, 99–100, 102, 105, 106, 107, 108, 110, 112, 117, 173–4, 176, 189, 198
Lestringant, Frank 45, 93, 95
Lévi-Strauss, Claude 89
Lévy-Bruhl, Lucien 41
Lewis, I. M. 186
Lima, third Ecclesiastical Council of 190
literature, songs read as 32
llamas, role in Inca ritual 148–51, 161–2
Loayza, Francisco A. 133
Lockhart, James 9, 25–6, 27, 54, 55–6, 61, 62, 64, 71, 83
logocentrism 10–13, 17–18
   influence on European views of indigenous Americans 18
Louis XIV of France 156, 157

McClary, Susan 169
MacCormack, Sabine 48, 134, 143, 150–1, 152, 166
McGillycuddy, V. T. 198–9
Maldonado, Angel, Bishop 90, 91
Mama Ocllo (legendary Inca ancestor) 136, 143
Manco Capac (legendary Inca ancestor) 136, 143
Manco Inca 130–1, 133
   festival celebrations 154–7 (*see also* Inca Raimi)
   political agenda 155, 156
   political background 154
   sources of power 156–7
maracas 94, 111–12, 116–20
   duality of role 119, 120
   heightening of voice 120
   religious/metaphysical significance 116, 117–19, 120
Marcus, Joyce 9
Martí, Samuel
   Canto, danza y música precortesianos 4, 32–3
   Instrumentos musicales precortesianos 4
Martín, Gerónimo 188
Martín, Mariana 91
material objects, presence in song 39, 63, 64–7, 71, 75
   mixing of 68–9

Index

See also birds; flowers, relationship with song; precious stones, as theme of song
Mauss, Marcel 101–4, 106
Maya, *see* Yucatán, enforcement of Christianity in
Mendez, Diego 171
Mendoza, Vincente 43–4
merchants, *see* banquets, songs performed at
metals, mentioned in song 67–8
metaphor 15–16, 27
  Mexica use of 23–5, 40–2
  role in history of language 15–16
  separation in 39–40
metonymy 27, 73–5, 78
Métraux, Alfred 118
Mexica (Aztecs):
  as basis of study 11
  nomenclature 8
  religion 41–2; role of song in ceremonies 31, 39, 75–6, 91–2; Spanish suppression of 178–81, 189–90
  worldview 30–2, 41–2, 73–5, 80
  See also cantares
"Mexica-Otomi Song" (*cantar no.*) 2–3, 76–8, 81
  style 76
  vocabulary 76–9
Middle Ages, musical traditions 55
Mignolo, Walter D. 9, 10
Miller, Arthur G. 32
missionaries 80, 139, 176–90
  ambivalent attitude to local religions 181–2
  decline in success/enthusiasm 178–9, 180–1, 182–3, 190–1, 192; blamed on Indians 178–9; blamed on Spaniards 178
Mixtec people/language 34–5
Molina, Alonso de 53, 63, 66, 71, 78
Molina, Cristóbal de, "el Almagrista" (possible author of *Relación de muchas cosas asaescidas en el Piru*) 133
Molina, Cristóbal de, "el Cuzqueño," *Relación de las fábulas y ritos de los Incas* 133, 136–7, 143, 144–5, 148, 150–1, 152, 184–6, 187, 188–9
Monaghan, John 9, 34
Montaigne, Michel de
  lack of musical commentary 94
  Of Cannibals 6, 7, 93, 94; critical commentary 95, 97, 102; on ethics of cannibalism 95–8, 102–3; lessons for Europe 97, 98, 103; on singing 94–5, 103, 105, 107, 108, 109
  Of Coaches 95–6
  Of Moderation 96
Mooney, James 198–9, 200

Motolinía (Toribio de Benavente) 20, 21, 44
mourning, songs of 128–9
Murúa, Martin de, Fray 144–5
music:
  ethnographic studies 4–5
  role in Western culture 196–7
  See also fear, induced by music/song; instruments, musical; notation, musical; song
musical history, studies of 4
  in the Americas 4–5, 177
  balance of approaches 5

Nahuatl (language) 8
  European comments on 21, 24
  grammatical structures 29–30, 61–2, 72–8, 87
  limitations 77
  "missionary" 76
  orthography 8
  (problems of) translation 51, 75
  songs written in 44
  system of writing 30–4
Narváez, Pánfilo de 172
Neubauer, John 12
"New World," use of term 7
Nez Perce War 197–9
Nezahualcoyotl 23, 24–5, 26, 85, 86
Nezahualpilli (son of Nezahualcoyotl) 24–5
Niles, Susan A. 130
Nimuendajú, Curt 119
nonalphabetic writing, early European encounters with 11–12
North America, *see* ghost songs; Hopi; Nez Perce War; Sioux
notation, musical:
  European 18, 45
  Mexican song glyphs viewed as 42
  use to transcribe Mexica songs 46
  See also percussion cadences

Olmec people/artifacts 36
Olsen, Dale A., *Music of El Dorado: The Ethnomusicology of Ancient South American Cultures* 4
Olvera, Luis de 184–6, 187, 188–9
Ong, Walter J. 29, 30
Otomi song 63

Pachacuti Inca Yupanqui 126, 128, 129, 130–1, 132, 137, 141, 153
  self-promotion through song 128

217

Index

painting, relationship with song 39, 69–70
panacas (Inca social groups) 137–8, 158
   threat of dismantling 155–6
Paso y Troncoso, Francisco del 21–2
Pauw, Cornelius de 19
percussion cadences:
   appearance in sung words 87–90
   interpretations 32, 43–4
   notation 42–3, 45, 56, 91
Pérez de Ribas, Andrés 43–4
Peter Martyr 18
phonography 17
pictographs 17, 18–20, 30–7
   associations with song 71
   contrasted with alphabetized song 33
   relationship with things 31–2
Pizarro, Francisco 126, 130–1, 133, 154
Pizarro, Pedro 138, 155
Plácido, Don Francisco, Governor 59
Platonism 31, 32
poetry:
   primitive vs. modern 16
   relationship with song 15–16, 17–18
   role in history of language 15–16
Pohl, John M. D. 20
Polo de Ondegardo, Juan 140, 190
polygamy 96, 99, 108
Pomar, Juan Bautista 23
possession, cults of 185–7; *see also* demonic possession
poststructuralism 27
potlatch exchange system 101
Pozos, Luis Alveláis 24–5
precious stones, as theme of song 67–9
Prescott, William 133, 143–4
"prestation" 101, 103
puns/wordplay 88–9

Quechua 135
   orthography 8
   translation into Spanish 131
   vocabulary 184, 187
quetzal plumes, presence in song 67, 69
Quint, David 95, 97, 102
quipus 131, 159
Quiroga, Vasco de 20, 21, 22

Rameau, Jean-Philippe 14
Ramirez, Diego 2, 3, 4

rattles, *see* leg rattles, Tupinamba use of; maracas
Relación de muchas cosas asaescidas en el Piru (Molina/Segovia?) 133, 135, 136, 138–9, 142, 143, 144, 145–6, 153
religious ceremonies, indigenous 176–7, 180
   blamed for decline of mission 179
   continuity 181, 192
   European responses to 179, 190–1, 192–3, 195–6; *see also* demonic possession
   role/power of song within 178, 179, 180, 184
   synthesis with Christian festivals 181–2, 190
   See also Christianity; Inca; Mexica; Tupinamba
"Ribald's Flower-Song" (*cantar* no.) 65–6
Robertson, William 19
Romances de los señores de la Nueva España 25, 42, 51
Rosier, James 174–5
Rousseau, Jean-Jacques 11, 20, 23, 24, 27, 93, 193
   Essai sur l'origine des langues 10–11, 12–18
   musical theory 13–15
Rowe, John H. 127, 165

Sahagún, Bernadino de 20, 21, 23, 37, 70, 180–1, 183
   Florentine Codex 44, 57–8, 59, 61, 75, 84, 91, 172–3, 178–81
   Psalmodia Christiana 59, 60, 80, 81–2
Sahlins, Marshall 122
Said, Edward 191, 192
Salomon, Frank 131, 159, 160, 161
Sangro, Raimondo de, prince of Sansevero 131
Sarmiento de Gamboa, Pedro 126
Saturiba, Chief 171
Sausero (Inca site) 151–2
Saussure, Ferdinand de 11, 27
"savages," European view of 13–14, 15–16, 168
schematism, *see* Inca: art
Seeger, Anthony 5
Segala, Amos 26–7
Segovia, Bartolomé de 133
Seler, Eduard 21–2
self:
   interplay with Other, theories of 191–2
   negation in Tupinamba culture 121–3
   place in Mexica culture 41–2
   presence in Tupinamba culture 123
"semiophagy" 122
Shakespeare, William, *The Tempest* 2–3
shamans, role in societies 117, 164–5
Shipibo-Conibo people 164–5
Sioux, massacre of (Wounded Knee) 198–9

Index

song:
  centrality to human culture 5–6, 201
  colonial mediation 7
  critical neglect 3–4, 10; reasons for 4, 5–6
  distinguished from music 14–15
  division into poetry and music 20–3, 32–3, 107
  essential characteristics 49
  European 160–1
  importance in European/native encounters 3
  interrelationship with other modes of expression 17–18
  metaphysical force 176–7
  as mode of remembrance 131–2
  origins 78–80, 81
  pictorial representations 35–7
  political significance 129–31, 132
  (possibility of) reconstruction 4, 50
  religious polarization 180
  religious significance 124
  role in history of language 13–15
  as source of communion 106–7
  spatial situation 124–5
  special powers 5, 6–7, 175–7, 180–1, 193–6
  temporal situation 124–5
  as theme of songs 63–4, 77, 85–7
  as threat to logocentrism 12–13
  See also cannibalism; *cantares*; Christianity; Inca; music; religious ceremonies; speech; *taki onqoy*; Tupinamba
"song " (on origins of song) 1, 79–80, 81
"song " (threnody) 7, 80, 81
songbooks, mentioned in song 70–1
sound, representation of, *see* phonography
Soustelle, Jacques 31, 41
Spanish:
  colonization of New World 1–2
  exploitation of indigenous people 186
  slaughter of Indian nobles (1520) 172–3, 192
  See also Christianity; missionaries
speech:
  distancing from song 98–9, 123, 162–4, 175–6, 194, 196
  relationship with song 36–9, 48–9
  ritualized 37–9
"speech-act" theory 104
Staden, Hans 103, 108, 112, 115–17, 118, 119, 120
stereotypes 191–2, 194
Stevenson, Robert 54
  Music in Aztec and Inca Territory 4, 21, 32–3

Stoicism (in Montaigne's philosophy) 96, 97, 98, 105
Sullivan, Lawrence L. 5
"Summer Song" (*cantar* no. 81)
  generic characteristics 62
  structure 61, 62
  text 51–3
  themes 62, 63, 64
  variants 53
  vocabulary 71
sun, role in Inca worship 135, 141–2, 143, 145, 151, 152–3, 156–8, 161, 162, 165–6
supplementarity 13, 22–3, 46, 110–11

taki, *see* Inca: festivals; Inca: songs; sun, role in Inca worship
taki onqoy ("song-dance sickness"), supposed anti-Catholic movement 184–90
  alleged practices 185–6
  compared with other indigenous movements 191, 198, 200
  evolution of Spanish attitudes to 187–90
  role of song in 187
  See also informaciones de servicios
Tavárez, David 90–1
Tecayehuatzin, Prince 25
technology, musical 124–5, 197
Tenochtitlan, battle for 171–2
Teotihuacan murals 35–6
teponaztli, *see* drums, drumming
Thevet, André 19, 98, 99–100, 102, 103, 105, 106, 112–15, 118
"three ages" theory of society 22
"three worlds" view of cosmos 121–2
Titu Cusi (exiled Inca leader) 185
Toledo, Francisco de 190
Toltec people 22
Topa Huallpa 133
Topa Inca Yupanqui 128–9, 132, 138
torture, Christian practice of 183, 184
Totoquihuatzin 88
"Toto-Song" (*cantar* no.) 8, 87–90
Treitler, Leo 45
Trobriand people 101
True Declaration of the Estate of the Colony in Virginia, A 2
Tupinamba:
  economy 97, 98, 100–5, 108, 121
  ethical/ritual systems 93–4, 96–8, 102–3, 105–6, 109–10, 118, 121, 122–3

219

Index

Tupinamba (*cont.*)
  musical instruments 111–20; pictured 111–12; *see also* leg rattles, Tupinamba use of; maracas
  oratory 93–4
  religion 117, 118, 121
  songs 45–8, 93–4, 98–101, 102–8, 173–4; role in ritual 94

Urban, Greg 5
Urton, Gary 9, 127, 131

Valeriano, Don Antonio, Governor 59
Vico, Giambattista 22, 193
Viracocha Inca 126–7
Viveiros de Castro, Eduardo 103, 108–9, 119–20, 121–3
vocables 54, 83–5, 87, 162–4, 194
  infixed 83–4
  liminal status 85
  percussive 87–90
  "quasi-lexical" 83, 84–5
  special usages 85–7
  standard forms 83, 87, 91
voice, role in human imagination 2–3
volutes 35–7, 39

Wafer, Lionel 175
Warburg, Aby 200–1
warfare, as theme of song 62–3, 69–70
weeping, representations of 86–7
women:
  role in cannibalistic rituals 110, 115–16
  role in social order 109–10

Wounded Knee, *see* Sioux
Wovoka (Paiute Indian) 198
writing:
  impact on spoken/sung word 28
  Mesoamerican, history of 20
  modern studies 9
  reasons for study 10
  relationship with song 160–1
  relationship with speech 196
  Rousseau's view 17–18
  as threat to Christian order 180–1
  as threat to logocentrism 12–13
written sources (of American song) 6, 10
  Eurocentric nature 6

Ximénez, Cristóbal 189
Xiuhtlamin, Cristóbal de Rosario 59
Xochicalco, pyramids of 35
xochicuicatl 24–5

Yamque Yupanqui (son of Pachacuti) 128–9
Yucatán, enforcement of Christianity in 181–4, 189–90
Yupanqui, Doña Angelina (Señora Betanzos) 126, 132

Zapotec people 90
  songs 90–1, 92; influence on later traditions 92; similarity to Mexican *cantares* 91, 92
Zappullo, Michele 21
Zuidema, R. Tom 127, 137, 165

For EU product safety concerns, contact us at Calle de José Abascal, 56–1°,
28003 Madrid, Spain or eugpsr@cambridge.org.

www.ingramcontent.com/pod-product-compliance
Lightning Source LLC
LaVergne TN
LVHW080312260326
834688LV00038B/1073